SETON HALL UNIVERSITY

QL737.C432 D65 1986   MAIN

Dolphin cognition and behavior :

3 3073 00256792 1

D1525467

DATE DUE

MAR 2 2 1993		
NOV 2 3 1994		
MAY 1 4 1996		
A L A form	JUN 2 1 1997	
GAYLORD		PRINTED IN U.S.A.

Dolphin Cognition and Behavior:
A Comparative Approach

COMPARATIVE COGNITION
AND NEUROSCIENCE

Thomas G. Bever, David S. Olton, and
Herbert L. Roitblat, Series Editors

Roitblat/Bever/Terrace: Animal Cognition

Nilsson/Archer: Perspectives on Learning and
Memory

Kendrick/Rilling/Denny: Theories of
Animal Memory

Schusterman/Thomas/Wood: Dolphin
Behavior and Cognition

DOLPHIN COGNITION AND BEHAVIOR: A COMPARATIVE APPROACH

Edited by

RONALD J. SCHUSTERMAN
California State University, Hayward, and
University of California, Santa Cruz

JEANETTE A. THOMAS
Hubbs Marine Research Institute, San Diego

FORREST G. WOOD
Naval Ocean Systems Center, San Diego

SETON HALL UNIVERSITY
McLAUGHLIN LIBRARY
SO. ORANGE, N. J.

 LAWRENCE ERLBAUM ASSOCIATES, PUBLISHERS
1986   Hillsdale, New Jersey   London

QL
737
C432
D65
1986

Copyright © 1986 by Lawrence Erlbaum Associates, Inc.
All rights reserved. No part of this book may be reproduced in
any form, by photostat, microform, retrieval system, or any other
means, without the prior written permission of the publisher

Lawrence Erlbaum Associates, Inc., Publishers
365 Broadway
Hillsdale, New Jersey 07642

Library of Congress Cataloging in Publication Data

Dolphin cognition and behavior.

(Series in comparative cognition and neuroscience)
Bibliography: p.
Includes index.
1. Dolphins—Behavior. 2. Dolphins—Psychology.
3. Cognition in animals. 4. Mammals—Behavior.
5. Mammals—Psychology. I. Schusterman, Ronald J.
II. Thomas, Jeanette A. III. Wood, Forrest G.
(Forrest Glenn), 1918– . IV. Series.
QL737.C432D65 1986   599.5'3   86-4440
ISBN 0-89859-665-3
ISBN 0-89859-594-0 (pbk.)

Printed in the United States of America
10 9 8 7 6 5 4 3 2 1

Contents

viii   CONTENTS

Foreword

The conference on dolphin cognition and behavior held at the Hubbs Marine Research Institute at Sea World in June, 1983 led to a stimulating and productive exchange of data and ideas. I am sure I speak for all the participants in thanking the organizers and sponsors for making this possible. The resulting papers (which are far too numerous and diverse for any meaningful review here) include both first-hand reports of dolphin behavior strongly suggesting cognition, and reviews of experiments with other animals whose abilities are relevant and helpful to those planning further investigations of dolphin mentality. While parrots and apes are obviously very different from cetaceans, the eye-opening discoveries made in the past few years about their apparently intentional communication provide significant comparisons with the emerging picture of cognition in dolphins and other marine mammals. It is obvious that dolphins' behavior is complex and versatile. Despite the lack of hands they can learn to carry out a variety of manipulative tasks. Complex communicative exchanges take place under natural conditions, and in captivity they can learn to understand a variety of visual and acoustic signals.

A highly significant but neglected question is whether dolphins are consciously aware of what they are doing. To many people the versatility and complexity of their behavior makes it obvious that they must often be acting intentionally, with some understanding of the likely results of their behavior. For example, dolphins are often kept together in small groups from which only one is trained to perform a complex set of maneuvers to entertain the public. In some cases when the trained animal is removed, another immediately performs the complex actions without prior experience or practice (Herman 1980). Perhaps one dolphin can learn the gymnastic tricks of another without thinking about them, but it seems more likely that such an observing companion is consciously aware of what the trained dolphin is doing and how he might perform if given the opportunity.

On the other hand, it has become customary for behavioral scientists to ignore the question of animal consciousness, and some even minimize the significance of human thoughts and feelings. Although overt behavior is easier to observe, this does not mean that subjective, conscious mental experiences are nonexistent or unimportant. One can never prove with absolute and logical certainty that another person or animal is consciously thinking; but such extreme standards of proof are seldom if ever required in other areas of science. Given the obvious reality and importance of our own thoughts and feelings, together with the similarity of basic elements that make up all central nervous systems, it is at least as difficult to prove the nonexistence of mental experiences in dolphins, apes, or other animals as to establish their presence.

If and when dolphins do experience conscious thoughts, it may well be adaptive to communicate them to their companions. The coordination of social interactions is surely facilitated by exchange of information about any thoughts and feelings that may be important to the participants. Therefore the interpretation of their communicative signals may well be a long step towards literally reading the minds of dolphins. While it is possible that all dolphin behavior is comparable to the large fraction of our own behavior that goes on without conscious awareness, conscious thinking may be the most economical and efficient way to deal with complex and constantly changing situations, as I have suggested elsewhere (Griffin 1984). This is why it is so important to learn just what the communicative capabilities of dolphins really are.

It has been widely held that animal communication conveys only relatively crude emotional states aroused in the communicator by the immediate stimulus situation. But recent studies of primates both under natural conditions (reviewed in a symposium edited by Harré & Reynolds, 1984), and in captivity (reviewed by Ristau & Robbins, 1982), show that they sometimes communicate semantic information. This may include information about objects and events that are not currently available to stimulate the communicating animals. This is why the data presented in Herman's chapter in this volume are especially significant. Dolphins can learn to comprehend messages from their trainers about objects not visible or otherwise detectable at the time the message is received. As the lingering taboos of behaviorism are relaxed, it seems likely that investigators of other animals will begin to inquire how extensive this sort of communication may be.

One of the most important attributes of human language is what George Miller (1967) appropriately described as "combinatorial productivity." This means the addition of new and important meaning by rule-governed combinations of words, ordinarily into sentences. Until recently this seemed to be a unique human accomplishment. But Herman demonstrates that dolphins can learn to comprehend relationships encoded in sentence-like sets of commands. It remains to be seen whether they can also learn to produce rule-governed messages, but an ability to understand and respond appropriately to messages whose meaning requires comprehension of the rules as well as of the individual elements is certainly an important step in the direction of combinatorial productivity in animal communication.

In the thoughtful discussion of Herman's experiments at the conference, it was pointed out that we scientists whose native language is English tend to assume that grammatical rules providing combinatorial productivity must necessarily involve word order or the temporal sequence of other signals. This type of rule is easy to manipulate experimentally, but it is by no means universal among human languages. Many languages use inflection of key words to convey grammatical relationships, such as which noun is actor or object and who performs a certain action. The fact that this sort of grammatical rule is so widespread might mean that it is in some ways a simpler and perhaps even an easier way to combine words meaningfully. Would apes, parrots, dolphins or other animals learn more readily to communicate with combinatorial productivity if the rules involved modifications of signals rather than their temporal order? This notion was one of many potentially fruitful ideas that took shape during the conference, and readers of the following chapters will find abundant and comparable food for thought.

Donald R. Griffin
The Rockefeller University

REFERENCES

Griffin, D. R. (1984). Animal thinking. Cambridge, MA: Harvard University Press.

Harré, R., & Reynolds, V. (Eds.). (1984). The meaning of primate signals. New York: Cambridge University Press.

Herman, L. M. (1980). Cognitive capacities of dolphins. In L. M. Herman (Ed.), Cetacean Behavior mechanisms and functions New York: Wiley.

Miller, G. A. (1967). The psychology of communication. New York: Basic Books.

ACKNOWLEDGMENTS

From October 3–5, 1980, Hubbs Marine Research Institute in San Diego hosted a workshop entitled "Potentials for Research on Cognition in Dolphins and Human-Dolphin Communication." About 15 scientists discussed problems in characterizing the perceptual world of dolphins, comparative learning capacities of dolphins and chimpanzees, the significance of brain size in relation to intelligence, and training methodologies in dolphins. At that time the need to address these topics at a larger conference was established.

On July 6–8, 1983, about 30 scientists from many disciplines within the broad areas of the brain and behavioral sciences participated in a conference called "Dolphin Cognition and Behavior: Comparative and Ecological Aspects." The conference was hosted by Hubbs Marine Research Institute. Robert Buhr organized the conference with assistance by William E. Evans, Ronald J. Schusterman, and Forrest G. Wood. This book is based to a large extent on papers given at the conference or generated as a result of discussion at the conference.

Both meetings were funded by the Office of Naval Research under the Oceanic Biology Program. Dr. Bernard J. Zahuranec and Dr. Donald Woodward from the Office of Naval Research provided valuable assistance in organizing and participating in the meetings.

Information in this book relates to Department of Navy Grant N00014–83–G–0011 issued by the Office of Naval Research. The United States Government has a royalty-free license throughout the world in all copyrightable material contained herein.

Dolphin Cognition and Behavior:
A Comparative Approach

BRAIN AND SENSES OF DOLPHINS

Theodore H. Bullock

Cetaceans present unique opportunities for new insights into the mammalian brain—the highest achievement of evolution. Some species possess the greatest brains in nature, at least in respect to size. The brains are remarkably specialized in many ways, compared to those of other mammals. They have been evolving separately from other mammals for a long time. Their cognitive achievements, although not yet fully assessed, their special sensory capacities, acoustic signaling, songs, and other behavioral features add reasons that the correlates in brain anatomy, physiology, and chemistry should be studied for clues to understanding how brains mediate cognition and behavior.

In spite of these strong reasons and the great interest in dolphins and whales, their brains are relatively little studied and our knowledge lags well behind that for other orders of mammals. Extraordinary difficulties lie in the path of investigation of cetaceans, even of anatomy. The overriding difficulty is scarcity of material and access permitting the use of modern methods. A quite proper reluctance to sacrifice specimens of these magnificent species has almost completely prevented the use of the most revealing modern techniques of experimental anatomy for tracing connections by allowing the living nerve cell to distribute substances it takes up into all it axonal and dendritic processes—methods

1

which provide the main body of information for establishing homologies and functional interrelations of parts of the brain in other mammals.

The same factors, plus some reluctance even to record physiological activity in the brain of cetaceans with chronically implanted electrodes in the alert and cooperating animal—by the same techniques used on humans for many years for the benefit of the patient—have kept the progress of this branch of research down to a handful of papers. In both anatomical and physiological approaches it is vastly more difficult to learn something about cetacean brains than about those of the great apes.

Whales and dolphins which are taken in the course of the still extant commercial operations are wasted as far as research use is concerned because, in addition to other factors, the cost of bringing scientists and their tools to the surviving but doomed animals is beyond the research funds of the competent people. The opportunities due to these remaining fisheries, hopefully soon to be abolished, should not be wasted. Without encouraging the fisheries in any way, humane research upon doomed or dying animals should be greatly accelerated before it is too late, in the interest not only of human welfare, which this knowledge would surely benefit, but of a real appreciation of the cetaceans themselves.

Chapters in this section demonstrate that some significant results can be obtained in spite of the difficulties. Occasional opportunities arise to preserve a brain freshly and suitably, at least for the older, classical stains. More rare are the qualified anatomists who will devote the time necessary to work up and examine such material and see it through to publication. Peter Morgane and his coauthors are among these few; they have made the most of long and laboriously collected, well-fixed brains of many species. They provide here the most advanced analysis to date, including cell anatomy based on staining by the Golgi method, of the degree of evolutionary achievement of the dolphin cortex, reaching rather surprising conclusions from the point of view of prevailing views based upon inadequate and premature anatomy.

A small number of electrophysiological recording experiments have been done, beginning in the early 60s on anesthetized, mostly doomed animals, in Japan and the U.S.S.R., and on chronically implanted animals in the U.S. and the U.S.S.R. Most recently the technique has been used, based upon standard clinical methods, of recording from outside the skull, in the "far field," averaging hundreds of responses over several minutes. S. H. Ridgway reviews the short latency, relatively more stimulus-bound responses, as well as studies revealing a unique pattern of sleeping. D. L. Woods and coauthors report a preliminary study showing that long latency electrical waves can be found when a dolphin is presumably engaged in cognitive processes of a moderately high level, hence that this active and promising field of research on humans can be extended to cetaceans.

Behavioral evidence is the main grist for the next two chapters which review particularly the sensory capacities. P. Nachtigall compares vision, hearing and the chemical senses among marine mammals, pinnipedes and otters as well as cetaceans. C. S. Johnson examines more closely the evidence on hearing in the best studied dolphin and its specialized form used in echolocation.

The net result of these five chapters is to reinforce our appreciation of the need for further study of the capacities and of the morphological, physiological and, it should be added, the chemical correlates of cognition and behavior in these remarkable mammals, among other reasons because they have independently evolved so different a brain from most mammalian orders.

1 Evolutionary Morphology of the Dolphin Brain

P. J. Morgane
Worcester Foundation for Experimental Biology

M. S. Jacobs
New York University Dental Center

Albert Galaburda
Harvard Medical School and Beth Israel Hospital

INTRODUCTION

Studies of the cetacean brain are expected to shed considerable light on mammalian brain evolution and, in particular, on how the brain has adapted to markedly differing environments, such as between land and water. To date, although there have been numerous studies on different aspects of cetacean brain anatomy, what has been lacking is integration of this information with that available from studies of evolutionary neuroanatomy. Relative to this, the cetacean brain has historically often been given special status based on its size and fissural complexity rather than on the microscopic appearance of the cortical formations comprising its main divisions.

Before considering the status of the dolphin brain, it should be noted that development and formation of the neocortex of mammals and reptiles took place in a land environment, which shows much more diurnal and seasonal variation than does an aqueous environment. The cetaceans are a major Order of mammals showing a complete secondary return to an aqueous medium. Genetically related to all terrestrial mammals, the cetaceans are of particular evolutionary value and uniqueness, since they have adapted themselves to activity in an aqueous medium according to evolutionary laws characteristic of the whales alone. In doing so they exemplify the potential possibilities of environmental changes on the structural organization of the brain, in particular, the great adaptability of the cortical formations of the cerebral hemispheres. In this regard, analysis of comparative anatomical material reveals that the most important morphologic changes that occur in the mammalian nervous system in the process of evolution can be demonstrated primarily in the telencephalon and, especially, in the cortical formations (Filimonoff, 1949).

Development of the chordate nervous system has followed the path of a progressive development of rostral regions in relation to the caudal ones. It is the development of cortical areas and especially of the neocortex that is of particular

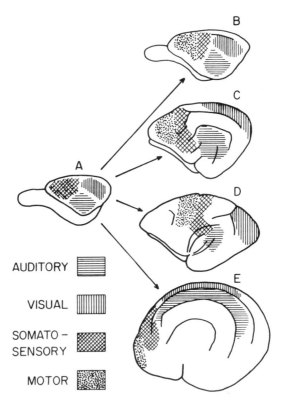

FIG. 1.1.   Schema showing sensorimotor areas projected onto the brain surface in a variety of mammals. The brain of the hypothetical common ancestor or "initial" type is indicated in A. In this regard, we view the hedgehog brain as a possible model of the brain of the initial ancestor of mammals. The representations of sensorimotor areas are shown in B: rabbit; C: cat; D: rhesus monkey and E: dolphin brain. Note in the dolphin the displacement of the visual and auditory areas onto the dorsolateral convexity of the hemisphere and the lack of intervening cortex between visual and auditory areas and between visual-auditory areas and sensorimotor areas (as indicated by electrophysiological mapping studies of Ladygina et al., 1978).

interest. Filimonoff's fundamental studies (1947, 1949) have made it possible to visualize the hypothetical original type of the mammalian cortex and has provided support for morphological regularities of departures from this original or "initial" type of cortical organization (Fig. 1.1). Of these departures from the prototype, the primate type of cortex has so far been studied most thoroughly. This type is characteristic of monkeys and man who have primitive Insectivora at the root of their phylogenetic tree. In evolution the departure from primitive Carnivora belonging to the group of Creodonta, an extinct suborder of the order of Carnivora, has received the least study. This group has often been proposed as including modern Orders of Ungulata, Carnivora, Pinnipedia, and Cetacea. However, Gingerich, Wells, Russell and Ibrahim Shah (1983) have evidence that whales may have evolved from a family of archaic ungulates called Condylarthra and entered the shallow seas in the early Eocene Period (approximately 60 million years ago). They completely adapted themselves to the new conditions and appear to have preserved characteristic features of the original structure of the brain of primitive mammals in greater measure than have the land animals. At the same time the cetaceans were in a position to develop specific features of adaptation not characteristic of land mammals. Thus, studies of the cetacean brain structure make it possible to move closer to solving some of the most important problems of evolution of the mammalian brain.

SUBDIVISIONS OF THE CORTICAL FORMATIONS

Before elaborating and discussing the basis of our subdivision of the cetacean brain it is essential to review some of the basic principles of Filimonoff (1947, 1949) dealing with what he terms a rational division of the cerebral cortex. Using these concepts we can better interpret the organization of the dolphin brain as revealed by our recent studies.

Filimonoff (1949) emphasized that the study of comparative anatomical data is essential to unraveling the problems of a rational classification of cortical formations. Such a classification represents one of the basic tasks of architectonic analysis of the cerebral cortex as a morphological discipline proper as well as a discipline of considerable value in the solution of the problems of localization of function.

In the classification of Filimonoff various types of cortical formations can be identified. The *paleocortex* (semicortex or cortex semi-separatus) is phylogenetically and ontogenetically the most ancient type of cortex and is characterized by an incomplete separation of the cortical lamina from the subcortical cellular aggregates. The *archicortex* or old cortex is characterized by a cortical lamina which has already become fully separated from the subcortex. It is, however, considerably less complex in its structure than that of the final stage of cortical evolution, the *neocortex*. Via so-called transitional cortex the archicortex passes into the lower level of the intermediate or periarchicortex (the pre-subicular and entorhinal areas), whereas the neocortical lamina passes into the upper level of the latter (superlamination). As noted, the *intermediate cortex,* separating the ancient and old cortex from the new cortex, is divided correspondingly into two major zones which are termed peripaleocortical and periarchicortical formations (Fig. 1.2). It is emphasized that the new, ancient, and old cortex, sharply differing from each other in terms of cellular organization and stratification during the process of development, as well as in the adult organism, are not directly adjacent but are separated from each other by transitional areas which cannot be related either to the new, old, or ancient cortex and which we can single out, on this basis, as special areas which are termed the intermediate cortex.

The clear identification of the intermediate cortex as one of the basic cortical types together with the ancient, old and neocortex, corresponds to Filimonoff's earlier formulated concept of intermediate cortical formations which is one of the basic principles in interpreting development of the cerebral cortex. In dealing with cortical formations strongly differing from each other either structurally or genetically, there is always found between them these intermediate formations, the structure of which represents a certain transition of basic formations from one

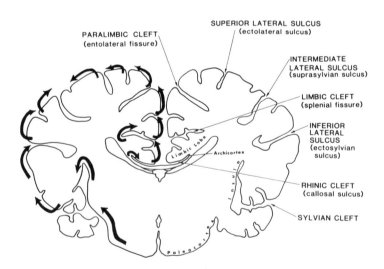

FIG. 1.2.   Schema of dolphin brain (frontal section) indicating Evolutional directional trends of cortical growth outwards from two primitive cortical moieties, archicortex medially and paleocortex laterally. The different cortical fields extending outward from the primitive cortical moieties represent successive waves of circumferential architectonic differentiation in evolution (also see Fig. 1.3). The arrows represent directions of cortical differentiation outward from primitive cortices in Evolution.

to the other, although these may remain under these circumstances sharply and linearly separated from one another. Importantly, by means of this principle, we can establish basically the subdivision of cortical zones into areas and the areas into individual cortical fields. The comparative anatomical study of architectonic structures in the mammalian Orders show that there are always present, without exception, the same basic zones which can be singled out by studies of ontogenetic material and that also here the principle of intermediate formations is of basic importance. In accordance with this principle, within the whole mammalian Class the neocortex is separated along its entire length from the paleo- and archicortex by the intermediate cortex.

In summary, the cerebral cortex is thus divisible into five principal zones: ancient cortex (paleocortex), old cortex (archicortex), intermediate cortex (peripaleocortex and periarchicortex), and the new cortex (neocortex). As the basic studies of Filimonoff (1947, 1949) demonstrate, the concept of intermediate or transitional cortical formations can be regarded as one of the leading principles underlying processes of cerebral cortex formation and, correspondingly, it serves as the basis for division of the cortex into its fundamental areas and into more functional structural units.

In studying the evolution of the cerebral cortex, analysis of the development of the ancient and old cortical areas and of the intermediate cortical areas which separate them from the new cortex is of particular interest. Neocortex appears in phylogenesis in typical form only in the mammalian Class (Filimonoff, 1949). Here it plays a greater role the further we get away from the initial forms of animals, i.e., from those archetypal forms (see Fig. 1.1) which are of particularly great importance to the understanding of the entire evolutional process. At the same time, only within the limits of the ancient, old, and intermediate cortices can we find precise homologies of their component structural units which provides for their correct quantitative evaluation. This latter is absolutely essential to the elucidation of the dynamics of evolution of the cerebral cortex, to the correct characterization of changes which are taking place, and to the determination of directions in which these changes occur.

It is possible, by studies of corresponding data, to express in definite terms the structural characteristics, based on quantitative and topographic correlations, of the cerebral cortex in the representatives of various Orders of the mammalian Class. A comparison of these formulas with those characterizing the so-called initial type, which can be constructed on the basis of the studies of ontogenetic material, permits approaches to the solution of the problem concerning the degree of proximity of individual investigated structural types of the cerebral cortex to the initial type. Using these approaches will permit solution of the problem concerning the presence or absence in each investigated type of various features deviating from the initial type as well as the trend of corresponding deviations. The solution of these problems also provides us with the data needed to evaluate the ways and means of cerebral cortical evolution within the mammalian Class.

In the evaluation of the essence of individual features characterizing the cerebral cortical structure in a given Order, of basic significance is their comparison with features which characterize this structure in the so-called "initial" type (see Fig. 1.1). At present, the true initial type does not exist in nature but a certain idea of it can be obtained on the basis of embryogenetic studies, though only in a general way and in a somewhat conjectural sense. A comparison of any investigated species with this archetype shows that high degrees of deviation from the initial type may be limited to specific individual features and appear as a sharp contrast against the basic features which are closer to those of the initial type. This sharp contrast may attest, to a greater or lesser extent, to the primitive character of the cortical structure of the corresponding brain as a whole. On the other hand, even in cases of high organization of the cerebral cortex, against a basic background of deviating features, individual characteristics inherent in the initial type may similarly appear as a sharp contrast.

The simultaneous presence, in cases with a primitive and in cases with a complex organization of the cerebral cortex, of characteristics which deviate from the initial type, as well as features which are similar to it, attests to a certain independence of the evolution of various features from each other. At the same time, this diversity attests to the highly important role of idioadaptations in the evolution of the cerebral cortex, i.e., adjustments to specific environmental conditions. In this regard, it is important to stress that cortical formations, due to their extreme plasticity, react particularly strongly by means of changes in structure to environmental changes. They react under these conditions by showing modifications of a differentiated nature, i.e., modifications involving not the cortex as a whole but mostly in special cellular groups in various combinations, corresponding to alterations in various environmental conditions of existence.

CONCEPTS OF NEOCORTICAL EVOLUTION: APPLICATION TO STUDIES OF ARCHITECTURE OF THE CETACEAN CEREBRAL CORTEX

In considering the evolution of the brain it is of paramount importance to determine both the extent and direction of evolutionary development of the different cortical formations. By studying the direction of differentiation outward from the archicortical and paleocortical cortices into the limbic and insular cortices and, thence, into the paralimbic and parinsular cortices and, finally, into highly specialized motor and sensory cores (primary cortex), we may be able to better establish the directionality of evolutionary changes in the brain and perhaps determine the extent to which evolution has taken place in the specific cortical formations. We have been applying just such approaches recently to a study of the evolutionary anatomy of the whale brain. These studies clearly show the importance of understanding the underlying morphogenetic sequences in order to phylogenetically reconstruct the cortical formations.

Before interpreting the organization of the cortical formations of the dolphin brain based on our recent studies, we need first to stress several points in relation to cortical growth and development. These principles have been elaborated in considerable detail by Sanides in a series of studies (1970, 1972) and we have applied them to the analysis of the cerebral cortex of the dolphin. The essence of these principles can be summarized as follows: The limbic lobe is a derivative of archicortex while the insular cortex is a derivative of paleocortex. This principle of the basically "dual" nature of neocortex means that there are two neocortical moieties, one differentiated in stages away from the hippocampus and the other in stages away from the piriform cortex. Thus, there are successive waves of circumferential cortical differentiations away from both archicortex and pal-

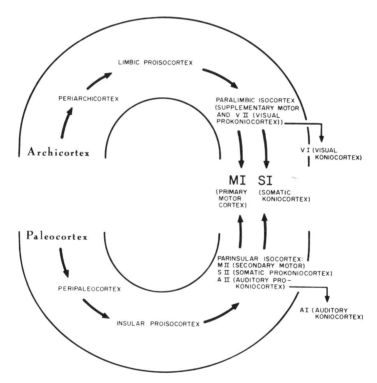

FIG. 1.3. Schema indicating directional trends of growth of cerebral cortex outward from archicortex and paleocortex through several cortical growth ring stages. This schema shows all four cortical growth rings extending outward from each primitive cortical moiety culminating in most mammalian species in the fourth cortical growth ring represented by Motor I (primary motor cortex, MI), Somatosensory I (primary sensory cortex, SI), Auditory I (primary auditory cortex, AI), and Visual I (primary visual cortex, VI). In the convexity cortex of the dolphin we find no evidence of the fourth cortical growth ring, the leading edge of cortical differentiation in the dolphin cortex being represented by the paralimbic and parinsular isocortices.

eocortex (Figs. 1.2 and 1.3) that result in the formation of two different moieties of neocortex. These outwardly extending cortical formations have been referred to as "growth rings" of the neocortex (Sanides 1970, 1972). These studies of evolutional direction of cortical differentiation shed considerable light on how the brain is organized and constitute basic approaches to tracing the evolution of, and eventually defining, the mammalian neocortex. This approach has so far been used as a tool for tracing differential trends of evolutionary significance in a series of primates and lower mammals (Sanides 1970, 1972), and we are now for the first time beginning to apply such approaches to studies of the organization of the whale brain. In our recent work (Morgane, Jacobs & Galaburda, 1985) we began to elaborate a concept of neocortical evolution in the dolphin (*Tursiops truncatus*) by histological analysis of successive growth rings of cerebral cortex in this species using both Nissl and Golgi material. In our earlier studies, using primarily cytoarchitectonic analysis, we have described the paleocortex (Jacobs, Morgane & McFarland, 1971), and archicortex (Jacobs, McFarland & Morgane, 1979), whereas in later studies on the limbic lobe (Morgane, McFarland & Jacobs, 1982) and the insular formation (Jacobs, Galaburda, McFarland, & Morgane, 1984) we have stressed the quantitative approach to cortical cytoarchitecture.

Growth Rings of the Neocortex

The concept of growth rings of the neocortex, based on circumferentially changing characteristics of the cortex from more primitive cortices outward toward the convexity can be described as follows: The first stage of a laminated cortex is the two-strata periarchicortex medially and peripaleocortex laterally which, together, comprise the periallocortex. This periallocortex represents the first incipiently laminated cortex and is the first growth ring of neocortex (see Fig. 1.3). The periallocortex is thus considered the first step of neocortical evolution or what we term the primary stage of neocortex. The second growth ring, which is the proisocortex of the limbic lobe medially and insular cortex laterally, appears outside of the first growth ring. The third growth ring is formed also of two moieties, a paralimbic one medially and parinsular one laterally. These are the sites of additional, so-called secondary and supplemental sensory and motor representations (Fig. 1.3). The fourth or last stage of cortical evolution comprises, in the case of sensory cortex, special cores of koniocortex appearing within the sensory regions. In this last stage of cortical evolution koniocortex appears as a core rather than a ring within the cortical sensory regions. In the case of motor cortex the area gigantopyramidalis appears. The principle to keep in mind is that the gradations originating from phylogenetically older cortices determine the structure of more recent cortices and, therefore, they appear to represent directions of cortical differentiation during evolution.

Features of Progressive Cortical Differentiation

It is important first to summarize various features which form the basis of progressive cortical differentiation. These features relate to the continuing trends we see in animals with more highly evolved brains and represent changes that have occurred in the brain in progressing from lower mammalian forms to higher forms such as primates, including man.

The major prevailing trends in progressive cortical differentiation are: (1.) A shift in emphasis from the inner (layers V and VI) to the outer (layers II, III and IV) strata of the cortex, i.e., greater development of the outer layers. The most advanced stage of cortex is one with high granularization and showing an externo-pyramidal character, i.e., there is diminishment of band-like layer V (a "limbic" feature) associated with an increase in cell number, particularly in the outer pyramidal layer III and, especially, a relative increase in lamina IIIc cells; (2.) A stepwise appearance of granular cells, this stepwise granularization or stellarization process being a main trend in higher neocortical evolution. In this process there is emergence of an incipient inner granular layer IV, via a dysgranular stage in which granule cells are intermingled with small pyramidal cells. Overall, in progressive cortical evolution there is an increase in number of Golgi type II granular neurons relative to type I pyramidal neurons. Granule cells actually make their first appearance in the limbic and insular proisocortices; (3.) An overall thickening of cortex with special development and sublamination of the upper cortical laminae; (4.) A clear accentuation of lamination and; (5.) Extensive development of the basal dendritic skirt, this basal arborization of dendrites being a major progressive feature of pallial neuron evolution.

Features of Conservative Cortical Differentiation

Our recent Golgi studies have shown that the dolphin brain displays primarily features of conservative cortical differentiation. These will, therefore, be summarized and briefly discussed as a basis for interpreting the status of the dolphin brain. Some of the major prevailing trends in conservative cortical differentiation are: (1) Agranularization or what we term priority of the agranularity principle: The dolphin cortex is largely of the agranular type and there is a limited granularization trend seen over the entire cortex of the dolphin brain. In the dolphin there appears to be only an incipient development of layer IV which may be considered a primitive cortical feature and is, by definition, a sign of an intermediate-type cortex. Since layer IV is barely identifiable over the entire dolphin cortex and still has immature pyramidal cells in it from adjacent layers we term it "dysgranular" which represents the weakest degree of incipient granularization of the cerebral cortex; (2) Accentuation and strong pyramidalization of layer II. In the dolphin cortex, we have found a strong pyramidal character of layer II and, for that matter, strong pyramidalization of all layers of the dolphin cortex over all

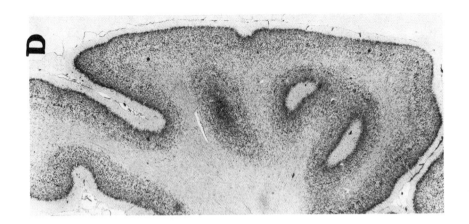

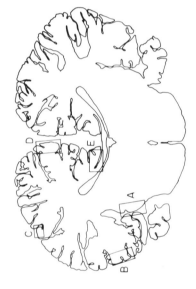

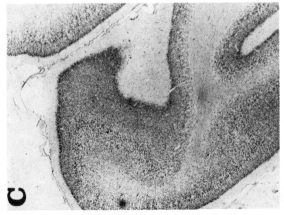

14

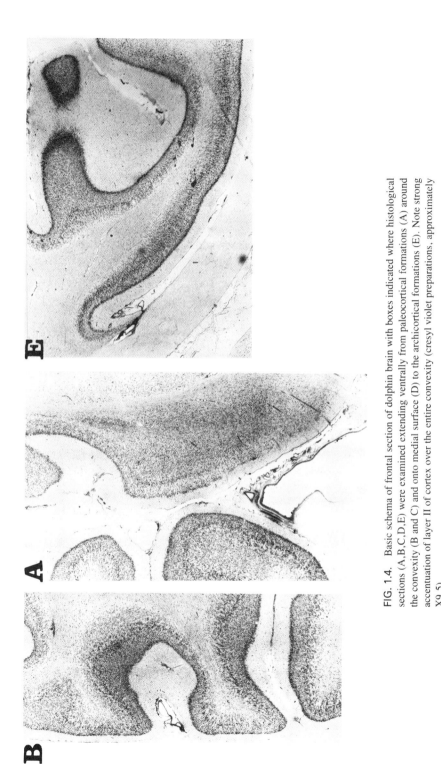

FIG. 1.4.   Basic schema of frontal section of dolphin brain with boxes indicated where histological sections (A,B,C,D,E) were examined extending ventrally from paleocortical formations (A) around the convexity (B and C) and onto medial surface (D) to the archicortical formations (E). Note strong accentuation of layer II of cortex over the entire convexity (cresyl violet preparations, approximately X9.5).

areas so far examined. Thus, Golgi type I neurons clearly predominate relative to type II neurons in all cortical laminae. Layer II is also strongly accentuated over the entire cortical formation of the dolphin brain (see Fig. 1.4). An accentuated layer II in the convexity cortex is considered largely a protoneocortical (periallocortical and proisocortical) mark expressing the originally prevailing layer I input of the axodendritic type. This effectively means the cortex in the dolphin is entirely covered over with a paleo-archicortical type of organization which represents a primitive architectonic feature. Thus, the horizontal fibers of the cortex, to which a highly organized associative function is ascribed, are located in man in the phylogenetically recent layers of the cortex, predominantly in layer III, whereas in the dolphin they are in the older and functionally primitive layer I. This latter is a characteristic of periallocortex in other mammals. Most of the cells in layer II in the dolphin brain are transitional pyramidal or multiform cells which are larger than granules. The presence of transitional intermediate type neurons is evidence of weak differentiation of the cortex. In this regard, most of the pyramids we have examined in the dolphin cortex are of the atypical or indeterminate type. This lack of specialization of neurons, with most being transitional or immature in type, is a strongly conservative feature in the dolphin brain. The pyramidalization layer II is actually quite similar in its structural organization to the external layer of the periarchicortex. Kesarev, Malofeyeva and Trykova (1977), in particular, have pointed out that the cetacean neocortex has numerous similarities to periarchicortex and, on the basis of our recent findings, we generally concur with this analysis; (3) Strong development of layers I and VI, the more primitive layers of cortex, along with underdevelopment of layers II, III and IV, the phylogenetically newer layers of the cortex. The dolphin brain shows exceptionally strong development of layers I and VI with some concomitant reduction of layers II and III. Layer IV is, at best, incipient. (4) Widespread dendrites in layer I (zonal arborization of dendrites) from so-called "extraverted" neurons in layer II over the entire cortex is a conservative feature of pallial neuron evolution. These extraverted neurons are a common feature of dolphin cortex and are prominent over the entire convexity cortex (see Fig. 1.5). They have apical dendrites that characteristically divide dichotomously at varied wide angles and terminate in layer I. Since these "extraverted neurons" very much resemble those of the superficial cell condensations of the first and second growth rings of the neocortex (the periallocortex and proisocortex) we recognize them as ancient type cortical neurons. In reality, the extreme example of the extraverted type goes back even to the amphibian level of brain evolution before a cerebral cortex has developed (see Fig. 1.6). In the cerebral cortex of most mammals this type of neuron is preserved only in the primitive allocortices, the most typical cell of its type being the granule cells of the dentate gyrus; (5) Little areal variability which can be characterized as the "uniformity" effect and which Kesarev et al. (1977) term a monotonous character or single structural design of dolphin cortex. Heightening of structural heterogeneity is characteristic of more evolved brains such as in primates. This

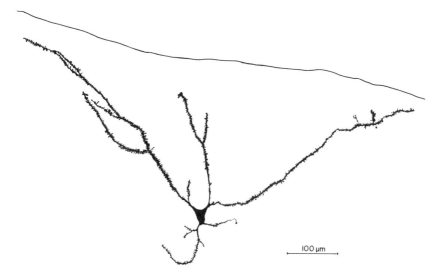

100 μm

FIG. 1.5.   Camera lucida drawing of cell of bandlike layer II in convexity cortex of dolphin brain. Accentuated layer II consists of polymorphic cells of the overall pyramidal type which are darkly staining and larger than granule cells. The peculiar "extraverted" character of these cells is revealed primarily by the Golgi method. The cells in layer II in dolphin convexity cortex have a well-developed dendritic pattern which is not found in isocortical laminae of the rat or cat, but is found in convexity cortex of hedgehog and bat brains (Sanides, 1972). These wide angle tufted cells in the convexity cortex are mostly atypical pyramidal cells with a short apical shaft from which dendrites spread widely into layer I or show direct widespreading of apical dendrites from the perikaryon into lamina I. In all of these cells the under-developed basilar dendrites never have reached development or spread like the apical dendrites. There is extensive overlapping of the external dendritic fields of the accentuated layer II cells within the zonal layer, the perikaryon of layer II cells appearing shaped by the extraversion and wide dendritic spread. As is known, extraversion in the allocortical and periallocortical formations is an expression of the fact that the zonal layer still represents the main afferent and association plexus of the cortex. This arrangement is a conservative feature agreeing with the observation in the hedgehog brain that thalamic terminations reach the zonal layer. The pial surface of the cortex is represented by the wavy line above the neuron.

homogeneous appearance of wide areas of the cortical formations of the dolphin brain is a decided feature of dolphin cortex in Nissl material we have examined (Morgane et al., 1980, 1982; Jacobs et al., 1984). The projectional regions of the cortex in cetaceans appear to directly interlock with each other and do not appear to be widely separated by associative regions, as in most other mammals. These projectional areas of the cortex in cetaceans are, however, arranged in the very same order as in the hypothetical ancestor of mammals (see Fig. 1.1): the visual region is retromedial, the auditory region is lateral and the somatosensorimotor area is rostral; (6) Arcuate pattern of main sulci and gyri on the lateral convexity

FIG. 1.6.   Schema from Ramon y Cajal showing phylogenetic trends of development of pallial neurons in A (frog), B (lizard), C (mouse) and D (man). Note how
this phylogenetic trend is paralleled by the ontogenesis of a pyramidal neuron of
the mouse (a-e). From: S. Ramon y Cajal: Histologie du systeme nerveux de
l'homme et des vertébres, Paris, Maloine, 1909. Note the striking resemblance of
cortical cells in frog (A) and lizard (B) brains to the extraverted neurons (Fig. 1.5)
seen in layer II on the convexity cortex of the dolphin brain.

of the hemisphere suggestive of the pattern seen in carnivores and ungulates.
This is a distinct feature of all cetacean brains we have examined; (7) Coexistence of progressive and conservative characters in the brain, so-called "mo-
saic" evolution of the brain. Kesarev (1970, 1975) has emphasized that dolphin
cortex is of a special character exhibiting combinations of features of very high
and primitive organization, though the progressive features he referred to mostly
relate to the expanse of cortex and extensive gyrification rather than to specific
intrinsic, histological features; (8) Generally indistinct areal boundaries. This is
the usual feature in the dolphin cortex as seen in our studies and those of Kesarev
(1970, 1975) and Kesarev et al. (1977); (9) Generally poor lamination over the
entire cortical surface. This is particularly related to an incipient layer IV which
is characteristic of all whale brains we have so far examined.

RECENT STUDIES OF CETACEAN CORTEX

In the past most workers seem to have been overcome by the vast expansion of
the cortex in the whale brain, particularly the convexity, so-called "associa-

tion,'' cortex. Our recent studies, using Golgi material, indicate that the dolphin brain has not reached the definitive final evolutionary stage of cortical development represented by the primary sensory and primary motor cortex. Thus, we find no hypergranular cores (koniocortex) in the dolphin and no evidence of primary motor cortex. Accentuated layer II, with many dendrites of extraverted neurons extending into layer I, is characteristic of the entire convexity cortex in the dolphin brain. In earlier evolutionary stages, before the primary motor and primary sensory cortices are elaborated, the paralimbic and parinsular representations are still contiguous. Our preliminary findings indicate that this contiguity of paralimbic and parinsular cortices appears to be the situation in the dolphin brain. The hedgehogs, which are survivors of the Paleocene epoch when archaic mammals were dominant, did not reach the stage of primary sensory and motor cortex evolution (Sanides, 1970, 1972). Whales are thought to have returned to water some 70–90 million years ago (Kesarev et al., 1977) and, related to this,

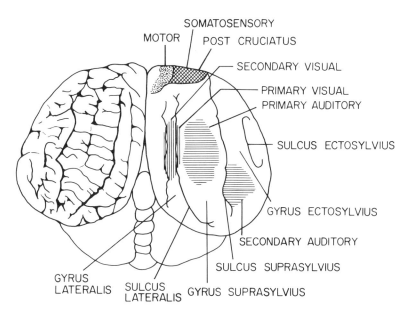

FIG. 1.7.   Map of electrophysiological localization in dolphin brain described by Sokolov et al. (1972). In these studies they claimed to be able to distinguish primary from secondary auditory and visual areas as shown in the map. In this figure, redrawn from the earlier Sokolov et al. (1972) work, areas of nonresponsive cortex between the auditory and visual areas, as well as between the somatosensory and motor areas, is indicated. This differs somewhat from the later Russian work (Sokolov et al., 1978) indicating that these various areas are in close proximity with little intervening cortex. This latter would agree more with the concept of the ''initial'' type brain shown in Fig. 1.1E.

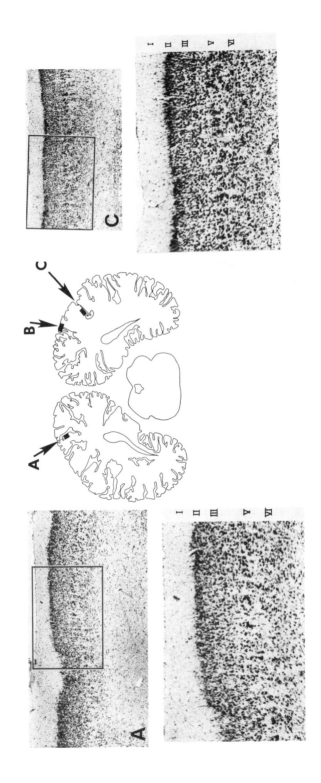

FIG. 1.8. Cytoarchitectonic organization of the cortex of the suprasylvian gyrus of *Tursiops truncatus* shown at three locations: (A) along the medial wall of the gyrus forming the external bank of the lateral sulcus, (B) on the free surface of the gyrus and (C) on the lateral wall of the gyrus forming the medial bank of the suprasylvian sulcus. The locations of these cortical fields (A, B, C) are shown by arrows on the orienting section outline. The higher magnifications of cortical areas represented by A, B and C (below each) show the cytoarchitectonic details. The suprasylvian cortex is extremely thin (0.97 ± .03 mm) and the percentage ratio of the width of its layers (I:II:III:V:VI) is 31:7:32:12:18, indicating dominance of layer III in the cortical plate (cortical plate = layers II+III+V+VI). The suprasylvian cortex is densely cellular (cortical cell density = 36,300 ± 2,800 neurons/mm³), far denser than the cortices we have previously quantified in the limbic lobe (Morgane et al., 1982) and insula (Jacobs et al., 1984). The laminar packing density of neurons in the cortical plate exhibits a decreasing density gradient from layer II through layer V (laminar density, L.D., layer II = 103,400 cells/mm³; L.D. layer IIIa = 91,400 cells/mm³; L.D. layer IIIb = 61,400 cells/mm³; L.D. layer IIIc = 47,600 cells/mm³; L.D. layer Va = 39,300 cells/mm³; L.D. layer Vb = 26,200 cells/mm³; L.D. layer VIa = 38,700 cells/mm³; and L.D. layer VIb = 21,200 cells/mm³). The predominant cell type throughout the cortex has a transitional pyramidal shape, with only approximately 11% of the neurons examined in Nissl preparations appearing to be stellate cells. Subsequent Golgi studies have verified this. The majority of these are scattered among the pyramids of layer III, especially in layer IIIc. A typical layer IV containing stellate cells, present in most land mammals, is not seen in the dolphin. Although the cortical plate is composed chiefly of small pyramidal-type cells throughout, variations in cell size are present in the different horizontal layers. The mean size dimensions (major cell axis by minor cell

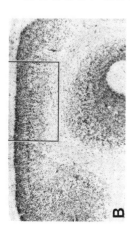

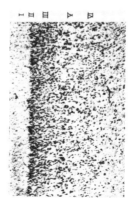

axis) of neurons in the various layers exhibit a narrow range. The predominant size of the pyramidal cell population is small superficially in the cortex (layer I = 13.4 μ by 9.2 μ, layer II = 13.8 μ by 9.0 μ, layer IIIa = 13.2 μ by 8.8 μ, layer IIIb = 12.8 μ by 10.2 μ). At deeper levels of the cortex, however, the mean size of pyramidal cells increases (layer IIIc = 15.6 μ by 11.8 μ, layer Va = 15.0 μ by 10.2 μ, layer Vb = 15.8 μ by 11.0 μ, layer VIa = 15.2 μ by 11.0 μ, layer VIb = 14.2 μ by 10.0 μ). The difference between mean sizes of the pyramids of layers IIIc and Va is not significant (P < 0.70) indicating an equopyramidal type cortical organization. The small population of stellate cells throughout the cortex remains essentially unchanged in size, with mean sizes in the different layers ranging only from 9.2 μ by 9.0 μ in layer II to 10.8 μ by 10.2 μ in layer VIa. From the medial wall of the suprasylvian gyrus (A) to the free surface (B) and, thence, to the lateral wall of the gyrus (C), layers II and III become increasingly more compact and the borders shared by layers II and III and also by layers III and V become more difficult to distinguish. Decreasing clarity of the III-V border results from the appearance of scattered pyramidal and some stellate-type neurons in layer IIIc and the equopyramidal relationship existing between layers IIIc and Va. The size relationship between pyramids of layer IIIc and Va reflects whether a particular cortex is oriented toward motor (emphasis on layer V pyramids) or a sensory-association (emphasis on layer IIIc pyramids) type of organization. At this general location in the lateral edge of the suprasylvian gyrus the shortest latency evoked responses of neurons to sound (click) stimuli have been elicited, indicating this to be the site of the primary auditory cortex in the dolphin (Ladygina et al., 1978). The equopyramidal relationship between layer IIIc and Va present in suprasylvian cortex of dolphins contrasts with the strongly externopyramidal relationship present in primary sensory and association cortices of land mammals. It is apparent that in the evolution of the cetacean auditory cortex differentiation has occurred in a different manner from that in land mammals, the latter involving the proliferation of large numbers of stellate cells and elaboration of layer IV (granularization). In view of the paucity of stellate cells in certain extant insectivores which may have had ancestors phylogenetically closer to those of modern cetaceans, cortical differentiation and specialization in the dolphin appears to have depended upon changes in existing populations of modified pyramidal cells. In the case of the auditory cortex, as indicated by our quantitative data, cortical specialization is associated in the dolphin not only with a greatly increased cell density, particularly in layers II and III and by an overall decrease in pyramidal cell size, but also by the appearance of larger pyramids in the deeper layers of the cortex, beginning with layer IIIc. The hyperpyramidalization occurring in the dolphin auditory cortex appears to parallel the various parameters of hypergranularization present in the auditory and other sensory cortices of most terrestrial mammals in which, in addition to increased cell density of layer IV, greatly increased numbers of stellate cells also appear in layers II and III. It would appear that in evolution of the dolphin, the region of cerebral cortex identified electrophysiologically as primary auditory cortex became specialized in a different way than in terrestrial mammals. In the aquatic environment auditory cortex of dolphin has been densely populated chiefly with transitional pyramidal cells that exhibit a decreased density gradient from superficial to deep levels of the cortical plate. The relative absence of neurons of stellate type and lack of typical layer IV further support the hypothesis that cortical specialization has occurred in a different manner in the dolphin. All fields illustrated stained by cresyl violet. Survey fields A,B,C, approximately 15.7X, enlargements 35.4X.

also apparently did not reach the final stage of sensory and motor cortex evolution. Actually, the general resemblance of the structural organization of the cetacean type cortex to the so-called "original architectonics" of the neocortex of primitive mammals (Creodonta) makes it possible to suggest that granularity of the neocortex of land mammals developed much later than at the time at which the ancestors of the Cetacea had already descended into the sea. The comparative studies of Sanides (1970, 1972) in insectivores and bats suggest that the formation of the koniocortices, as well as of the area gigantopyramidalis, i.e., the latest steps in sensory and motor cortex evolution, occurred in somewhat advanced mammals about 50 million years ago in the Eocene epoch with the rise of modern Orders and Suborders of mammals. By this time the whales had long since returned to the sea.

It should be emphasized that expansion and differentiation of neocortex has proceeded independently in the major mammalian lines of descent. The whales, having left terrestrial life many million of years ago, at about the same time as the Chiroptera, seem to reflect in their present neocortical structure the conservative features of those early mammalian stages that were perhaps preserved because of the decisive lack of further somatic sensory experience of land life for both groups of animals. Lacking this possible stimulus for higher neocortical differentiation, the neocortical evolution in the whales may, therefore have taken a different path leading, among other things, to the enormous surface spread of the neocortex, compensating or even hypercompensating in this manner for the reduced level of cortical differentiation.

We have only recently been able to acquire adequate Golgi impregnated material of dolphin brain suitable for studies of the various types of neuron families in the different cortical areas and for analysis of the architecture of their dendritic processes. Of particular importance is that our preliminary Golgi analyses of several types of cortical formations (growth rings), including convexity cortex, is not, by any of the criteria described above, indicative of progressive cortical differentiation of the dolphin brain. In the case of the dolphin brain, in particular, and the whale brain, in general, we have observed that: (1) the cortex is highly agranular; (2) layer II consists largely of transitional pyramidal cells, particularly extraverted neurons with wide dendritic ramifications in layer I; and (3) layer IV, if seen, lacks typical granule cells and contains only poorly differentiated or immature pyramidal-type neurons.

In contrast to primates where lateral integration is so well known, convexity cortex in whales, like in carnivores, has not been adequately defined cytoarchitecturally or by Golgi analysis of cell structure and dendritic characteristics. Interestingly, in the convexity cortex of the dolphin there is no dominant development of layer IIIc pyramids which is a hallmark of association cortex in man and primates. On the other hand, there is some evidence from studies of the thalamus that there might be a prominent elaboration of association cortices in dolphin brain. Thus, the lateral, posterior and pulvinar complexes, which project to posterior association cortex in all known species, are large in dolphin (Kruger, 1959). Based on development of the thalamus, association or "intrinsic" cortical fields should be extensive in the cetacean brain. However, regardless of the status of association type cortex, we emphasize, as has Sanides (1970, 1972) that association does not appear to be the leading edge of cortical evolution.

Kesarev et al. (1977) and others in the Russian school prefer to term the entire cetacean cortex as proisocortex, i.e., not true neocortex. We generally disagree with this conclusion, preferring to think in terms of successive rings of cortical differentiation with the second and third growth rings (insulo-limbic and parinsular-paralimbic cortex, respectively) representing earlier types of true neocortex. This parinsular-paralimbic cortex appears to comprise most of the convexity cortex in the dolphin. Thus, our findings to date indicate that the final stage of neocortical evolution as seen in most land mammals has not apparently been reached in the dolphin brain. In these terms, the dolphin brain, therefore, exhibits many similarities to the brain growth ring development seen in hedgehogs, and, in some ways, in bats. As already noted, the hedgehog brain may possibly be viewed as a model of the brain of the initial ancestor of mammals. In this regard, our recent Golgi studies have also shown, as is the case in the hedgehog and bat cortex, a strong development of extraverted neurons in layer II over the entire cortex of the dolphin brain. An accentuated layer II in the cortex is

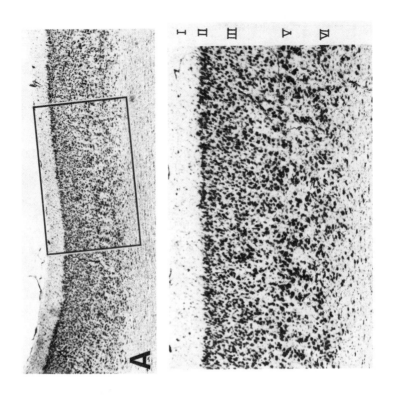

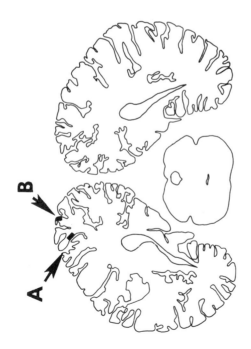

24

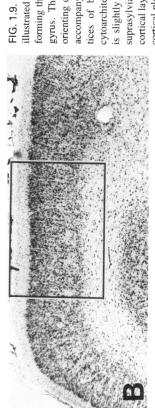

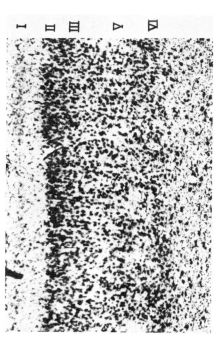

I

II
III

V

VI

FIG. 1.9. Organization of the cortex of the lateral gyrus in *Tursiops truncatus* as illustrated in two cortical fields: (A) in the external wall of the lateral gyrus forming the medial bank of the lateral sulcus, and (B) near the free surface of the gyrus. The locations of cortical fields A and B are shown by arrows on the orienting drawing. Boxes outlining portions of cortex on A and B are shown in accompanying photomicrographs (below each) at higher magnification. The cortices of both the lateral wall and free surface have an essentially similar cytoarchitectonic organization. Although the cortex is thin (1.14 ± .01 mm), it is slightly (0.17 mm), but significantly (P = <.001), thicker than that of the suprasylvian gyrus (0.97 ± .03 mm). In common with the suprasylvian gyrus, cortical layer III of the lateral gyrus percentagewise is also the broadest layer of the cortical plate (cortex other than layer I). The percentage ratio of the width of the cortical layers in the lateral gyrus (I:II:III:V:VI) is 20:7:37:15:21, indicating again the strong likelihood that this cortex is dominated by afferent rather than efferent cortical mechanisms. The cortical plate in the lateral gyrus is especially compact at the level of layers II and III and consists, as in the case of the suprasylvian gyrus, chiefly of small cells mostly of transitional pyramidal type that range in size from 9.2 um by 8.4 um to 17.6 um by 11.8 um. The overall cortical cell density is slightly higher (37,500 ± 1,800 neurons/mm³) than that of the suprasylvian gyrus, but the difference between the means is not significant (P < 0.70). The same decreasing gradient pattern of laminar densities from layer II through layer V, present in the suprasylvian gyrus, is also present in the lateral gyrus (laminar density, L.D., layer II = 105,000 cells/mm³; L.D. layer IIIa = 75,400 cells/mm³; L.D. layer IIIb = 54,500 cells/mm³; L.D. layer IIIc = 43,500 cells/mm³; L.D. layer Va = 35,800 cells/mm³; L.D. layer Vb = 20,000 cells/mm³; L.D. layer VIa = 33,100 cells/mm³; and L.D. layer VIb = 16,700 cells/mm³). Throughout the cortex of the lateral gyrus the great majority of cells are modified pyramids that appear somewhat immature or transitional in nature. Approximately 13% of the neurons appear to be stellate cells and, as in the suprasylvian cortex, these cells are located mainly in layer III, especially IIIc. Obviously, the final classification of these cells cannot be made except in Golgi analysis. The cells in layer IIIc that may be of stellate type, however, are scattered among the more numerous pyramidal cells and are present neither in sufficient numbers or concentrations to be considered as a distinct layer such as the internal granular layer of terrestrial mammals though we are continuing to study this issue. Considering the overall small size of neurons throughout the cortex, it is of interest that neurons of pyramidal type exhibit broader ranges of mean sizes (from 11.8 to 17.6 um by from 7.6 um to 11.8 um) than do the stellate cells (from 9.2 to 12.2 um by from 8.4 to 11.2 um). Moreover, a statistical comparison of pyramidal cell size in the cortex reveals that the pyramids of layers IIIb, IIIc and Va are significantly larger than those of layers II and IIIa, with P values being from 0.05 to less than 0.001 (layer I = 12.2 um by 7.6 um, layer II = 11.8 um by 8.2 um, layer IIIa = 13.4 um by 10.0 um, layer IIIb = 15.4 um by 10.0 um, IIIc = 15.8 um by 11.4 um, layer Va = 17.6 um by 11.8 um, layer Vb = 14.6 um by 10.6 um, layer VIa = 12.6 um by 8.8 um, and layer VIb = 15.2 um by 10.8 um). It is important to point out, however, that there is no statistically significant size difference between layer IIIc and Va pyramids (P <.30) indicating that, like the suprasylvian region, the cortex of the lateral gyrus has an equopyramidal type organization. In view of their similar equopyramidal organization, it is significant that most of the lateral gyrus has been shown to give rise to multiple evoked responses to light flashes (Ladygina et al., 1978). In general, the cortical cytoarchitecture of the lateral gyrus repeats the patterns present in the suprasylvian gyrus. Thus, as in the case of auditory cortex the visual cortex of the dolphin is essentially microcellular, hyper-pyramidalized, agranular and is characterized by extremely dense layers II, IIIa and b, and an equopyramidal organization. Nevertheless, in spite of overall similarities, morphometric differences, especially involving layers III and V, are present and reflect organizational and functional differences between the two adjacent cortical regions. It is of additional interest that the cortex extending onto the medial surface of the hemisphere beyond the lateral gyrus in the dolphin, and comprising part of the medial occipital area (Kesarev et al., 1977), has been partially included in the visual projection zone by Ladygina et al (1978) based on limited electrophysiological evidence with exploring electrodes. In Loyez myelin material we have traced fibers from the lateral geniculate nucleus to this medial cortex which in *Tursiops* covers a prominent oval shaped lobule. As in the lateral gyrus, the cortex of the oval lobule is thin (1.2 ± .05 mm) and the percent ratio of width of its layers (I,II,III,V,VI) is 13:5:32:22:28, again indicating the dominance of layer III. Although a number of architectonic differences from the lateral gyrus can be demonstrated morphometrically the overall cortical architecture of the oval lobule is of the same fundamental type as that of lateral and suprasylvian gyri. Both fields of lateral gyrus shown are stained by cresyl violet. Survey fields approximately 20X, enlargements approximately 50X.

clearly a protoneocortical mark indicating the originally prevailing layer I input of the axodendritic type. Of course, the extreme thickness of layer I and its strong content of horizontal fibers does not, in itself, serve as conclusive evidence of a phylogenetic closeness between dolphin brain and brains of insectivores. However, considered along with the many other conservative features we and others have defined in the dolphin brain, the accumulated evidence in no way points to signs of progressive evolution of the whale brain or to any evidence that the final cortical growth rings have developed in these brains.

ELECTROPHYSIOLOGICAL MAPPING STUDIES
OF THE CETACEAN BRAIN

With regard to the relative size and positions of specific types of cortex on the convexity of the brain in whales little is presently known. Sokolov, Ladygina and Supin (1972) and Ladygina, Mass and Supin (1978) have carried out a series of electrophysiological mapping studies on convexity cortex of the dolphin and a map summarizing their findings is shown in Figs. 1.1E, and 1.7. They have even claimed, on the basis of evoked potential work, to have been able to define both primary and secondary auditory and visual cortex in the dolphin (see Fig. 1.7). We have followed up this work with a cytoarchitectonic analysis of these same areas and, to date, have not on these grounds been able to demonstrate any koniocortices indicative of primary sensory cortex. In Figs. 1.8 and 1.9 we indicate the cytoarchitecture of similar cortical fields mapped by the Russians (as shown in Fig. 1.7). We are presently carrying out Golgi analyses of these same formations and, to date, these have revealed in these areas extremely extraverted neurons of accentuated layer II with dendrites extending at wide angles into accentuated layer 1 (see Fig. 1.5). Our Golgi analyses indicate that layer II is composed largely of immature-type pyramidal neurons with strong development of apical branches into layer I and poorly developed basilar dendrites. In general, our evidence to date in no way distinguishes a primary sensory cortical area on the convexity of the hemisphere. It appears that the parinsular/paralimbic type cortices we have identified as forming the main mass of convexity cortex may contain the equivalents of secondary sensory-motor areas, though none of these are clearly definable by cytoarchitectonic or Golgi analyses.

SUMMARY

The whale cortex does not appear to have developed the last or phylogenetically latest stage of cortical evolution characteristic of primates and many other mammals. It is possible that hypergranular cores (koniocortex) and area gigantopyramidalis developed about 50 million years ago in land mammals, whereas whales returned to water some 70–90 million years ago before granularization of the cortex occurred. The leading stage in cortical differentiation in whales seem to be the paralimbic-parinsular stage which is the most primitive of somatomotor representation. It is obvious that Golgi studies combined with evolutionary and ontogenetic analyses, along with physiological approaches, are needed to shed further light on fundamental cortical types and their extent in the whale brain. Though the whale brain has taken a different course of evolution it retains all conservative characters seen in primitive terrestrial and aerial forms such as hedgehogs and bats. Given that the whale returned to water many million of years ago as a totally aquatic mammal, continued studies of the cetacean brain may help in the understanding of mammalian brain evolution in general and the effects of environment on cortical development.

ACKNOWLEDGMENT

Supported by National Science Foundation Grant BNS 82–42356 and BNS 84–14523.

REFERENCES

Filimonoff, I. N. (1947). A rational subdivision of cerebral cortex. *Archives of Neurology & Psychiatry, 58,* 296–311.

Filimonoff, I. N. (1949). *Comparative anatomy of mammalian cerebral cortex.* Moscow: Edition of the Academy of Medical Sciences (Russian Edition).

Gingerich, P. D., Wells, N. A., Russell, D. E., & Ibrahim Shah, S. M. (1983). Origin of whales in epicontinental remnant seas: New evidence from the early Eocene of Pakistan. *Science, 220,* 403–406.

Jacobs, M. S., Galaburda, A. M., McFarland, W. L., & Morgane, P. J. (1984). The insular formations of the dolphin brain. Quantitative cytoarchitectonic studies of the insular component of the limbic lobe. *Journal Comparative Neurology, 225,* 396–432.

Jacobs, M. S., McFarland, W. L., & Morgane, P. J. (1979). The anatomy of the brain of the bottlenose dolphin (*Tursiops truncatus*). Rhinic lobe (rhinencephalon): The archicortex. *Brain Research Bulletin, 4* (Supp. 1), 1–108.

Jacobs, M. S., Morgane, P. J., & McFarland, W. L. (1971). The anatomy of the brain of the bottlenose dolphin (*Tursiops truncatus*). Rhinic lobe (rhinencephalon). I. The paleocortex. *Journal Comparative Neurology, 141,* 205–272.

Kesarev, V. S. (1970). Certain data on neuronal organization of the neocortex in the dolphin brain. *Arkh. Anat. Gistol. Embriol., 59,* 71–77.

Kesarev, V. S. (1975). On the problem of homologization of the cerebral neocortex in cetaceans. *Arkh. Anat. Gistol. Embriol., 68,* 5–13.

Kesarev, V. S., Malofeyeva, L. I., & Trykova, O. V. (1977). Ecological specificity of cetacean neocortex. *Journal Hirnforschung, 18,* 447–460.

Kruger, L. (1959). The thalamus of the dolphin (*Tursiops truncatus*) and comparison with other mammals. *Journal Comparative Neurology, 111,* 133–194.

Ladygina, T. F., Mass, A. M., & Supin A. Ia. (1978). Multiple sensory projections in the dolphin cerebral cortex. *Zh. Vyssh. Nerv. Deiat. 28,* 1047–1054.

Morgane, P. J., Jacobs, M. S., & McFarland, W. L. (1980). Anatony of the brain of the bottlenose dolphin (*Tursiops truncatus*). Surface configuration of the telencephalon of the bottlenose dolphin with comparative anatomical observations in four other cetacean species. *Brain Research Bulletin, 5* (Supp. 3), 1–107.

Morgane, P. J., McFarland, W. L., & Jacobs, M. S. (1982). The limbic lobe of the dolphin brain: A quantitative cytoarchitectonic study. *Journal Hirnforschung, 23,* 465–552.

Morgane, P. J., Jacobs, M. S., & Galaburda, A. (in press, 1985). Evolutionary aspects of cortical organization in dolphin brain. In M. Bryden & R. J. Harrison (Eds.), *Research on dolphins.* Oxford: Oxford University Press.

Sanides, F. (1970). Functional architecture of motor and sensory cortices in primates in the light of a new concept of neocortex evolution. In C. R. Noback & W. Montagna (Eds.), *The primate brain (Advances in Primatology, Vol. I)* (pp. 132–208). New York: Appleton-Century-Crofts.

Sanides, F. (1972). Representation in the cerebral cortex and its areal lamination patterns. In E. H. Bourne (Ed.), *Structure and function of nervous tissue, Vol. 5* (pp. 329–453). New York: Academic Press.

Sokolov, V. E., Ladygina, T. F., & Supin A. Ia. (1972). Localization of sensory zones in the dolphin's cerebral cortex. *Doklady Akademy Nauk SSSR, 202,* 490–493.

2 Physiological Observations on Dolphin Brains

Sam H. Ridgway
Naval Ocean Systems Center, San Diego

Physiological observations can possibly contribute to the understanding of cognition from at least three approaches. First, understanding of biological phenomena often results from correlation of apparently unrelated findings in anatomy, behavioral science, and physiology. Therefore, it seems appropriate to present some findings on the physiology of the dolphin brain in a conference on dolphin cognition and behavior. Second, because our best examples of mental events rest in our own conscious experiences, similarities of brain structure and function between animals and human adults have been suggested as a possible basis for inferring mental process (Neville & Hillyard, 1982). Third, mental processes must occur within the nervous system and there cause some change. If such changes are measurable, we might be able to assess the dolphin's cognitive ability. These processes, however, are difficult to measure because so much goes on within the nervous system that is not necessarily either conscious, mental, or cognitive—e.g., the regulation of body functions (breathing, circulation, homeostasis), proprioceptive adjustments (posture, balance, orientation), sensory coordination and involuntary reflexes, to name a few. Recently, methods have been devised for measuring ''event related potentials'' (ERP) from the human brain. Some averaged waves recorded from the scalp such as the ''P300'' and ''N400'' appear to be associated with cognition (Callaway, Tueting, & Koslow, 1978; Kutas & Hillyard, 1980). Work on dolphin ERP is discussed in another chapter (Woods, Ridgway, Carder, & Bullock).

Physiological methods such as the ERP offer potential as a nonbehavioral means of investigating animal cognition that may be especially valuable if the ERP can be correlated with behavior. Although it has been asserted that cognitive characteristics can only be measured through behavioral experiments and observations (cf. Herman, 1980), we know from our own mental experience that overt behavior does not always reflect our mental processes. Humans given a paralytic agent such as curare or succinylcholine are capable of no overt motor behavior, yet, their minds are active and they are able to give complete descriptions of their experience after the paralysis has worn off. For the present, behavioral experiments and observation are certainly the best methods we have for comparing the cognitive characteristics of species; yet, we must not ignore the structure and function of the brains from which the behavior comes. We should be especially alert for structural and functional brain characteristics that can be correlated with behavior and vice versa (Bullock, 1984).

In this chapter, I present some of our findings about the size, form, and physiology of the dolphin brain, and occasionally draw some comparisons from the literature about the brains of orangutans, gorillas, chimpanzees, and humans.

DOLPHIN BRAIN SIZE

"Long before the human species or even the vertebrates appeared, the greatest achievement of evolution was the brain" (Bullock, 1984). During evolution, it appears clear, larger brain size has been a selective advantage. There is an inverse correlation between the age of appearance of a group in earth history and the size of its brain (Bonner, 1980).

In searching for some brain component or characteristic that sets us apart from other species, neurobiologists have often mentioned the large size of the human brain expressed in terms such as encephalization, the relative enlargement of the cerebral cortex, and the extreme fissurization or convolution of the cortex. Dolphins, like humans, have large brains with a greatly expanded, highly fissurized neocortex. This factor more than any other has led many of us to consider the animal's mental life.

When we speak of the large dolphin brain, we should not consider as equal all toothed whales sometimes called porpoises or dolphins. Just as there are great variations in primate brain size, there are differences within the odontocetes: Two species with members of similar body size may have widely different brain weights. For example, in each case—*Grampus* and *Kogia, Orcinus* and *Ziphius, Lagenorhynchus* and *Plantanista,* or *Cephalorhynchus* and *Pontoporia*—the former has a brain two to three times as large as the latter despite similar body size (see Ridgway & Brownson, 1984). The zenith of cetacean brain size seems to lie in the family Delphinidae. Only in this family do we have animals in the human size range with brains as large as the human brain.

Wood and Evans (1980) have compared several odontocetes using the EQ (encephalization quotient, Jerison, 1973). In their EQ series, *Tursiops* and *Lagenorhynchus* lie only slightly below the human. In a larger series using only adult animals, Ridgway and Brownson (1982, 1984) reported a mean brain weight of 1587 grams for *Tursiops* and 1256 grams for *Lagenorhynchus*. EQ's of both species were between 4.0 and 5.0, below human values but roughly double the EQ of higher primates including gorillas, chimpanzees, and orangutans. Thus, when brain size is considered in relation to body size, the most highly encephalized of the dolphins rank between humans and other higher primates.

CONVOLUTEDNESS—SURFACE AREA OF THE DOLPHIN BRAIN

It is generally assumed that the human brain is more convoluted (cf. Teyler, 1977) than that of all other mammals; however, Elias and Schwartz (1969) and Haug (1970) have shown that the brains of some odontocetes have more surface area per unit of volume than the human brain, and thus are more convoluted. In the first study, the "index of folding," another measure of convolution, was found to be 2.86 for a series of human brains and 4.47 for a bottlenosed dolphin brain of similar size. In a series of 19 *Tursiops* brains, Ridgway and Brownson (1982, 1984) found an average cortical surface area of 3745 cm² while Elias and Schwartz (1969) gave a mean value of 2275 cm² for the 20 human brains they measured.

Therefore, odontocetes exceed humans, and all other groups as well, in convolutedness or fissurization of the cerebral cortex (Fig. 2.1). Cortical surface area is directly related to brain size (Jerison, 1982; Ridgway & Brownson, 1984). Small odontocete brains are just as convoluted as larger ones.

VOLUME OF THE DOLPHIN CORTEX

Although the dolphin brain is highly convoluted with a large cortical surface area, the cortex is thin (see also Morgane, Jacobs, & Galaburda, this volume). Haug (1969) gives values of 2.9 mm and 1.4 mm for cortical thickness in *Homo* and *Tursiops* respectively. His dolphin specimen weighed 110 kg and was probably immature. Kesarev (1971) reported 1.60 mm cortical thickness in *Tursiops*. Ridgway and Brownson (1984) found a range of mean cortical thickness in adult *Tursiops* from 1.30 mm in visual cortex to 1.76 mm in motor areas. Thus, it appears that the thickness of the cerebral cortex of humans is about twice that found in dolphin. From this, we can see that, although the dolphin cerebrum is considerably larger in surface area, the total average volume of its cortex (560 cc) is just over 80% of the average (660 cc) human brain's cortex. This measure again places *Tursiops* below *Homo* but above such highly encephalized land mammals as chimpanzees (Haug, 1970).

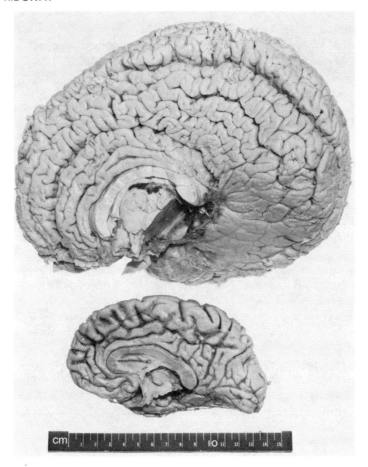

FIG. 2.1.   Medial view of right prosencephalon of the largest delphinid, the killer whale *Orcinus* (above) compared to right prosencephalon of a human brain below. This *Orcinus* brain is about five times as large as the human brain, but there is only a slight difference in size of the corpus callosum.

THE DOLPHIN BRAIN AND VISCERAL FUNCTION

The massive development of the neocortex in dolphins might be related to the more active participation of their central nervous system, in comparison with that of terrestrial mammals, in the regulation of visceral functions and the correlation of visceral and somatic functions (Kesarev, 1971; Kesarev & Malofeyeva, 1969). Lilly (1964), for example, has proposed that dolphin respiration may be controlled by the nucleus ellipticus of the thalamus and that, presumably, this nucleus has projections to and from the cortex. Thus, the fully aquatic cetaceans may devote more brain to controlling respiration than terrestrial mammals. Even so, visceral and somatic functions required for coping with the marine environment are common to all marine cetaceans. Yet, the EQ of some odontocetes is 1 or less, placing them on a par with terrestrial mammals such as ungulates, prosimians, and carnivores (Jerison, 1973) while in others the EQ is 4 or 5, placing them almost as high as humans. Moreover, Wirz (1950) has measured various parts of the brain, comparing them with the brain stem (where visceral and somatic functions must be represented). Her system placed the odontocete brains on a par with those of humans. Ridgway, Flanigan, and McCormick (1966) studied a similar index, the ratio of brain weight to spinal cord weight. Here again, dolphins ranked just below humans and considerably above other higher primates. Considering these findings, the suggestion by Kesarev and Malofeyeva (1969) and by Kesarev (1971) that the massive development of the cetacean neocortex has resulted from the greater participation of the neocortex, compared to that of terrestrial mammals, in regulating visceral and somatic function seems unlikely. We must look for other reasons for the great expansion of the neocortex in dolphins.

GROWTH OF THE DOLPHIN BRAIN

"In man there seems to be an extraordinary prolongation of youth, and this permits the brain to continue its expansion. The period of dependency on parents is increased so that the period when learning can occur becomes relatively long" (Bonner, 1980). The human brain grows from just under 25% of its adult weight at birth to full development in about 17 or 18 years. Kesarev (1971) has pointed out that while human cortex development is mainly in the postnatal years, some lower primates are born with cortical formation about 80% of the adult complement. He says, "the earliest to appear and the latest to conclude their development in man are those formations of the neocortex which may be considered phylogenetically as the most recent and are associated with the most complex forms of cerebral activity, present only in man, the integrative and analytical functions" (Kesarev, 1971).

Delphinids are also born with brains at a more advanced stage of development. A longer gestation period, about 12 months in *Tursiops,* is needed so that the neonate can swim and engage in activities that might require a more developed brain. Neonatal brain weight averaged 42.5% of mean adult weight in eight Atlantic coastal *Tursiops,* and over 50% in two *Orcinus* and two *Delphinus* (Ridgway & Brownson, 1984). By weaning time at 18 months, Atlantic coastal *Tursiops* have brains over 80% of mean adult weight, a stage not reached by human brains until year three or four. Male *Tursiops* do not reach sexual maturity until about 13 years-of-age, while the females mature slightly earlier (Sergeant, Caldwell, & Caldwell, 1973). From the sparse data available, I estimate that

BRAIN GROWTH

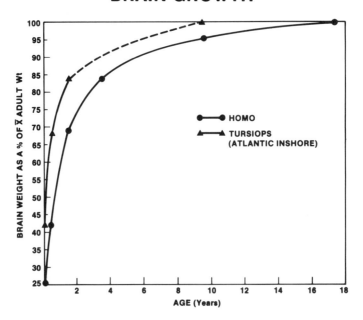

FIG. 2.2.   Approximate growth curves for humans (*Homo*) and dolphin (*Tursiops*) brains. The dolphin data are from my files while the human curve was drawn from average values given by Spector (1956). Laird (1969) gives a more precise curve showing human brain growth reaching 95% by age five. Irrespective of which human values are used, the dolphin brain is larger at birth and and at any age continues to be larger as a percentage of adult weight.

Atlantic coastal *Tursiops* reach full brain development in 9 or 10 years, about half the total growth period required for human brains (Fig. 2.2) but considerably longer than for most higher mammals. Regarding the time period during which the brain develops to full adult size, it appears that *Tursiops* again ranks between humans on the one hand, and gorillas and chimpanzees on the other.

DOLPHIN BRAIN METABOLISM

"Brains are metabolically expensive and don't get bigger (phylogenetically) unless in some fashion they are more than paying for their upkeep" (Hockett, 1978). This statement is supported by measures of brain metabolism in many vertebrates. Might the cetacean brain represent a departure from this general trend? Could the dolphin brain be large, but metabolically less active than the brains of other mammals?

Many authors have found that dolphins have a higher metabolic rate than terrestrial mammals of similar size (Hampton, Whittow, Szckercezes, & Rutherford, 1971; Irving, Scholander, & Grinnell, 1941; Kanwisher & Sundnes, 1965; Pierce, 1970; Ridgway & Patton, 1971; Scholander, 1940). The high protein diet (dolphins consume almost no carbohydrates) contributes considerably to a high metabolic rate. Those species studied have large thyroid glands (Harrison, 1969) and a high level of circulating thyroid hormones (Ridgway & Patton, 1971). Long-term food consumption of captive animals correlates well with observed levels of oxygen consumption. The *Tursiops* studied by Ridgway and Patton (1971) required over 6000 Kcal/day to maintain body weight. Feeding rates of several species of odontocetes have been summarized by Sergeant (1969).

Marine delphinids are diving mammals. Some, at least, are capable of reaching depths of 300 to 600 m and remaining submerged for 5 to 20 min. Alveolar gas tensions after longer dives by Atlantic coastal *Tursiops* (Ridgway, Scronce, & Kanwisher, 1969) suggest that the brain may be capable of short periods of anaerobic metabolism, a capability not found in higher adult land mammals. Since this observation in *Tursiops,* anaerobic metabolism by the seal brain during the later stages of a maximal dive has been demonstrated (Kerem, Elsner, & Wright, 1971; Simon, Robin, Elsner, Van Kessel, & Theodore, 1974).

I was not able to show anaerobic metabolism during hypoxic periods up to 6 min in anesthetized dolphins. Arterio-venous differences in oxygen and glucose across the dolphin brain were as high or higher than in anesthetized humans. Based on my own data and those of Soviet researchers, I conclude that there is no basis for assuming dolphin brains have a lower overall rate of metabolism. The great fissurization of the dolphin brain creates a large cortical surface area that may be essential to provide surface contact with the abundant meningeal blood supply (Ries & Langworthy, 1937; Wilson, 1933) to support oxygen and glucose needs of the cortex. The proposition that brain size and fissurization in odontocetes may be connected with diving and the need to sustain brain function during prolonged hypoxia is, however, weakened by the observation that seals (Scholander, 1940) and sirenians (Irving et al., 1941), animals that also dive for long periods, have smaller, less convoluted brains and a thicker cortex.

HEMISPHERIC INDEPENDENCE

Total Crossing of Optic Nerve Fibers

In most mammals, each eye projects the majority of its nerve fibers to the opposite (contralateral) cerebral hemisphere (crossed fibers); however, considerable numbers of fibers (uncrossed fibers) project to the cerebral hemisphere on the same side (ipsilateral side). The dolphin may be an exception to the general rule that crossed and uncrossed fibers arise from each eye. Each of the dolphin's

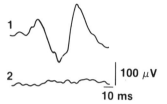

FIG. 2.3.   Evoked responses from visual cortex of a dolphin to photic stimulation
to one eye (1. contralateral hemisphere; 2. ipsilateral hemisphere). These responses support the earlier anatomical evidence that optic nerve fibers from each
eye project only to the opposite hemisphere of the brain (figure redrawn from
Supin et al., 1978).

eyes probably projects only to the contralateral hemisphere. This conclusion is
somewhat tenuous because it results mainly from two anatomical studies of one
animal each. First, Hatschek (1903) studied the brain of a captured dolphin that
had lost one eye. Using a Weigert stained series of brainstem sections, he
observed total decussation of the optic nerve across the optic chiasm. From this
information, he concluded that dolphins lacked binocular vision. Second, Jacobs, Morgane, and McFarland (1975) reported on a silver degeneration study
carried out on a male *Tursiops truncatus* that had been enucleated and then
vitually perfused after 14 days survival. With some reservations concerning the
long survival time and a 19% discrepancy between numbers of fibers in the optic
nerve and optic tract of their specimen, the researchers concluded that the dolphin exhibited an apparently total decussation of optic nerve fibers, a condition
highly atypical of mammals but common in other vertebrates.

Some physiological evidence also supports complete crossing of optic nerve
fibers. Supin et al. (1978) mapped the sensory projection zones on the dorsal and
dorsolateral surface of dolphin cortex. They found that large evoked potential
responses were obtained from visual cortex when light flashes were presented to
the contralateral eye, but no such responses were obtained when equivalent
flashes were presented to the ipsilateral eye (Fig. 2.3).

The Visual Field and Disconjugate Eye Movement

Langworthy (1932) like Hatschek (1903) doubted that *Tursiops* had stereoscopic
vision saying that "the development of the visual cortex compares well with that
described by Mott for other mammals having panoramic vision." It appears to
me that *Tursiops* has some degree of visual overlap ventrally and rostrad as well
as dorsally and slightly caudad. Despite these small areas of overlap in the visual
field, the eyes appear to move independently. McCormick (1969) observed that
one eye might look forward and dorsally, while the other might look rearward
and ventrally. Physiologic investigations have confirmed that dolphin eye movements are not conjugate. Power spectral density analyses of the dolphin eye

movements showed maximal power around 0.1 Hz, lower than the human counterpart (Dawson, Carder, Ridgway, & Schmeisser, 1981).

Dolphin Sleep

Shurley, Serafetinides, Brooks, Elsner, and Kenney (1969; see also Serafetinides, Shurley, & Brooks, 1972) were the first to find evidence supporting John Lilly's claim that cetaceans could sleep with half the brain awake (Lilly, 1964). More extensive research was done by Soviet investigators (Mukhametov, 1984; Mukhametov, Supin, & Polykova, 1977). They reported marked asymmetries in electroencephalograms (EEG) from right and left hemispheres of *Tursiops* (Fig. 2.4). My observations of *Tursiops* EEG tend to support most of these findings.

   Mukhametov (1984) recognized three stages in the dolphin EEG: stage 1, desynchronization; stage 2, intermediate synchronization including sleep spindles and theta and delta waves; stage 3, maximal synchronization, when delta waves of maximal amplitude occupied not less than 50% of each scoring interval. Stages 1 and 2 occurred bilaterally or unilaterally. Stage 3 occurred in only one hemisphere at a time. Wakefulness or bilateral EEG desynchronization (EEG stage 1 in both hemispheres) occupied 50 to 60% of the recording time. Stage 2, intermediate synchronization, was sometimes recorded bilaterally, and at such times dolphins displayed EEG patterns typical of terrestrial mammals. "The whole sequence of respiratory movements of dolphins may be observed during bilateral intermediate EEG synchronization without arousal." Bilateral intermediate EEG synchronization (stage 2 in both hemispheres) occupied only a small percentage of the recording time. Unihemispheric slow wave sleep (stage 3 in only one hemisphere), the main type of sleep observed in the dolphin brain, occupied 30 to 40% of recording time. "We have never recorded bilateral delta waves in the dolphin brain during natural sleep. The unilateral sleep episodes can last more than 2 h. . . . Simultaneous recordings from the parietal, occipital, and frontal fields of the hemispheres confirm that a hemisphere is always syn-

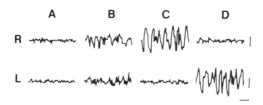

FIG. 2.4.   Electroencephalographic tracings from right (R) and left (L) cerebral hemispheres of a dolphin brain (figure redrawn from Mukhametov, 1984). A: bilateral desynchronization. B: bilateral intermediate synchronization. C, D: unilateral delta waves. Unipolar recordings from roughly symmetrical areas of the parietal cortex. Time calibration 1 s, amplitude calibration 200 μV.

chronized or desynchronized as a unit. Records from thalamic nuclei demonstrate that the thalamus can also generate slow wave activity unilaterally and concurrently with the ipsilateral neocortex. Thus, unilateral slow wave sleep is not only a cortical, but also a subcortical phenomenon'' (Mukhametov, 1984).

Separate Blood Supply for the Two Hemispheres

In most mammals, the internal carotid artery is the major supplier of blood to the brain. This is not the case in the dolphin which supplies its brain through the massive thoracico-spinal retia (Viamonte, Morgane, Galliano, Nagel, & McFarland, 1968). In its course from heart to brain, blood passes through the retia. This arrangement is thought to have a pressure-damping function for the cerebral circulation (Nagel, Morgane, McFarland, & Galliano, 1968).

Neither the internal carotid artery nor vertebral arteries supply blood to the dolphin brain, and the circle of Willis is absent (McFarland, Jacobs, & Morgane, 1979). The entire cerebral blood supply comes through a thoracico-spinal rete, supplied by intercostal and posterior thoracic arteries. Vogl and Fisher (1981a), in a study of *Delphinapterus* and *Monodon,* concluded that the carotid artery is closed at a level just proximal to the carotid rete and has no direct involvement with the cerebral blood supply. Vogl and Fisher (1981b) summarize additional findings as follows:

> Circulation to the brain is effected by two pairs of arteries originating from intracranial retia. The rostral pair supplies most of the forebrain (prosencephalon) and hindbrain (rhombencephalon). The circulatory pattern is characterized by (1) complete independence of anterior cerebral arteries (no anastomoses); (2) extensive cortical supply by the anterior choroidal arteries; (3) absence of subdural communicating vessels between rostral and caudal trunks; (4) union of caudal trunks to form a small basilar artery; and (5) absence of vertebral arteries and hence of a vertebral basilar system.

Thus, in *Tursiops, Delphinapterus,* and *Monodon,* and probably in cetacea in general, there is a lack of connecting vessels that in most mammals make up the circle of Willis. "The absence of these anastomoses forms the anatomical basis for the complete subdural independence of blood supply to each of the two cerebral hemispheres, of which the functional significance is not known'' (Vogl & Fisher, 1981b).

Kovalzon and Mukhametov (1982) have shown that temperature varies during unihemispheric slow wave sleep in dolphins. The variation in temperature may result from changes in the circulation. Independent circulation may be essential for the development of such marked asymmetries in brain wave patterns as have been observed (Fig. 2.4).

ABSENCE OF REM SLEEP IN DOLPHINS

Dreams can certainly be regarded as mental events, and dreaming in humans has been firmly connected to physiological events described as rapid eye movement sleep (REM). REM (also called paradoxical or dream sleep) has been reported in many mammals but in the dolphin there is definitely room for controversy about its presence. Mukhametov (1984) states flatly that he has never observed REM in many days and nights of dolphin EEG recording involving 30 experimental subjects over a period of 8 years. *"Tursiops truncatus* and *Phocoena phocoena* are with the echidna among the three species, in which no paradoxical sleep has been revealed. It is noteworthy that the echidna is a secondary terrestrial mammal and its ancestors were aquatic mammals." (Mukhametov, 1984; the basis for this last assertion is not given). Six minutes of REM were observed in a single night's recording of a pilot whale (Shurley et al., 1969). Flanigan (1974, 1975) observed nocturnal erections during apparent sleep in male dolphins (*Tursiops* and *Orcinus*), a sign of REM in man and other mammals.

LATERALIZATION OF THE DOLPHIN BRAIN

In recent years, few features of the human brain have received more attention than its lateralization. Seventy to 80% of human brains have a larger planum temporale in the left hemisphere than in the right (Geschwind & Levitsky, 1968; Witleson, 1977). Studies of normal and brain-damaged people have demonstrated that the two cerebral hemispheres are specialized for different mental abilities. The body of literature on human laterality is extremely large. I can mention the findings only in a brief generalization. In most right-handed adults, language material is processed in the left hemisphere, and material concerned with spatial relationships is more dependent on right hemisphere processing (Levy, 1982; Neville & Hillyard, 1982). "Some authors have proposed that cerebral laterality occurs in direct proportion to the evolution of language, of handedness, of executive control, or the existence of a conscious self" (Hillyard & Bloom, 1982).

Human cortical specializations do not mature until at least puberty (Neville & Hillyard, 1982). Most of the dolphins used in behavioral experiments have been immature animals, thus we might not expect a full display of lateral specialization. In addition, I am aware of no attempt to demonstrate any lateral specializations in behavioral experiments and only one study on anatomical differences between the hemispheres. However, there are at least two observations that may suggest laterality preferences—first, the marked proclivity in confinement to swim in a counterclockwise direction and, second, the tendency to favor one eye. Studies of cortical surface area have revealed that the right hemisphere is slightly larger in at least two species, *Tursiops truncatus* and *Delphinus delphis* (Ridgway & Brownson, 1979, 1982).

Counterclockwise Swimming

Townsend (1914) observed that three newly captured *Tursiops* circled counterclockwise and two went clockwise. Kellogg and Kohler (1952) observed six animals at Marineland, Florida "almost always swimming in a clockwise direction against the current." Lilly (1962) observed that two dolphins, one female and one male, in his laboratory always circled to the left (counterclockwise). Reports from three different oceanaria in Florida (Caldwell, Caldwell, & Siebenaler, 1965) revealed that newly introduced *Tursiops*, and *Stenella*, swam counterclockwise around the pool regardless of direction of water flow. At one oceanarium, all newly introduced *Tursiops* swam counterclockwise between 1954 and the winter of 1964, but in the winter of 1964 six of seven animals circled clockwise (Caldwell et al., 1965). In concrete tanks at Point Mugu, California and in wooden tanks in San Diego, California, I noticed that all newly introduced dolphins (27 *Tursiops* and 8 *Lagenorhynchus*) recently captured in the wild swam in a counterclockwise direction. Newly captured dolphins at Point Mugu swam in counterclockwise circles even when they were apparently asleep (Ridgway, 1972). After the animals had been in captivity for a time the direction of swimming became less stereotyped; however, the counterclockwise direction usually predominated, especially during after hours periods when the animals swam in a leisurely manner neither chasing, playing, nor attending to their human trainers. With seven *Tursiops* in three different tanks at Point Mugu I observed that switching the direction of water current in the pool after the dolphin's swimming direction had been well established did not change the direction of swimming.

Soon after capture the *Tursiops* swam almost continuously, even while apparently asleep; however, as time passed most ceased this continuous swimming and settled into a surface hanging behavior (see Flanigan, 1974; McCormick, 1969; Ridgway, 1972) during periods of rest or sleep. I have observed six females, adapted to such surface hanging behavior, which became pregnant and delivered live offspring. In each case, the surface hanging behavior ceased immediately after parturition and mother and calf swam continuously in a counterclockwise circle. Only occasionally did the animals reverse direction. Females that had relatively straight dorsal fins developed a distinct leftward tilt in the fin as did their offspring.

The majority of *Tursiops* and *Lagenorhynchus* at Sea World in San Diego had left-tilted dorsal fins and swam counterclockwise. Eight *Orcinus* had left-tilted dorsal fins and swam counterclockwise and two had right-tilted dorsal fins and swam clockwise. Four *Pseudorca* from Japan and twelve *Cephalorhynchus* captured in Chile (Southern Hemisphere) swam counterclockwise when first confined (L. H. Cornell, Pers. Comm., 1984).

According to Balonov et al. (1981; also see Harnad & Doty, 1977) the direction of rotational tendencies reflect the greater activity of the opposite hemisphere. When dolphins swim in a counterclockwise direction, the rotational tendency is toward the left and away from the right hemisphere, presumably the one with greater activity. Those dolphins that circle while asleep should have alternation of activity between the hemispheres according to the findings of Soviet investigators (Mukhametov, 1984; Mukhametov et al., 1977) yet, they do not change the direction of circling. These findings seem to confound the idea that the dolphins turn in the opposite direction from the hemisphere with greater activity.

The Case for Eye Preference

Maxwell (1960) observed wild bottlenosed dolphins with calves off the coast of Northern Scotland. He noted that the calves swam to the mother's right. I have seen *Lagenorhynchus* at sea with calves on either side; however, only animals that approached our boat to ride the left bow wave had calves on the left. With captive *Tursiops* that I have observed, the neonate, especially in the hours soon after birth, usually swam on the mother's left, the side away from the enclosure walls, as she swam counterclockwise.

Right eye preference seems consistent with the counterclockwise swimming that we observe in the majority of captive dolphins. This direction of swimming places the right eye toward the enclosure wall and toward any human outside the tank who might provide food, etc. Because the optic chiasma is completely crossed, right eye preference may suggest a leading role for the left hemisphere in vision, whereas the counterclockwise turning might suggest a leading role for the right hemisphere in that movement. The case for counterclockwise turning is certainly much stronger than that for right eye preference.

In 1964, Adolph Frohn (then of the Miami Seaquarium, an early dolphin trainer who trained at the first oceanarium, Marine Studios of Florida) told me, referring to *Tursiops,* "a porpoise has a looking eye and it is more often the right one." I have not made a thorough study of eye preference, but of 27 recently captured *Tursiops,* 19 approached and examined my outstretched hand (Fig. 2.5) with the right side and eye facing me. Right eye preference is by no means universal, and the animals often appear to attend the trainer with both eyes. In the early stages of training the animal often stations in front of the trainer and since the majority of humans are right handed, a bias toward the left eye might be expected.

There are also two observations of great whales that might suggest right eye preference. First, the California gray whale, a baleen whale that feeds from the

FIG. 2.5.   In my experience, captive dolphins have a slight disposition to favor
the right eye. Of 27 recently captured *Tursiops*, 19 approached and examined my
outstretched hand with the right side and eye facing me. Right eye preference is by
no means universal and the animals often appear to attend their trainers using the
left eye or both eyes.

bottom, shows greater wear of the baleen on the right side suggesting that gray whales swim with their right side down while feeding (Kasuya & Rice, 1970). Although certainly not the only possible explanation, such behavior would be consistent with a predilection for using the right eye. Second, the fin whale, an animal that often feeds near the surface on krill, other zooplankton, or small schooling fish, is strongly but asymmetrically countershaded, externally and within the oral cavity (Mitchell, 1972). The lower jaw is consistently white on the right and dark on the left. The whale has been observed at the surface,feeding on its right side. In this posture the lightly pigmented right jaw conforms to the usual light color pattern of the underbody (Gambel, 1985) and the right visual field is downward in the direction of escaping food, competing whales, or possible predators. The fin whale is, however, not consistently a right side feeder (Watkins & Schevill, 1979). If there is any basis to my suggestion that right eye preference is associated with fin whale countershading, it might be revealed by considering the behavior and escape modes of prey species. Some prey might be more easily engulfed by approaching from above while other prey might be more readily attacked from below, forcing its entrapment against the ocean surface. While the idea of eye preference is based on meager evidence and largely speculative at this point, it does deserve consideration by those who study the behavior and ethology of cetaceans in captivity and in the wild.

Anatomical Asymmetry of the Dolphin Brain

Toothed whales, but not baleen whales, generally have an asymmetrical cranium (Ness, 1967). The nasal opening is shifted to the left of the cranial midline in varying degrees, and several skull and head structures on the right are larger than those on the left. There is no known reversal of the family-specific asymmetries among any individual odontocete. A few early authors have also reported asymmetries of the brain (Breathnach, 1960). These observations have often been discounted because of the possibility that such large brains might be liable to deformation during long periods of fixation.

Sleptsov (1939) has proposed an interesting explanation for the asymmetry of skull and brain of odontocetes based on his studies of *Delphinus, Delphinapterus,* and *Phocoena.* Embryonic odontocetes have olfactory bulbs, nerves, and tracts but these degenerate and by the late fetal stage are absent. Postnatal odontocetes do not have these olfactory structures. Sleptsov (1939) argued that, in the embryonic state, the left olfactory nerve and lobe degenerate more rapidly than those on the right resulting in the cerebral and cranial asymmetries.

Ridgway and Brownson (1979, 1984) have shown that in *Tursiops* the right hemisphere has a larger surface area (T test: $P < 0.05$). *Delphinus* gave a similar result though with less certainty (T test: $P < 0.07$). Although the mean values for *Stenella* showed a small advantage to the right, the difference was not found to be significant (T test: P> 0.1). There were no significant differences in thickness of the cortex between any functional areas of left or right hemispheres.

In addition, in *Tursiops* the echolocation beam is projected slightly to the left (Au, 1980). Ridgway and Brownson (1984) speculate that the right hemisphere advantage in cortical surface area has something to do with the left ear receiving the first echoes from the left-deviated sonar beam.

Turning preference may also be involved in the right-dominant asymmetry in cortical surface area. The majority of captive *Tursiops* and *Delphinus* that I have observed showed a distinct preference for counterclockwise circling. Turning toward the left in a counterclockwise direction suggests a dominant role for the opposite right hemisphere (see Balonov, Deglin, Kaufman, & Nikolaenko, 1981; Harnad & Doty, 1977). Mukhametov (1984) has not mentioned turning preference in sleeping dolphins. It would be interesting to learn if turning preference changed with changes in EEG activity. My observation that sleeping dolphins continue to swim counterclockwise, while presumably their EEG activity is periodically alternating between the two hemispheres, would seem to go against the idea that turning preference is away from the most active hemisphere.

Summary of Dolphin Brain Lateralization

Bogen (1969), who cites cases of humans who lived normal lives with one cerebral hemisphere absent, data from hemispherectomy patients, and animal experiments, has hypothesized that each cerebral hemisphere is a separate brain capable of analysis and adaptation to environmental conditions. In one animal experiment, Wenzel, Tschirgi, and Taylor (1962) observed that kittens with one hemisphere removed suffered behavioral losses that were "extremely small or even undetectable."

It appears to me that the dolphin cerebral hemispheres may be even more "separate" than those of the human. Several probable manifestations of lateralization have been observed in dolphins; however, no functional asymmetries comparable to the dominance of the human left hemisphere for speech have been shown. In fairness it must be pointed out that studies of functional asymmetry are often difficult to carry out and none have really been undertaken with dolphins.

In monkeys and humans the right hemisphere shows a leading role in spatial orientation (Balonov et al., 1981). Our finding (Ridgway & Brownson, 1979, 1984) of greater surface area in the right cerebral hemisphere of *Tursiops* and *Delphinus* may be a reflection of such right dominance in dolphins. More and more the generalities about functional dominance in one or the other of the two hemispheres of the human brain are being discovered in animals. Balonov et al. (1981) sum up their judgment of these findings in their recent review:

> In our opinion, the facts point to a remarkable similarity between the functional asymmetry of the brain in human beings and animals. This is seen in the similar

role of the leading extremity and the leading eye and ear in adaptive behavior; in the fact that communication in both humans and animals is controlled by the left hemisphere, while all forms of spatial orientation are controlled by the right hemisphere. . . .

SOMATOSENSORY OBSERVATIONS
ON THE DOLPHIN

Lende and Welker (1972) attempted studies of dolphin skin sensitivity, recording evoked potentials from an area of cerebral cortex. Using stimuli such as tapping or lightly touching or stroking the skin or by allowing water droplets to fall on the skin contralateral to the area of somatosensory cortex under study, the investigators produced a map of skin sensitivity based on recordings from this area of cortex. The greatest sensitivity was found in "a broad zone extending below both eyes and ventrally around the neck. . . ."

The somatosensory evoked potential (SEP) method was also used by Ridgway and Carder (1984) to obtain a gross, but more complete map of dolphin skin sensitivity. The dolphin SEP was small (about one-fifth as large) compared to responses from the same leads evoked by sound stimulation. With electrode leads placed over the right side of the dolphin's brain, SEP's were recorded only to stimuli on the left side of the body. When the snout was stimulated on the left side near the tip, a robust SEP was observed, but when the stimulus was moved only 3 cm, over to the right side, the SEP vanished. Figure 2.6 shows a rough map of dolphin skin sensitivity based on the SEP.

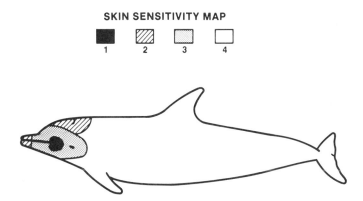

FIG. 2.6.   Dolphin skin sensitivity map based on somatosensory evoked potentials. The belly and genital area were not tested. 1. most sensitive, followed by 2., 3., and 4. in descending order (from Ridgway & Carder, 1984).

Nerve endings are especially prominent around the dolphin's eyes, blowhole, genital area, and along the snout where the greatest sensitivity was observed. The SEP measurements cannot be used to compare the magnitude of dolphin skin sensitivity with that of other species. However, Kolchin and Bel'kovitch (1973) made measurements of a different kind and compared them to human sensitivity. They used the galvanic skin response (GSR) to stimuli produced by a 0.3-mm weighted wire to make a partial map of body skin sensitivity in the common dolphin *Delphinus delphis*. They did not study the genital region, but of the body portions studied found the dolphin to be most sensitive (< 10 mg/mm^2) in separate circular areas of about 5 cm diameter around the blowhole and eyes. The snout, lower jaw, and melon were found to be somewhat less sensitive (10 to 20 mg/mm^2) while still less sensitivity (20 to 40 mg/mm^2) was observed along the back both anterior and posterior to the dorsal fin. The authors state that "from an ecological point of view the results we obtained are not unusual. The values for the threshold of sensitivity to touch in dolphins are 10—40 mg/mm^2; this is close to the figures for a human being in the most sensitive skin areas, the tactile surfaces of the fingers, the skin of the eyelids, and the lips."

THE AUDITORY SYSTEM

Hypertrophy of the auditory system may be the primary reason for the dolphin's large brain. The medial geniculate is about 7 times as large as that of the human, the inferior colliculus is 12 times as large, and the nucleus of the lateral lemniscus of the dolphin is over 250 times as large as the equivalent structure in humans. Enlargements of great magnitude are also present in other brainstem nuclei (see Bullock & Gurevich, 1979). Langworthy (1932) points out that "large numbers of acoustic fibers reach the cerebral cortex. The cerebral cortex may be said to have reached its great development on the basis of these acoustic impulses." More recently, Wood and Evans (1980) have hypothesized that "the high degree of encephalization of odontocetes reflects, to some considerable extent at least, their known or presumed acoustic attributes and capabilities."

Mapping the Auditory Cortex

Supin et al. (1978; also see Bullock & Gurevich, 1979) located extensive auditory projection areas on the dorsal surface of each hemisphere about 1.5 to 3.0 cm lateral to the sagittal suture. Thus, compared to most land mammals, there is in the dolphin brain an apparent shifting of the auditory area from the temporal to the parietal lobe and the dorsum of the hemisphere (Fig. 2.7). Evoked potential data suggest the presence of both primary and secondary auditory cortex (Supin et al., 1978) whereas histological investigation does not (Morgane et al., this volume). On physiological grounds the bat also exhibits complex organization of the auditory cortex (Suga, 1984) yet, like the dolphin, shows the histologist a more primitive level of cortical development (see Morgane et al., this volume). The extent of auditory cortex in dolphins may be greater than that indicated in the mapping experiments previously mentioned. A tonotopic map of the cochlea's projections on the dolphin cortex has not been done; therefore, it is entirely possible that further auditory projection areas will be found in temporal cortex, which, in the dolphin, is less accessible than the dorsal area that has been mapped (Fig. 2.7).

In their studies of the dolphin cortex, Supin et al. (1978) noticed that evoked potentials were almost never recorded from the cortical surface. Responses occurred only when the electrodes were submerged to a depth of at least several mm. The investigators point out that the sections of cortex on the surface of the hemisphere are thinner than the submerged ones and suggest that differences in development and possibly in numbers of afferents arriving in submerged sections (those sulci and gyri buried beneath the surface) compared to those on the surface could account for the observed difference (Supin et al., 1978). They also noted that "no classic patterns of reversal of the evoked potential are observed during intersection of the cortex by the recording electrode. These features can be explained by the nature of the electrical field distribution in the densely packed gyri of the dolphin cerebral cortex" (Supin et al., 1978).

Suga's (1984) research has revealed an intricate organization of auditory cortex in bats; he has suggested that equally complex organization may be present in other auditory systems of animals and that human auditory cortex may show similar arrangements for processing the complex sounds of speech. In Suga's bats, complex sounds are processed by neurons tuned to combinations of information-bearing elements or parameters in the sounds. For example, areas of cortex are tuned to particular echo delays and particular echo amplitudes. Neurones tuned to specific information bearing parameters (IBP) or combinations of

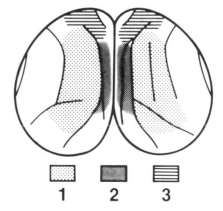

FIG. 2.7. Depiction of dorsal aspect of dolphin brain showing 1. auditory, 2. visual, and 3. somatosensory cortex as determined by evoked potential studies (figure redrawn from Supin et al., 1978).

IBP's are clustered in areas of the cerebral cortex and systematically arranged along axes or in coordinate systems for representation of sounds that are biologically important to the species (Suga, 1984).

It seems likely that equally complex sound processing takes place in the dolphin cortex. If so, the mapping experiments conducted to date (Supin et al., 1978), though they showed certain differences of response in three areas of auditory cortex, may not have been of sufficient acoustic detail to reveal systematically arranged axes of specific delay-sensitive or amplitude-sensitive neurones and thus do not reveal the full extent of cortical organization. Possibly, surface segments that were not responsive in the mapping experiments (Supin et al., 1978) contain neurones tuned to more specific acoustic paramaters than those tested.

Detailed organization of auditory cortex described for owls (Knudsen & Konishi, 1978) and bats (Suga, 1984) may be equally or even more complex in dolphins. If so, the dolphin cortex must map an extensive surrounding area of the environment with specific acoustic parameters. According to Suga (1984),mustached bats map an area of only about three meters, and target distances of 50 to 140 cm are best represented, whereas dolphins, with an echolocation range of 100 m or more, probably map a large area of their surroundings for specific acoustic parameters. Since sound travels about four times as fast in water, neurons performing equal echo delays of X ms will represent Y m in a bat and 4 Y m in a dolphin. Specific neurones forming such axes may take up considerable space in the cortex and could be a major reason for the great expansion of neocortex in the dolphin.

Bullock and Gurevich (1979) pointed out substantial claims for fine discrimination of target distance and azimuth by Soviet dolphin echolocation researchers and presented a table comparing dolphin and bat performance based on the Soviet reports. The Soviet data show dolphins performing distance and azimuth discriminations even finer than those by bats. "If these comparisons are correct and fair, they may help in accounting for the vast difference in absolute (though not relative) size of the inferior colliculus and other auditory structures of the brain . . ." (Bullock & Gurevich, 1979). In addition, Bullock has suggested to me (Pers. Comm., 1984) that dolphins make more quantitative discriminations than bats, e.g., echo quality and social signal quality—like timbre and individual's calls. Besides neurophysiology, relevant experiments on the behavioral discrimination of subtle differences in calls or echoes from targets of slightly different texture, shape, or density are needed.

Evoked Potentials and Dolphin Hearing

Although Johnson (1966) had presented a behavioral audiogram, Bullock et al. (1968) were the first to use evoked potential techniques in the study of dolphin hearing and auditory processing. They studied the auditory evoked potentials

(AEP) from midbrain auditory structures. This was a landmark study that deserves careful reading, but some findings of major importance can be summarized as follows:

1. Temporal resolution of successive sounds was found to be extremely rapid;
2. There was no evidence of facilitation of response to the second of two identical stimuli as had been observed in echolocating bats;
3. Small changes in stimulus frequency altered AEP amplitude and waveform;
4. Frequency-modulated (FM) tones were more likely to produce a large AEP than were constant-frequency tones. In one case, a 100 kHz tone produced a weak AEP, while a 135 kHz tone produced none. An FM pulse starting at 100 kHz and sweeping upward to 135 kHz caused a large AEP. This result was also observed for tones sweeping down in frequency.
5. An AEP to a given tone could be masked only by a relatively narrow band of frequencies surrounding that stimulus (Bullock et al., 1968).

Bullock and Ridgway (1971, 1972) recorded and telemetered electrical activity from the inferior colliculus or nucleus of the lateral lemniscus and from a few locations in the cerebral cortex of alert dolphins. Electrodes were placed by stereotaxic means with the animal under anesthesia (Ridgway & McCormick, 1967).

The experimental animals used by Bullock and Ridgway (1972) were trained to emit on command a series of clicks (similar, at least, to echolocation clicks) at a rate of 15 to 300 per sec. The voluntary clicks resulted in AEP's. However, the clicks of highest intensity often evoked modest AEP's while clicks of weaker intensity gave maximal AEP's, suggesting important differences in click composition. Experiments with artificial echoes showed recovery to be more rapid (0.5 ms including the duration of the click) following the animal's own click than following an artificial conditioning tone burst of equal evoking power.

The typical midbrain AEP was specialized for ultrasonic, ultrabrief, fast-rising, closely spaced sounds like the echolocation clicks. No potential was evoked if the frequency was below 5 kHz or if the rise time was above 5 ms. However, at several cerebral locations (mainly in the posterior lateral temporal cortex) long latency, long duration, slowly recovering potentials were evoked by frequencies below 5 kHz, whether fast or slowly rising acoustic envelopes were used (Bullock & Ridgway, 1971, 1972). Soviet investigators have recently confirmed many of these findings in the harbor porpoise (Popov, Ladygina, & Supin 1984).

Bullock and Ridgway (1972) suggested that the dolphin brain might possess two separate auditory systems, one specialized for ultra-brief, fast-rising sounds like echolocation clicks while the other was specialized for longer, slower rising sound like dolphin whistles.

In humans and laboratory animals a series of far field waves can be recorded from the surface of the scalp or skull without penetrating the brain with electrodes. Clicks evoke a series of seven waves cresting in the first 10 ms that have been identified and appear remarkably similar in several species. The auditory brainstem response (ABR) has also been recorded in dolphins (Ridgway et al. 1981).

The dolphin ABR's were larger than those of other mammals previously investigated—about 10 times larger than the human (Ridgway et al. 1981). The click-evoked dolphin ABR consisted of 7 waves within 10 msec., numbered by the positive peaks at the vertex (Fig. 2.8) and corresponding well with waves in other mammals. The pattern was consistent in all dolphins tested (six *T. truncatus* and two *D. delphis*). At higher sound intensities, 30 dB above threshold and more, wave IV was consistently large, sometimes reaching an amplitude of 10 μV. Though seldom surpassing 3 μV in amplitude, wave VI was often equal to wave IV near threshold, and waves IV and VI usually disappeared simultaneously as clicks were attenuated to below threshold. Wave V was usually absent at the highest levels of sound stimulation but was prominent over a range

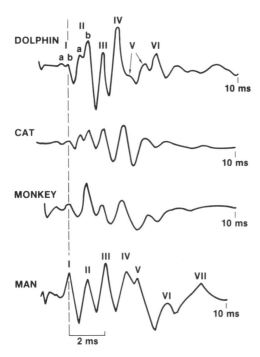

FIG. 2.8.   Dolphin averaged brainstem response (ABR) compared to those of cat monkey and human. Dashed line is through Wave I for each species. Dolphin Wave's I and II contain dual peaks (a, b). Dolphin Wave V becomes a prominent single wave 20 to 30 dB below the level of stimulation resulting in the ABR seen here (from Ridgway et al., 1981).

from 20 dB below maximum to about 10 dB above threshold. In general, however, the waves decrease in amplitude and increase in latency as click stimuli are attenuated. The amplitude decrease is significantly unequal for different waves, being maximal for IV, yet all seven are visible considerably below maximal or even moderate stimulus levels.

For 66 kHz clicks, the latency change with intensity approximates 4.5 μsec/dB of attenuation. The values of 6 and 124 kHz clicks are 12 and 3.7 μsec/dB respectively. The value generally given for humans is 40 μsec/dB (probably mainly due to the 2 to 5 kHz stimuli used). Equal intensity stimuli at the three frequencies gave different latencies for each wave of the dolphin ABR. The difference averaged about 1 msec between 6 kHz and 124 kHz for each individual wave. These differences are compatible with an interpretation that various parts of the cochlea differ in the speed at which auditory nerve impulses are aroused in and conducted by the auditory nerve fibers (Ridgway, 1983). It is not yet proven whether the waves of the ABR come more from auditory brainstem nuclei or from axon bundles between them. In either case, dolphin auditory transmission is fast, not only in the cochlea but in the CNS as well. Wave I is thought to arise from the 8th nerve and wave IV from the lateral lemniscus (see Ridgway et al., 1981, for references on these points). Transmission time from wave I to wave IV or any other wave is likely a function of CNS rather than cochlear conduction speed. Brain stem transmission time (BTT) is considerably faster in *T. truncatus* (a dolphin species with mean brain weight around 1500 g) than in humans or domestic cats and is similar to that of the rat. Despite a much longer nerve pathway, BTT in the dolphin is equal to or faster than that in much smaller brained species.

Instead of accepting that a large discrepancy in elapsed time due to the longer conduction distance is exactly compensated for by faster processing in the nuclei, Ridgway et al. (1981) suggested that the nuclear delays might be relatively uniform at each level through the several orders of mammals and that the axonal conduction velocity is higher by just enough to compensate for a longer path in the dolphin.

Soviet investigators have reported fiber diameters in the dolphin 8th nerve about twice as large (5–7 μm) as in other species (Bullock & Gurevich, 1979). A doubling in fiber diameter of myelinated axons in laboratory mammals approximately doubles conduction speed. If we assume that all fibers conducting to the dolphin lateral lemniscus are equivalently enlarged—fiber diameters up to 12 μm have been traced from the cochlear nucleus to the lemniscus in another odontocete, a bottlenosed whale (DeGaaf, 1967)—a reasonable guess is that wave I to wave IV conduction delay in the dolphin could be up to 1 msec less than in humans.

Jacobs and Jensen (1964) have compared 8th nerve fiber diameters in sperm whales (odontocetes that are probably good echolocators) and fin whales (mysticetes which may not have an active echolocation system). In the fin whale the largest population of fibers at a single dimension had a diameter of 6 μm, and the maximum diameter was 11 μm whereas the sperm whale 8th nerve contained the most fibers at a 9 μm diameter with a maximum of 14 μm. It would be interesting to determine the distribution of fiber sizes serving different levels of the basilar membrane of the cochlea. Mean fiber diameters for afferent nerves serving the basal end may be larger to provide for more rapid conduction of the high-frequency impulses resulting from sonar target echoes.

A tantalizing problem that might be investigated with the ABR concerns the increase in fiber diameter with increasing brain size. The largest delphinid, the killer whale *Orcinus orca,* has a brain about four times as large as that of *T. truncatus* (6000 vs 1500 g). I am interested to learn if BTT in this large brain is kept short by increased fiber diameters in the auditory pathway. (Dawson, Hawthorne, Jenkins, & Goldston, 1982, have reported large diameter fibers in the dolphin optic nerve and retina.)

Another characteristic of the dolphin ABR that differs from that in other mammals studied is the influence of stimulus repetition rate on the response (Ridgway et al., 1981). In adult humans, for example, latency increases by about 0.5 msec for each rate increase of 10 per sec (Don, Allen, & Starr, 1977). The dolphin ABR latencies increase only slightly as stimulus rate is increased from 0.5 to 200/sec. In the cat, clicks at 80/sec reduce all components to about 50% of recovered amplitudes, while dolphin ABR wave amplitudes show only little change at rates of 160/sec. Faster CNS recovery times were previously demonstrated (Bullock et al., 1968; Bullock & Ridgway, 1972) but cochlear anatomy and physiology might play roles as well in this feature of dolphin audition.

MacKay (1967) has suggested that dolphins may employ phase information in sonar detection. Johnson (1967) has elaborated on the advantages of phase detection for echolocation by dolphins. No proof existed, however, that the dolphin auditory system is sensitive to phase at the high frequencies used in echolocation target detection (Au, 1980; Evans and Powell, 1967). Wever et al. (1971) suggested that ''the representation of detailed high frequency sounds, and especially their time and phase relations, may well be the basis for the dolphin's remarkable facility in echolocation.''

We attempted to test the dolphin capability for phase detection using the ABR (Ridgway et al.,1981). Reversing the phase of single sine waves delivered to the hydrophone revealed a small but consistent alteration of response. This was attributed to a shift of the whole ABR—i.e., a longer latency to initial compression clicks. Rarefaction clicks consistently produced ABRs with waves I through IV at least 40 μsec earlier than those to compression clicks. This seemed to account adequately for the result of point-by-point subtraction of compression ABRs from rarefaction ABRs, which was a complex battery of waves about a tenth of the amplitude of the ABR waves (Ridgway et al., 1981).

Because at 66 kHz one-half of a cycle is about 7.5 usec in duration, the 40 μsec difference in latency seen is over 5 times what would be expected from simply the difference in arrival time of the excitatory rarefaction. These data are evidence for phase detection by the dolphin auditory system at least to 66 kHz. The above findings suggest that the dolphin brain is specialized for rapid processing of auditory stimuli (see also Bullock et al., 1968; Bullock & Ridgway, 1972). If given enough time, the human auditory system seems to perform as well on some echolocation tasks (Fish, Johnson, & Ljungblad, 1976). Indeed, when pulses similar to dolphin echolocation pulses were projected at targets by instrumented divers and the received echoes stretched (tantamount to a slowed down tape recording and therefore reduced equivalently in frequency) 128 times, human divers performed with as few errors as *Tursiops* in distinguishing metal targets of copper, brass, or aluminum and geometrical aluminum shapes covered with neoprene rubber (Fish et al., 1976).

Studies with static metal targets may give only limited detail of the dolphin's echolocation processing ability. However, if the findings of Fish et al. (1976) are a fair comparison of echolocation ability and based on a sonar discrimination task that is difficult for dolphins, we must conclude that the major accomplishment in the sonar processing component of the dolphin auditory system is the ability to process sound rapidly. In this paper I have reviewed a number of other findings, for example, the large diameter of auditory nerve fibers, the short latency and the relatively flat latency-intensity function of the dolphin ABR waves, and the rapid temporal resolution of successive sounds, that lend support to my view that much of the great hypertrophy of the dolphin auditory system—and perhaps the entire cerebrum—results from the animal's need for great precision and speed in processing sound.

REFERENCES

Au, W. L. (1980). Echolocation signals of the Atlantic bottlenose dolphin (*Tursiops truncatus*) in open waters. In R. G. Busnel & J. F. Fish (Eds.), *Animal Sonar Systems* (pp. 251–282). New York: Plenum.

Balonov, L., Deglin, V., Kaufman, D., & Nikolaenko, N. (1981). Functional asymmetry of the animal brain. *Journal of Evolutionary Biochemistry and Physiology, 17*, 163–170. (In Russian, English translation 1982, New York: Plenum).

Bogen, J. E. (1969). The other side of the brain II. An appositional mind. *Bulletin of The Los Angeles Neurological Society, 34*, 135–162.

Bonner, J. T. (1980). *The evolution of culture in animals.* New Jersey: Princeton University Press.

Breathnach, A. S. (1960). The cetacean central nervous system. *Biological Reviews, 35*, 187–230.

Bullock, T. H. (1984). Comparative neuroscience holds promise for quiet revolutions. *Science, 225*, 473–478.

Bullock, T. H., Grinnell, A. D., Ikezono, E., Kameda, K., Katsuki, K., Nomoto, M., Sato, O., Suga, N., & Yanagisawa, K. (1968). Electrophysiological studies of central auditory mechanisms in cetaceans. *Zeitschrift Für Vergleichende Physiologie, 59*, 117–156.

Bullock, T. H., & Gurevich, V. (1979. Soviet literature on the nervous system and psychobiology of Cetacea. *International Review of Neurobiology, 21,* 48–127.

Bullock, T. H., & Ridgway, S. H. (1971). Neurophysiological findings relevant to echolocation in marine animals. In K. Schmidt-Koenig & M. F. Thompson (Eds.), *Orientation and navigation in animals* (pp. 373–395). Washington, DC: American Institute of Biological Sciences.

Bullock, T. H., & Ridgway, S. H. (1972). Evoked potentials in the central auditory system of alert porpoises to their own and artificial sounds. *Journal of Neurobiology, 3,* 79–99.

Caldwell, M. C., Caldwell, D. K., & Siebenaler, J. B. (1965). Observations on captive and wild Atlantic bottlenosed dolphins, *Tursiops truncatus,* in the Northeastern Gulf of Mexico. *Los Angeles County Museum Contributions in Science, 91,* 1–10.

Callaway, E., Tueting, P., & Koslow, S. (Eds.). (1978). *Event-related brain potentials in man.* New York: Academic Press.

Dawson, W. W., Carder, D. A., Ridgway, S. H., & Schmeisser, E. T. (1981). Synchrony of dolphin eye movements and their power density spectra. *Comparative Biochemistry and Physiology, 68A,* 443–449.

Dawson, W. W., Hawthorne, M., Jenkins, R., & Goldston, R. (1982). Giant neural systems of the inner retina and optic nerve of small whales. *Journal of Comparative Neurology, 205,* 1–7.

DeGaaf, A. S. (1967). *Anatomical aspects of the cetacean brain stem.* Assen, Netherlands: Von Gorcum.

Don, M., Allen, R., & Starr, A. (1977). Effect of click rate on the latency of auditory brain stem responses in humans. *Ann. Otol. Rhinol. Laryngol., 86,* 186–196.

Elias, H., & Schwartz, D. (1969). Surface areas of the cerebral cortex of mammals determined by stereological methods. *Science, 166,* 111–113.

Evans, W. E., & Powell, B. A. (1967). Discrimination of different metallic plates by an echolocating deophinid. In R. G. Busnel (Ed.), *Animal sonar systems* (pp. 363–383). Jouy-en-Josas, France: Laboratoire De Physiology Acoustique, INRA—CNRZ.

Fish, J. F., Johnson, C. S., & Ljungblad, D. K. (1976). Sonar target discrimination by instrumented human divers. *Journal of The Acoustical Society of America, 59,* 602–606.

Flanigan, W. F. (1974). Nocturnal behavior of captive small cetaceans. I. The bottlenosed porpoise, *Tursiops truncatus. Sleep Research, 3,* 84.

Flanigan, W. F. (1975). More nocturnal observations of captive, small cetaceans. I. The killer whale, *Orcinus orca. Sleep Research, 4,* 139.

Geshwind, N., Levitsky, W. (1968). Human brain: Left-right asymmetries in temporal speech region. *Science, 161,* 186–187.

Gambel, R. (1985). The fin whale. In S. H. Ridgway & R. J. Harrison (Eds.), *Handbook of marine mammals, Vol. III, Sierenia and Mysticeti* (pp. 171–192). London: Academic Press.

Hampton, I. F. G., Whittow, G. C., Szekercezes, J., & Rutherford, S. (1971). Heat transfer and body temperature in the Atlantic bottlenosed dolphin, *Tursiops truncatus. International Journal of Biometeorology, 15,* 247–253.

Harnad, S., & Doty, R. (1977). Introduction. In S. Harnad, R. Doty, L. Goldstein, J. Jaynes, & G. Krauthamer (Eds.), *Lateralization of the nervous system.* (p. 17). New York: Academic Press.

Jerison, H. J. (1973). *Evolution of the brain and intelligence.* New York: Academic Press.

Jerison, H. J. (1982). Allometry, brain size, cortical surface, and convolutedness. In E. Armstrong & D. Falk (Eds.), *Primate brain evolution: Methods and concepts* (pp. 77–84). New York: Plenum.

Johnson, C. S. (1966). Auditory thresholds of the bottlenosed dolphin (*Tursiops truncatus* Montagu). U. S. Naval Ordinance Test Station, NOTSTP 4178. 25 pp.

Johnson, C. S. (1967). Discussion. In R. G. Busnel (Ed.), *Animal sonar systems* (pp. 384–398). Jouy-en-Josas, France: Laboratoire de Physiology Acoustique, INRA—CNRZ.

Kanwisher, J., & Sundnes, G. (1965). Physiology of a small cetacean. *Hvalradets Skrifter, 48,* 45–53.

Kasuya, T., & Rice, D. W. (1970). Notes on baleen plates and on arrangement of parasitic barnacles of gray whales. *Scientific Reports of The Whales Research Institute, 22*, 39–43.

Kellogg, W. N., & Kohler, R. (1952). Reactions of the porpoise to ultrasonic frequencies. *Science, 116*, 250–252.

Kerem, D., Elsner, R., & Wright, J. (1971). Anaerobic metabolism in the brain of the harbor seal during the late stages of a maximum dive. *Federation Proceedings, 30*, 484.

Kesarev, V. (1971). The inferior brain of the dolphin. *Soviet Science Review, 2*, 52–58.

Kesarev. V. S., & Malofeyeva, L. I. (1969). Structural organization of the dolphin motor cortex. *Arkhiv Anatomii Gistologii i Embriologii, 56*, 48–55. (Neuroscience Translations No. 12, Federation of American Societies for Experimental Biology).

Harrison, R. J. (1969). Endocrine organs: Hypophysis, thyroid, and adrenal. In H. T. Anderson (Ed.), *The biology of marine mammals* (pp. 349–389). New York: Academic Press.

Hatschek, R. (1903). Schnervenatrophie bei einem delphin. *Arb. Neurol. Inst. Univ. Wien, 10*, 223–229.

Haug, H. (1969). Vergleichende, quantitative untersuchungen an den gehiren des menschen, des elefanten und einiger zahnwale. *Medizinsche Monatschrift, 23*, 201–205.

Haug, H. (1970). Qualitative und quantitative untersuchungen an den gehirnen des menschen, der delphinoideae und des elefanten. *Ergebnisse der Anatomie und Entwicklungsgeschichte, 43*, 1–70.

Herman, L. M. (1980). Cognitive characteristics of dolphins. In L. M. Herman (Ed.), *Cetacean behavior* (pp. 149–209). New York: Wiley.

Hillyard, S. A., & Bloom, F. E. (1982). Brain functions and mental Processes. In D. R. Griffin (Ed.), *Animal mind-human mind* (pp. 13–32). Dahlem Konferenzen, Berlin: Springer-Verlag.

Hockett, C. F. (1978). In search of Jove's brow. *American Speech, 53*, 243–313.

Irving, L., Scholander, P. F., & Grinnell, S. W. (1941). The respiration of the porpoise, *Tursiops truncatus. Journal of Cellular and Comparative Physiology, 17*, 145–168.

Jacobs, M. S., & Jensen, A. V. (1964). Gross aspects of the brain and fiber analysis of cranial nerves in the great whale. *Journal of Comparative Neurology, 123*, 55–72.

Jacobs, M. S., Morgane, P. J., & McFarland, W. L. (1975). Degeneration of visual pathways in the bottlenosed dolphin. *Brain Research, 88*, 346–352.

Knudsen, E., & Konishi, M. (1978). Center surround organization of auditory receptive fields in the owl. *Science, 202*, 778–780.

Kolchin, S. & Bel'kovitch, V. (1973). Tactile sensitivity in *Delphinus delphis. Zoologicheskiy Zhurnal, 52*, 620–622.

Kovalzon, V. M., & Mukhametov, L. M. (1982). Temperature variations in the brain corresponding to unihemispheric slow wave sleep in dolphins. *Journal Evolutionary Biochemistry and Physiology, 18*, 307–309. (in Russian)

Kutas, M., & Hillyard, S. A. (1980). Reading senseless sentences: Brain potentials reflect semantic incongruity. *Science, 207*, 203–205.

Laird, A. K. (1969). The dynamics of growth. *Research/Development, 20*, 28–31.

Langworthy, O. R. (1932). A description of the central nervous system of the porpoise (*Tursiops truncatus). Journal of Comparative Neurology, 54*, 437–499.

Lende, R. A. & Welker, W. I. (1972). An unusual sensory area in the cerebral neocortex of the bottlenose dolphin, *Tursiops truncatus. Brain Research, 45*, 555–560.

Levy J. (1982). Mental processes in the nonverbal hemisphere. In D. R. Griffin (Ed.), *Animal mind-human mind* (pp. 57–73). Dahlem Konferenzen, Berlin: Springer-Verlag.

Lilly, J. C. (1962). In V. Mountcastle (Ed.), *Interhemispheric relations and cerebral dominance* (pp. 112–114). Baltimore: Johns Hopkins University Press.

Lilly, J. C. (1964). Animals in aquatic environments: Adaptation of mammals to the oceans. In D. B. Dill (Ed.), *Handbook of physiology-environment* (pp. 741–747). Washington, DC: The American Physiological Society.

58 RIDGWAY

MacKay, R. S. (1967). Experiments to conduct in order to obtain comparative results. In R. G. Busnel (Ed.), *Animal sonar systems* (pp. 1173–1196). Jouy-en-Josas, France: Laboratoire De Physiology Acoustique, INRA—CNRZ.

Maxwell, G. (1960). *Ring of bright water* London: Longmans.

McCormick, J. G. (1969). Relationship of sleep, respiration, and anesthesia in the porpoise: A preliminary report. *Proceedings of The National Academy of Sciences of The United States of America, 62,* 697–703.

McFarland, W. L., Jacobs, M. S., & Morgane, P. J. (1979). Blood supply to the brain of the dolphin, *Tursiops truncatus,* with comparative observations on special aspects of the cerebrovascular supply of other vertebrates. *Neuroscience and Biobehavioral Reviews, Suppl. 1,* 93 pp.

Mitchell, E. (1972). Whale pigmentation and feeding behavior. *American Zoologist, 12,* 60.

Mukhametov, L. M. (1984). Sleep in marine mammals. *Experimental Brain Research, Suppl. 8,* 227–238.

Mukhametov, L. M., Supin, A. Y., & Polyakova, I. G. (1977). Interhemispheric asymmetry of the electroencephalographic sleep patterns in dolphins. *Brain Research, 134,* 581–584.

Nagel, E. L., Morgane, P. J., Mc Farland, W. L., & Galliano, A. E. (1968). Rete mirabile of dolphin: Its pressure-damping effect on cerebral circulation. *Science, 161,* 898–900.

Ness, A. R. (1967). A measure of asymmetry of the skulls of odontocete whales. *Journal of Zoology (London), 153,* 209–221.

Neville, H. J., & Hillyard, S. A. (1982). Neurophysiological approaches, state of the art report. In D. R. Griffin (Ed.), *Animal mind-human mind* (pp. 333–353). Dahlem Konferenzen, Berlin: Springer-Verlag.

Pierce, R. W. (1970). *Design and operation of a metabolic chamber for marine mammals.* Doctoral dissertation. University of California, Berkeley.

Popov, V. V., Ladygina, T. F., & Supin, A. Y. (1985). Evoked potentials of the auditory cortex of *Phocoena phocoena. Journal of Comparative Physiology.*

Ridgway, S. H. (1972). Homeostasis in the aquatic environment. In S. H. Ridgway (Ed.), *Mammals of the sea: Biology and medicine* (p. 715). Springfield, IL: Thomas.

Ridgway, S. H. (1983). Dolphin hearing and sound production in health and illness. In R. Fay & G. Gourevich (Eds.), *Hearing and other senses: Presentations in honor of E. G. Wever* (pp. 247–296). Groton, CT: Amphora Press.

Ridgway, S. H., & Brownson, R. H. (1979). Brain size and symmetry in three dolphin genera. *Anatomical Record, 193,* 664.

Ridgway, S. H., & Brownson, R. H. (1982). Relative brain sizes and cortical surface areas of odontocetes. In A. Myllymaki & E. Pulliainen (Eds.), *Abstracts of Papers: Third International Theriological Congress.* Helsinki, p. 207.

Ridgway, S. H., & Brownson, R. H. (1984). Relative brain sizes and cortical surface areas of odontocetes. *Acta Zoologica Fennica, 172,* 149–152.

Ridgway, S. H., Bullock, T. H., Carder, D. A., Seeley, R. L., Woods, D., & Galambos, R. (1981). Auditory brainstem response in dolphins. *Proceedings of The National Academy of Sciences of The United States of America, 78,* 943–1947.

Ridgway, S. H., & Carder, D. A. (1984). Compliance of dolphin skin: Tactile sensitivity distribution and skin vibrations in the living dolphin.

Ridgway, S. H., Flanigan, N. J., & McCormick, J. G. (1966). Brain-spinal cord ratios in porpoises: Possible correlations with intelligence and ecology. *Psychonomic Science, 6,* 491–492.

Ridgway, S. H., & McCormick, J. G. (1967). Anesthesia for major surgery in porpoises. *Science, 158,* 510–512.

Ridgway, S. H., & Patton, G. S. (1971). Dolphin thyroid: Some anatomical and physiological findings. *Zeitschrift Für Vergleichende Physiologie, 71,* 129–141.

Ridgway, S. H., Scronce, B. L., & Kanwisher, J. (1969). Respiration and deep diving in a bottlenose porpoise. *Science, 166,* 1651–1654.

Ries, F. A., & Langworthy, O. R. (1937). A study of the surface structure of the brain of the whale (*Balaenoptera physalus* and *Physeter catodon*). *Journal of Comparative Neurology, 68*, 1–47.

Scholander, P. F. (1940). Experimental investigations on the respiratory function in diving mammals and birds. *Hvalradets Skrifter, 22*, 1–131.

Serafetinides, E. Shurley, J., & Brooks, R. (1972). Electroencephalogram of the pilot whale, *Globicephala scammoni*, in wakefulness and sleep: Lateralization aspects. *International Journal of Psychobiology, 2*, 129–135.

Sergeant, D. E. (1969). Feeding rates of Cetacea. *FiskDir Skrifter Ser HavUnders, 15*, 246–258.

Sergeant, D. E., Caldwell, D. K., & Caldwell, M. C. (1973). Age, growth and maturity of bottlenose dolphins (*Tursiops truncatus*). *Journal of The Fisheries Research Board of Canada, 30*, 1009–1011.

Shurley, J., Serafetinides, E., Brooks, R., Elsner, R., & Kenney, D. (1969). Sleep in cetaceans. I. The pilot whale, *Globicephala scammoni*. *Psychophysiology, 6*, 230.

Simon, L. M. Robin, E. D., Elsner, R., Van Kessel, A., & Theodore, J. (1974). A biochemical basis for differences in maximal diving time in aquatic mammals. *Comparative Biochemistry and Physiology, 47B*, 209–215.

Sleptsov, M. M. (1939). On the problem of the asymmetry of the skull in odontoceti. *Zoologicheskiy Zhurnal, 18*, 367–386.

Spector, W. S. (1956). *Handbook of biological data* (p. 162). Philadelphia: Saunders.

Suga, N. (1984). Neural mechanisms of complex-sound processing for echolocation. *Trends in NeuroSciences, 7*, 20–27.

Supin, A. Y., Mukhametov, L. M., Ladygina, T. F., Popov, V. V., Mass, A. M., & Poliakova, E. G. (1978). *Electrophysiological study of the dolphin brain*. Moscow: Nauka. (in Russian)

Teyler, T. J. (1977). An Introduction to the Neurosciences. In M. C. Wittrock (Ed.), *The human brain* (p. 5). Englewood Cliffs, NJ: Prentice Hall.

Townsend, C. H. (1914). The porpoise in captivity. *Zoologica, 1*, 289–299.

Viamonte, M., Morgane, P. J., Galliano, R. E., Nagel, E. L., & McFarland, W. L. (1968). Angiography in the living dolphin and observations on blood supply to the brain. *American Journal of Physiology, 214*, 1225–1249.

Vogl, A. W., & Fisher, H. D. (1981a). The internal carotid artery does not directly supply the brain in Monodontidae (Order Cetacea). *Journal of Morphology, 170*, 207–214.

Vogl, A. W., & Fisher, H. D., (1981b). Arterial circulation of the spinal cord and brain in the Monodontidae (Order Cetacea). *Journal of Morphology, 170*, 171–180.

Watkins, W. A., & Schevill, W. E. (1979). Aerial observation of feeding behavior in four baleen whales: *Eubalaena glacialis, Balaenoptera borealis, Megaptera novaeangliae*, and *Balaenoptera physalus*. *Journal of Mammalogy, 60*, 155–163.

Wenzel, B., Tschirgi, R., & Taylor, J. (1962). Effects of early postnatal hemidecortication on spatial discrimination in cats. *Experimental Neurology, 6*, 332–339.

Wever, E. G., McCormick, J. G., Palin, J., & Ridgway, S. H. (1971). The cochlea of the dolphin *Tursiops truncatus*: Hair cells and ganglion cells. *Proceedings of The National Academy of Sciences of The United States of America, 68*, 2908–2912.

Wilson, R. B. (1933). The anatomy of the brain of the whale (*Balaenoptera sulfurea*). *Journal of Comparative Neurology 101*, 19–51.

Wirz, K. (1950). Studien über die cerebralization: Zur quantitativ en bestimmung der rangordnung bei saugetiere. *Acta Anatomica, 9*, 134–196.

Witelson, S. F. (1977). Anatomic asymmetry in the temporal lobes: Its documentation, phylogenesis, and relationship to functional asymmetry. In S. J. Dimond, & Blizard, D. A. (Eds.), *Evolution and lateralization of the human brain* (pp. 328–354). Annals of the New York Academy of Science, *299*, 1–501.

Wood, F. G., & Evans, W. E. (1980). Adaptiveness and ecology of echolocation in toothed whales. In R. Busnel & J. Fish (Eds.), *Animal sonar systems* (pp. 381–426). New York: Plenum.

3

Middle- and Long-Latency Auditory Event-Related Potentials in Dolphins

David L. Woods
University of California, Davis

Sam H. Ridgway
Donald A. Carder
Naval Ocean Systems Center, San Diego

Theodore H. Bullock
Scripps Institution of Oceanography

INTRODUCTION

Following the presentation of an auditory stimulus a series of electrical deflections, event-related potentials or ERPs, can be recorded from the scalp of humans and other animal species (Corwin, Bullock, & Schweitzer, 1982). ERPs have been widely used for monitoring human sensory and cognitive processing (Hillyard & Woods, 1979), and hold the promise of elucidating sensory and cognitive processes in other species (Bullock, 1981). In the human, short- and middle-latency auditory ERPs (latencies 1.5–30.0 msec) are *exogenous* in that their amplitudes and latencies are determined primarily by the characteristics of the evoking stimulus and are little affected by manipulations in processing strategy. In contrast, long-latency components change with attention and have been related to a variety of higher cognitive functions (Hillyard & Kutas, 1983). One of these components, the P3 or P300, is thought to be wholly *endogenous,* in that it reflects higher order optional cognitive operations which may be elicited by a stimulus (Donchin, 1981).

Short-latency ERPs have revealed specialized mechanisms of acoustic processing in the cochlea, brainstem, and cortex of the bottlenose dolphin and other dolphin species (Bullock et al., 1968; Bullock & Ridgway, 1972; Bullock & Gurevich, 1979; Ladygina & Supin, 1977; Ridgway et al., 1981). Recently, comparative studies of endogenous long-latency components, particularly the P3 or P300, have been undertaken on other species including the rat (O'Brien, 1982), cat (Farley & Starr, 1983; Wilder, Farley, & Starr, 1981), and monkey (Arthur & Starr, 1984; Neville & Foote, 1984).

One purpose of the current experiments was to determine if P300-like activity might be evident in the dolphin. In humans, the P300 can be elicited when infrequent stimuli are novel and unpredictable or when they cue an infrequent response (Courchesne, Hillyard, & Galambos, 1975). Our first two experiments were designed to determine if P300-like activity would be elicited in the dolphin under either of these circumstances.

Our third experiment was designed to compare the effects of stimulus repetition on dolphin and human ERPs. Recovery functions (changes in amplitude as a function of interstimulus interval) of human ERPs show two properties that have not consistently been reported in the recovery cycles of ERPs from other animal species. First, the duration of the recovery cycle of the human N100-P200 is extremely long; at interstimulus intervals (ISIs) less than 20 sec the N100-P200 is still not fully recovered (Nelson & Lassman, 1973). Second, it is partially specific for the stimulus repeated. For example, when a probe tone is inserted into a train of conditioning tones the amplitude of the ERP that it elicits is increased if it is different in frequency from the conditioning tones (Butler, 1973; Picton, Woods, & Proulx, 1978; Woods & Elmasian, 1984). An examination of the recovery cycle of the dolphin ERP was of particular interest since dolphin ERPs show long-latency components whose relative amplitudes are similar to those of the N100-P200 (Seeley, Flanigan, & Ridgway, 1976). Moreover, since the recovery function of the human N100-P200 has been related to the persistence of short-term acoustic memory (Picton, Campbell, Baribeau-Braun, & Proulx, 1978), it was felt that investigations into the recovery cycle of ERPs in the bottlenose dolphin might also provide some insight into the structure of acoustic memory in this species.

METHODS

A 22-year-old female dolphin was studied. The animal had been used in previous behavioral experiments and was accustomed to the restraining tank used for recording. Brainstem auditory evoked potentials previously obtained (Ridgway et al., 1981) had revealed normal peripheral auditory function.

Experimental Procedure

After the animal was hoisted from its home tank, wire electrodes (0.1 mm Jelliff alloy C) were loaded into a 20 gauge needle which was inserted to the skull. The needle was then gently withdrawn, leaving the bare-tipped wire hooked in place on fascia near the skull surface. The procedure was carried out rapidly using local anesthetic and focal cooling and resulted in little apparent discomfort to the animal. The electrodes were inserted so as to overlay the primary auditory areas of parietal cortex as mapped by Soviet researchers (Ladygina & Supin, 1977). Reference electrodes were placed on the ipsilateral mastoid process and the snout.

Following electrode implantation, the animal was partially submerged in the restraining tank with the lower jaw underwater (see Seeley et al., 1976 for further details). In order to prevent chafing and irritation of the dorsal skin, the animal was periodically sprayed with cool water. Stimuli were presented in water through an LC-10 hydrophone acting as a speaker 50 cm in front of the lower jaw.

Data Analysis

Wideband EEG (bandpass 1.0–3000 Hz) was recorded on an FM tape recorder along with trigger codes for subsequent analysis by computer. The EEG was digitized off-line (213 Hz/channel) after anti-alias filtering (- 3 dB at 100 Hz). Prior to averaging it was scanned for artifacts (excessive peak-to-peak deflections or amplifier blocking).

EXPERIMENT I. EFFECTS OF STIMULUS PROBABILITY

In humans, P300 components are produced by deviant auditory stimuli in ongoing trains of tones (Knight, 1984). In Experiment I, we presented novel auditory stimuli in an effort to produce a P300-equivalent in the dolphin. The stimuli were either computer-synthesized tones (8 or 12 kHz) or sounds which the dolphins had encountered in their environment (dolphin calls or a tone-signal used for training). The environmental sounds were digitized and edited by computer.

All stimuli had 300 msec durations (5 msec rise and fall times) and were presented at fixed 1.5 sec interstimulus intervals (ISIs). There were six conditions (Table 3.1) each lasting 8 min. In each, three stimuli were presented—probable stimuli on 80% of the trials, and two different infrequent stimuli on 10% of the trials each. The stimuli were presented in random order, with probabilities counterbalanced so that the frequent stimulus in one condition was the infrequent stimulus in another. Each condition had been recorded on an audio tape recorder. During the experiment, these were presented through the LC-10 hydrophone after amplification. Trigger pulses indicating the timing and occurrence of different stimuli were recorded along with EEG data for subsequent decoding by computer.

Six stimulus sets were used in all with five different stimuli—tones at 8.0 and 12.0 kHz, two different dolphin calls (FM sweeps), and a 7.5 kHz "bridge tone" which had served as a conditioned reinforcer during the training for experiment II, which follows.

Results

Figure 3.1 shows the grand mean ERPs (averaged over stimuli) recorded from a parietal-mastoid electrode pair in response to frequent (solid line) and infrequent (the two dashed lines) stimuli. The ERPs evoked by both stimulus classes consisted of a sharp P25 component (a relative positivity at the parietal electrode 25 msec after sound onset), a small negative component (N200), and a broad late positivity (P550), followed by a still later negativity (not illustrated) and a positivity which was present prior to the start of the next sample (1.1 sec after sound onset). The P550 component was larger to the infrequent stimuli in every stimulus set (Table 3.1), while the N200 component showed a more variable enhancement. The P25 component was similar in amplitude to frequent and infrequent stimuli.

Although enhanced P550 amplitudes were elicited by infrequent stimuli in every condition of Experiment I, the greatest enhancements were observed in

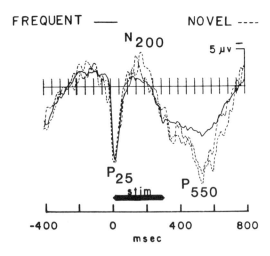

FIG. 3.1.   ERPs averaged over the five different stimuli when presented with 80% probabilities (solid line) and when they were presented as deviant stimuli with 10% probabilities (dashed lines). Note the enhanced amplitude of the P550 component to the deviant stimuli. All ERPs from this and following figures are from the parietal-mastoid derivation on the left hemisphere.

TABLE 3.1
Amplitudes (in uV) of the P550 Component Recorded from Parietal-
Left Mastoid Derivations in the Different Stimulus Conditions of
Experiment I

	Condition					
	1	2	3	4	5	6
Frequent stim (80%)	8.0 kHz	12.0 kHz	8.0 kHz	8.0 kHz	Call 1	Call 2
	4.6	6.3	3.7	4.4	3.4	5.7
Deviant-1 (10%)	Bridge tone	Bridge tone	12.0 kHz	12.0 kHz	Call 2	Call 1
	16.6	13.0	8.0	9.4	4.6	15.7
Deviant-2 (10%)	—	8.0 kHz	Call 1	Call 2	Bridge tone	8.0 kHz
	—	11.7	9.4	6.6	8.0	14.3

Peak amplitudes were measured within the latency range of 300–600 msec with respect to the mean voltage during a 400 msec prestimulus interval.

conditions 1 and 2 (where the bridge tone was presented infrequently), and condition 6 (with different dolphin calls serving as frequent and infrequent stimuli, see Table 3.1). Enhanced P550 amplitudes were most prominent in the parietal-mastoid placements, and were not observed at parietal-snout derivations.

EXPERIMENT II. ERPs TO CONDITIONED TONE SEQUENCES

Although the human P300 is usually associated with low probability of stimulus delivery, if one stimulus in a train of low probability stimuli requires a differential response it will elicit larger P300s than equally improbable nontallied stimuli (Courchesne, Courchesne, & Hillyard, 1978). In Experiment II, we examined the response to a differentially reinforced stimulus in a random sequence, in order to determine if it would elicit an enhanced P550 component.

Stimuli

The stimuli were five complex tones which had been synthesized by computer and recorded on a high fidelity audio tape recorder. They consisted of sine waves at a selected fundamental frequency mixed with first and second harmonics of equal energy and zero phase lag. The fundamentals were selected in one octave steps from 1.0 to 16.0 kHz. Although the tones had comparable RMS voltages, they were not equated in acoustic energy as monitored in the tank near the dolphin's head. All stimuli were 300 msec in duration with 5 msec rise and fall times.

The third tone in the sequence (4.0 kHz fundamental) was differentially reinforced. A series of audio tapes was constructed for the conditioning procedures. First, the animal was conditioned to associate the presentation of the bridge tone (7.5 kHz) with the delivery of fish during the feeding period. Then, the target tone was presented in isolation at long (20–30 sec) ISIs with each presentation followed by the presentation of the bridge tone and fish. Subsequently, two tone sequences were used (tone 3 and tone 1), with differential reinforcement of tone 3. At this point in the training, another tape was constructed with all of the tones except the target randomly presented at 1.5 sec ISIs. This tape was presented periodically between feedings so that responses to nontarget tones would not be associated with reinforcement. Finally, the test tape was constructed with all of the stimuli, including the target, presented randomly (20% probability for each) at fixed 1.5 sec ISIs.

Results

The animal developed a conditioned response to the bridge tone characterized by immediate orienting, and was reported by the trainer to orient to the target tone. The ERPs elicited by the equiprobable stimuli are shown in Fig. 3.2. Components with similar latencies and scalp distributions were produced by each of the stimuli. The differentially reinforced target tone (tone 3) elicited enhanced N200 and P550 components in comparison with tones 1, 2, and 5, but somewhat smaller N200-P550s than those elicited by tone 4 (8 kHz). A small late positive component was elicited by tones 1 and 2, while the target and tones 4 and 5 elicited a larger P550 component which was comparable in amplitude for the target and tone 4.

In experiment II, we found enhanced late positive activity (P550) to the target tone and an adjacent nonreinforced tone as well. However, the results are difficult to interpret for several reasons. First, the intensities of the tones possibly differed due to the resonances of the tank. Second, the higher frequency tones would be expected to elicit larger responses at comparable intensities because of the increased sensitivity of the dolphin auditory system to high frequency sounds (Bullock & Ridgway, 1972; Johnson, 1966). Third, because of the harmonic structure of the stimuli they may have been difficult for the dolphin to discriminate, particularly in the restraining tank with acoustic resonances that were unfamiliar to the dolphin. Finally, although only tone 3 was differentially reinforced, the tone which produced the largest N200 and P550 components (tone 4) was closest in fundamental frequency to the bridge tone (7.5 kHz), which had been directly paired with reinforcement.

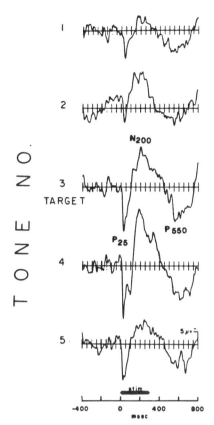

TONE NO.

FIG. 3.2. ERPs elicited by the different complex tones used in the conditioning sequence. The tones had been generated by computer and consisted of a fundamental and two harmonics at equal energies. The target tone (no. 3) had been associated with the delivery of a conditioned reinforcer (bridge tone, frequency 7.5 khz) and with food reinforcement. All tones were presented with equal probabilities.

EXPERIMENT III. THE RECOVERY CYCLE OF THE DOLPHIN ERP

Experiment III was designed to examine the effects of stimulus repetition on auditory ERPs in the dolphin. An audio tape was constructed to control the timing of function generators which delivered tones, clicks, or FM sweeps. Stimuli were presented in trains of six. On 50% of the trials the inter-stimulus intervals (ISIs) within the trains were fixed at 0.5 sec, and on the remainder of the trials ISIs were 1.0 sec. Trains with different ISIs occurred randomly. Longer intertrain intervals (ITIs, also random, and either 2.0 or 6.0 sec) were inserted between trains to permit the ERPs at the beginning of the trains to recover more fully.

Three different stimuli occurred on a random basis in the trains:

1. *Standard stimuli* were presented in the first four positions on all of the trains, on 50% of the trains in the fifth position, and on 80% of the trains in the

6th position. The ERPs elicited by these stimuli were used for evaluating recovery cycles.

2. *Probe tones* (*of a different pitch*) were presented in the 5th position on 50% of the trains in order to examine the specificity of the recovery process.

3. *FM sweeps* (going from the frequency of the standard tone to the frequency of the deviant tone or vice versa) were presented on 20% of the trials in the sixth position.

Each condition lasted 5.25 min and contained a total of 250 stimuli. The stimuli in each of the three categories (standards, probes, and FM sweeps) remained constant during a given condition. Standard stimuli were tones, or brief clicks similar to dolphin sonar pulses. The probe stimuli were identical to the standard tones used in other conditions. For example, when the standard tone was 30 kHz, the probe tone was 80 kHz, and vice versa. The tones were 200 msec in duration with rise and fall times of 5 msec, and frequencies of 10, 20, 30, and 80 kHz. The broad-band clicks were produced by ringing the LC-10 hydrophone with a square wave (20 μsec). Most stimulation was performed at 140 dB re 1 micropascal.

FREQUENCY

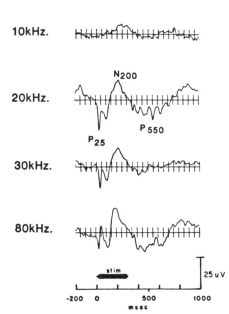

FIG. 3.3.   Grand mean ERPs elicited by 300 msec duration tone bursts ranging in frequency from 10 kHz (top) to 80 kHz (bottom). The ERPs were averaged over the different stimulus positions and trains used in Experiment III.

Results

The components typically elicited by the tone burst stimuli are shown in Fig. 3.3 for a parietal-left mastoid placement. At least five components could be reliably identified: middle-latency positive and negative waves (P25 and N65), a small subsequent positivity (P110), and two prominent long-latency components, the N200 and P450. The P450 component was followed by a broad positivity in response to deviant probe tones (P550), which was seen to a lesser extent following the tones at train onset. Comparisons of ERPs from left and right hemisphere sites showed that the components were symmetrically distributed over the two hemispheres. P25, N65 and P110 components were seen at all sites, but N200 and P450/P550 components were more clearly observed in parietal-mastoid than in parietal snout electrode pairs. A small off-potential, consisting mainly of middle-latency components, occurred at the higher tone frequencies. The 10 kHz tone produced small and delayed late components without evident middle-latency activity, probably in part because of its lower intensity (due to the bandpass characteristics of the hydrophone). The 20, 30, and 80 kHz tones produced middle- and long-latency responses with comparable amplitudes and latencies.

The effects of stimulus intensity were examined on ERPs elicited by 20 kHz tones and click stimuli (Fig. 3.4). Click stimuli elicited prominent middle-laten-

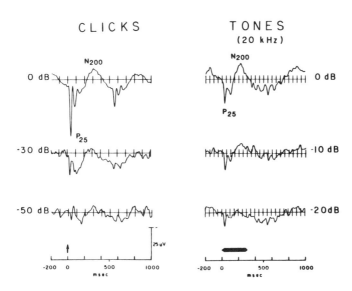

FIG. 3.4   Grand mean ERPs at different stimulus intensities elicited by brief broadband clicks (left) and 20 kHz tones (right). Long-latency components were elicited by both types of stimuli, but middle latency components were more prominent in response to the click stimuli. The ERPs shown were averaged over the different stimulus positions and trains used in Experiment III.

cy components with P25 amplitudes in excess of 40 μV. As stimulus intensities were reduced amplitudes decreased for both middle- and long-latency components, with click ERPs showing a broader dynamic range than tone responses.

The recovery functions of peak-to-peak measures of the N200-P450 were comparable for the different tone frequencies and are shown in Fig. 3.5a (averaged over all tones). N200-P450 amplitudes declined markedly with stimulus repetition. In trains with tones separated by 1.0 sec ISIs, amplitudes declined to 30% of those recorded at the beginning of the train. In trains with 0.5 sec ISIs, amplitudes declined to 15% of control values. In response to click stimuli, the middle-latency components showed short refractory periods, and did not vary systematically with ISI in the range tested.

The refractory effects produced by stimulus repetition were highly specific to the conditioning stimulus. Probe tones had N200-P450 amplitudes more than 500% larger than conditioning tones in the same train position (Fig. 3.5a). Indeed, probe N200-P450s were larger than ERPs at train onset, suggesting that the refractory effects produced by the conditioning tones may have been specific to that stimulus.

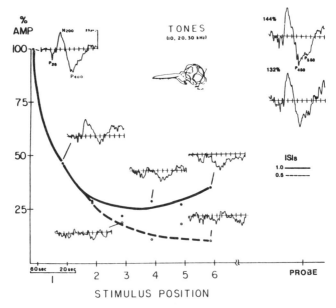

FIG. 3.5a.   The recovery functions of the N200-P400 component elicited by 300 msec tone bursts. The results shown were averaged over ERPs obtained with 10, 20 and 30 kHz tone bursts in Experiment III. ERPs are shown for stimulus trains with 1.0 sec ISIs (top, solid line) and 0.5 sec ISIs (botton, dashed line). ERPs to the probe stimuli are shown as inserts on the upper right, but data points for these traces are off-scale.

A late positive component (P550), seen as a shoulder on the P450 to baseline, was produced by probe stimuli and stimuli at train onset. Both the P550 and the P450 were reduced in amplitude during the conditioning train sequence. ERPs produced by FM-sweeps (not shown) also elicited enhanced and slightly prolonged P550 components, but because of the small numbers of trials in this category the ERPs were noisy and less consistent than those in other stimulus classes.

Several parallels were evident between the recovery cycles of human ERPs obtained in a similar paradigm (Fig. 3.5b) and dolphin responses. First, both the dolphin N200-P450 and the human N100-P200 were reduced in amplitude to asymptotic levels by the first several stimuli in a train. Second, in both species the ERPs were largest at the longest ISI.

However, several differences were also observed. First, the degree of refractoriness was greater for dolphin than human ERPs. For example, amplitudes in

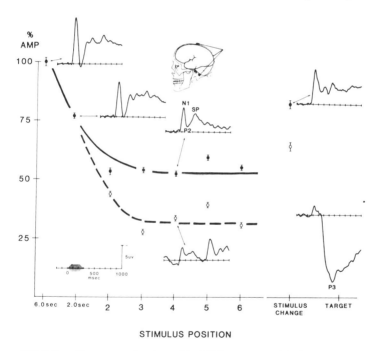

FIG. 3.5b.   The recovery functions of the N100 component of the human ERP in a group of 12 human subjects in a paradigm similar to that of Experiment III. Grand mean ERPs are averaged over subjects and different evoking stimuli, including pure and complex tones, vowels and consonant-vowel-consonant syllables. ERPs are shown for stimulus trains with 1.0 sec ISIs (top, solid line) and 0.5 sec ISIs (bottom, dashed line). ERPs to deviant nontarget stimuli are shown on the top right. ERPs to target stimuli (requiring a button press response) are shown on the bottom right. Note the occurrence of a large P300 to the target stimuli.

the 0.5 sec ISI trains were reduced to about 15% of initial amplitudes in the dolphin vs. about 30% in humans. Second, a larger difference was observed between ERPs following 6.0 and 2.0 sec intertrain intervals for the dolphin than for humans, suggesting that the refractory period may have been more prolonged in the dolphin. Third, the refractory process was more specific in the dolphin. In humans, tone pips of one pitch reduce N100-P200 amplitudes to tone pips separated by several octaves. In the dolphin no such reduction was evident; probe N200-P450 amplitudes were larger than those at train onset.

The probe tones also produced additional late positivity in man (P300) and dolphin (P550). In humans, when stimulus order is counterbalanced across subjects, probe P300 amplitudes are seen to be reduced over successive stimulus blocks (Woods & Elmasian, 1985). In the dolphin, we were unable to determine if similar amplitude reductions of the P550 occurred, or otherwise operationally dissociate it from the P450. However, the P550 elicited by the frequency-shifted tones appeared to be relatively larger than to tones with similar P450 amplitudes at train onset.

DISCUSSION

The components of the dolphin auditory ERP could be divided into three groups. *Middle-latency components* (*P25, N60*) were most prominent in responses to ultrasonic, broad-band clicks similar to the sonar pulses emitted by free swimming dolphins. The P25 was recorded equivalently in parietal-mastoid and parietal-snout placements over an intensity range of more than 50 dB, and was resistant to stimulus repetition. We have found middle-latency ERPs with similar properties, including a broad dynamic range and resistance to stimulus repetition, in previous studies using indwelling electrodes (Bullock et al., 1968; Bullock & Ridgway, 1972; Ridgway et al., 1981). The relative prominence of middle latency ERPs evoked by clicks suggests that the dolphin brain may show a similar specialization for the processing of sonar signals as found in other echolocating mammals (O'Neill & Suga, 1982).

Long-latency N200 and P450 components were elicited by tones from 10–80 khz. These components were comparable in amplitude for tones and clicks, and could be recorded over a limited range of stimulus intensities. Unlike the middle-latency components, the N200-P450 showed a prolonged and highly specific refractory period. These refractory properties have not been reported for ERPs in the cat (Buchwald, Hinman, Norman, Huang, & Brown, 1981; Wilder et al., 1981) or monkey (Arthur & Starr, 1984), but are similar to those of human long-latency N100-P200 components (Picton et al., 1977; Woods & Elmasian, 1985).

In humans, the refractory period of the N100-P200 has been suggested to reflect the degree of memory excitation required by a stimulus (Picton, Campbell, Baribeau-Braun, & Proulx, 1978). When a stimulus has been presented its representation in memory is primed so that its repetition produces only a small additional N100-P200. With increasing ISIs the memory representation decays so that N100-P200 amplitudes are enhanced. When a tone follows another of a different pitch, portions of its representation will have been excited so that its N100-P200 amplitude will be only partially recovered. Following this line of reasoning the discreteness of the neuronal representation of a sound in memory would be reflected in the degree of specificity of the refractory process. If so, the mnemonic representation of tones would appear to be more discrete in the dolphin than in man, since the ERP recovery functions are more specific.

A second difference between dolphin and human acoustic memory is also suggested by the data. In humans, ERPs show large increases in amplitude as ISIs are extended up to several seconds, and then smaller increases as intervals are lengthened further. For example, in humans only small differences in N100-P200 amplitude are observed between 2.0 and 6.0 sec. In the dolphin marked differences were observed in the N200-P450 at these intervals. This suggests that in the dolphin the neural excitation may still have been in the rapidly changing phase (similar to that observed in humans at shorter intervals) at 2.0-6.0 sec ISI. In any case, these characteristics of the ERP are consistent with a precise and persistent representation of acoustic features in the memory of the dolphin (Herman, 1980).

In the dolphin a *long-latency positive component* (*P550*) was elicited in all three experiments by infrequent or task-relevant stimuli. It was difficult to distinguish this component operationally from the P450 since both were enhanced by the low probability of stimulus delivery. For example in experiment III both P450 and P550 activity were enhanced following deviant stimuli. In humans the same relationship is observed between the P300 (emitted in response to deviant stimuli) and the P200 (enhanced to infrequent stimuli because of the specificity of the refractory process discussed above). However, the P550/P450 ratio appeared higher to deviant stimuli than to other stimuli in the train, as would be expected if the P550 were correlated with the processing of startling or deviant stimuli.

The relatively small amplitude of the P550 components recorded in experiment II, which most closely resembled human P300 paradigms, may have been related to several factors. First, the harmonic structure of the stimuli may have made them confusing to the dolphin because of echoes and distortion in the restraining tank. Second, the animal had never been presented with the stimuli while restrained and half submerged, and may have experienced difficulty in generalizing across different conditioning and test environments. Indeed, in the absence of an overt motor response we could not be certain that the animal was differentially responding to the target tone.

The small amplitude of the P550 in experiments I and III may be due to other factors. First, unless infrequent stimuli cue responses, the P300 components that they elicit are reduced in amplitude with repeated presentations in humans

(Courchesne, 1978) and monkeys (Arthur & Starr, 1984). Habituation may have similarly reduced P550 amplitudes in the dolphin. Second, in P300 experiments requiring auditory discriminations, humans with perfect pitch have small P300s (Klein, Coles, & Donchin, 1984). The small P550s in the dolphin may similarly reflect a highly evolved capacity for pitch discrimination.

The latency of the P550 component also deserves comment. In humans, P300 latencies are related to the time required to recognize (McCarthy & Donchin, 1981), and respond to stimuli (Woods, Courchesne, Hillyard, & Galambos, 1980). Insofar as the latency of the P300-equivalent is indicative of the time required for processing auditory stimuli in different species, the dolphin would at first glance appear to process at least some auditory stimuli more slowly than humans, cats (Wilder et al., 1981), or monkeys (Arthur & Starr, 1984). However, several other factors may also have contributed to the prolonged latencies of the P550 component which we observed. First, reflections and resonances in the small restraining tank may have made acoustic discriminations more difficult. In humans P300 latencies in difficult tasks may exceed 600 msec (Pritchard, 1981). Second, human P300 latencies are longer than those of equivalent potentials in animals with smaller brains. Thus, there may be a relationship between the time of tranmission between certain neuroanatomical structures and the latency of the P300-like component. The prolonged latency of the P550 in the bottlenosed dolphin is consistent with the large brain size (1500 grams) of this species, and suggests that the P300 pathways may have increased in length in comparison with terrestrial mammals. Third, different species may vary in the extent to which stimuli are used for "context updating" (Donchin, 1981). A deeper and more thorough updating may be associated with longer latency P300s. If so, the long latency of the P300 equivalent in dolphin would be consistent with a thorough analysis of acoustic inputs. Fourth, P300 latencies in man increase (by up to 120 msec) with aging (Goodin, Squires, Henderson, & Starr, 1978). If a similar relationship holds in dolphins the relatively advanced age of our animal (22 years) may have contributed to the prolonged latencies of the P300-like potentials that we observed.

SUMMARY

We recorded event-related potentials (ERPs) from the skull surface of a bottlenose dolphin (*Tursiops truncatus*) in response to a variety of auditory stimuli including pure and complex tones, FM sweeps, clicks, and dolphin calls. The effects of stimulus repetition and probability on ERPs were examined in three experiments. In each experiment, infrequent, deviant sounds (such as dolphin calls mixed with trains of tones) or task-relevant stimuli (associated with reinforcement) were presented at low probabilities in an effort to elicit endogenous potentials similar to those which occur in humans following the presentation of infrequent or surprising stimuli.

Three classes of responses were recorded. *Middle-latency components (P25-N60)* showed short refractory periods and were maximal in amplitude to brief click stimuli similar to echolocation pulses. *Long-latency components (N200-P450)* showed comparable amplitudes for click and tone stimuli. When stimuli were repeated, the N200-P450 was markedly reduced in amplitude at all intervals tested (up to 6.0 sec). This refractory process was specific to the stimulus because conditioning tones of one frequency did not reduce N200-P450 amplitudes to probe tones of another frequency. The dolphin N200-P450 showed more marked and specific refractory effects than the human N100-P200 recorded in a comparable paradigm. The differences may reflect a more precise representation of auditory stimuli in dolphin short-term acoustic memory.

Deviant stimuli produced an enhanced *long-latency positive component (P550)* in the dolphin, similar in some respects to the ''decision-related'' P300 wave in humans.

REFERENCES

Arthur, D. L., & Starr, A. (1984). Task-relevant late positive component of the auditory event-related potential in monkeys resembles P300 in humans. *Science, 223,* 186–188.

Buchwald, J., Hinman, C., Norman, R. J., Huang, C., & Brown, K. A. (1981). Middle- and long-latency auditory evoked responses recorded from the vertex of normal and chronically lesioned cats. *Brain Research, 205,* 91–109.

Bullock, T. H. (1981). Neuroethology deserves more study of evoked responses. *Neuroscience, 6,* 1203–1215.

Bullock, T. H., Grinnell, A. D., Ikezono, E., Kameda, K., Katsuki, K., Nomoto, M., Sato, O., Suga, N., & Yanagisawa, K. (1968). Electrophysiological studies of central auditory mechanisms in cetaceans. *Zeitschrift fur Vergleichende Physiologie, 59,* 117–156.

Bullock, T. H., & Gurevich, V. S. (1979). Soviet literature on the nervous system and psychobiology of Cetacea. *International Review of Neurobiology, 21,* 47–127.

Bullock, T. H., & Ridgway, S. H. (1972). Evoked potentials in the central auditory system of alert porpoises to their own and artificial sounds. *Journal of Neurobiology, 3,* 79–99.

Butler, R. A. (1973). Frequency specificity of the auditory evoked response to simultaneously and successively presented auditory stimuli. *Electroencephalography, and clinical Neurophysiology, 33,* 277–282.

Corwin, J. T., Bullock, T. H., & Schweitzer, J. (1982). Auditory brainstem responses in five vertebrate classes. *Electroencephlography and clinical Neurophysiology, 54,* 629–641.

Courchesne, E. (1978). Changes in P3 waves with event-repetition: Long-term effects on scalp distribution and amplitude. *Electroencephalography and clinical Neurophysiology JR, 45,* 754–766.

Courchesne, E., Courchesne, R., & Hillyard, S. (1978). The effect of stimulus deviation on P3 waves to easily recognized stimuli. *Neuropsychology, 18,* 189–199.

Courchesne, E., Hillyard, S., & Galambos, R. (1975). Stimulus novelty, task relevance, and the visual evoked potential in man. *Electroencephalography and clinical Neurophysiology.* *39*, 131–143.

Donchin, E. (1981). Surprise!. . . Surprise? *Psychophysiology* . *18*, 493–513.

Farley, G. R., & Starr, A. (1983). Middle and long latency auditory evoked potentials in cat. I. Component definition and dependence on behavioral factors. *Hearing Research*, *10*, 117–138.

Goodin, D., Squires, K., Henderson, B., & Starr, A. (1978). Age related variations in evoked potentials to auditory stimuli in normal human subjects. *Electroencephalography and clinical Neurophysiology* , *44*, 447–458.

Herman, L. M. (1980). Cognitive characteristics of dolphins. In L. M. Herman (Ed.), *Cetacean behavior* (pp. 363–429). New York: Wiley.

Hillyard, S. A., & Kutas, M. (1983). Electrophysiology of cognitive processing. *Ann. Rev. Psychol.*, *34*, 33–61.

Hillyard, S., & Woods, D. (1979). Electrophysiological ananysis of human brain function. In M. Gazzaniga (Ed.), *Handbook of behavioral neurobiology* (pp. 345–377). New York: Plenum.

Johnson, C. S. (1966). Auditory thresholds of the bottlenose dolphin (*Tursiops truncatus* Montagu). *U.S. Naval Ordinance Test Station TP, 4178.*

Klein, M., Coles, M. G. H., & Donchin, E. (1984). People with perfect pitch process tones without producing P300. *Science, 223,* 1306–1309.

Knight, R. T. (1984). Decreased response to novel stimuli after prefrontal lesions in man. *Electroncephalography and clinical Neurophysiology* , *59*, 9–20.

Ladygina, T. F., & Supin, A. Y. (1977). Localization of the projectional sensory areas in the cortex of the Atlantic bottlenose dolphin (*Tursiops truncatus*). *Zhurnal Evoliutsionnoi Biokhimii Fiziologii*, *13*, 712–718.

McCarthy, G., & Donchin, E. (1981). A metric for thought: A comparison of P300 latency and reaction time. *Science, 211,* 77–80.

Nelson, D., & Lassman, F. (1973). Combined effects of recovery period and stimulus intensity on the human auditory evoked vertex response. *Journal of Speech and Hearing Research* , *16*, 297–308.

Nelson, D., & Lassman, F. (1973). Combined effects of recovery period and stimulus intensity on the human auditory evoked vertex response. *Journal of Speech and Hearing Research* , *16*, 297–308.

Neville, H. J., & Foote, S. L. (1984). Auditory event-related potentials in the squirrel monkey: Parallels to human late wave responses. *Brain Research* , *298*, 107–116.

O'Brien, J. H. (1982). P300 wave elicited by a stimulus-change paradigm in acutely prepared rats. *Physiology & Behavior, 28,* 711–713.

O'Neill, W. E., & Suga, N. (1982). Encoding of target range and its representation in the auditory cortex of the mustached bat. *The Journal of Neuroscience JR, 2,* 17–31.

Picton, T., Campbell, K., Baribeau-Braun, J., & Proulx, G. (1978). The neurophysiology of human attention. A tutorial review. In J. Requin (Ed.), *Attention and performance VII* (pp. 429–467). Hillsdale, NJ: Lawrence Erlbaum Associates.

Picton, T., Woods, D., Baribeau-Braun, J., & Healey, T. (1977). Evoked potential audiometry. *Journal of Otolaryngology* , *6*, 90–119.

Picton, T., Woods, D., & Proulx, G. (1978). Human auditory sustained potentials II. Stimulus relationships. *Electroencephalography and Clinical Neurophysiology, 45,* 198–210.

Pritchard, W. S. (1981). Psychophysiology of P300. *Psychology Bulletin, 89,* 506–540.

Ridgway, S. H., Bullock, T. H., Carder, D. A., Seeley, R. L., Woods, D. L., & Galambos, R. (1981). Auditory brainstem response in dolphins. *Proceedings of the Natural Academy of Science, 78,* 1943–47.

Seeley, R. L., Flanigan, W. F., & Ridgway, S. H. (1976). A technique for rapidly assessing the hearing of the bottlenoised porpoise, *Tursiops truncatus. Naval Undersea Center Report, San Diego California, NUC TP 522.*

Wilder, M. B., Farley, G. R., & Starr, A. (1981). Endogenous late positive component of the evoked potential in cats corresponding to P300 in humans. *Science, 211*, 605–607.

Woods, D. L., Courchesne, E., Hillyard, S., & Galambos, R. (1980). Split-second recovery of the P3 component in multiple decision tasks. *Progr. Brain Research , 54*, 322–330.

Woods, D. L., & Elmasian, R. (1984). The Short and long-term habituation of event-related potentials to speech sounds and tones. *Electroencephalography and clinical Neurophysiology,* in press.

4

Vision, Audition, and Chemoreception in Dolphins and Other Marine Mammals

Paul E. Nachtigall
Naval Ocean Systems Center,
Kailva, Hawaii

INTRODUCTION

Marine mammal brains are active vital centers for the perception and interpretation of environmental information received through a variety of sensory modalities. While it may be difficult to directly examine the question of animal consciousness or self-awareness (Griffin, 1983) quantifiable objective techniques exist for examining the abilities of animals to perceive their environments. Most definitions of consciousness include a statement of awareness to sensations and most definitions of "cognitive processes" include sensation and perception (Mayer, 1983). The techniques of animal psychophysics allow an examination of sensation through the interpretation of an animal's behavior. Carefully interpreted experimental designs and psychophysical procedures have allowed us a fascinating view of the sensory processes, and thus the perceptual world, of dolphins and other marine mammals.

To optimize feeding, reproduction, and predator avoidance the sensory systems of animals must accurately gather available information. Rich sources of sound, light, and chemical stimuli fill the marine environment. Neurophysiological and psychophysical research with marine mammals has primarily concentrated on the study of audition and vision but taste reception experiments have recently been done. An examination of the sensory capabilities of a number of marine mammal species provides a comparative perspective to the variety of solutions to common problems that dolphins and other marine mammals encountered when returning to an aquatic environment.

VISION

Marine mammals present a unique opportunity to examine the course of evolutionary development of visual processes in their adaptation from a terrestrial to an underwater environment. The extent of this adaptation varies with the species. Dolphins normally spend all of their lives in water while otters and pinnipeds are amphibious and divide their time between aquatic and terrestrial environments. All marine mammals so far examined have specific adaptations for vision in both mediums.

The mammalian eye may be considered analogous to a camera. In a camera, light rays are bent or focused to project a clear image and that image is then recorded on the film. The focusing process of the eye is accomplished by its accommodating or dioptric mechanisms: the pupil, cornea, and lens. The light-sensitive retina is roughly analogous to film. Electromagnetic energy of light is coded, transferred to nerve impulses at the retina, and then processed by the central nervous system. Both optic mechanisms and the retinal structures of marine mammal eyes show specific adaptations aiding aerial and underwater vision.

Focusing light rays onto a retina is quite different under water than it is in air due to the differences in speed of light in the two media. Because water is optically denser than air, light travels slower in water. Light is therefore bent when it passes through air and into water or any medium that is as optically dense as water. The cornea and most of the interior of the eye are optically as dense as water (Riggs, 1966). Thus, light waves traveling through the air are bent by the cornea so that two-thirds of the focusing power of an air-adapted human eye occurs at the cornea (Christman, 1971). When an air adapted cornea is placed under water the focusing power of the cornea is therefore lost. Human skindivers overcome this loss by wearing a face mask to keep the eye in an aerial medium. Each of the marine mammal groups so far examined has independently evolved a unique solution to this focusing or accommodating problem. These solutions are presented in conjunction with behavioral evidence collected from psychophysical studies on vision.

Most of the studies of marine mammal vision have been done in the last 25 years, and recently, most of those studies have examined some form of visual acuity. Visual acuity was defined by Riggs (1966) as ". . .the capacity to discriminate the fine details of objects in the field of view. Good visual acuity implies that a subject can discriminate fine detail; poor acuity implies that only gross features can be seen" (p. 321).

A variety of visual problem-solving tasks have been used, with at least one of the tasks now standard enough for valid visual *acuity* comparisons to be made.

Otters

According to Walls (1963) the otter eye is able to accommodate under water without the aid of corneal accommodation by well developed ciliary muscles and an enormous sphincter in the iris, which squeezes the anterior portion of the lens. The otter's normal (emmetropic) vision occurs in the air but these adaptive accommodating processes cause the lens to be shaped to enable the otter to see quite well under water.

Three behavioral studies of otter vision have been conducted. Gentry and Peterson (1967) examined underwater visual size discrimination in the sea otter (*Enhydra lutris*). The animal was trained to choose the larger of two simultaneously presented black circular targets on a white background. Sea otters were, at one time, difficult to maintain in captivity and Gentry and Peterson had only 2 weeks to run the experiment. It is difficult to accurately determine a quantitative measure of visual acuity with a size-discrimination task, so Gentry and Peterson compared their results to those of a similar study of underwater vision of the California sea lion (Schusterman, Kellogg, & Rice, 1965). The otters performance was not as good as the sea lion's. However, a number of sources have indicated that the visual size-discrimination task is contaminated as a test for acuity by the brightness differences created by different sized targets (Balliet & Schusterman, 1971; Fobes & Smock, 1981; Nachtigall, 1969; Schusterman, 1968).

Although it was obvious in 1969 that the visual size-discrimination problem was not a pure acuity task, it was the predominately used visual task for marine mammals and could therefore be used as a comparative tool. Nachtigall (1969) used this task to compare visual size discrimination in a river otter, the clawless otter *Amblyonyx cineria,* in air and under water. Using the same black targets on a white background that had previously been used by Gentry & Peterson (1967), Nachtigall found no difference in visual size-discrimination ability in air and under water. This was the first behavioral evidence to support Walls' (1963) assumption of the relatively good underwater accommodating ability of the otter. A comparison of data from the three studies indicates that the sea lion is superior to the clawless otter and the clawless otter is in turn better than the sea otter at making visual size discriminations.

In order to more precisely examine visual acuity, Balliet and Schusterman (1971) obtained the otters previously used by Nachtigall (1969) to test visual acuity on a task which required the resolution of targets made up of equally spaced horizontal alternating black and white stripes. These Ronchi ruling targets were specifically designed to measure visual acuity (Riggs, 1966). The targets varied by line width and had equal areas of black and white on each target in order to control for brightness differences. In addition to controlling for brightness, Ronchi targets also allow a quantitative measure of visual acuity in the form of the minimum angle of resolution (MAR). The MAR is determined by

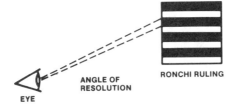

ANGLE OF
RESOLUTION

RONCHI RULING

EYE

FIG. 4.1. Schematic of the quantitative measure of visual acuity using ronchi ruling targets and calculated minimum angle of resolution.

measuring the size of the lines at the animals' threshold and the distance from the target (see Fig. 4.1) and calculating the threshold angle. Balliet & Schusterman (1971) found the aerial and underwater visual acuity to be about the same with a mean MAR of 14.85 min when the river otters (*Amblyonyx cineria*) were tested in bright light.

It is apparent that the adaptation of the dioptric or focusing mechanisms has enabled the otter to accommodate equally well in air or under water in bright light. The fact that they do not see as well as sea lions must be attributed to the retinal and neural elements of the otter eye.

Pinnipeds

The anatomical structures of the eyes of sea lions and other pinnipeds have evolved for underwater vision in a way different from that of otters. Walls (1963) states that the pinniped eye functions normally (is emmetropic) under water. The cornea does not function well as a focusing device in air, and the sea lion should be quite astigmatic out of the water. The astigmatism is overcome, Walls (1963) indicates, by a much constricted pupil that closes down to a narrow vertical slit for aerial vision. Focusing is accomplished in a manner similar to that of a pinhole camera.

Most of the interest in psychophysical research on pinniped vision was initiated by the work done by R. J. Schusterman and his coworkers (e.g., Schusterman, Kellogg, & Rice, 1965). Schusterman (1968, 1971) has quite nicely summarized his early visual acuity work. The early visual tasks were not measures of acuity but were, as has been indicated with the otters, size-discrimination problems. According to Schusterman (personal communication), the original visual size-discrimination problems developed from early attempts to examine possible echolocation in pinnipeds and the size-different targets were constructed originally as echolocation stimuli. Vision proved to be the more dominant sensory modality (Schusterman, 1971) and subsequent visual problems became progressively more refined.

In the first attempt to determine MARs, Schusterman (1971) used patterns consisting of broken and solid black rectangles, 1.5 cm wide and 10.0 cm long, on a white background. Both the harbor seal (*Phoca vitulina*) and sea lion MARs were determined in a simultaneous two-choice task requiring the animal to choose the broken rectangle. The MARs were estimated to be 2 min for both species under water. It then became apparent that the broken rectangle task also did not represent visual acuity accurately due to the differential pinpoint brightness of the break in the black rectangle on the white background.

As Schusterman (1971) stated:

> Visual acuity measured in this way probably involves a brightness or intensity discrimination. In view of these considerations, and in the light of our present results, it seems quite likely that with the types of test patterns used in our earlier attempts to obtain underwater visual actuity thresholds in pinnipeds, the obtained threshold values considerably overestimated their visual resolving power. (p. 491)

In light of this observation, Schusterman (1971) repeated the tests using Ronchi rulings and found the MAR for the sea lion to be around 6 min of arc for both aerial and underwater vision. Using the same task, Schusterman also measured the underwater visual acuity of the Stellers sea lion (*Eumetopias jubatus*) and the harbor seal (*Phoca vitulina*) and found MARs of 7.1 and 8.3 min, respectively.

All the pinniped visual studies so far mentioned were conducted in open sunlight. If Walls' (1963) statement that the aerial focusing requires the pupil to close down to create a pin-hole lens is correct, then logically at low luminance levels acuity in air should not be as good as it is under water where the pupil remains dilated. Schusterman and Balliet (1971) examined this assumption by testing sea lion aerial and underwater acuity at various luminance levels. The animal was tested in a darkened chamber with background luminance to the plexiglass Ronchi patterned targets varied. The results confirmed Walls' assumptions because as the luminance level was lowered, aerial acuity became increasingly poor as compared to underwater acuity at the same luminance level. Underwater acuity remained remarkably good down to 10^{-4} millilamberts. The sea lion's MAR at that level was found to be around 10 min of arc which is nearly as good as those of the Rhesus monkey and baboon in air at the same light levels.

This excellent acuity under water at low illumination levels is of course not totally due to the fact that the sea lion's pupil remains dilated under water. Pinnipeds have generally adapted to seeing at low luminance levels, as indicated by the structure of the retina and tapetum. The tapetum is essentially a reflective surface just behind the retina. A reflective surface has obvious advantage for vision at low luminance levels. Landau & Dawson (1970) histologically examined the retinal cell structure of the sea lion. They found a primarily rod-filled retina with no apparent fovea centralis. The rods were widespread and relatively densely packed, but the ganglion cell densities were lower in the periphery with peripheral receptory ganglion cell ratios of about 200 to 1, while central areas showed receptor/ganglion ratios near 50 to 1. They also concluded that the ". . .eyes in Pinnipedia are apparently cone free" (p. 699). But they were not entirely sure if ". . .the receptors in this family of aquatic mammals are indeed rods or only look like them" (p. 701). There has been no psychophysical examination of color vision in the sea lion.

Despite the adaptations for dim light acuity, no experimental studies have examined the threshold for dim light absolute sensitivity in the sea lion. A study of absolute sensitivity of the harp seal (*Pagophilus groenlandicus*) was done by Lavigne & Ronald (1972). They examined thresholds of a single harp seal for a variety of monochromatic lights under both light- and dark-adapted conditions. Light-adapted sensitivity was found to be quite similar to that of humans except that the sensitivity curve was bimodally distributed with peaks near 500 and 550 nm and a dip near 525. The dark-adapted curve showed sensitivity increased by eight log units (as compared to light adapted) with the peak occurring at 525 nm. According to Lavigne & Ronald, this Purkinje Shift "implies that the harp seal has a duplex retina and suggests that at least two types of photo-pigments with different obsorption spectra must be present. . ." (p. 1203). This behavioral evidence for a duplex retina was not expected. Nagy & Ronald (1970) had previously examined harp seal photo-receptors with an electron microscope and found that the outer segments resembled those typically found in rods and most terminated in typical rod-like spherules. Subsequent work, summarized by Lavigne, Bernholz, & Ronald (1977), provided additional evidence for duplicity in pinniped retinas, including dual functions in dark-adaptation curves, critical flicker frequency (Bernholz & Mathews, 1975) of a harp seal and reanalysis of visual acuity functions under different light levels for a California sea lion.

Dolphins

While there is no doubt that dolphins echolocate extremely well, they also have the capability for fine visual discrimination. A blindfolded dolphin may have difficulty finding fish at very close range even while echolocating vigorously. Given that dolphins may open their eyes under water at great depths and also look through the air in bright sunlight, their visual systems must indeed be accommodating.

Anatomy and Optics. Walls (1963) was quite uninformed about whale eyes in general and odontocete eyes in particular. He believed that the whale eye ". . .has reverted to the fish type—perfectly so in the odontocetes," and that "no whale is known to be able to rotate the eyeball. . ." (p. 412). He also assumed that the odontocete eye is ". . .probably. . .completely useless in air" (p. 412). His description of the basic anatomical structure was more accurate. Walls stated that the odontocete eye is generally ellipsoidal, with a spherical lens and a cornea which is thickened at its margin. A reflective tapetum is also present behind the retina.

Kellogg and Rice (1963, 1966) were the first to show that the eye of one odontocete, the bottlenose dolphin (*Tursiops truncatus*) is not "completely useless in air." Although their study was not a parametric examination of dolphin visual acuity, the results of their shape discrimination study indicated that the subject could discriminate two-dimensional shapes both in air and under water.

It is obvious to anyone who observes a captive bottlenose dolphin that their eyes are quite readily movable. Dral (1972) observed this ocular mobility and examined a living dolphin's eye. He noted that when the dolphin looks under water it often views an object to the side with a single eye but when the animal views an object in air it "faces" the object in a nasal-ventral direction. The cornea is not spherically curved, but is thickened at the margins. Dral's opthalmoscopic measurements indicated that the dolphin may see quite well in a dorso- or ventro-temporal direction (through the thickened portion of the cornea) in air. He concluded that "under water the animal can use the whole range of its eye, whereas in air vision is restricted to its nasoventral part" (p. 511). Dral examined a total of seven dolphin eyes and found that, contrary to Walls' assumptions, not all of the lenses were spherical, and some had a distinct oval shape. He also noted that the iris operculum has strong muscles and lies closely against the lens and therefore could provide a mechanism for accommodating similar to that found for the otters. He also noted that in-air bright-light conditions, "the operculum is lowered by which action, together with a small lowering of the iris, the pupil is divided into two small apertures, a nasal and a temporal one" (p. 512).

Dawson, Birndorf, and Perez (1972) examined both living and fixed dolphin eyes with a retinoscope, opthalmoscope, and fundus camera. They were apparently unaware of Dral's work and formulated an independent, but different, view of the focusing mechanism of the dolphin eye in air. On the basis of their calculations of the curvature of the cornea and the distances within the eye, they determined that the dolphin would require 5.1 diopters of lens accommodation to clearly focus an image for the retina *under water* but that . . .no amount of accommodation would correct for the additional power provided by the cornea in air, indicating that optically, the dolphin is hopelessly myopic when he is out of water" (p. 8). They did not specify precisely which part of the cornea the animal would presumably be viewing through and did not mention its irregular shape, as did Dral (1972), but the calculations were based on a radius of curvature of approximately 14.8 mm, which implies a regularly curved cornea.

When Dawson et al. examined pupil constriction under bright light they did not come to the same conclusion as Dral. While Dral said the pupil closes down into two apertures, Dawson et al. stated that the pupil closes down into a U-shaped slit. On the basis of this pupilary slit and the adaptations for dim-light sensitivity (e.g., large pupil and tapetum), Dawson et al. proposed that the dolphin overcomes its myopia in air the same way that the sea lion compensates for its astigmatism—by focusing with a very narrow opening analogous to a pin-hole camera.

Retinal Structure.   Perez, Dawson, and Landau (1972) examined the retinal anatomy of the bottlenose dolphin. They concluded that, like the sea lion, the receptor to ganglion cell ratio was near 100:1, but unlike the sea lion, cones were quite obviously present. The ganglion cells, however, were unusually large. Very large ganglion cells are not that unusual among mammals. In the cat 5 to 10% of the ganglion cells are of the giant variety. Perez et al. stated that "in contrast to the cat, the ganglion cell population of *Tursiops truncatus,* as seen by interference microscopy, appears to be almost entirely composed of ganglion cells of the giant variety" (p. 6). No functional significance of the giant ganglion cells was proposed. According to additional microscopic work (Dawson & Perez, 1973) the giant cell bodies range up to 150 μm in diameter and appear to predominate in the central 40° of the retina. They apparently give rise to large dendritic processes and large optic nerve fibers. Dawson and Perez suggested that giant cells and large fibers must lead to rapid communication with the brain but that they might also be used to sustain anaerobic metabolism. Dral (1977), while noting Dawson and Perez's speculation, believed that the function of the giant cells remained an open question. Dawson (1980) stated that the giant fibers may well be a part of a "transient" detector system with great value in the detection of movement in the peripheral visual fields and subsequent orientation towards the source of movement, but Dawson, Hope, Ulshafer, and Jenkins (1983) once again stressed the supportive function.

Behavioral Psychophysics.   Madsen (1972) examined both aerial and under-water acuity in the bottlenose dolphin and found the MAR in water to be about 12 min, and in air about 22 min. She was not particularly confident in her results, noting that part of the experiment was performed hastily and before the animal was fully trained to the new discrimination. Madsen used Ronchi grid patterns presented simultaneously, collecting data by a combined method of descending limits and tracking. In spite of Madsen's trepidation concerning her results, another study of bottlenose dolphin aerial acuity (Pepper, Simmons, Beach, & Nachtigall, 1972), using Ronchi rulings successively presented by a method of constants, indicated that the bottlenose dolphin has a MAR of 18 min in air under bright light conditions—not that much different from Madsen's 22 min.

It should be noted that all three of the aforementioned studies of aerial vision (Kellogg & Rice, 1966; Madsen, 1972, and Pepper et al., 1972) conducted with bottlenose dolphins were collected with some difficulty. For some reason it is quite difficult to get a dolphin to attend to static visual stimuli presented in air. Kellogg and Rice, for instance, report that aerial discriminations could only be accomplished after the animal had learned the task under water. A great deal of training was required before Pepper et al.'s animal properly attended to the visual stimuli. Despite this difficulty, the results generally indicate that cetaceans are capable of resolving the details of targets in air fairly well.

Spong and White (1971) attempted to examine the visual acuity of the Pacific white-sided dolphin (*Lagenorhynchus obliquidens*) under water. The task consisted of a simultaneous discrimination between two stimuli presented on a white background. Each variable stimulus was made up of two black vertical lines separated by a gap, while the standard was a black rectangle equal in area to the sum of the two vertical lines on each variable target. The animal was trained to choose the variable target containing the gap. The MAR determined by the method of constant stimuli was found to be 6 min in bright light. White, Cameron, Spong, and Bradford (1971) examined underwater visual acuity of the killer whale (*Orcinus orca*) using a task and methods similar to that used with the white-sided dolphin. In an attempt to control for possible brightness differences, White et al. changed the standard target from a solid black rectangle to two vertical black lines with a gap width well below the presumed acuity of the whale. The MAR was estimated to be 5.5 min of arc in relatively bright light.

Although the procedures in both of these underwater acuity studies appear sound, the MARs may be an overestimate of true underwater acuity. When Schusterman (1968) presented a similar task to sea lions he found a MAR of about 2 min. Subsequent testing of sea lions with Ronchi patterns indicated an actual MAR of 6 min. Schusterman (1971) stated that his first overestimate was probably due to the point source of light occurring when a single white space is presented between two larger black spaces on the variable target. Schusterman further stated that it seems quite probable that the underwater acuity of at least the Pacific white-sided dolphin had been overestimated in Spong & White's (1971) work. Herman, Peacock, Yunker and Madsen (1975) examined the visual acuity of the bottlenose dolphin both in air and under water using Ronchi grid targets presented either 1 or 2.5 m away. They found that at 1 m aerial vision was poor, as compared with underwater vision, but that at 2.5 m the acuity in air and under water was about the same at 12.5 min of arc. Expanding on Dral's and Dawson's earlier hypotheses, Herman et al. postulated that vision was equally good in the two media due to a double-split pupil model of the dolphin eye in bright light conditions.

Although rod- and cone-like receptor cells are present in cetacean eyes, Madsen and Herman (1980) reported that prolonged training by several different techniques yielded no success in teaching a dolphin to discriminate among blue, green, or red monochromatic light. This lack of dolphin ability to discriminate colors was supported by Madsen's spectral sensitivity data demonstrating no Purkinje Shift when examining absolute thresholds with monochromatic light of different wavelengths (as reported in Madsen & Herman, 1980).

AUDITION

As in the visual system, the auditory structures of marine mammals have adjusted and adapted from an aerial to an underwater environment. As was noted previously, marine mammals have adapted to the aquatic environment in different degrees. Pinnipeds spend time both in air and under water, while cetaceans are wholly acquatic. Differential adaptations of the auditory systems of the two groups naturally reflect the environmental conditions encountered in their habitats. There is little behavioral information on the auditory abilities of the otters, but there has been a good amount of work conducted with pinnipeds and odontocete cetaceans. Work with these two groups reflects an interest due to the confirmed echolocation ability of the odontocetes (e.g., Evans, 1973) and the proposed (Poulter, 1963, 1966, 1969; Shaver & Poulter, 1967; Renouf & Davis, 1983) but contested (Evans & Haugan, 1963; Schusterman, Gentry, & Schmook, 1967; Schusterman, 1966, 1968; Schevill, 1968; Wartzok, Schusterman, & Gailey-Phipps, 1984) echolocation of some pinnipeds. Echolocation involves an active process of emitting sounds and locating objects by the returning echoes. Here, studies of echolocation are referred to only in the context of hearing (for reviews of echolocation performance by dolphins, see Busnel & Fish, 1980, and Nachtigall, 1980).

Sound travels through water almost five times faster than through air due to water's greater density. This density difference also creates an impedance mismatch when sound travels through air and into water. In an aerially adapted mammalian ear, the middle ear functions as an impedance matching transformer. Sound pressure waves travel through the air, strike the tympanic membrane and are amplified by the lever actions of the three ossicles of the middle ear. Thus amplified, the waves enter the cochlear fluid via the oval window and proceed to stimulate the receptor cells of the organ of corti. In the human middle ear the pressure wave is magnified about twenty times to approximate the impedance of the cochlear fluid. Under water this elaborate impedance matching mechanism becomes unnecessary because the impedance mismatch between water and some structures of the head is very slight. Sound might enter the head and proceed directly to the organ of corti (Reppening, 1972). Sound traveling to reach the inner ear through this tissue route, rather than through the middle ear, is usually termed bone conduction. Bone conduction may cause fluid motion within the inner ear by one of two ways; by moving the entire cochlear capsule, thus creating inertial lag in the fluid, or by distorting one part of the capsule causing the fluid to adjust to changes within the confinement of the capsule walls. The first way may be termed resonant reaction, while the second is called conductive reaction (Reppening, 1972). Bone conduction of one type or the other is a functional mechanism for the underwater hearing of at least some marine mammals.

Pinnipeds

Anatomical Structure.   The outer ear structures of pinnipeds have undergone considerable modification. The external ear (pinna) of the sea lion is very reduced and may serve primarily as a valve to close off the ear canal as the sea lion dives (Reppening, 1972). True seals (phocids) do not have external pinnae. In comparison to terrestrial mammals, the external ear opening (auditory meatus) is quite small and the ear canal is long and narrow. Pinniped middle ears are characterized by relatively large ossicles, especially in the phocids (Møhl, 1968). The phocid inner ear shows particular modifications with a greatly enlarged basal whorl of the cochlea, a relatively large aqueduct of the cochlea, and greatly enlarged oval and round windows. Reppening (1972) reported that the pinniped ear is well adapted for bone conductional hearing due to: (1) an enlarged cochlear round window three times the size of the oval window, (2) a petrosum (bone casing of the ear) that is detached from all other skull bones except the mastoid, and (3) arrangement of temporal bones to aid in a conductive reaction type of bone conduction. Despite these modifications the pinniped's ear must also function in air. Aerial sound transmission is apparently accomplished in the typical mammalian pattern—from the tympanic membrane via the middle ear to the oval window.

Evoked Potentials.   All of the abovementioned mechanical structures function to transmit energy to the receptor cells on the cochlea. Sensations from the cochlear receptor cells are, of course, passed on to the central nervous system. Bullock, Ridgway, and Suga (1971) examined, to a limited extent, the location of auditory function in the sea lion midbrain using implanted electrodes to record evoked auditory potentials. Evoked potentials were recorded in the inferior colliculus and in the region of the lateral lemniscus. They measured evoked potentials for a variety of sound stimuli and discribed different wave forms in response to different stimuli. The results showed that the sea lion's midbrain was not very specialized for extremely short duration, fast rise time sounds needed for echolocation.

Sound Localization.   Møhl (1964) was the first to examine pinniped hearing using behavioral techniques. He was primarily interested in whether or not the harbor seal (*Phoca vitulina*) was capable of directional hearing in air and under water in order to determine whether the seal heard via its external auditory meatus or through bone conduction. His assumption was that if the seal heard via bone conduction it would be unable to localize sound under water due to masking of tympanum-transmitted sounds by the faster bone conducted sounds. This assumption was based on human localization under water which was reported to be quite poor. A detailed picture of the functional anatomy of the pinniped inner ear was not available at that time.

Møhl found the seal could make directional discriminations both in air and under water, but specific thresholds for minimum angle of discrimination were not computed. In a brief attempt to determine the seal's upper frequency limit, Møhl found that the seal was able to make underwater directional discriminations with sounds up to 160 kHz—the limit of Møhl's equipment and the highest reported frequency capable of being heard by any previously tested animal. On the basis of this evidence he concluded that "...it seems unlikely that these animals hear by bone conduction . . . ,'' (p. 291) but instead suggested that the seal accommodates to waterborne sound by muscular tension on the ossicles of the middle ear.

Gentry (1967) examined underwater auditory location in the California sea lion. Thresholds for angular discriminations, Minimum Audible Angles (MAA), were determined for 3.5 and 6 kHz sine wave presentations. Gentry found MAA's of 15 and 10°, respectively, and suggested that the adaptation for sea lion localization under water may not be osteological as proposed by Møhl (1964), but might be neurological, based on an increased ability to discriminate interaural time differences. A comparison of localization of the harbor seal and sea lion showed that the harbor seal is capable of finer angular discriminations. Although Gentry's hypothesis was not disproved, Reppening's (1972) comparison of middle ear functions of seals and sea lions indicated that the difference between the two may well have been due to osteological development. It seems obvious that both osteological and neurological adaptations would be necessary for fine angular discriminations under water. Moore (1975) and Moore and Au (1975) presented various types of signals to a sea lion that was trained to position within a nose-cup and choose whether a signal came from a transducer located on its midline or from one positioned at various angles to its left. Moore (1975) found that with click-type signals, similar to those produced by sea lions, the Minimum Audible Angle was 5.5°. Performance with various pure tone signals, with a preset angle of 20°, showed good performance below 1 kHz and poor localization ability at 2 or 4 kHz. Moore and Au's (1975) follow-up work demonstrated that performance at 8 and 16 kHz was nearly as good as that at frequencies below 1 kHz. These performance differences were interpreted as being due to different auditory localization processes. Phase differences were used to explain performance below 1 kHz while intensity differences accounted for performance above 4 kHz. Subsequent work by Moore and Schusterman (1976) on the discrimination of pure-tone intensities by the California sea lion supported the notion that its intensity discrimination is well developed, demonstrating a difference threshold of 3 dB at 16 kHz.

The angular discrimination capabilities of the harbor seal (*Phoca vitulina*) were examined by Terhune (1974). Terhune compared seal performance in air and under water with both click trains and sinusoidal or low frequency noise stimuli. Differences in performance on these types of stimuli led Terhune to believe that well-defined time cues, or differences in the arrival time of sounds to the two ears, were more important for sound localization by seals than were cues of phase or intensity.

Frequency Discrimination.   Møhl's (1964) finding of directional discrimination ability at frequencies as high as 160 kHz prompted him to undertake further work on the upper frequency limit of seal hearing. Human subjects had been reported to hear "ultrasonics" (above 20 kHz) when submerged, due to bone conduction, and Møhl (1967) was interested to learn if the seal had also been hearing "ultrasonics" in his previous work. Human subjects hearing "ultrasonics" had reported that high-frequency sounds were not discriminable in pitch but were heard as if they were all the same high-frequency sound. Møhl reasoned that an adequate analogous measure of the upper-frequency limit of the seal would be that point at which the seal could still hear sounds but could no longer discriminate differences in tonal frequency.

Two types of pulsed sound stimuli were presented to the seals under water. In the first type all pulses were of the same frequency, while the second type was made up of alternating pulses varying in frequency. The frequency differences of the pulses in the second type of stimulus were systematically varied from 2 to 250% of the standard stimulus frequency. Thresholds for pitch discrimination were taken from the point at which the animal could no longer discriminate the two types of stimuli in a two-choice response. Although the seal could hear sounds as high as 160 kHz, frequency differences above 60 kHz could not be discriminated. The Weber ratio remained relatively constant from 1 through 57 kHz at 13×10^{-3}. Møhl assumed that the upper-frequency limit of the seal, if compared to traditional analogous upper-frequency limits of humans, was around 60 kHz. Some sort of bone conduction hearing apparently occured above 60 kHz.

Audiograms.   In order to further investigate the upper-frequency limit of the harbor seal and compare it to more traditional approaches, Møhl (1968) examined the absolute sensitivity of the seal to both air and waterborne sine waves with frequencies ranging from 1 to 180 kHz. A comparison of the aerial and underwater audiograms (Fig. 4.2) demonstrated that the seal's threshold under water is lower than in air by about 15 dB at comparable frequencies and that hearing extends to a higher range under water than in air. On the basis of these data Møhl concluded that the seal's ear is "water-adapted" relative to air adaptation, but not completely so. He reasoned that if the ear were totally water-adapted the impedance differences of air and water would dictate a constant 30 dB difference between thresholds in the two media. He therefore concluded that some sort of unknown accommodation was taking place which ". . . allows for serviceable hearing in air without sacrificing sensitivity in water" (p. 36). Møhl

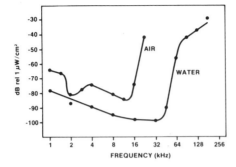

FIG. 4.2. Audiograms of the harbor seal both in air and under water from Møhl (1968).

also suggested that the seal may hear under water via bone conduction, but that seal bone conduction must be different from humans as indicated by the human's reported inability to localize sound under water. As was predicted from his previous work on frequency discrimination, the underwater audiogram shows a very sharp decrease in sensitivity around 60 kHz.

Using behavioral methods very similar to Møhl's (1968), Terhune & Ronald (1971) examined the absolute sensitivity, to airborne sine waves, of the harp seal (*Pagophilus groenlandicus*). Eleven tones ranging from 1 to 32 kHz were presented. The resulting aerial audiogram was compared to that of the harbor seal (Møhl, 1968) and humans in air and under water (see Fig. 4.3). Terhune & Ronald found that both the human and the harbor seal show a distinct region of maximum sensitivity, but the harp seal does not. Sensitivity remained relatively constant from 1 to 32 kHz. Terhune & Ronald also ran a brief experiment on seal critical ratios by testing thresholds of 2, 4 and 8.6 kHz sine-wave tones masked by a continuously presented 35 dB (re .0002 dynes/cm²) white noise. Critical ratios, as a percentage of the center frequency, were at 10% for both the 2 and the 4 kHz tones and 35% from the 8.6 kHz tone. They reported that the animals' behavior became erratic during the critical ratio tests and that ''During the testing at 8.6 kHz, the seal often pushed the initial switch without following up by pressing the other switches'' (p. 387). This implies that the differences in critical ratios obtained were due to the behavioral breakdown in the animal's response. The critical ratios obtained were not unlike those of the cat or human at comparable frequencies, and ''In general, the critical ratios of *P. groenlandicus* are similar to those of other terrestrial and marine mammals. This indicates that the inner ear of *P. groenlandicus* functions in a typically mammalian manner'' (p. 389).

Terhune & Ronald (1972) continued auditory measurements of the harp seal by determining its audiogram under water. The audiogram was compared to the underwater audiogram of the harbor seal and the in air audiograms of both harbor seal (Mohl, 1968) and harp seal (Terhune & Ronald, 1971) as shown in Fig. 4.4. Underwater audiograms indicate similar hearing in the two species.

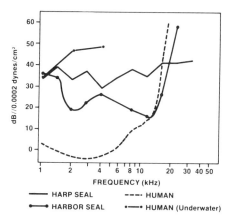

FIG. 4.3. Audiograms of the harp seal, harbor seal and human in air, and the human under water from Terhune and Ronald (1971).

The underwater audiogram of the California sea lion was obtained by Schusterman, Balliet, & Nixon (1972). Instead of using a place or lever response indicator, they trained a sea lion to emit clicks in the presence of an auditory stimulus and remain silent in its absence. Conditioned vocalization was shown to be a reliable response indicator. The resulting audiogram is presented in Fig 4.5.

An observational note by Schusterman et al. indicates that if the sea lion hears by bone conduction it perceives bone-conducted sound differently from conventionally heard sounds. They note that at 32 kHz the sea lion performed in a manner similar to that in testing at lower frequencies. But when 48 kHz sounds were presented, even at very high intensities, the sea lion did not respond. Finally after a "good deal of exposure" the sea lion responded to 48 kHz sounds. When the animal was retrained to 8kHz, nonresponding again occurred and additional training was necessary. Two additional crossovers from frequencies above and below 32 kHz gave similar results. After extensive training at 68 kHz the animal responded to very intense signals at frequencies up to 192 kHz.

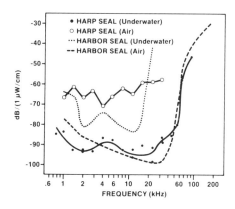

FIG. 4.4. Aerial and underwater audiograms of the harp seal and harbor seal from Terhune and Ronald (1972).

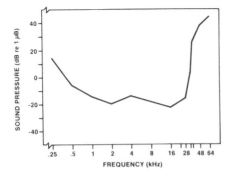

FIG. 4.5. Underwater audiogram of the California sea lion from Schusterman et al. (1972).

Schusterman & Balliet suggested that 32 kHz may be the point at which the sea lion begins to hear "ultrasonics" (bone-conducted sounds) similar to those noted by Møhl (1967). If this is true then the sea lion should also be incapable of fine frequency discriminations above 32 kHz. Schusterman & Moore (1978) found this to be true.

The aerial audiogram for sounds between 4 and 32 kHz of the California sea lion was obtained by Schusterman (1974) using the same animal and essentially the same procedures as those used in the Schusterman et al. (1972) underwater work. Sensitivity beyond 4 kHz decreased gradually to 24 kHz with a rapid loss of sensitivity at higher frequencies. A comparison of the two audiograms indicated that generally, like the seal, the sea lion hears better under water than in air with an average loss of 15 dB in air as compared to underwater.

Gray seal (*Halichoerus grypus*) hearing in air and under water was examined by Ridgway & Joyce (1975) using cortical evoked potential measurements. Peak sensitivity in air was around 4 kHz, with peak sensitivity underwater around 25 kHz. Absolute sensitivity was generally about 15 dB better underwater when comparing the two peaks. Underwater hearing of the ringed seal (*Phoca hispida*) measured by Terhune & Ronald (1975) using behavioral techniques was found to be quite similar to that of the gray seal and the harp seal; so similar in fact that Terhune and Ronald predicted that all members of the seal (phocid) family or subfamily will have "virtually identical hearing abilities" (p. 230).

Based on available data it seems well established that both otarid and phocid pinnipeds have ears adapted to hearing both in air and underwater. Underwater hearing is better in both groups, and phocids generally hear higher frequencies than do otarids. Both groups hear sounds of higher frequency than can be discriminated, indicating that some type of bone conduction most likely occurs.

Dolphins

The acoustical reception and processing abilities of the dolphins have generally been shown to be among the most sophisticated of any animal so far examined

(Popper, 1980). Dolphins not only possess a highly refined echolocation ability but also live in tightly organized schools that appear to be organized by sound communication (Norris, 1968), perhaps recognizing individual conspecifics by whistle signatures (Caldwell, Hall, & Caldwell, 1971). The recognition of echolocation prompted a great deal of both research and speculation about the dolphin's auditory system, but only within the last 20 years has enough experimental evidence been gathered to support a viable theory of the sound pathway to the inner ear.

Fraser and Purves (1960) concluded that dolphins receive sound via the external auditory meatus while Norris (1964) suggested that sound is received via bone conduction through the fat layer of the lower jaw. Subsequent electrophysiological recordings (Bullock, Grinnell, Ikezono, Kameda, Katsuki, Nomato, Sato, Suga, & Yanagisawa, 1968) and cochlear microphonic work (McCormick, Wever, Palin, & Ridgway, 1970) have demonstrated that sounds passing through the lower jaw excite cochlear and midbrain regions with greater intensity than those sounds presented in the area of the external auditory meatus. This support for Norris' theory of sound conduction prompted additional interest in the pathways sound travels to reach the inner ear.

Sound Paths.   As has been noted by Reppening (1972) the term bone conduction could more adequately be termed tissue conduction. In the water-adapted cetacean, tissue conduction appears to be the primary route of sound conduction to the middle ear. The isolation of the bullae shows an adaptation for tissue-conducted sound (Norris, 1968). The lower jaw contains fat which is closely matched to the impedance of sea water. The lower jawbone of most odontocetes becomes broadened and quite thin posteriorily, and the fat forms an oval shape that closely corresponds to the area of minimum thickness of the jaw. Norris (1968) labeled this an "acoustic window." The fat body leads directly to the bulla. Norris proposed that the function of this anatomy is to produce a "wave guide" or sound path to the ear structures located deep within the head.

The placement and supporting structures of the ear complex itself indicates adaptation for tissue conduction. According to Fraser & Purves (1960), paired and single air sacs are scattered throughout the head. Norris (1968) indicated that these air sacs may serve to channel tissue-conducted sounds. One air sac, the peribullary sinus, almost completely isolates the cochlea-bearing periotic bone from the adjacent skull, thus effectively isolating tissue conducted sounds to particular incoming pathways. The pathway for transmission of sound energy once it reaches the general area of the bulla is not clear. The function of the middle ear, and the type of bone conduction occurring within the bulla, has not been precisely established and remains the subject of some discussion.

Anatomy and Function of the Middle Ear.   The cetacean middle ear contains the same basic elements as that of terrestrial mammals, but the parts show considerable modification. McCormick, Wever, Palin and Ridgway (1970) found that the tympanic membrane has been modified to form a ligamentous structure 0.5 mm thick. The thick tympanic membrane is attached to a true tympanic ligament which extends to the malleus. The malleus is very large and is mainly supported by a fusion of its anterior process to the tympanic bone. This fusion is a true bony union (syntosis) that can only be separated by breaking it. A second smaller ligament runs from the posterior wall of the tympanic bone to the malleus. The malleus is fused with the incus and the incus is connected to the stapes through a movable joint. The footplate of the stapes lies in the oval window. It fits closely and is supported by a narrow angular ligament. The stapes is *not* fused to bone surrounding the oval window.

McCormick et al. (1970) were careful to point out that the connection between the tympanic membrane and the malleus is not direct but rather is indirect through the tympanic ligament. They proposed that the tympanic ligament functions primarily as a suspensor for the malleus. This is a crucial point. If the primary function of the tympanic ligament is suspensory, it seems to be unnecessary. The malleus is primarily supported by fusion to the tympanic bone. The function of the tympanic ligament is the key to some debate over the function of the dolphin middle ear.

The basic controversy is whether the dolphin middle ear functions by conductive bone conduction or by resonant bone conduction. Basically, a conductive reaction could occur by the transfer of mechanical energy from the tympanic ligament (which is tightly stretched) to the malleus and from the malleus through the incus and stapes to the oval window. The theory of resonant bone conduction holds that the tympanic ligament is primarily suspensory and that bone mechanical energy is transferred through the surrounding bone structures. These bone structures vibrate the capsule containing the inner ear, thus producing movement in the cochlear fluid in a resonant reaction. Norris (1968) implied and McCormick et al. (1970) proposed, that energy is transmitted to the inner ear via resonant reaction. On the other hand, Fraser and Purves (1960) and Fleischer (1973) stated that a conductive reaction through the middle ear is the effective process. Purves (1966) concluded that resonant vibrations of the bulla play no part in cetacean hearing.

McCormick et al. (1970) based their assumption of resonant reaction on their series of experiments in which cochlear microphonics were monitored on live dolphins under deep anesthesia. Structures of the middle ear were progressively removed. A surgical avenue to the bulla was opened to give access to the tympanic ligament. Levels of cochlear microphonics were recorded before and after surgery, and no differences were noted. The tympanic ligament was severed and *no change in the magnitude of the potentials* to a 23.4 kHz tone was apparent. They concluded that "a sound-conductive function for the tympanic ligament is therefore excluded." Using another animal, with frequencies ranging from 3 to 100 kHz, a metal hook was placed around the tympanic ligament with a

30-gm weight. When tension was applied, cochlear microphonics were reduced by 18 dB (differential response to varying frequencies was not observed). This loss was explained by "elastic restraint and damping" of the ossicular complex. The resonant sound conduction occurs, according to McCormick et al. by "acoustic vibrations of the cochlear capsule. These vibrations involve the auditory ossicles also, but to a different degree and probably in different phase relations" (p. 1427). McCormick et al. continued, stating that "the result is a relative motion between the footplate of the stapes and the cochlear capsule, producing displacement of fluid in the cochlea, which is the usual condition for cochlear stimulation." Thus, placing tension on the tympanic ligament held the entire ossicular chain under tension and impeded the resonantly produced motion of the stapes at the oval window.

McCormick et al. examined the functional parts of the middle ear by removing them. The malleus was broken away from the tympanic bone, its connection to the incus was severed, and the tensor tympanic tendon was cut. Finally, the malleus was removed. All this damage resulted in a loss of only 4 dB on cochlear microphonic measurements. They concluded that "the malleus can be dispensed with without serious consequences."

Fleischer (1973) examined the anatomical structure of the dolphin middle ear. He did not make cochlear microphonic measurements of live anesthetized dolphins as McCormick et al. had done, but rather relied on measurements of the function of preserved specimens of the ear of *Tursiops*. Fleischer attached a smaller transducer to the base of the stapes and stimulated various parts of the ear structure to measure transmission of vibration across the middle ear. When the tympanic bone was stimulated the movement of the stapes was "10 to 22 dB" more than that of the periotic bone. When frequencies up to 100 kHz were applied to the tympanic bone, the most sensitive points of transfer were found directly around the tympanic ligament. Although Fleischer had intended to determine the effects of severing the tympanic ligament he found it impossible to do so with the tools available to him. Instead he broke the goniole (a connection between the malleus and the process sigmoidus). When the goniole was broken the ossicles no longer transmitted vibrations. As Fleischer stated: "It seems that the whole ossicular chain with its muscles and ligaments has some kind of natural tension which is lost when the goniole is broken" (p. 148). Fleischer (1973) explained the lack of significant transfer function of the middle ear noted in McCormick et al.'s work by stating that:

> In the experiments of McCormick et al. (1970), a hole was made into the outside of the tympanic bone. According to the author's experience it seems nearly impossible that the goniole was not broken during such a preparation. The assumption that the goniole was broken in these experiments would explain that the greatest sensitivity was found at much lower frequencies than in other studies and that the malleus and tympanic ligament could be removed without impairing the effectiveness of the ear as tested by means of the cochlear microphonics. (p. 154)

Unfortunately, Fleischer made no comment on the reported fact that measurements of cochlear microphonics can be made without entering the tympanic bone, and, in fact, McCormick et al. measured cochlear microphonics before and after the auditory bulla was opened and found that: "There were no significant changes" (McCormick et al., 1970, p. 1427). The evidence to date thus seems to indicate that vibrations are transferred to the cochlea via resonant bone conduction.

Cochlear Structure. Following their work on cochlear microphonics, Wever, McCormick, Palin, and Ridgway presented a series of papers (1971a, 1971b, 1972) on the structure of the dolphin inner ear. Ears of both the bottlenose dolphin (*Tursiops truncatus*) and the Pacific white-sided dolphin (*Lagenorhynchus obliquidens*) were examined and compared to the human ear. The number of cochlear turns was found to be 1.75 in *Lagenorhynchus* and about 2 in *Tursiops;* the typical human ear has about 4½ turns. The ratio of the width of the basilar membrane at its widest point to its narrowest point was 11 in *Lagenorhynchus* and 14 in *Tursiops,* as compared to 6.25 in humans. Estimates of the total number of inner hair cells showed *Lagenorhynchus* to have 3,272, *Tursiops* 3,451, and man 3,475. Outer hair cells numbered 12,899 for *Lagenorhynchus,* 13,933 for *Tursiops,* compared to 11,500 for man. The estimated number of ganglion cells showed a sharp difference between humans and cetaceans. *Lagenorhynchus* showed about 65,000 ganglion cells while *Tursiops* had approximately 95,000. Humans typically have about 30,500 ganglion cells. The ratio of hair cells to ganglion cells is therefore about 4:1 in *Lagenorhynchus,* and about 5:1 in *Tursiops,* compared with a ratio of 2:1 in man. Wever et al. (1972) suggested that the high ratio is ". . .aiding the representation of high frequency information and of fine details of cochlear events to higher centers of the auditory nervous system. . ."(p. 661).

Evoked Potentials from the Central Auditory Nervous System. Bullock et al. (1968) examined evoked potentials from the inferior colliculi, medullary auditory centers and medial geniculate bodies of 29 terminal specimens of four species of dolphins. The dolphins were obtained from Japanese fishermen who captured the animals as a human food source. Electrodes were inserted into the midbrain region of anesthetized dolphins 4–5 cm below the tentorium. Sound stimuli were presented both in air and under water or by a hydrophone pressed against the surface of the dolphin's head. Most stimuli were brief high-frequency pulses lasting from 0.3 to 10.0 msec and having a rise and decay time of .1 msec or more. A variety of relatively complex waveforms were recorded as a function of the auditory stimuli, but a series of positive and negative deflections commonly appeared. Changes of frequency often changed the wave form.

Audiograms from the inferior colliculus were obtained by varying intensity, for a variety of frequencies, to establish thresholds for evoked potentials. The duration of tone presentation was either 0.1 msec or 1.0 msec. The resulting audiogram for the two durations was quite similar. A summary audiogram taken from various points in the inferior colliculus of one *Stenella* was found to be quite similar to the behaviorally determined audiogram in *Tursiops* (Johnson, 1966).

Decrease in stimulus intensity generally showed a decrease in evoked potential amplitude without drastically changing its form. Frequency differences were more apt to change the evoked response wave form than were intensity differences, indicating that the population of cells recorded, and therefore contributing to the compound evoked response, was quite heterogeneous. Frequency-modulated tones produced a larger evoked potential than were tones of continuous frequency. In one case a 100-kHz tone pulse produced a weak evoked response, and a 135-kHz pulse produced none. A frequency modulated pulse starting at 100 kHz and sweeping upward to 135 kHz caused a large evoked potential.

Masking experiments indicated relatively narrow critical bandwidths. As noted previously, stimuli applied to the lower jaw were most effective in producing evoked potentials. Sounds presented in front of the animal indicated peak sensitivity when they were presented 30° to the side and 20° below the horizon.

Sound travels much faster in water than in air, so echolocation underwater should show very fast recovery times for evoked potentials. Bats show evidence of neural adaptation that speeds response recovery following the initial sound. Bullock et al. expected to find faster recovery for evoked potentials than those reported for bats because of the air-water speed difference. They did not find what they expected; complete recovery of the collicular response normally required 3 to 5 msec. No indication of facilitation was evident. When recovery was measured, with the first and second tones being different frequencies, recovery became faster. Recordings from individual neurones may be required to fully understand recovery times (see Ridgway, this volume).

Bullock and Ridgway (1972) continued the examination of evoked potentials. Instead of using anesthetized terminal animals, they surgically implanted the electrodes and allowed anesthesia to wear off before recording evoked potentials. Electrodes were multiple linear arrays, usually with seven electrodes, which were implanted in either the area of the inferior colliculus or in various "cerebral" locations. The different locations gave at least two distinct forms of response. Those in the inferior colliculus gave evoked potentials quite similar to those shown in Bullock et al.'s (1968) earlier work, while those above the tentorium in "cerebral" (either in the temporal cortex or white matter) areas were distinctly different. Evoked potentials in the area of the inferior colliculus responded to high frequency signals with very fast rise times. Full evoked potentials were evident, with signals as fast as 50 microsec. Potentials in this area could not be evoked with long-duration low-frequency signals. "Cerebral" evoked potentials showed opposite characteristics. The best frequency for evoking responses in these areas was about 5 kHz, with an upper limit around 10–15 kHz. The evoked responses had slow long-latency wave forms and slow recovery times. The fast high-frequency pulses did not evoke responses in these areas. Bullock and Ridgway postulated that these differential evoked responses represent the two types of auditory information processed by the dolphin, with echolocation clicks being processed at the level of the inferior collicus while lower frequency whistles are processed in the temporal lobe. Potentials from the area of the tentorium were mixed with characteristics of both types of responses.

Behavioral Psychophysics. Knowledge of the dolphin's ability to detect high-frequency sounds was available as early as 1952 (Kellogg & Kohler) but a detailed audiogram was not obtained until 1966. Johnson (1966) determined the audiogram for *Tursiops* by presenting sine-wave sounds ranging in frequency from 75 Hz to 150 kHz and using a go—no-go procedure. The animal was trained to swim to a stationing area within a ''stall'' and to watch for a light to come on. Following the light presentation a sound was sometimes presented. If the dolphin heard the sound, its task was to leave the area and push a lever. If no sound was presented the animal was occasionally reinforced for staying. Sound intensity levels were varied by a staircase method with 1, 2, or 3 dB steps. The resulting audiogram, compared to the human aerial audiogram, is presented in Fig. 4.6. The comparison indicates that at regions of best sensitivity for each, thresholds for human and dolphin are quite similar but separated by about 50 kHz in frequency. The bottlenose dolphin's high-frequency hearing is excellent.

Andersen (1970a) determined the audiogram of the harbor porpoise *Phocoena phocoena* in a go—no-go paradigm. The resulting audiogram, presented in Fig. 4.7, indicates thresholds similiar to those of *Tursiops,* with an upper frequency limit near 150 kHz but with slightly lower thresholds between 8 and 16 kHz.

Although sensory comparisons across species are included throughout this review these comparisons must be considered as approximations. The effects of

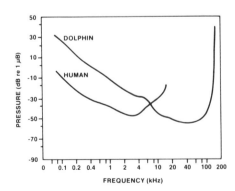

FIG. 4.6. Underwater audiogram of the bottlenosed dolphin from Johnson (1966).

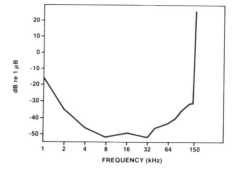

FIG. 4.7. Underwater audiogram of the Harbor porpoise from Anderson (1970).

differing psychophysical methods and the reward parameters associated with these methods probably produce variations in obtained thresholds independent of actual sensitivity of the subject. Without experimental evidence on the effects of differential procedures, it is difficult to precisely determine the magnitude of differences due to factors other than actual sensitivity.

Hall & Johnson (1972) examined auditory thresholds of the killer whale (*Orcinus orca*). The experimental method was similar to that used by Johnson (1966) with *Tursiops*. The resulting audiogram, with background noise recorded, is presented in Fig. 4.8. In contrast to the to the other cetaceans the killer whale's upper frequency limit is much lower, around 30 kHz. Killer whale echolocation has not been specifically tested nor proven.

Cetaceans are a diverse group. One species, *Inia goeffrensis,* known from rivers in Brazil, possesses a sophisticated echolocation ability (Penner & Murchison, 1970). Jacobs and Hall (1972) obtained the animal used by Penner and Murchison in order to determine the behavioral audiogram. They used procedures closely similar to those used by Johnson (1966). Sine-wave tones ranging from 500 Hz to 105 kHz were presented. The resulting audiogram, shown in Fig. 4.9, shows maximum sensitivity between 20 and 60 kHz with an upper frequency limit near 100 kHz. At its best frequencies the absolute sensitivity of *Inia* appears to be as good as that of other dolphins underwater and man in air.

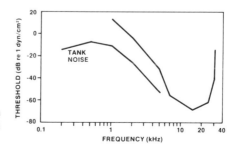

FIG. 4.8. Underwater audiogram of the killer whale from Hall and Johnson (1972).

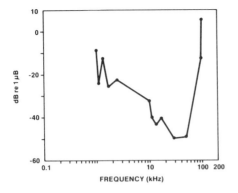

FIG. 4.9. Underwater audiogram of the Amazon river dolphin from Jacobs and Hall (1972).

The high-frequency cutoff is apparently lower than that of other dolphins but well above that of the killer whale.

The audiograms of two beluga whales (*Delphinapterus leucas*) were obtained by White, Norris, Ljungblad, Baron, and di Sciara (1978). Pure tones ranging between 1000 Hz and 123 khz were presented individually using methods similar to Johnson's (1966). Both animals demonstrated peak sensitivities near 30 khz, good hearing between 20 and 90 khz, and a rapid decrease in sensitivity above 120 khz.

Johnson (1968a) continued the examination of bottlenose dolphin auditory thresholds by varying the length of the stimulus presentation. In his original (1966) work a standard 3-sec duration was used. In the later work the duration of the stimulus was varied from intervals slightly shorter than 1 msec up to 8 sec for six frequencies varying from 250 Hz to 100 khz. Johnson generally found an increase in sensitivity with increase in stimulus duration. By applying these data to an appropriate formula, Johnson approximated critical bandwidths for 20 and 40 khz tones. To more precisely determine critical bandwidths, Johnson (1968b) measured thresholds in the presence of masking noise. The animal and apparatus were essentially the same as those of his first two experiments. The animal's task was to report any tone heard above the level of the broadband "white" masking noise. Absolute thresholds at 5, 10, 20, 50 and 100 khz were obtained in the presence of six different masking levels ranging from −90 through −50 dB (re 1 microbar). Masked thresholds were also obtained at the −40 dB level for 6, 8, 12, 15, 23, 30, 40, 60, 70 and 80 khz. Plotting the thresholds and calculating the critical bandwidths, Johnson estimated that *Tursiops* had approximately 40 critical bandwidths compared to 24 in humans. Noise effectively raised thresholds and Johnson concluded: ". . .the animal's inner ear functions is very much the same way as the human inner ear" (p. 967).

Herman & Arbeit (1972) examined the frequency discrimination ability of *Tursiops*. The animal was trained to station in front of two emitting hydrophones. While one hydrophone projected a sine-wave pure tone, the other projected the same tone modulated by 1 or 2 Hz. The animal's task was to choose the pure tone. The frequency difference (i.e., magnitude of the modulation) was systematically varied according to the animal's behavior, using a tracking procedure to determine frequency difference discrimination ability. Using pure tone frequencies of 1, 6, 12, 19, 27, 36, 50 and 70 khz. Herman and Arbeit found very good discrimination ability between 6 and 50 khz, with Weber ratio values around .002 to .003. This region of peak discrimination ability closely corresponds to the region of maximum snsitivity on the dolphin's audiogram (Johnson, 1966) and is as good as that of any animal previously tested, including *Homo sapiens.* Additional work by Thompson and Herman (1975), using a similar procedure and the same animal, tested the dolphin's frequency discrimination ability for frequencies up to 140 khz. Frequency discrimination ability remained remarkably good at high frequencies with Weber ratios never exceeding .008 between 2 and 130 khz. The only other marine mammal similarly tested is the harbor seal with lowest Weber ratios equal to .013 (Møhl, 1964).

Sound Localization.   The use of echolocation would seem to require a finely tuned system for auditory localization. Dolphin sound localization was first examined by Andersen (1970b) in the harbor porpoise *Phocoena phocoena.* Although Anderson was unable to complete his experiment due to animal illness, he presented the results he did obtain. The animal was trained to swim through two hoops located directly in front of a dividing barrier. A transducer was located on each side of the barrier net, and the animal was rewarded for swimming to the transducer emitting the 2 khz signal. Andersen stated that: "Due to the rather primitive experimental setup the author does not find it worthwhile to treat the response values statistically" (p. 262). But he did estimate a minimum audible angle of 3°.

Renaud & Popper (1975) examined sound localization in *Tursiops.* They noted that earlier work on the harbor porpoise had examined sound localization only at frequencies below any dolphin's peak sensitivity. Consequently, they presented a localization task for frequencies ranging from 20 to 100 khz. The animal was trained to hold its head stationary by biting a bar. Sounds were presented from one of two transducers located 18 meters from the bite bar. Paddles were positioned to either the right or the left of the subject. Responses to the paddle corresponding to the position of the transducer emitting the sound were correct and reinforced. The initial angle of presentation was 6° with subsequent angles varied by the staircase method.

With the animal facing the transducers directly, minimum audible angles of between 2 and 4 degrees were found for sine-wave tones between 2 and 100 khz. When the animal was turned 15% off center, performance was better with MAAs of 1.3° and 1.51°. Placing the animal 30° off center, however, lowered performance to a MAA of 5°. When click-type sounds were presented straight on, MAAs dropped to 0.7 to 0.8°, particularly remarkable in comparison to the

MAA of the California sea lion, previously shown to be 5.5° (Moore & Au, 1975). One would, however, expect an echolocating animal to have a very good ability to locate sound position.

Au & Moore (1984) examined the bottlenose dolphin's ability to hear as a function of sound direction. Using the same animal previously tested by Renaud and Popper, Au and Moore measured the receiving beam pattern for 30, 60, and 120 kHz sounds presented in the vertical and horizontal planes. Using a tracking procedure and differential noise-masked thresholds, they found that the animal heard best when sounds were presented 5 to 10° above the midline of its mouth in the vertical plane and directly in front in the horizontal plane. Moore and Au also found that the receiving beam patterns narrowed with increased frequencies in both planes and that the animal remained sensitive to sounds *below* the midline of its jaw in the vertical plane, while sensitivity dropped off rapidly to sounds presented from above. These are strong behavioral data confirming Norris' (1964) hypothesis that sound is received through the lower jaw.

The work on dolphin auditory psychophysics has generally shown a finely adapted sound reception system. These findings would be expected on the basis of the demonstrated echolocation ability of some cetaceans. Results of work on absolute thresholds, critical bandwidths, frequency discrimination, and sound localization all indicate that the dolphin auditory system is at least as good or better than the human system in spite of the fact that sound travels five times as fast under water as it does in air.

CHEMORECEPTION

Smelling substances dispersed in air and tasting others dissolved in water are two examples of sensory chemoreception. It seems likely that dolphins have no sense of smell in the form that exists in most mammals (Donaldson, 1977) because they lack the peripheral olfactory apparatus, including olfactory nerves, bulbs, and tracts (Jacobs, Morgane, & McFarland, 1971). The sense of taste is present in dolphins (Nachtigall & Hall, 1984) but it may differ somewhat from traditional mammalian taste reception (Yablokov, 1961).

The sense of smell may exist among the pinnipeds. Neurologically, the olfactory apparatus is "variably reduced" but more reduced for true seals than for sea lions and walruses (Harrison & Kooyman, 1968). Peterson and Batholomew (1967) assumed that olfaction was present in California sea lions due to the frequency and persistence with which females nuzzled and sniffed their pups. They also noted that taste reception is possible but ". . .does not appear to be of major importance" (p. 43). Unfortunately, the statement by Evans and Bastian (1969) that ". . .little or no experimental information on the gustatory and olfactory capabilities of pinnipeds is available" (p. 462) has remained accurate over the past 15 years.

Yablokov (1961) wrote that it was common knowledge to game specialists and those who study beluga whales (*Delphinapterus leucas*) that the animals react to blood in the water by either trying to quickly escape or by becoming unusually excited. He postulated that these small odontocete whales detected the blood by a water-borne sense of "smell" and that if belugas could detect blood they might also be capable of perceiving other dissolved substances. Yablokov also noted that large number of preputial gland ducts open to the urinary channel of male cetaceans, that cetacean bladders are relatively small, and that odontocetes may well leave a "scent" in the water that can be perceived by other animals. The perceiving structure was assumed to be located in the V-shaped series of pits or grooves found at the base of the dorsal surface of the beluga whale's tongue. Neuroanatomical support for Yablokov's notion that odontocetes possessed a chemoreception capability was provided by Jacobs et al. (1971) who demonstrated that in the bottlenose dolphins even though peripheral olfactory structures are not present, "prominent olfactory lobes" are found in the rhinencephalon possibly activated via the trigeminal nerve.

In other mammals taste buds are found within the epithelium of mushroom-shaped fungiform papillae, in the grooves of the foliate papillae, and in the chevron-like row of circumvallate papillae found on the dorsal furface of the root of the tongue (Pfaffman, 1959). Although once assumed to not exist, dolphin taste buds have been located and described within a series of grooves or pits located in a position analogous to the circumvallate papillae in humans. Suchowskaja (1972) described taste buds for *Delphinus delphis* and *Tursiops truncatus,* Donaldson (1977) provided photomicrographs of the taste buds of *Tursiops,* while Yamasaki, Komatsu, and Kamiya (1978) found taste buds in the tongue of *Stenella coeruleoalba,* though Komatsu and Yamasaki (1980) de scribed degeneration of taste buds with age in that species. Some individual taste buds in humans exhibit multiple sensitivity (Arvidson & Friberg, 1980), being responsive to all four basic tastes: salt, sweet, sour, and bitter. The receptors for taste perception are apparently present in the bottlenose dolphin and other odontocetes.

Sokolov and Kuznetzov (1971) were the first to report a behavioral demonstration of dolphin taste reception. A female Black Sea bottlenose dolphin (*T. truncatus*) was trained to throw a ball after receiving "pure water" or to go to a feeding place after receiving a "stimulant." Few details are provided, but the animal reportedly detected trimethylamine (which tastes and smells quite fishy), camphor, and indole (which smells strongly of feces). Kuznetsov (1974) subsequently reported that the substances were delivered from a rubber bulb to an animal trained to hold its open mouth out of the water. Kuznetsov also stated that "there were times when the dolphin did not perform well," and since the next stage of the experiment was to attempt to obtain thresholds a more reliable method was required. He attempted to establish a "negative differentiation" by providing no reinforcement following water presentations and fish reinforcement for lever pressing following "substance" presentations, but (not surprisingly) Kuznetzov found that the animal continued to paddle press regardless of the stimulus condition. A third method was devised. Each of two female dolphins was trained to individually come to an experimenter's platform in response to its own sonic cue. Salt water or chemical solutions were randomly and successively delivered from glass jars located 1 meter above the water into the animal's mouth at 3 min intervals. Ten to 20 sec following delivery a ring and a bowling pin tied to the ends of a T-shaped stick were presented. If salt water had been presented the animal was to toss up the bowling pin, and if a chemical solution was presented the animal was to toss the ring. The data suggested that the animals could distinguish valeric and oxalic acid and beta-phenylethyl alcohol from salt water, but Kuznetzov stated that the "flaw of this method is that the number of correct responses is largely determined by the dolphin's ability to solve problems, rather than the extent to which the animals distinguished between different stimuli" (p. 153). A similar procedure, however, (Kuznetsov, 1978) was used to examine the abilities of a male and female bottlenose dolphin to discriminate extracts of secretions of the prostate gland in ethyl alcohol diluted in salt water, from salt water.

The fourth method described by Kuznetsov (1980) for measuring dolphin sensitivity to chemical compounds used a Pavlovian conditioned response procedure. Rather than having the swimming and freely responding dolphins choose between rings and bowling pins, individual animals were placed in "tubs" of sea water. Composite galvanic skin responses (GSRs), electrocardiograms, and respirations were recorded. A tube was "fastened" to the mouth of an animal with sea water flowing constantly at 7-10 ml/sec. At intervals of 3 to 7 min 5–10 milliliters of a chemical stimulus was presented in the flowing sea water paired with an unspecified level of electric current. Although not stated, the shock caused by the electric current most likely produced a measurable increase in the galvanic skin response. With repeated pairing of the current and the chemical, the chemical alone soon resulted in an elevated GSR, thus measures of the animal's sensitivity to the chemicals could be measured by observing changes in the GSR. The results of data from nine harbor porpoises (*Phocoena phocoena*), two common dolphins (*Delphinus delphis*), and three Black Sea bottlenose dolphins *T. truncatus*) showed that *Phocoena* reportedly detected trimethylamine at a concentration of 8.5×10^{-7} M; skatole at 1.7×10^{-6} M; and camphor at 3×10^{-6}M. *Tursiops* reacted to hydrochloric acid at 0.15 M; valeric acid at 1×10^{-4}M; quinine chloride at 1×10^{-4} M and a solution of male *Tursiops* urine at 1%. While this Pavlovian method revealed that these chemicals were, in some way, sensed; it did not provide answers to questions about taste sensitivity and behavior. Psychophysical threshold levels were not obtained.

In a fifth method, Kuznetsov (1979) trained two male bottlenose dolphins using a sort of go—no-go procedure. If an animal touched a metal lever after receiving water it received a fish; if the animal touched the lever after being given a chemical stimulus it would get an electric shock. Although little procedural detail is provided, this method apparently worked. The animals were shown to be capable of detecting the following chemicals dissolved in fresh water: indole, valeric acid, caproic acid, citric acid, oxalic acid, hydrochloric acid, quinine chloride, picric acid, and common salt. The animals were "insensitive" to saccharose and glucose.

Psychophysical detection thresholds are normally established by first determining that some level of chemical dissolved in water produces some indicator response reliably. The concentration of that chemical is then decreased to find a second level at which the chemical is not detected. Various concentrations between those two extremes are then examined to determine the animal's detection performance as a function of concentration level. Normally, when an animal detects some concentration correctly 75% of the time a threshold is established. Unfortunately, none of the five reported procedures used by Sokolov and Kuznetsov provided differential correct response levels to different concentrations, and therefore no psychophysical detection thresholds were obtained.

We at the Naval Ocean Systems Center have recently examined the Pacific bottlenose dolphin's ability to taste dilute solutions of what, to humans, are chemicals that produce the four basic tastes of sour, bitter, salty, and sweet and have determined psychophysical thresholds for those solutions.

A 141.4 kg male bottlenose dolphin, captured off the coast of Oahu and estimated to be 3–5 years old, was initially trained to station in front of the experimenter with an open mouth so that various solutions could be presented. We noticed, however, that a pocket of sea water usually remained in the animal's mouth around the base of the tongue. To eliminate the possible confounding effects of this remaining water we switched to a solution presentation method which required the animal to swim out of the water and beach himself. This placed the animal in a prone position allowing remaining water to drip out of the side of his mouth. Once beached, the animal was required to bite on a polymide plastic bite plate shaped to fit his mouth. Holes were drilled into the bite plate so that silicone tubes could be connected to deliver liquids directly over the taste bud area at the base of the tongue. Peristaltic pumps were calibrated daily to deliver liquids at a constant flow rate of 9 ml/sec. Plastic connecting tubes and the bite plate were flushed between each trial with air followed by distilled water. Each trial consisted of two steps. In the first step 70 ml of distilled water was delivered over an 8-sec period. This step provided a flushing of the animal's mouth. Five sec after the first step, a second solution delivery occurred. On half the randomly predetermined trials, the second step was identical to the first. On the other half of the trials, distilled water plus the chemical to be detected was delivered. On those trials in which distilled water was delivered twice, the animal was required to hold on to the bite plate. After, the animal was required to hold on to the bite plate for 5 additional sec, a 9 kHz tone was presented signaling a correct no-go response and the animal left the beaching tray to receive fish reinforcement. On those trials where the second delivery contained the chemical, the animal was required to release the bite plate indicating that it tasted the chemical. On these correct "go" responses the animal immediately left the beaching tray and received fish reinforcement.

Various bracketing sessions were conducted to determine the range of sensitivity before conducting each experiment. Once the threshold range was approximately bracketed, six concentrations were chosen for the subsequent experiment arranged as a modified method of constants. Two 18-trial sessions were normally conducted each working day. Three concentration levels were presented in each session, and each level was presented within a six-trial block. Each concentration level was tested at least 17 times within the experiment, yielding a minimum of 102 trials per level.

The results of the bracketing sessions indicated that the threshold for detection of citric acid in distilled water lay somewhere between .026 and .016 M. Six molarity levels between these values where chosen: .026, .024, .022, .020, .018, and .016; these yielded mean performance levels of 95, 99, 96, 96, 78, 70% correct respectively. Interpolation of these data yielded a calculated 75% correct threshold level at .017 M.

Training the animal to detect quinine sulfate occured quite rapidly and bracketing sessions revealed a possible threshold between 2.86×10^{-5}M and 0.81×18^{-5}M. The following six molarities (each $\times 10^{-5}$) were chosen: 2.86, 2.45, 2.04, 1.63, 1.22, and .81; these yielded mean performance levels of 98, 89, 84, 80, 72, and 54% correct, respectively. Interpolation of these data yielded a calculated 75% correct threshold of 1.36×10^{-5}M.

The calculated thresholds revealed that the bottlenose dolphin's ability to taste chemicals, perceived by humans as sour and bitter, is very good. Pfaffman's (1959) review gave a range of human thresholds for citric acid from .0013 to .0057 M, and for quinine sulfate from 0.4×10^{-6} to 1.1×10^{-5}M. the dolphin's thresholds for citric acid at .0173 M and for quinine sulfate at 1.36×10^{-5}M fall just above the human range, indicating that the dolphin's ability to taste these substances is nearly as good as that of humans.

Given that a dolphin normally spends its time in salt water and frequently opens its mouth, the detection of salt in distilled water becomes a particularly interesting question. Is the animal tasting salt or is the animal tasting the difference between salt and distilled water? Seen in traditional terms, our animal detected salt in distilled water at 97, 95, 82, 78, 70 and 65% correct for concentrations of 0.3, 0.2, 0.15, 0.10, 0.05, and 0.03 M, respectively. When the fact that the animal slid off the test tray and into the salt water between trials, thus returning to a salt water environment, is taken into account these data might be elevated by adaptation. In order to further examine the question, a dolphin would either have to be kept in fresh water or allowed longer times out of salt water between trials.

While Kuznetsov (1979) found that the Black Sea bottlenose dolphin was insensitive to saccharose and glucose, we found that the Pacific bottlenose dolphin did report the presence of sucrose. Sucrose levels of 0.2, 0.15, 0.08, 0.04, and 0.02 M were reported at 92, 96, 71, 81, 76, and 65% correct respectively. These levels show that dolphins detect sucrose, they do not detect it nearly as well as do humans.

While we now know that dolphins detect chemicals which humans report as producing sensations of sour, bitter, salty, and sweet, we still know very little about dolphin chemoreception. Chemicals which to us taste bitter and quite unappealing did not seem to bother the dolphin in the slightest. Further the possibility of pheromonal communication by cetaceans has not been examined. There is much work for future patient researchers in the area of dolphin, and other marine mammal, chemoreception.

REFERENCES

Andersen, E. (1970a). Auditory sensitivity of the harbor porpoise *Phocoena phocoena*. In G. Pilleri (Ed.), *Investigations on Cetacea*, Vol. 2. (p. 255–259). The Brain Anatomy Institute, University of Berne.

Andersen, S. (1970b). Directional hearing in the harbor porpoise *Phocoena phocoena*. In G. Pilleri (Ed.), *Investigations on Cetacea*, Vol. 2. (pp. 260–263). The Brain Anatomy Institute, University of Berne.

Arvidson, K., & Friberg, V. (1980). Human taste: Response and taste bud number in fungiform papillae. *Science, 209*, 807–808.

Au, W. W. L., & Moore, P. W. B. (1984). Receiving beam patterns and directivity indices of the Atlantic bottlenosed dolphin *Tursiops truncatus*. *Journal of the Acoustical Society of America, 75*, 255–262.

Balliet, R. F., & Schusterman, R. J. (1971). Underwater and aerial visual acuity in the Asian "clawless" otter (*Amblyonix cineria cineria*). *Nature, 234*, 305–306.

Bernholz, C. D., & Mathews, M. L. (1975). Critical flicker frequency in a harp seal; evidence for duplex retinal organization. *Vision Research, 15*, 733–736.

Bullock, T. H., Grinnel, A. D., Ikezono, E., Kameda, K. Katsuki, Y., Nomoto, J., Sato, O., Suga, N., & Yanagisawa, K. (1968). Electrophysiological studies of central auditory mechanisms in cetaceans. *Zeitschrift für Vergleichende Physiologie, 59*, 17–156.

Bullock, T. H., & Ridgway, S. H. (1972). Evoked potentials in the central auditory system of alert porpoises to their own and artificial sounds. *Journal of Neurobiology, 3*:79–99.

Bullock, R. H., Ridgway, S. H., & Suga, H. (1971). Acoustically evoked potentials in midbrain auditory structures in sealions (Pinnipedia). *Zeitschrift für Vergleichende Physiologie, 74*, 372–387.

Busnel, R.-G., & Fish, J. R. (Eds.). (1980). *Animal sonar systems.* New York: Plenum Press.

Caldwell, M. M., Hall, N. R., & Caldwell, D. K. (1971). Ability of an Atlantic bottlenosed dolphin to discriminate between, and respond differentially to, whistles of eight conspecifics. *Proceedings of the Eighth Annual Conference on Biological Sonar and Diving Mammals, 8*, 57–67.

Christman, R. J. (1971). *Sensory experience.* Scranton, PA: International Textbook Co.

Dawson, W. W. (1980). The cetacean eye. In L. M. Herman (Ed.), *Cetacean behavior: Mechanisms and functions* (pp. 58–100). New York: Wiley.

Dawson, W. W., Birndorf, L. A., & Perez, J. M. (1972). Gross anatomy and optics of the dolphin eye (Tursiops truncatus). Cetology, 10, 1–12.

Dawson, W. W., Hope, G. M., Ulshafer, M. N., & Jenkins, R. L. (1983). Contents of the optic nerve of a small cetacean. Aquatic Mammals, 10, 45–56.

Dawson, W. W., & Perez, J. M. (1973). Unusual retinal cells in the dolphin eye. Science, 181, 747–749.

Donaldson, B. J. (1977). The tongue of the bottlenosed dolphin. In R. J. Harrison, (Ed.), Functional anatomy of marine mammals Vol 3. (pp. 175–198). London: Academic Press.

Dral, A. D. G. (1972). Aquatic and aerial vision in the bottlenosed dolphin. Netherlands Journal of

Dral, A. D. G. (1977). On the retinal anatomy of cetacea. In R. J. Harrison (Ed.), Functional anatomy of marine mammals, Vol. 3 (pp. 81–134). London: Academic Press.

Evans, W. E. (1973). Echolocation by marine delphinids and one species of freshwater dolphin. Journal of the Acoustical Society of America, 54(1), 191–199.

Evans, W. E., & Bastian, J. (1969). Marine mammal communication: Social and ecological factors. In H. T. Anderson (Ed.), The biology of marine mammals (pp. 425–473). New York: Academic Press.

Evans. W. E., & Haugen, R. M. (1963). An experimental study of echolocation ability of a California sea lion, Zalophus californianus (Lesson). Bulletin of the Southern California Academy of Science, 63, 167–175.

Fleischer, G. (1973). On structure and function of the middle ear in the bottlenosed dolphin (Tursiops truncatus). Proceedings of the Ninth Annual Conference on Biological Sonar and Diving Mammals, 9, 137–180.

Fobes, J. L., & Smock, C. C. (1981). Sensory capacities of marine mammals. Psychological Bulletin, 89, 288–307.

Fraser, F. C., & Purves, P. E. (1960). Hearing in cetaceans. Bulletin of the British Museum (Natural History), 7, 1–140.

Gentry R. L. (1967). Underwater auditory localization in the California sea lion (Zalophus californianus). The Journal of Auditory Research, 7, 187–193.

Gentry, R. L., & Peterson, R. S. (1967). Underwater vision of the sea otter. Nature, 216, 435–436.

Griffin, D. R. (1983). Prospects for a cognitive ethology. In J. de Luce & H. T. Wilder (Eds.), Language in primates: Perspectives and implications. New York: Springer-Verlag.

Hall, J. D., & Johnson, C. S. (1972). Auditory thresholds of a killer whale Orcinus orca Linnaeus. Journal of the Acoustical Society of America, 51, 515–517.

Harrison, R. J., & Kooyman, G. L. (1968). General physiology of the pinnipedia. In R. J. Harrison, R. S. Hubbard, R. S. Peterson, C. E. Rice, & R. J. Schusterman (Eds.), The behavior and physiology of pinnipeds (pp. 211–296). New York: Appleton-Century-Crofts.

Herman, L. M., & Arbeit, W. R. (1972). Frequency difference limens in the bottlenose dolphin: 1–70 kHz. Journal of Auditory Research, 12, 109–120.

Herman, L. M., Peacock, M. F., Yunker, M. P., & Madsen, C. J. (1975). Bottlenosed dolphin: Double-split pupil yields equivalent aerial and underwater diurnal acuity. Science, 189, 650–652.

Jacobs, D. W., & Hall, J. D. (1972). Auditory thresholds of a fresh water dolphin, Inia geoffrensis, Blainville. Journal of the Acoustical Society of America, 51, 531–533.

Jacobs, M. S., Morgane, P. J., & McFarland, W. L. (1971). The anatomy of the brain of the bottlenosed dolphin. Journal of Comparative Neurology, 141, 205–272.

Johnson, C. S. (1966). Auditory thresholds of the bottlenosed porpoise. Naval Ordinance Test Station Technical Report (NOTS TP 4178).

Johnson, C. S. (1968a). Relation between absolute threshold and duration-of-tone pulses in the bottlenosed porpoise. Journal of the Acoustical Society of America, 43, 757–763.

Johnson, C. S. (1968b). Masked tonal thresholds in the bottlenosed porpoise. Journal of the Acoustical Society of America, 44, 965–967.

Kellogg, W. N., & Kohler, R. (1952). Responses of the porpoise to ultrasonic frequencies. *Science, 116,* 446–450.

Kellogg, W. M., & Rice, C. (1963). Visual discrimination in a bottlenose dolphin. *Psychological Record, 13,* 483–498.

Kellogg, W. N., & Rice, C. (1966). Visual discrimination and problem solving in a bottlenose dolphin. In K. S. Norris (Ed.), *Whales, dolphins and porpoises* (pp. 731–754). Berkeley: University of California Press.

Komatsu, S., & Yamasaki, F. (1980). Formation of the pits with taste buds at the lingual root of the striped dolphin *Stenella coeruleoalba. Journal of Morphology, 164,* 107–119.

Kuznetsov, V. B. (1974). A method of studying chemoreception in the Black Sea bottlenose dolphin (*Tursiops truncatus*). In V. Ye Sokolov (Ed.), *Morfologiya, fiziologia i akustika morskikh mlekopitayushchikh* (pp. 147–153). Moscow: Nauka. (in Russian)

Kuznetsov, V. B. (1978). Chemical communication and capacity of the bottlenosed dolphin to transmit information on a chemical stimulus. In V. Ye Sokolov (Ed.), *Morkiye meklopitayushchiye: Rezul'taty imetody issledovaniy* (pp. 213–221). Moscow: Nauka. (in Russian)

Kuznetsov, V. B. (1979). Chemoreception in dolphins of the Black Sea. *Doklady Akadamii Nauk SSR. 249(6),* 1498–1500. (Translated by Plenum Publishing Corp., 1980)

Landau, D., & Dawson, W. W. (1970). The histology of retinas from the pinnipedia. *Vision Research, 10,* 691–702.

Levigne, D. M., Bernholz, C. D., & Ronald, K. (1977). Functional aspects of pinniped vision. In R. J. Harrison (Ed.), *Functional anatomy of marine mammals, Vol. 3* (pp. 135–173). London: Academic Press.

Lavigne, D. M., & Ronald, K. (1972). The harp seal, *Pagophilus groenlandicus* (Erxleben 1777). XXIII. Spectral sensitivity. *Canadian Journal of Zoology, 50,* 1197–1206.

Madsen, C. J. (1972, Sept.). *Visual acuity in marine mammals.* Paper presented at the American Psychological Association Meeting, Honolulu.

Madsen, C. J., & Herman, L. M. (1980). Social and ecological correlates of cetacean vision and visual appearance. In L. M. Herman (Ed.), *Cetacean behavior: Mechanism and functions* (pp. 101–147). New York: Wiley.

Mayer, R. E. (1983). *thinking, problem solving, cognition.* New York: W. H. Freeman.

McCormick, J. G., Wever, E. G., Palin, J., & Ridgway, S. H. (1970). Sound conduction in the dolphin ear. *Journal of the Acoustical Society of America, 48,* 1418–1428.

Møhl, B. (1964). Preliminary studies on hearing in seals. *Vidensk. Medd. Fra Dansk Naturh. Foren. Bd., 127,* 283–294.

Møhl, B. (1967). Frequency discrimination in the common seal and a discussion of the concept of upper hearing limit. In V. A. Albers (Ed.), *Underwater acoustics, Volume 2.* (pp. 43–54). New York: Plenum Press.

Møhl, B. (1968). Hearing in seals. In R. J. Harrison (Ed.), *The behavior and physiology of pinnipeds* (pp. 172–195). New York: Appleton-Century-Crofts.

Moore, P. W. (1975). Underwater localization of click and pulsed pure tone signals by the California sea lion. *Journal of the Acoustical Society of America, 2,* 406–410.

Moore, P. W., & Au, W. W. L. (1975). Underwater localization of pulsed pure tones by the California sea lion. *Journal of the Acoustical Society of America, 58,* 721–727.

Moore, P. W. B., & Schusterman, R. J. (1976). Discrimination of pure-tone intensities by the California sea lion. *Journal of the Acoustical Society of America, 60,* 1405–1407.

Nachtigall, P. E. (1969). Visual size discrimination in the East Asian clawless otter (*Amblyonyx cinerea*) in air and underwater. *Proceedings of the Sixth Annual Conference on Biological Sonar and Diving Mammals, 6,* 83–86.

Nachtigall, P. E. (1980). Odontocete echolocation performance on object size, shape and material. In R.-G. Busnel & J. F. Fish (Eds.), *Animal sonar systems* (pp. 71–95). New York: Plenum Press.

Nachtigall, P. E., & Hall, R. W. Taste reception in the bottlenosed dolphin. *Acta Zoologica Fennica, 172,* 147–148.

Nagy, A. R., & Ronald, K. (1970). The harp seal, *Pagophilus groenlandicus* (Erxleben, 1777). VI. Structure of the retina. *Canadian Journal of Zoology, 48,* 367–370.

Norris, K. S. (1964). Some problems of echolocation in cetaceans. In W. N. Tavolga (Ed.), *Marine bioacoustics* (pp. 317–336). New York: Pergamon Press.

Norris, K. S. (Ed.). (1966). *(Whales, dolphins and porpoises.)* Berkeley: University of California Press.

Norris, K. S. (1968). The evolution of acoustic mechanisms in odontocete cetaceans. In E. T. Drake (Ed.), *Evolution and environment* (pp. 297–324). New Haven, CT: Yale University Press.

Penner, R. H., & Murchison, A. E. (1970). Experimentally demonstrated echolocation in the Amazon River porpoise, *Inia geoffrensis* (Blainville). *Proceedings of the Seventh Annual Conference on Biological Sonar and Diving Mammals, 7,* 17–35.

Pepper, R. L., Simmons, J. V., Beach, F. A. III, & Nachtigall, P. E. (1972). In air visual acuity of the bottlenose dolphin. *Proceedings of the Ninth Annual Conference on Biological Sonar and Diving Mammals, 9,* 83–89.

Perez, J. M., Dawson, W. W., & Landau, D. (1972). Retinal anatomy of the bottlenosed dolphin *(Tursiops truncatus).* Cetology, *11,* 1–11.

Peterson, R. S., & Bartholomew, G. A. (1967). *The natural history and behavior of the California sea lion.* Special Publication #1, The American Society of Mammalogists.

Pfaffman, C. (1959). The sense of taste. In J. Field, H. W. Magoun, & V. E. Hall (Eds.), *Handbook of physiology* (pp. 507–553). Baltimore: Williams and Wilkins.

Popper, A. N. (1980). Sound emission and detection by delphinids. In L. M. Herman (Ed.), *Cetacean behavior* (pp. 1–52). New York: Wiley.

Poulter, T. C. (1963). Sonar signals of the sea lion. *Science, 193,* 753–755.

Poulter, T. C. (1966). The use of active sonar by the California sea lion. *Journal of Auditory Research, 6,* 165–173.

Poulter, T. C. (1969b). Sonar of penguins and fur seals. *Proceedings of the California Academy of Science, 36,* 363–380.

Purves, P. E. (1966). Anatomy and physiology of the outer and middle ear in cetaceans. In K. S. Norris (Ed.), *Whales, dolphins and porpoises* (pp. 320–376). Berkeley: University of Calfornia Press.

Renaud, D. L., & Popper, A. N. (1975). Sound localization by the bottlenose porpoise *Tursiops truncatus. Journal of Experimental Biology, 63,* 569–585.

Renouf, D., & Davis, M. B. (1983). Evidence that seals may use echolocation. *Nature, 300,* 635–637.

Reppening, C. A. (1972). Underwater hearing in seals: Functional morphology. In R. J. Harrison (Ed.), *Functional anatomy of marine mammals* (pp. 307–331). New York: Academic Press.

Ridgway, S. H., & Joyce, P. L. (1975). Studies on seal brain by radiotelemetry. *Rapp. P.v. Reun. Cons. int. Explor. Mer., 1969,* 81–91.

Riggs, L. A. (1966). Visual Acuity. In C. H. Graham (Ed.), *Vision and visual perception* (pp. 321–349). New York: Wiley.

Scheville, W. E. (1968). Sea lion echo ranging? *Journal of the Acoustical Society of America, 43,* 1458–1459.

Schusterman, R. J. (1971). Visual acuity in pinnipeds. In H. E. Winn & B. L. Olla (Eds.), *Behavior of marine animals, Vol. 2* (pp. 469–492). New York: Plenum Press.

Schusterman, R. J. (1966). Underwater click vocalizations by a California sea lion: Effects of visibility. *Psychological Record, 16,* 129–136.

Schusterman, R. J. (1968). Experimental laboratory studies of pinniped behavior. In R. J. Harrison (Ed.), *The behavior and physiology of pinnipeds* (pp. 87–171). New York: Appleton-Century-Crofts.

Schusterman, R. J. (1974). Auditory sensitivity of a California sea lion to airborne sound. *Journal of the Acoustical Society of America, 56,* 1248–1250.

Schusterman, R. J., Balliet, R. F., & Nixon, J. (1972). Underwater audiogram of the California sea lion by the conditioned vocalization technique. *Journal of the Experimental Analysis of Behavior, 17,* 339–350.

Schusterman, R. J., Gentry, R., & Schmook, J. (1967). Underwater sound production by captive California sea lions, *Zalophus californianus. Zoologica, 52,* 21–24.

Schusterman, R. J., Kellogg, W. N., & Rice, C. E. (1965). Underwater visual discrimination by the California sea lion. *Science, 147,* 1594–1596.

Schusterman, R. J., & Moore, P. W. (1978). The upper limit of underwater auditory frequency discrimination in the California sea lion. *Journal of the Acoustical Society of America, 63,* 1591–1595.

Shaver, H. N., & Poulter, T. C. (1967). Sea lion echo ranging. *Journal of the Acoustical Society of America, 42,* 428–437.

Sokolov, V. Ye, & Kuznetsov, V. B. (1971). Chemoreception in the Black Sea bottlenose dolphin, *Tursiops truncatus (Montague). Doklady Akademii Nauk SSSR, 201,* 998–1000.

Spong, P., & White, D. (1971). Visual acuity and discrimination learning in the dolphin *(Lagenorhynchus obliquidens). Experimental Neurology, 31,* 431–436.

Suchowskaja, L. I. (1972). The morphology of the taste organs in dolphins. In G. Pilleri (Ed.), *Investigations on cetacea, IV* (pp. 201–204). Brain Anatomy Institute, Berne.

Terhune, J. (1974). Directional hearing of a harbor seal in air and water. *Journal of the Acoustical Society of America, 56,* 1862–1865.

Terhune, J. M., & Ronald, K. (1971). The harp seal, *Pagophilus groenlandicus* (Erxleben, 1777). X. The air audiogram. *Canadian Journal of Zoology. 49,* 385–390.

Terhune, J. M., & Ronald, K. (1972). The harp seal, *Pagophilus groenlandicus* (Erxleben, 1777). II. The underwater audiogram. *Canadian Journal of Zoology, 50,* 565–569.

Terhune, J. M., & Ronald, K. (1975). Underwater hearing sensitivity of the ringed seal *(Pusa hispida). Canadian Journal of Zoology, 53,* 227–231.

Thompson, R. K. R., & Herman, L. M. (1975). Underwater frequency discrimination in the bottlenosed dolphin (1–140kHz) and human (1–8kHz). *Journal of the Acoustical Society of America, 57,* 943–947.

Walls, G. L. (1963). *The vertebrate eye and its adaptive radiation.* New York: Hafner.

Wartzok. D., Schusterman, R. J., & Gailey-Phipps, J. (1984). Seal echolocation? *Nature, 308,* 753.

Weaver, E. G., McCormick, J. G., Palin, J., & Ridgway, S. H. (1971a). Cochlea of the dolphin, *Tursiops truncatus:* The basilar membrane. *Proceedings of the National Academy of Science, USA., 68,* 2708–2711.

Wever, E. G., McCormick, J. G., Palin, J., & Ridgway, S. H. (1971b). The cochlea of the dolphin, *Tursiops truncatus:* Hair cells and ganglion cells. *Proceedings of the National Academy of Science, USA, 68,* 2908–2912.

Wever, E. G., McCormick, J. G., Palin, J., & Ridgway, S. H. (1972). Cochlear structure in the dolphin, *Lagenorhynchus obliquidens. Proceedings of the National Academy of Science, USA. 69,* 657–661.

White, D., Cameron, N., Spong, P., & Bradford, J. (1971). Visual acuity of the killer whale *(Orcinus orca). Experimental Neurology, 32,* 230–236.

White, M. J., Norris, J., Ljungblad, D., Baron, K., & di Sciara, G. (1978). *Auditory thresholds of two beluga whales.* Hubbs Sea World Technical Report 78–109. San Diego, CA.

Yablokov, A. V. (1961). Trudy soveshchaniy ikhtiologicheskoy komissii. (The "sense of smell" in marine mammals.) *Akademii Nauk SSSR, 12,* 87–93. (in Russian)

Yamasaki, F., Komatsu, S., & Kamiya, T. (1978). Taste buds in the pits of the posterior dorsum of the tongue of *Stenella coeruleoalba. Scientific Reports of Whales Research Institute, 30,* 285–290.

5 Dolphin Audition and Echolocation Capacities

C. Scott Johnson

Naval Ocean Systems Center,
San Diego

INTRODUCTION

We know considerable information about audition and echolocation in several delphinid species, but have the most complete data on *Tursiops truncatus*. Therefore, my discussion will concentrate on audition and echolocation in *T. truncatus*.

A few basic physical concepts will assist the reader. The pressure (p, in dynes/cm²) of a plane sound wave is related to particle velocity (u, in cm/sec) by (cf. Urick, 1967, p. 12.):

$$p = \rho cu \tag{1}$$

where ρ is the density of the fluid (in gm/cm³) and c is the velocity of sound in the fluid (in cm/sec). The product ρc is called the specific acoustic impedance of the fluid. Particle displacement (y, in cm) is related to pressure, acoustic impedance, and frequency (f, in Hz) by (cf. Heuter & Bolt, 1955, p. 52):

$$y = \frac{p}{2\pi\rho cf}. \tag{2}$$

Sound intensity (I, in watts/cm²) in a plane wave is related to instantaneous pressure by:

$$I = \frac{p^2}{\rho c}(10^{-7}). \tag{3}$$

When sound in one medium havng an acoustic impedance of $\rho_1 c_1$ is transmitted into a second medium of a differing acoustic impedance of $\rho_2 c_2$, part of the incident wave's intensity is reflected back into the first medium. Assuming a

115

plane boundary between the two semiinfinite media, the fraction of energy reflected for normal incidence to the boundary is (cf. Officer, 1958, p. 78):

$$R = \frac{(\rho_2 c_2 - \rho_1 c_1)^2}{(\rho_2 c_2 + \rho_1 c_1)^2} \quad (4)$$

The transmission coefficient (T) is related to R by R + T = 1. For each watt/cm^2 of acoustic power incident on the boundary, R and T respectively are the fraction of that power reflected and transmitted. For examples, the approximate acoustic impedance of salt water is 1.5×10^5 gm/(cm^2)(sec) and of air is 42 gm/(cm^2)(sec). For bone, c = 3.4×10^5 cm/sec (Chivers & Parry, 1978) and ρ = 2.6 gm/cm^3 (Lakes et al. 1983). Using Eq. (4), a sound propagation from water to air will result in R = 0.9989 and T = 0.0011. The values of R and T are the same whether going from air to water or vice versa. For sound transmission from water to bone, R = 0.504 and T = 0.496. In this case, about the same amount of power is transmitted as is reflected. Air in water is a fine reflector of sound while bone is not nearly as good. This is why, except for air filled locations, sound is easily transmitted through delphinid heads and bodies. More complicated calculations can be made using the frequency of the sound and the shape of the objects, but these calculations are beyond the scope of this article. Compressional bone conduction, which is different from bone sound transmission, is discussed in the next section.

Acousticians frequently express sound propagation in terms of the dimensionless parameter ka (cf. Hicklings, 1962). Here ka = $\frac{2\pi}{\lambda}$ where λ is the wavelength of sound in the target material and "a" is the radius in the case of a spherical target. For a spherical target, k is just the circumference at the largest diameter divided by the wavelength of the incident sound wave. Spherical targets reflect poorly below ka = 1 (wavelength of sound is less than its circumference). Because of low internal sound velocities, bubbles in water are more efficient scatterers than solid spheres. For example, the velocity of sound in air is approximately 4.5 slower than in water. Because λ = c/f, the wavelength in air is 4.5 times shorter than the same frequency in water. Bubbles near the surface of water have a ka = 0.0136 (Urick, 1967, p. 201). A bubble will affect sound waves in water at frequencies more than 70 times lower than a similar size solid sphere.

Hearing is measured in decibels (dB) because the sensation of loudness is linear on a dB scale and because of the wide range in hearing sensitivities and frequencies. Decibels are used most often for pressure measurements, but can be used to scale any dimensionless number. To convert pressure, p, (in dynes/cm^2) to dB relative to 1 microPascal (μPa), the standard underwater sound reference unit (10^{-5} dyne/1 cm 2 = 1 μPa), the following formula is used:

$$dB = 20 \log_{10} (p/10^{-5} \text{ dyne/cm}^2). \quad (5)$$

One should conclude from the above discussion the following points:

1. Echolocation in water is very different from echolocation in air. Water has acoustic properties similar to those of most targets. Therefore, less energy is reflected from targets while greater target penetration by sound is achieved allowing internal structures to be examined.

2. Air is the greatest impediment to underwater sound transmission. Targets containing air or other gases, e.g., fish with swim bladders, return much larger echoes than other targets.

EAR ANATOMY AND TRANSDUCTION MECHANISMS

Delphinids have no outer ear (pinna). The inner ear and vestigial external auditory meatus of *Tursiops truncatus* are shown in Fig 5.1. Underwater hearing in delphinids has been studied for many years. Delphinids probably hear about the same way humans hear under water, by compressional bone conduction (McCormick, Wever, Ridgway, & Palin, 1980). To hear in air, humans translate large movements of air molecules from sound waves into the much smaller displacements required by the inner ear. This is accomplished, following von Békésy (1957), by conduction through the ear drum (tympanic membrane) and the middle ear bones: incus (I), maleus (M), and stapes (S). The ear drum and ear canal (meatus), which are both vestigial in cetaceans, are not necessary for underwater hearing because sound waves travel through the delphinid skull and directly to the inner ear. The middle ear bones are still necessary, although their role is not entirely understood. McCormick, Wever, Ridgway, & Palin (1970) showed that *T. truncatus* can hear at high frequencies after removal of the maleus. The air in the middle ear cavity is necessary if the cochlea is to function as a frequency analyzer as with humans. Compressional bone conduction is illustrated in Fig. 5.2. We can estimate the displacement of the round window due to compression of the petros bone containing the cochlea (von Békésy, 1960, p. 173). This model assumes stimulation by pressure waves, not mechanical bone stimulation.

Assuming a cylindrical (not hemispherical) displacement of the round window,

$$A = \frac{Vp}{\rho c^2 S'},$$ (6)

where A is the displacement (in cm), p is the applied pressure (in dynes/cm^2), V is the cochlear volume (in cm^3), s' is the area of the round window (in cm^2), and ρ and c are, respectively, the density (in gm/cm^3) and speed of sound (in cm/sec) in the petros bone. Values for some parameters are not known and values for humans (Littler, 1965, p. 327) will be used. Substituting these values in Eq. 6 and the value of p for the measured threshold of hearing in *T. truncatus* at 50kHz, (45 dB re 1 µPa = 1.8×10^{-3} dynes/cm^2) (Johnson, 1967)

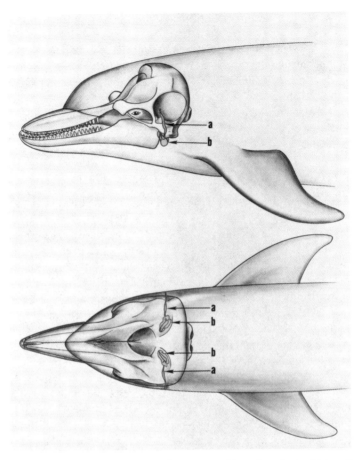

FIG. 5.1. The skull, external auditory *meatus* (a), and ear bones (b) in a *T. truncatus*.

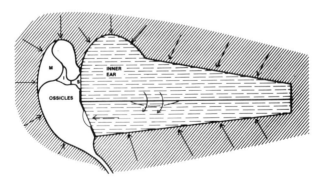

FIG. 5.2. Schematic representation of the reception of sound to the ear of a dolphin (underwater).

$$A = \frac{(0.0981)(8.1 \times 10^{-3})}{(2.6)(3.4 \times 10^5)^2(.02)} = 2.9 \times 10^{-14}\text{cm.} \tag{7}$$

This is close to the extrapolated displacement of the basilar membrane at the minimum hearing threshold at 3200 Hz in humans (Littler, 1965, p. 30). This value also is similar to the displacement of water particles as calculated using Eq. 2.

$$y = \frac{1.8 \times 10^{-3}}{2\pi(50 \times 10^3)(1.0)(1.5 \times 10^5)} = 3.8 \times 10^{-14}\text{cm.} \tag{8}$$

In this case, f is the acoustic frequency (50 kHz), ρ and c are the density of water and speed of sound in water, 1.0gm/cm^3 and 1.5×10^5 cm/sec, respectively.

We have assumed in the above comparison that the displacement of the round window and the basilar membrane are the same. The relationship between the amplitudes of the two are not known in delphinids. However, in humans the amplitude of the stapes and round window are both less than or equal to that of the basilar membrane (von Békésy, 1960, p. 173) and we have no reason to assume otherwise here. In delphinids, and all cetaceans for that matter, the stapes is much more rigidly fixed in the oval window, which is very important for stimulation of the cochlea in compressional bone conduction, as illustrated in Fig. 5.2.

The importance of air in the middle ear cavity is now very apparent, for if this cavity were fluid- or bone-filled the round window could not move and the sound analyzing capabilities of the cochlea would be lost. The entire basilar membrane would be stimulated by relatively large amplitude motions of the particles of the cochlear fluid, as in a hydrophone. It is through these particle motions that sharks, which have no swim bladder, apparently detect sound (Banner, 1968).

The delphinid cochlea is of a more sturdy structure than that of terrestrial animals and appears well adapted for high-frequency hearing (Wever, Palin, & Ridgway, 1971). Further evidence of the importance of high-frequency hearing in delphinids is the size of the auditory nerve. In *T. truncatus* the auditory nerve has more than twice the nerve fibers as that of a human: 112,500 as compared with 50,000 (Morgane & Jacobs, 1972).

Sound Transmission to the Ear

Reyesenbach de Haan (1957) and Fraser & Purves (1954) suggest that the vestigial external auditory meatus in delphinids functions to transmit sound to the ear. However, the work of Bullock et al. (1968) and McCormick et al. (1970) rule out this function. Norris (1964) suggested that sounds entered the lower jaw through the mandibular nerve foramen and were transmitted through the fat body of the mandibular canal to the inner ear. Norris (1968) later changed the entrance area to the posterior part of the mandible. Bullock et al. (1968), using electrophysiological methods, reported that the primary pathway of sound to the inner ear is via the lower jaw. This was later supported by McCormick et al. (1970) using the cochlear potential measurements. However, data from the Bullock et al. (1968) and McCormick et al. (1970) studies need to be interpreted with a degree of caution. In all cases the animal's mouth was open and its larynx connected to a gas-filled tube (described by Nagel, Morgane, & McFarland, 1964), which is extremely unnatural. Fig. 5.3 shows the location of air spaces in *T. truncatus*. There may or may not be air in the mouth in normal conditions. Under the conditions of the measurements by Bullock et al. (1968) and McCormick et al. (1970), air in the mouth could extend further back and to each side, blocking sounds transmitted from the lower parts of the melon to the bullae. Data Bullock et al. (1968) obtained in water show the greatest sensitivity at angles of 5° to 30° from the midline of the head. Underwater hearing data of 85 kHz are plotted on a polar scale in Fig. 5.4, with data taken by Norris and Harvey (1974) using a "freshly dead" *T. truncatus* head and a hydrophone implanted at two locations in the head. In both, the sound projector was pivoted with center at the blow hole and at jaw level. The pivoting arm holding the sound projector was 100 cm long for Bullock et al. (1968) who used pulsed, 85-kHz signals. Norris

a — VESTIBULAR SAC
b — TUBULAR SAC
c — PREMAXILLARY NASAL SAC
d — MOUTH
e — EUSTACHEAN TUBE
f — EAR BONE AREA
g — TRACHEA
h — LUNGS

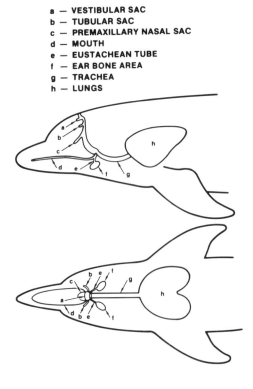

FIG. 5.3. Schematic drawing showing the various air-filled spaces in the body of a dolphin: (a) vestibular sac, (b) tubular sac, (c) premaxillary nasal sac, (d) mouth, (e) eustachean tube, (f) ear bone area, (g) trachea, and (h) lungs.

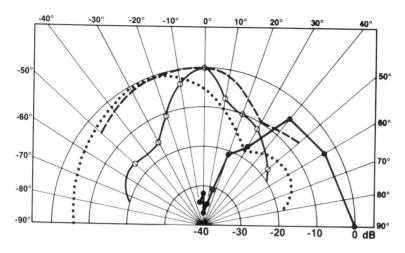

FIG. 5.4.   The solid dots connected by a straight line are a plot of the threshold data obtained by Bullock et al. (1968) at 85 kHz. The dashed curve and the dotted curve are data obtained by Norris and Harvey (1974) showing the relative sound transmission through a *T. truncatus* head with receiving hydrophone at the external auditory meatus (1.8 cm deep) and the mandibular fat body anterior to the bulla (6.8 cm deep), respectively. Open circles are the behavioral data of Au and Moore (1984).

and Harvey (1974) used a 83-cm arm and single 23 μsec pulses without carrier frequency. Evoked potential data of Bullock et al. (1968) are plotted as relative thresholds whereas the data plot of Norris and Harvey (1974) is of the receiving hydrophone voltage for a constant projector output, plotted in dB relative to the maximum voltage at this hydrophone. The data of Bullock et al. (1968) show a rapid increase in threshold with angle while data of Norris and Harvey (1974) show a relatively slow decline in transmission with increasing angle. Recent behavioral data taken by Au and Moore (1984) on directional hearing in the bottlenose dolphin are also shown plotted in Fig. 5.4. The stimulus used was 2.0-s-duration pure tone bursts at 120 kHz. They also took data at 30 kHz and 60 kHz which gave broader reception curves. Data were also taken at these frequencies in the vertical plane. Maximum sensitivity in the vertical plane was between 5° and 10° above the midline of the animal's mouth. Bullock et al. (1968) conclude that "sound coming from above the horizontal is probably much reduced in effectiveness," which is not born out by the Au-Moore data. These results taken together suggest that the directionality observed in *T. truncatus* (see sound localization below) hearing is caused by directional reception by the ear, by signal processing in the central nervous system, or both, and not by directional paths through the head as suggested by Norris (1980). The shape of the mellon may aid sound reception (see following discussion of Fig. 5.8).

AUDITORY THRESHOLDS

Behavioral auditory thresholds have now been measured in six delphinid species (Ljungblad, Scoggins, & Gilmartin, 1982). The audiogram for *T. truncatus* is similar to that for humans, but shifted up on the frequency scale by a factor of ten. While the ear is considered to be a pressure transducer, sound detection, depends on the duration of the signal and, therefore, on energy.

The important features to note about delphinid hearing thresholds are the upper frequency limit, the high sensitivity of hearing, and the extremely sharp cutoff of hearing at the upper limit. In terms used in electronic filter design, this sharp cutoff represents a low-pass filter with a cutoff of 495 dB per octave for *T. truncatus*, which is far greater than can be produced by any electronic analog. The reasons for this sharp cutoff are unknown. The middle ear bones may contribute to the sharp upper limit cutoff. Parnell (1963) has shown that there is an approximately linear relationship between the upper frequency limit of hearing and the density of middle ear bones from humans, guinea pigs, bats, and delphinids.

Similar sharp cutoffs have been observed with individual human listeners (Rice, Schubert, & West, 1969). Unfortunately, the practice is to average results of several individuals, masks the effect of a given individual's sharp cutoffs. The average roll-off for ten subjects was approximately 104 dB per octave.

Threshold Versus Stimulus Duration

Detection thresholds for *T. truncatus* vary with the duration of acoustic stimulus (Johnson, 1968b). Results from similar experiments with human subjects indicate that the variation of threshold intensity with stimulus duration is approximated by:

$$I/I_\infty = 1 + \tau/t, \tag{9}$$

where I is the pure tone threshold intensity, t (sec) is the stimulus duration, I_∞ is the threshold for a long tone, and τ is a constant. For short tones with $\tau/t \gg 1$ the threshold decreases inversely with tone duration, and complete integration of signal energy is necessary for detection. For long tones, ($\tau/t \ll 1$), threshold is constant and equal to I_∞. Equation 9 is not an accurate representation of data for short pulses because the bandwidth of the signals increases inversely with signal duration, and the ear has finite receiving bandwidths. There is an added increase in the threshold due to shorter signals.

Frequency and Intensity Discrimination

Thompson and Herman (1975) measured the auditory frequency discrimination ability of *T. truncatus*. Thompson and Herman's data are the most complete and are plotted in Fig. 5.5 with similar measurements on human subjects by Shower and Biddulph (1931). Differential frequency discrimination depends on stimulus loudness and the way the changing frequencies are presented to the subjects. However, the effect of loudness on frequency discrimination is small for stimuli 40 dB or more above threshold, which was the case for the data in Fig. 5.5. A sine-wave frequency-modulated signal was used in both sets of data in Fig. 5.5. Discrimination also varies with the frequency of modulation. In both cases shown here, the modulation frequency was 2 Hz for direct comparisons with data taken with human subjects. It has been noted (C. S. Johnson, 1980) that the method of frequency modulation may be much more important for discrimination by *T. truncatus* than for human subjects. In the referenced case two *T. truncatus* could not be trained to discriminate pulse signals of alternating and widely differing frequencies from a pulsed single tone, but one of them rapidly learned to discriminate a sine-wave-modulated from a continuous tone.

Masked Thresholds

An auditory phenomenon related to frequency discrimination is critical bands. The concept of critical bands first was proposed by Fletcher (1940). According to

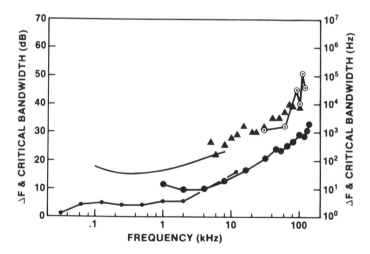

FIG. 5.5.   The solid triangles are the critical ratios measured by Johnson (1968a), the circles points connected by a straight line are the critical ratios measured by Moore and Au (1982), and the large solid circles connected by a straight line are the differential frequency discrimination data from Thompson and Herman (1975). The solid line depicts the critical ratios for humans by French and Steinberg (1947) and Hawkens and Stevens (1950), and the small solid dots connected by a straight line are the differential pitch sensitivity measurements made on human subjects by Shower and Biddulph (1931).

the critical band theory, only noise in a finite band bracketing a tone is effective in masking the tone, and the tone is just audible when the acoustic power is equal to that noise in the critical band. A critical band is, therefore, defined as the ratio of the intensity of a tone at threshold to the intensity per Hertz of the masking noise at that frequency. This is only strictly true for a flat or "white" noise spectrum.

Critical bands have been measured for *T. truncatus* by Johnson (1968a) and more recently by Moore and Au (1982). Data from both are plotted in Fig. 5.5 with the binaural data from human listeners collected by French and Steinberg (1947) and Hawkins and Stevens (1950). These data indicate 40 critical bands in the *T. truncatrus* auditory system, whereas there are 24 in the human auditory system (Zwicker, 1961).

In humans the minimum detectable tone change (ΔF) is closely related to critical bandwidth at the same frequency (Fletcher, 1940; Zwicker, Flottorp, & Stevens, 1957). If the same relationship holds true for *T. truncatus*, ΔF would be approximately the critical bandwidth divided by 20, which is approximately true with the bottlenose dolphin. It should be noted that what we have been referring to as critical bands in humans are more accurately called critical ratios; critical bands are larger than critical ratios by a factor of 2.5 (Sharf, 1970). Au and Moore (1983) measured critical bandwidths in *T. truncatus* at 30, 60, and 120 kHz and found the critical bandwidth was 10 times wider than the critical ratio at 30 kHz, 8 times wider at 60 kHz, and at 120 kHz the critical bandwidth was approximately the same as the critical ratio.

Another type of masking experiment has been done with *T. truncatus;* masking one pure tone by a second pure tone (Johnson, 1971). Instead of noise, a pure tone at a given level above threshold was played continuously and the thresholds for a second pure tone were determined at various frequencies above and below the masking tone. Data were collected for a 70 kHz masking tone at 40 dB and 80 dB above threshold. Data for the 80 dB masking level are significantly different. Apparently, the animal was responding to different thresholds in the two cases. Above 30 kHz something unexplained happened. Human subjects experience many different sound sensations due to the mixing of two tones (Wegel & Lane, 1924), especially at higher masking levels. Perhaps the animal experienced something similar and was responding to different acoustic sensations in the two cases.

The results of the dual tone masking experiment are in general agreement with those obtained for human subjects (Wegel & Lane, 1924; Munson & Gardner, 1950; Egan & Hoke, 1950), showing that low-frequency tones are more effective at masking high frequencies and high frequencies are less effective at masking low frequencies. As with the human data, dips in the thresholds occurred near 70 kHz. For humans this decrease is attributed to the presence of beats. Assuming that this is the case for *T. truncatus*, we can estimate the just perceivable sound level difference from the following relation,

$$\Delta L = 20 \log_{10}(\frac{1 + 10^{-M}}{1 - 10^{-M}}), \tag{10}$$

where ΔL is the variation in sound pressure level accompanying beats in dB, and M is the difference in level of the beating tones, also in dB. M values from data (25 dB, 34 dB and 18 dB) in Eq. 10 give ΔL values of 1.0, 0.35 and 2.0 dB, respectively. These ΔL values are consistent with those obtained for human just-noticeable-level differences.

Sound Localization

The most complete measurements on sound localization in delphinids have been made by Renaud and Popper (1975), also see Popper (1980) for references to later work. They worked with *T. truncatus* and measured minimum audible angles (MAA) in both the horizontal and vertical planes using both tonal pulses and broadband clicks. They found for frequencies between 20 kHz and 90 kHz the MAA was 2° to 3°, which is similar to human listeners (Erulkar, 1972; Mills 1958, 1972). MAAs for sounds above and below the animal were similar. Humans have difficulty in locating sounds with respect to elevation unless they can move their heads (Butler, 1969). Renaud and Popper (1975) suggested that *T. truncatus* used intensity clues to make its judgments. Using short (35 μsec) pulses with energy centered at about 63 kHz, Renaud and Popper measured a MAA of 0.9°. As with humans, broadband signals are easier for *T. truncatus* to locate.

Important Areas for Future Study

1. The upper hearing limit of humans decreases with age, (von Békésy, 1957). It would be useful for various reasons to know if this also occurs with delphinids.

2. Masked auditory thresholds are needed from more delphinid species, as well as studies with frequency-modulated signals and the reported critical time interval discussed by C. S. Johnson (1980).

3. Masked auditory thresholds for human subjects at the upper frequency limits are needed for comparison with dolphin data.

DELPHINID ECHOLOCATION SOUND PRODUCTION

The location and operation of the sound generating system or systems of *T. truncatus* are still not precisely known. However, it is most likely that the sounds originate from the air passage system above the bony nares (Evans & Maderson, 1973; Ridgway, 1983). We do know (Au, Floyd, Penner, & Murchison, 1974) that the bottlenose dolphin can emit very intense sonic pulses (220 dB re 1 μPa at 1 meter) having peak frequencies between 120 kHz and 130 kHz. We do know (Au, 1980) that for *T. truncatus* the beam-width of some echolocation clicks is quite narrow, with a broadband 3-dB beam-width of 10° in both the horizontal and vertical planes. The center of the beam is directed up in the vertical plane at about 20° with respect to the animal's mouth-line. In the vertical plane the beam is slightly asymetrical with more energy emitted below than above the center-line. In the horizontal plane the beam is directed slightly to the left. Au, Floyd, and Haun (1978), showed that the beam pattern for some single pulses is similar to that of a 7.5-cm diameter circular piston transducer.

Evans (1973) showed that the beam pattern for different pulses can vary greatly, and that *T. truncatus* can emit two simultaneously, one 20° to left of center and one 20° to the right, separated in time by about 80 μsec, with both appearing together at 0°.

Reznikov, claims to have found that the emitted sonic beam is rotated at high speed independently of head motion (see Bullock & Gurevich, 1979, p. 87; this reference contains an excellent review of the Soviet biosonar work with ceta-ceans.) Reznikov is quoted as having measured angular scanning rates of 3.5×10^5 deg/sec; unfortunately, little evidence is supplied to support this claim. Evans (personal communication, July, 1983) pointed out that a similar high scanning rate can be obtained for his data if one assumes the two pulses reported in this reference were one pulse rotated from the hydrophone 20° to the left to the one 20° to the right in 80 μsec i.e., 40°/80 μsec $= 5 \times 10^5$ deg/sec. In this case the hydrophone at 0° clearly shows two pulses, ruling out a single pulse being swept at high speed.

Au et al. (1978) also measured acoustic pressure versus range of broadband click from near field to far field. For a discussion of near field and far field effects see Harris (1964). In between the near field and the far field a transition region exists in which the relationship between particle velocity (u) and acoustic pressure (p) varies in a complicated way and Eq. 1 does not hold. In general, the relationship between u and p depends on the emitted frequency and, shape of the sound source, including reflecting and refracting components. In the far field the pressure falls inversely with range. The near- to far-field transition occurs at a range of about 0.5 m to 0.6 m (Au et al., 1978). The suggestion that beam directionality might be due in part to an acoustic lens in the animal's melon was first proposed by Wood (1964). Norris (1964) also proposed the presence of an acoustic lens and most recently restated this (Norris, 1980). Litchfield et al. (1979) proposed, based on the acoustic properties of the various melon oils, that the melon shape itself serves as a ''sound lens'' and not an internal lens as suggested by Norris. The role of the melon, skull, and various nasal sacs in producing and focusing sounds also has been extensively studied in the Soviet Union (Bel'kovich & Dubrovskiy, 1976; Dubrovskiy & Zaslavskiy, 1975; Ro-manenko, 1973).

Acoustic Lens and Alternatives

Figure 5.6 shows a mid-sagittal section of a *T. truncatus* head traced from a full-sized photograph used in Green, Ridgway, and Evans (1980). For convenience the vertical directivity pattern obtained by Au (1980) is plotted along with indices of refraction calculated from velocity measurements reported by Norris and Harvey (1974). Figure 5.7 shows a similar plot in the horizontal 20° beam direction. The index of refraction (n) is defined here as the ratio of the velocity of sound in water to that in tissue. Two of the numbers are underlined in Fig. 5.6 because there appear to be typographical errors in the velocity values reported by Norris and Harvey (1974). If this is not the case, then the value 1.00 should be 0.88 and 1.07 should be 0.82. All of the values are uncertain by ± 4% or ±.04 because of the ±0.1 cm uncertainty in the thickness of the 2.5 cm sections used. The location of the sound source is close to that suggested by Au et al. (1978). Data were taken by Norris and Harvey at a temperature of 22.9°C. Correcting these data to 37°C, using the "outer melon" velocity measured by Litchfield et al. (1979), yields n = 1.06 between the outer melon and surrounding water.

Snell's law (cf. Urick, 1967, p. 105) governs the direction changes as sound is refracted from a medium of one index to another. In general, for a convex lens to have focusing properties it must be made of material that has a velocity of sound less than that of the surrounding medium, i.e., an index of refraction greater than 1 (cf. Folds, 1973). The shape of a lens is important, e.g., the more convex a lens is the greater its focusing properties. Size is also important. A lens

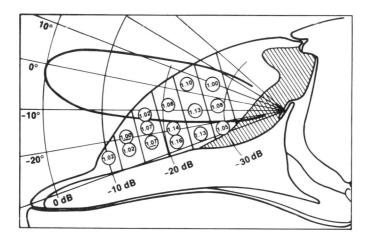

FIG. 5.6.   The sonar beam reported by Au (1980) and the indices of refraction at various locations in the melon as measured by Norris and Harvey (1974) superimposed on a mid-sagital tracing of a *T. truncatus* head.

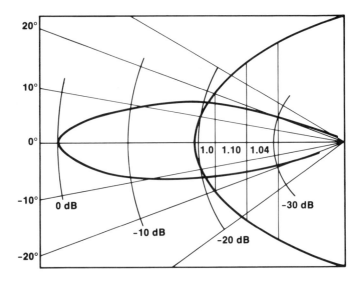

FIG. 5.7. A horizontal section along a plane 20° above the jaw-line of the *T. truncatus* in Fig. 5.6. The indices of refraction were extrapolated to this plane from those in Fig. 6 assuming that in the surrounding water n = 1.00. The beam shown is that measured by Au (1980) in this plane.

whose size is too small relative to the wave-length of the incidental sound will not focus well at long wavelengths (Anderson, 1950).

It is tempting to try to explain the production of the *T. truncatus* sound beam as a sound source, reflectors and lenses each acting independently as though each element of the system were in the far field. A strict application of the laws of physics does not permit this (Folds, June, 1983, personal communication). It is an approximation of unknown accuracy to consider the various parts of the animal's sound generating system independently, and the accuracy of this approach probably varies greatly with pulse bandwidth, pulse shape, pulse directivity pattern and pulse amplitude.

Au et al. (1978) showed that the transition point between the near- and far-fields for *T. truncatus* echolocation pulses is 0.5 m or more in front of the blow hole. Because this puts all of the animal's beam production apparatus in the acoustic near-field, the various parts of the system can not be considered independent in the strictest sense. The beam in Figs. 5.6 and 5.7 exists only in the far-field where it was measured, i.e., at ranges greater than 0.5 m. At ranges less than 0.5–0.6 m, the pulse shape may be quite different. Until this range is reached the various parts of the sound production mechanism are interacting with one another in a complex way to produce the far-field beam as observed by Au (1980). This does not mean that the animals can not echolocate at ranges less

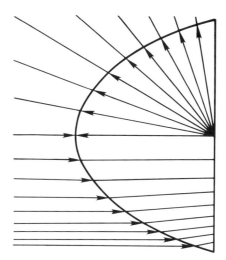

FIG. 5.8. The same section as in Fig. 5.7, showing ray paths leaving the melon from the center and parallel rays entering; n = 1.06 was the index of refraction used.

than 0.5–0.6 m, only that the sonar pulse intensity gets lower as the range is decreased from 0.5–0.6 m (see Hueter & Bolt, 1955, p. 69 for the simple example of a piston type projector). This may explain why Evans, Sutherland, and Beil (1964) were unable to get the narrow beams measured from live animals from a porpoise cadaver with an acoustic source located in its head.

This point also is illustrated in Fig. 5.8. Shown here is a section through the melon as in Fig. 5.7. Using an index of refraction of 1.06, rays are plotted radiating outward from the extrapolated position of the composite sound source. Very little effect on the rays is found. Also plotted are parallel rays shown entering the melon and being refracted inward. It is interesting to note that an extension of these latter rays at the downward 20° angle would bring them close to the bullae.

Echolocation Signals

Delphinid echolocation signals vary greatly in length, frequency content, intensity, and directionality (Au et al., 1974; Evans, 1973). Altes has derived a mathematical relationship with which he can reproduce the shapes of delphinid, bat and other biological signals (Altes, 1973; Altes, Evans, & Johnson, 1975). From this expression Altes is able to show that all these biological echolocation signals are linear period-modulated signals. This means that the intervals between zero-crossings by the signal waveform increase linearly from the beginning to the end of the signal; a fact that is not obvious from visual examination of delphinid click waveforms. Probably the single most important characteristic of clicks is their short duration. Signals of this type are good for range resolution, and, therefore, good target discrimination.

Murchison (1980) experimentally measured the range resolution of *T. truncatus* at ranges of 1m, 3m, and 7m and obtained minimum target separation thresholds of 0.9 cm, 1.5 cm, and 3 cm, respectively. Because of their good range resolution characteristics, short pulses also are good for sonar operation in locations where reverberation is high. Reverberation refers to the background "noise" made up of false echoes from the bottom, surface and other nontarget reflectors. The antithesis of a signal that has good range resolution is one that has good Doppler or velocity resolution. For good Doppler resolution, long duration, narrow-band signals are used. Some bats emit this type of pulse (Schnitzler & Henson, 1980).

Several target detection experiments have been done on *T. truncatus;* three of the most meaningful and recent were reported by Au and Snyder (1980), Au and Penner (1981), and Au and Turl (1983). These studies show that when making target detections, *T. truncatus* are limited by noise and reverberation in much the same was as man-made sonar systems.

Of the many biosonar target discrimination experiments performed on *T. truncatus* the one reported by Hammer and Au (1980) is the most recent. They trained a *T. truncatus* to report whether or not a target presented singly was a standard target. Their results indicated that the animal learned to recognize and remember the characteristics of the standard target echoes. A strong correlation was found between the behavioral results and a mathematical analysis that compared emitted porpoise-like pulses and recorded echoes from the various targets.

Morozov et al. (1971) and Penner and Kadane (1980) observed that *T. truncatus* emits a pulse and receives the echo before emitting another pulse, i.e., the interpulse interval is greater than the two-way transit time from animal to target. Au (1980) observed that this also was true when the target was absent and suggested that this may indicate that the animal is performing mental "range-gating." Range-gating is used in man-made sonars to eliminate all echoes except those in a given range interval.

THEORETICAL ECHOLOCATION MODELS

Floyd (1980) has discussed the principle theoretical models of delphinid biosonar systems. Two of these theoretical models were proposed by Altes (1980) and R. A. Johnson (1980). The former emphasizes correlation and matched filtering processing. Briefly, this means that the waveform of the emitted signal is somehow stored and compared with the echo. Hammer and Au (1980) used this type of theory to interpret their target recognition studies.

The second theory was proposed by Nordmark (1960) and is based on the phenomenon called time separation pitch (TSP). When pairs of correlated (similar) pulses are played repetitively to a listener a tone-like sound is perceived and the frequency of this tone-like signal is equal to 1 divided by the time separation between the pair of pulses. R. A. Johnson (1980) has conducted experiments with human subjects covering the same range of pulse intervals as the pulse-echo interval in the porpoise range resolution experiment (Murchison, 1980). Johnson's results are similar to the range resolution data obtained by Murchison. However, Murchison showed that the range resolution results are not explained by either a matched filter theory or a TSP theory.

In order for TSP to occur, the pairs of pulses must be somewhat similar in shape, i.e., correlated, so there is some commonality between the two theories. R. A. Johnson (1980) has shown that the TSP theory results in an energy frequency spectrum for the pairs of pulses taken together which has a number of peaks uniformly spaced along the frequency axis. These peaks are separated by a frequency that is equal to 1 divided by the pulse pair time separation. Ranging and target recognition are thus reduced in this theory to spectrum analysis.

The two basic theories then are reduced to whether the signal processing takes place in the time domain, the energy domain, or both. Neither theory fully explains all aspects of the porpoise biosonar system.

Electronic Models of Delphinid Biosonar System

Only one device based on a biosonar theory actually has been built. It is the U. S. Navy AN/SQQ-27(XN-2) "bionic sonar" (Floyd, 1980). Experiments have been conducted that might be considered modeling or pseudomodeling. In these experiments human subjects listened to and interpreted delphinid-like signals that have been transformed electronically. In the first of these (Fish, Johnson, & Ljungblad, 1976) human divers were equipped with a helmet housing, sending and receiving transducers, and high fidelity stereo earphones. Short delphinid-like pulses were projected through the sending projector located in front of the diver's face. Receiving hydrophones were located at either side of the helmet. Projected and received signals were communicated to electronic apparatus outside the experimental tank via coaxial cables. The target echoes were very short in time, some as short as 20 μsec. This means the signals had a bandwidth of 1/20 μsec or about 50 kHz, considerably greater than the human hearing range. To compensate for this the echoes were digitized and stretched in time by a factor of 128 and then played to the diver. The factor of 128 was chosen so that the length of the shortest echoes was at least 2 msec in duration. Green (1973) showed that 2 msec is the minimum pulse duration that humans can discriminate with high success scores between noise-type pulses. The targets used in this experiment were metal plates that had been used previously on a *T. truncatus* discrimination experiment (Evans & Powell, 1967). Similar results were obtained from divers and porpoises for this particular set of targets and conditions. For the divers to make their target discrimination it was necessary to scan the targets by moving their heads if they did not they had difficulty in making choices.

Other experiments have been conducted using human listeners and time-stretched echoes (Au & Martin, 1983; Martin & Au, 1983). In these experiments echoes from targets ensonified with dolphin-like signals were digitized and played back at slower rates to the subjects. No scanning was involved in these measurements. They found that, under controlled laboratory conditions, humans had discrimination scores about as good as dolphins under less controlled conditions.

Important Areas For Future Work

1. The actual operation of the sound source and sonar beam generation is not understood. Measurements using velocity detectors instead of pressure transducers in the near-field would be helpful. Also, measuring changes in the shape of the nasal sacs might help clarify their role in sound production. When the "state of the art" is more advanced, pulse interference laser holography could be a powerful tool to study melon and other displacements during phonations.

2. Experiments using human listeners and electronically transformed echoes are a useful method of studying echolocation and should be continued. The importance of target scanning needs to be determined.

3. Floyd's (1980) suggestion of using "electronic phantom" targets to test various theories is an extremely promising approach. In this type of experiment echoes are produced electronically and projected back to the dolphin in response to its own outgoing sonar pulses instead of using physical targets which simply reflect the outgoing signal. This approach allows the experimenter to check responses to specific changes in the echo.

REFERENCES

Altes, R. A. (1973). A theory for animal echolocation and its application to ultrasonics. *Ultrasonics Symposium Proceedings*, IEEE Cat. No. 73 CHO 807-8 SU, 67-72.

Altes, R. A. (1980). Models for echolocation. In R.-G. Busnel & J. F. Fish (Eds.), *Animal sonar systems* (pp. 625–671). New York: Plenum Press.

Altes, R. A., Evans, W. E., & Johnson, C. S. (1975). Cetacean echolocation signals and a new model for the human glottal pulse. *Journal of the Acoustical Society of America, 57*, 1221–1224.

Anderson, V. C. (1950). Sound scattering from a fluid sphere. *Journal of the Acoustical Society of America, 22*, 426–31.

Au, W. W. L. (1980). Echolocation signals of the Atlantic bottlenose dolphin (*Tursiops truncatus*) in open waters. In R.-G. Busnell & J. F. Fish (Eds.), *Animal sonar systems* (pp. 251–282). New York: Plenum Press.

Au, W. W. L., Floyd, R. W. & Haun, J. E. (1978). Propagation of Atlantic bottlenose dolphin echolocation signals. *Journal of the Acoustical Society of America, 64,* 411–422.

Au, W. W. L., Floyd, R. W., Penner, R. H., & Murchison, A. E. (1974). Measurement of echolocation signals of the Atlantic bottlenose dolphin, *Tursiops truncatus* Montagu, in open waters. *Journal of the Acoustical Society of America, 56,* 1280–1290.

Au, W. W. L., & Martin, D. W. (1983). Insights into dolphin sonar discrimination capabilities from broadband sonar discrimination experiments with human subjects. *Journal of the Acoustical Society of America* Suppl. 1, *74,* S73.

Au, W. W. L., & Moore, P. W. B. (1983). Critical ratios and bandwidths of the Atlantic bottlenose dolphin *(Tursiops truncatus). Journal of the Acoustical Society of America* Suppl. 1, *74,* S73.

Au, W. W. L., & Moore, P. W. B. (1984). Receiving beam patterns and directivity indices of the Atlantic bottlenose dolphin *(Tursiops truncatus). Journal of the Acoustical Society of America, 75,* 255–262.

Au, W. W. L., & Penner, R. H. (1981). Target detection in noise by echolocating Atlantic bottlenose dolphins. *Journal of the Acoustical Society of America. 70,* 687–693.

Au, W. W. L., & Snyder, K. J. (1980). Long-range target detection in open waters by an echolocating Atlantic bottlenose dolphin *(Tursiops Truncatus). Journal of the Acoustical Society of America, 68,* 1077–1084.

Au, W. W. L., & Turl, C. W. (1983). Target detection in reverberation by an echolocating Atlantic bottlenose dolphin *(Tursiops truncatus). Journal of the Acoustical Society of America, 73,* 1676–1681.

Banner, A. (1968). Measurements of the particle velocity and pressure of the ambient noise in a shallow bay. *Journal of the Acoustical Society of America, 44,* 1741–1742.

Bel'kovich, V. M., & Dubrovskiy, N. A. (1976). Sensory basis of cetacean orientation. *Izdaniya Nauka,* Leningrad. Joint Publications Research Service 7157, May 1977.

Bullock, T. H., Grinnel, A. D., Ikezona, E., Kameda, K., Katsuke, Y., Nomoto, M., Sato, O., Suga, N., & Yanogisawa, K. (1968). Electrophysiological studies of central auditory mechanism in cetaceans. *Zeitschrift für Vergleichende Physiologie, 59,* 117–156.

Bullock, T. H., & Gurevich, V. W. (1979). Soviet literature on the nervous system and psychobiology of cetacea. *International Review of Neurobiology, 21,* 47–127.

Butler, R. A. (1969). Monaural and binaural localization of noise bursts vertically in the median sagital plane. *Journal of Auditory Research, 3,* 23–25.

Chivers, R. C., & Parry, R. J. (1978). Ultrasonic velocity and attenuation in mammalian tissues. *Journal of the Acoustical Society of America, 63,* 940–953.

Dubrovskiy, N. A., & Zaslavskiy, G. L. (1975). Skull bone, dolphin sounding pulses, dolphin echolocation. *Izdaniya Nauka,* Leningrad, Joint Publications Research Service 65777, Sept. 1979.

Egan, J. P., & Hoke, H. W. (1950). On the masking pattern of a simple auditory stimulus. *Journal of the Acoustical Society of America, 22,* 622–630.

Erulkar, S. D. (1972). Comparative aspects of spatial localization of sound. *Physiological Reviews, 52,* 237–260.

Evans, W. E. (1973). Echolocation by marine delphinids and one species of freshwater dolphin. *Journal of the Acoustical Society of America, 54,* 191–199.

Evans, W. E., & Maderson, P. F. A. (1973). Mechanism of sound production in delphinid cetaceans: A review and some anatomical considerations. *American Zoologist, 13,* 1205–1213.

Evans, W. E., & Powell, B. A. (1967). Discrimination of different metallic plates by an echolocating delphinid. In R.-G. Busnel (Ed.), *Animal sonar systems: Biology and bionics* (pp. 363–382). Laboratoire de Physiologie Acoustique, Jouy-en-Josas *78,* France.

Evans, W. E., Sutherland, W. W., & Beil, R. G. (1964). The directional characteristics of delphinid sounds. In W. N. Tavolga (Ed.), *Marine bio-acoustics* (pp. 353–372). New York: Pergamon press.

Fish, J. F., Johnson, D. S., Ljungblad, D. K. (1976). Sonar target discrimination by instrumented human divers. *Journal of the Acoustical Society of America, 59,* 602–606.

Fletcher, H. (1940). Auditory patterns. *Reviews of Modern Physiology, 12,* 47–65.

Floyd, R. W. (1980). Models of cetacean signal processing. In R.-G. Busnel & J. F. Fish (Eds.), *Animal sonar systems* (pp. 615–623). New York: Plenum Press.

Fraser, F. C., & Purves, P. E. (1954). Hearing in cetaceans. *Bulletin of the British Museum (Natural History), Zoology, 2,* 103–116.

French, N. R., & Steinberg. J. C. (1947). Factors governing the intelligibility of speech sounds. *Journal of the Acoustical Society of America, 19,* 90–119.

Folds, D. L. (1973). Focusing properties of solid ultrasonic cylinderical lenses. *Journal of the Acoustical Society of America, 53,* 826–834.

Green, D. M. (1973). Temporal acuity as a function of frequency. *Journal of the Acoustical Society of America, 54,* 373–379.

Green, R. F., Ridgway, S. H., & Evans, W. E. (1980). Functional and descriptive anatomy of the bottlenose dolphin nasolaryngeal system with special reference to the musculature associated with sound production. In R.-G. Busnel & J. F. Fish (Eds.), *Animal sonar systems* (pp. 199–238). New York: Plenum Press.

Hammer, C. E., Jr., & Au. W. W. L. (1980). Porpoise echo-recognition: An analysis of controlling target characteristics. *Journal of the Acoustical Society of America, 68,* 1285–1293.

Harris, G. G. (1964). Considerations on the physics of sound production by fishes. In W. N. Tavolga (Ed.), *Marine Bioacoustics* (pp. 233–247). New York: Pergamon Press.

Hawkens, J. E., & Stevens, S. S. (1950). The masking of pure tones and speech by white noise. *Journal of the Acoustical Society of America, 22,* 6–13.

Hueter, T. F., & Bolt, R. H. (1955). *Sonics.* New York: Wiley.

Johnson, C. S. (1967). Sound detection thresholds in marine mammals. In W. N. Tavolga (Ed.), *Marine bioacoustics* (pp. 247–268). New York: Pergamon Press.

Johnson, C. S. (1968a). Masked tonal thresholds in the bottlenose porpoise. *Journal of the Acoustical Society of America, 44,* 965–967.

Johnson, C. S. (1968b). Relationship between absolute threshold and duration-of-tone in the bottlenose porpoise. *Journal of the Acoustical Society of America, 43,* 757–763.

Johnson, C. S. (1971). Auditory masking of one pure tone by another in the bottlenose porpoise. *Journal of the Acoustical Society of America, 49,* 1317–1318.

Johnson, C. S. (1980). Important areas for future cetacean auditory study. In R.-G. Busnel & J. F. Fish (Eds.), *Animal sonar systems* (pp. 515–518). New York: Plenum Press.

Johnson, R. A. (1980). Energy spectrum analysis in echolocation. In R.-G. Busnel & J. F. Fish (Eds.), *Animal sonar systems* (pp. 673–693). New York: Plenum Press.

Litchfield, C., Karol, R., Mullen, M. E., Dilger, J. P., & Luthi, B.(1979). Physical factors influencing refraction of the echolocative sound beam in delphinid cetaceans. *Marine Biology, 52,* 285–290.

Littler, T. S. (1965). *The physics of the ear.* New York: Pergamon Press.

Ljungbald, D. K., Scoggins, P. D., & Gilmartin, W. G. (1982). Auditory thresholds of captive eastern Pacific bottlenosed dolphins, *Tursiops* spp. *Journal of the Acoustical Society of America, 72,* 1726–1730.

Martin, D. W., & Au, W. W. L. (1983). Auditory detection of broadband sonar echoes from a sphere in white noise. *Journal of the Acoustical Society of America, 73,* S91.

McCormick, J. G., Wever, E. G., Palin, J., & Ridgway, S. H. (1970). Sound conduction in the dolphin ear. *Journal of the Acoustical Society of America, 48,* 1418–1428.

McCormick, J. G., Wever, E. G., Ridgway, S. H., & Palin, J. (1980). Sound reception in the porpoise as it relates to ecolocation. In R.-G. Busnel & J. F. Fish (Eds.), *Animal sonar systems* (pp. 449–467). New York: Plenum Press.

Mills, A. W. (1958). On the minimum audible angle. *Journal of the Acoustical Society of America, 30,* 237–246.

Mills, A. W. (1972). Auditory localization. In J. S. Tobias (Ed.), *Foundations of modern auditory theory* Vol. II. (pp. 303–348). New York: Academic Press.

Moore, P. W. B., & Au, W. W. L. (1982). Masked pure-tone thresholds of the bottlenosed dolphin (*Tursiops truncatus*). *Journal of the Acoustical Society of America, 72,* S42.

Morgane, P. J., & Jacobs, N. S. (1972). Comparative anatomy of the cetacean nervous system. In R. J. Harrison (Ed.), *Functional anatomy of marine animals* (pp. 117–244). New York: Academic Press.

Morozov, V. P., Akopian, A. I., Burdin, V. I., Donskov, A. A., Zaitseva, K. A., & Sokovykh, Yu. A. (1971). Audiogram of the dolphin (*Tursiops truncatus*). *Sechenov Phusiological Journal of the USSR, 57,* 843–848. (in Russian)

Munson, W. A., & Gardner, M. B. (1950). Loudness patterns—A new approach. *Journal of the Acoustical Society of America, 22,* 179–192.

Murchison, A. E. (1980). Detection range and range resolution of echolocating bottlenose porpoise (*Tursiops truncatus*). In R.-G. Busnel & J. F. Fish (Eds.), *Animal sonar systems* (pp. 43–70). New York: Plenum Press.

Nagel, E. L., Morgane, P. J., & McFarland, W. L. (1964). Anesthesia for the bottlenose dolphin, (*Tursiops truncatus*). *Science, 146,* 1591–1593.

Nordmark, J. (1960). Perception of distance in animal echolocation. *Nature* (Lond.), *188,* 1009–1010.

Norris, K. S. (1964). Some problems of echolocation in cetaceans. In W. N. Tavolga (Ed.), *Marine bioacoustics* (pp. 317–336). New York: Pergamon Press.

Norris, K. S. (1968). The evolution of acoustic mechanisms in odontocete. In Drake (Ed.), *Evolution and environment.* New Haven, CT: Yale University Press.

Norris, K. S. (1980). Peripheral sound processing in odontocetes. In R.-G. Busnel & J. F. Fish (Eds.), *Animal sonar systems* (pp. 495–509). New York: Plenum Press.

Norris, K. S., & Harvey, G. W. (1974). Sound transmission in the porpoise head. *Journal of the Acoustical Society of America, 56,* 659–663.

Officer, C. B. (1958). *Introduction to the theory of sound transmission, with application to the ocean.* New York: McGraw-Hill.

Parnell, J. E. (1963). *Estimates of auditory frequency response limits as a function of mammalian ossicular density.* Lockheed California Company Report No. 17080.

Penner, R. H., & Kadane, J. (1980). Biosonar interpulse interval as an indicator of attending distance in *Tursiops truncatus. Journal of the Acoustical Society of America, 68,* S97.

Popper, A. N. (1980). Behavioral measures of odontocete hearing. In R.-G. Busnel & J. F. Fish (Eds.), *Animal sonar systems* (pp. 469–481). New York: Plenum Press.

Renaud, D. L., & Popper, A. N. (1975). Sound localization by the bottlenose porpoise (*Tursiops truncatus*). *Journal of Experimental Biology, 63,* 569–585.

Reyesenback de Haan, F. W. (1957). Hearing in whales. *Acta Oto-laryngolica, 134* (suppl.) 1–114.

Rice, C. E., Schubert, E. D., & West, R. A. (1969). An auditory sensitivity at high frequency. *Psychological Record, 19,* 611–615.

Ridgway, S. H. (1983). Dolphin hearing and sound production in health and illness. In R. R. Fay & G. Gourevitch (Eds.), *Perspectives on modern auditory research: Papers in Honor of E. G. Wever.* Groton, CT: Amphora Press.

Romanenko, Y. V. (1973). Investigating generation of echolocation pulses in dolphins. *Zoologiya Zhurnal, 22,* 1698. Joint Publications Research Service 61553.

Schnitzler, H.-U., & Henson, O. W., (1980). Performance of airborne animal sonar systems. I. Microchiroptera. In R.-G. Busnel & J. F. Fish (Eds.), *Animal sonar systems* (pp. 109–195). New York: Plenum Press.

Sharf, B. (1970). Critical bands. In J. V. Tobias (Ed.), *Foundations of modern auditory theory.* New York: Academic Press.

Shower, E. G., & Biddulph, R. (1931). Differential pitch sensitivity of the ear. *Journal of the Acoustical Society of America, 3,* 275–287.

Thompson, R. K. R., & Herman, L. M. (1975). Underwater frequency discrimination in the bottlenosed dolphin (1–140 kHz) and the human (1–8 kHz). *Journal of the Acoustical Society of America, 57,* 943–948.

Urick, R. J. (1967). *Principles of underwater sound for engineers.* New York: McGraw-Hill.

von Bekesy, G. (1957, August). The ear. *Scientific American,* pp. 66–77.

von Bekesy, G. (1960). *Experiments in hearing.* Translated and edited by E. G. Wever. New York: McGraw-Hill.

Wegel, R. L., & Lane, C. E. (1924). The auditory masking of one pure tone by another and its probable relation to the dynamics of the inner ear. *Physiological Reviews, 23,* 266–285.

Wever, E. G., Palin, J. G., & Ridgway, S. H. (1971). The cochlea of the dolphin (*Tursiops truncatus*). *Proceedings of the National Academy of Sciences, 68,* 2381.

Wood, F. G. (1964). Discussion. In W. N. Tavolga (Ed.), *Marine bioacoustics* (pp. 395–396). New York: Pergamon Press.

Zwicker, E. (1961). Subdivision of the audible frequency range into critical bands (*Frequenzyruppen*). *Journal of the Acoustical Society of America, 33,* 248.

Zwicker, E., Flottorp, G., & Stevens, S. S. (1957). Critical bandwidth in loudness summation. *Journal of the Acoustical Society of America, 29,* 548–557.

COGNITION AND INTELLIGENCE OF DOLPHINS

Ronald J. Schusterman

How intelligent are dolphins? Compared with what other animals? What criteria should be used to judge intelligence? Are these intellectual standards set by humans or are they dictated by the life style and natural history of dolphins (i.e., by the nature of their feeding ecology, predator defense and social organization)? How do we study the intelligence and cognition of dolphins and what precisely do these terms mean? Should we emphasize the notion that intelligent behavior reflects various aspects of cognition (e.g., memory, expectancies, conceptualization, intentionality, etc.) or are we primarily concerned with long-term fitness maximizing behaviors? In what ways are the cognitive components, i.e., the short term aspects of intelligent behavior, related to those behaviors which, in the long haul, tend to maximize an individual's inclusive biological fitness? What cognitive characteristics do dolphins have in common with smaller brained creatures such as pigeons and rats, and what skills are unique to dolphins, i.e., what are their cognitive specializations?

The papers in this section deal with these and other knotty issues of animal intelligence in a most forthright and illuminating manner. Louis Herman, Karen Pryor, and Harry Jerison deal with proximal factors affecting the perceptual and cognitive worlds of dolphins. Herman approaches the subject empirically, using rigorous experimental techniques in a laboratory setting, while Pryor uses anecdotal observations from an oceanarium setting, and the piece by Jerison is intended to be essentially heuristic. Jerison focuses on the exotic notion that the "enhancement" of echolocation information from objects in the environment may result in group or consensual decision making before joint action is taken. This would be analogous, I suppose, to an electoral process in which an individual's wishes are deferred to the needs of the society. John Eisenberg discusses the selective forces resulting in higher levels of encephalization, and correlates these higher levels with greater cognitive skills. Theodore Bullock, Earl Hunt and Emil Menzel are concerned with the question of how to study and describe intelligence. The issues here are clearly delineated. Bullock and Menzel take a different position from that of Hunt. Menzel, in particular, articulates a nonreductionist, comparative, holistic, organismic, Darwinian approach to the study of intelligent behavior, while Hunt gives what I would characterize as a mechanistic, process-oriented, modeling or analogyzing account. I whole-heartedly agree with Menzel's warning about analogyzing between shaping pigeons to solve problems and the reasoning ability of chimpanzees, and about confusing problems of artificial intelligence with problems of biological intelligence. However, I do think that some experiments with simpler organisms, like pigeons and rats, enable us to focus our attention better on certain cognitive processes, like memory, with the aim of establishing continuity of species with regard to a particular cognitive ability. Moreover, Hunt suggests an exciting line of research in comparing the intelligence of man, animal and machine.

Although dolphins like some nonhuman primates may use semantic signaling under free-ranging conditions, we currently have no reason to believe, as apparently John Lilly did about a quarter of a century ago, that dolphins possess a sonic language which they use to communicate with one another about past and future events. Nor is there any evidence to date suggesting that dolphin sonic emissions reflect a language analogous to human spoken language which enables them to think in "words" as well as in "images". However, Herman does suggest that the brains of dolphins may be specialized for processing sights and sounds into temporal patterns, with the implication that dolphins have specialized cognitive skills. Do these skills play a role in language acquisition?

Questions about the linguistic behavior of animals and the extent to which man and other animals share mental abilities have been revived. There is little question that teaching artificial languages to anthropoid apes, which began in earnest in the late 1960s, played a major role in the revival of the Darwinian thesis for mental continuity and the recent burgeoning of research in comparative animal cognition. Herman's recent work on the ability of dolphins to comprehend the meaning and structural features of artificial acoustical and gestural languages is seen as a direct offshoot of the ape language research and should aid in assessing the cognitive abilities of dolphins relative to other highly encephalized species. One of the key questions here is the extent to which artificial language comprehension depends on the acquisition of conditional discriminations.

Other rigorous research efforts are needed to gain a wider appreciation of the intelligence of dolphins as well as other marine mammals. The expense of these efforts is enormous and comparative psychologists and behavioral biologists will need all the help they can get from public and private granting agencies. In particular, oceanariums and aquariums throughout the world can help by making some of their dolphins, pinnipeds, sea otters and other biological resources as well as facilities available for the noninvasive behavioral procedures currently in use or being devised for studying cognition and intelligence of marine mammals. Benefits from cognitive research accruing to the institutions displaying dolphins to the public will be of a dual nature. First, cognitive research will increase the educational aspects of the marine mammal exhibits. Second, show performances will be able to incorporate newly devised behavioral preparations to demonstrate first hand dolphin or sea lion reasoning abilities to the public. Indeed, the stage is set and the time is right for more intensive comparative study of cognition in dolphins and other marine mammals.

6 The Perceptual Worlds of Dolphins

Harry J. Jerison
University of California, Los Angeles

I have accepted the assignment to speculate about the way dolphins perceive the external world. The issue is the kind raised by Immanuel Kant in his "Critique of Pure Reason" (Kant, 1787/1934), parts of which can be read as an essay on the human perceptual world. In addition to his metaphysics, which need not concern us, Kant presented a useful psychological theory of the structure of the experience of reality, which he described as a priori knowledge. The data for the theory happened to be his personal experience, but it may be possible to suggest something comparable about the dolphin's world.

There are different constraints on theorizing that is to be based on behavioral rather than on experiential data, and there is only behavioral evidence for speculations ("theories") about the mind of the dolphin. One tactic is to imagine an animal's experiences, as suggested by its behavior and by the anatomy and physiology of its sensory and motor systems. The accepted (Lloyd Morgan's) canon for reconstructing an animal's perceptual world is to identify it with the simplest picture that is consistent with the data. A few unusual features of the world of the dolphin are made evident this way, but the result may be less satisfactory for dolphins than for members of most other species with which this strategy has been followed. Different experiences can be consistent with the same behaviors, and the simplest possible world may not be the world built by the dolphin's brain.

A true picture of the dolphin's perceptual world can be developed only if we accept an additional constraint. A "most parsimonious" explanation for a given behavior must account for the energetic investment of the organism in the neural control of the behavior, as well as for the behavior itself. We must keep in mind that the world of the dolphin is constructed by one of the largest information

141

processing systems that has evolved in vertebrates and that neural tissue is, energetically, the most costly tissue in which to invest. On the assumption that *evolution* is parsimonious we have to establish the benefits that have balanced this costly investment in neural tissue. Our speculations have to invoke brain mechanisms that are known to require large amounts of nervous tissue. We must, therefore, consider the way large, as opposed to small, amounts of neural tissue are invested in the control of behavior and experience. We must, in short, make a statement on the brain/mind problem as a problem in neurobiology.

Some Preliminaries on the Brain/Mind Problem

The following view of brain/mind relations, which is close to the consensus among neurobiologists who enjoy speculation, is implicit in my approach to the assignment: A brain is an organ that processes information from the external world, and large brains do this as hierarchically organized processing systems. At a very high level in the hierarchy the processing takes the form of a representation, or model, of a possible world (Craik, 1943/1967; cf. Jerison, 1973). At this level, neural activity is transformed into "chunks" (Simon, 1974) of information about "space" and "time," and about "objects" that include other individuals and the self.

Since the model that is constructed is based on physically defined information from the external world, and since it is processed by nerve cells and neural networks that are structurally similar in different animals, the models constructed by different individuals of the same species, or even of different animal species, are likely to be similar. The models would differ to the extent that sensory (including motor-feedback) systems differ, that environments differ, and that nervous systems differ. It seems natural, when applying this view to man, to consider the model as known directly as the "real world." The work of the brain is, therefore, at least partly to construct a reality, which is the ordinary real world of everyday experience. Kant described the structure of such a world for the human species, and his successors, the neoKantian biologists (von Uexküll, 1920, 1934/1957; cf. Lorenz, 1977), accepted the challenge of reconstructing perceptual worlds (*Umwelten*) of other animal species. This essay is on *Umwelt* in dolphins.

I undertake the analysis, then, with the basic assumption that perceptual worlds are creations of the brain. To this proposition I add two assertions. First, the construction of perceptual worlds is information processing that can be performed only by enormously large and complex neural networks. Second, such constructions account for the gross enlargement of the brain in "higher" vertebrates (birds and mammals), the enlargement beyond the requirements for controlling the body, which is called "structural encephalization." I have discussed these notions at length elsewhere (Jerison, 1973, 1982, 1983, 1985a, 1985b).

They imply that the large relative and absolute size of the dolphin's brain are important clues to this animal's perceptual world.

My assignment is to discuss perceptual worlds, but I have already used the word "mind" in discussing this problem. The usage was not a slip. The ideas of *Umwelt* and of mind in animals are, in my view, the same (cf. Walker, 1983). I do not believe that there are fundamental distinctions between perceptual and cognitive aspects of our knowledge of the external world, although we may wish to distinguish between perception and cognition in order to suggest something about the immediacy of the information processing that is going on. We would then recognize that there are cognitive dimensions of perception, for example, those that have been a feature of the psychophysics of recent decades as reviewed in Carterette and Friedman (1974, and other volumes in their 10 volume "Handbook of Perception"). Even very simple perceptual acts, such as the detection of weak lights or tones, involve complex decisions (Green & Swets, 1966; cf. Schusterman, 1980, on processes of this type in dolphins). Most of us would include such decision making among cognitive adaptations, even though it may involve "knowing" without awareness. Many of the classic topics on perception chosen for inclusion by Carterette and Friedman in their Handbook are more obviously cognitive, including the perception of speech and language.

Perceptual Worlds: *Umwelten*

We must now review some general features of *Umwelten* in animals, if we are to reconstruct the dolphin's world. The human *Umwelt* is especially important for this exercise, first, because we experience it as well as behave in it, and in using it as a point of reference we can avoid the behaviorist reductionism that may oversimplify our guesses about the perceptual world of another species. Second, our *Umwelt* is the only one we know that is created by a very large-brained animal. The worlds of all animals are exotic to us, however, and it will be enlightening to consider a few case histories in comparative psychology in which perceptual worlds, or *Umwelten,* of nonhuman species have been reconstructed (cf. von Uexküll, 1934/1957).

Some of the differences among *Umwelten* that have been established are, indeed, fantastic. Can you imagine an experience that might be correlated with the light-compass reaction? The information is a triangulation of external objects relative to an observer and the sun, and these data are correlated with information from an internal clock (Fraenkel & Gunn, 1940; Gould, 1980; Griffin, 1976). If the reaction were represented as a perceptual experience (beyond reflex activity), the experience would presumably be of immediate unquestioned knowledge of compass directions in addition to the three-dimensional Euclidian space that Kant described as known a priori. It would be part of our reality, if our lives were governed by sensory information of the kind available to ants and bees. The incorporation of two reference points, the self and the sun, rather that the unitary self as a single "origin" for a map of the external world, would almost certainly lead to different perspectives about the fundamental dimensions of reality. It is interesting to imagine the additional categories that Kant might have recognized as a priori were we equipped with this navigational system.

The construction of the self as one of the objects in the brain's "real world" undoubtedly requires a very large investment in neural processing machinery. Like all objects, the self is based on information processed by the brain. External information about reference axes of space and time, with the self at a center, and internal information about the position and orientation of the head and body, are obvious elements in the construction. Memories, expectations, plans, and so forth are additional elements. Were this kind of construction part of the dolphin's world, perhaps the most unusual features might arise from the role of echolocation as a source of information about the external world (Wood & Evans, 1980).

In later sections of this essay I will be concerned mainly with information about the external world provided by echolocation, but I do not wish to imply that only such an exotic sensing system would lead to major differences in *Umwelten*. Most land mammals live in worlds that would seem odd to us, because of shifts in the relative importance of information from the familiar modalities. In most species, for example, olfaction and nocturnal vision are much more important than in humans or other higher primates, and diurnal vision is less important (Eisenberg, 1981). Like adding an exotic sensing system, such as echolocation (Busnel & Fish, 1980), or the electric senses of many fish (Bullock, 1982), changing the balance of information among familiar modalities would also result in the differentiation of specialized perceptual worlds. In dolphins, current evidence on brain maps (Bullock & Gurevich, 1979; Wood & Evans, 1980) is consistent with the idea that auditory/vocal adaptations, presumably including those involved in echolocation, account for a significant fraction of the brain's enlargement, and it is natural to look at behavioral systems in which those adaptations are involved for clues about unusual features in the *Umwelt*.

Echolocation for Knowledge of the External World

When I think about animals that echolocate, such as bats and dolphins, I do what most of us do: I imagine their acoustic worlds as somehow equivalent to our visual worlds. I imagine that kind of world as built up of sequential (time-labeled) elements that are transformed into a spatial array the way a television raster generates a picture. Successive instants in time are labeled as x-values on a time-line abcissa, as it were, and the echolocation signals that are sent and received are correlated with those times. These become cues about the contents of a "pixel" (unit of dot-size) painted on a retina-like screen at that position of the x-coordinate. Kinaesthetic and proprioceptive data on the position and orientation of the head and body augment information about the x-coordinate and establish values of the y-coordinate, and data on intensity for the pixel could determine a z-coordinate and give information about brightness and distance. By analogy with the visual system we may assume that the constructed space is filled within perhaps 50–100 msec with a pointillistic representation of an external world. The required imagination is slightly more difficult than thinking about how we convert successive images on a movie screen into a knowledge (perception) of time and motion, but this may be because the idea of visual space is so natural for us that we have no sense of wonder about its construction from data at the retinas. The auditory system has to construct individual frames, as it were, and must also analyze the frames sequentially to create objects embedded in space and time.

The physical and biological basis for the construction of auditory space is reasonably well understood. For sensing a sound's location in space, the time interval between the sound's arrival at each ear, which may be as short as 10 μsec, is analyzed at a bulbar level in the brain as the basic datum for localizing the sound, although higher levels, including auditory cortex, are also involved (Erulkar, 1972). The point for perception is that the physical and neurophysiological data are of time differences, but the human experience is of space rather than time. The experience of a sound embedded in space is direct. Echolocation could, similarly, generate experiences of objects embedded in a three-dimensional world.

The information for echolocation is analyzed at tectal and cortical levels of the auditory central nervous system. This may raise another problem, because the experience of space (as a Kantian category, as it were) may be related to activities in the spatially organized visual central nervous system. Vision begins with activity of a two-dimensional retina, in which labels for x, y-coordinates are inherent in its structure. The spatial labels are maintained as the neural information is funneled centrally to midbrain and forebrain visual centers. Our imagery about external space appears to be visual (Kosslyn, 1980), even though many functional systems in the brain and body contribute information about space. It may be that the imagery reflects a space-construction function for regions in the brain conventionally called "visual" (rather than "spatial") and that space is constructed by that system even if inputs to it are from other sensory modalities. There would then have to be connections between the auditory and "visual" centers, if space is to be created by a brain in which the specialized systems for echolocation contribute to the construction. Whatever the neurobiology of its localization (perhaps as a "distributed" neural system [Mountcastle, 1978]), space as an experience is presumably constructed by all mammalian brains, and information from echolocation would reach the "space-construction" system in the brain.

Echolocation and Brain Size

Echolocation is an exotic function that requires unusual neural adaptations, but this does not explain the unusually large brain in dolphins and their relatives. The same sensorimotor specialization occurs in other groups, most notably in relatively small-brained insect-eating bats. We know that much of the bat's brain is devoted to supporting echolocation (Schnitzler & Ostwald, 1983; Suga, Niwa, & Taniguchi, 1983), but all of the neurons in this brain, which weighs less than a gram (Pirlot & Stephan, 1970), could be packed into a fraction of a convolution of a 1500-gram dolphin brain. If dolphins evolved an echolocation system no more elaborate in function than a bat's, the enlargement of their brains to accommodate the neural machinery of the system would not contribute measurably to their encephalization. We may, nevertheless, be on the right track in identifying echolocation as related to the expansion of the dolphin's brain, if we go beyond the simple sensorimotor adaptation. We have to suggest something about the way information from echolocation enters into the animal's world, the way it is used in the construction of reality.

Although specific sensory systems contribute to perceptual worlds of each species, the *Umwelt,* as discussed here, is based on information from all sensory systems. Auditory, visual, tactile, olfactory, gustatory, kinaesthetic and proprioceptive data contribute.

The human condition, in which language is also recognized as contributing to our *Umwelt* (cf. Kosslyn, 1980; Pavio, 1978; Whorf, 1956), suggests that there may be important dimensions in the *Umwelten* of other species, which are decoupled from the sensory surfaces. Appropriately enhanced, echolocation could be the basis for such a species-typical perceptual/cognitive dimension. If there are elaborate cognitive enhancements of echolocation in dolphins, they could be controlled only by a very enlarged brain.

Before considering such possible perceptual/cognitive dimensions, and to keep the matter of brain size in perspective, we should note how much information even small mammalian brains handle. If the neuron is the unit of processing, it is significant that a 1 gram brain would have more than 10^7 cortical neurons. (Between-species morphometrics of the brain are remarkably orderly [Jerison, 1985b], and this enables one to make the computation confidently.) The number of neurons in the whole brain is certainly much greater, since the quantitative data are from counts of cortical neurons only; the mammalian cerebellum, for example, contains several times as many neurons as the cerebral cortex (Eccles, 1973). It is evident that even small mammalian brains are large information processing systems. Distinguishing between the bat and dolphin brain with respect to size is a distinction between the large and almost inconceivably large. Although no one has actually counted them, the number of neurons in the human or dolphin brain, that is brains weighing about 1500 g, may be of the order of 10^{11} (cf. Mountcastle, 1978).

Large Brains and Perceptual/Cognitive Systems

Mammals are encephalized because of the evolution of functions that enhance an animal's knowledge of the external world. The evidence is from the enlarged brain in the earliest mammals (Jerison, 1973) and from the fact that sensorimotor projection systems account for much of the present enlargement of the mammalian brain (Jones & Powell, 1970). Projection systems in the most completely studied species include what were once labeled "association areas" (Bullier, 1983; Diamond, 1979; Merzenich & Kaas, 1980; cf. Welker, 1976), which suggests that advanced brain functions are enhancements of more elementary sensorimotor functions. The enhancements are presumably what we study when we study perception and cognition. If this argument is correct, encephalization in mammals is correlated with improved perceptual and cognitive processing. My task, then, is to be more specific about such processing in dolphins, but I have not yet presented a general enough view of the processing itself.

The processing can be thought of as the organization of the flow of neural information to control the body's activity in its environment. The amount of such information is extremely great, thousands of millions of events per sec, and the processing, at some level, consists of making a model of a world (the body and its environment) within which the activity of smaller units of neural information are placed. Craik (1943/1967) discussed the place of physical models in the structure of thought, and, among other things, his view anticipated modern ideas about how computers must be programmed to handle large amounts of information. The "external world" as a model may be thought of as, perhaps, the highest level of organization in a hierarchically organized information processing system.

In all very large processing systems, information must be organized in a hierarchical way (von Neumann, 1958). There are clusters of data with rules about their combination, which are "chunks" (programs or subroutines), each of which is small enough to be useful in the face of potential errors of analysis (Simon, 1974). Higher order chunks organized by the brain could refer to perceptual units such as the objects of the external world, a frame of reference such as three-dimensional space, a time-line, and a self that is at the center of a many-dimensional constructed world. This amounts to the construction by the brain of a possible world. The view is that we experience at least parts of the model directly as the reality that we are aware of or "know."

[This is also a way of looking at the idea of conscious and unconscious processes and the exchange of information between the conscious and unconscious: The highest order chunk is the most complete model of a possible world, which can be "scanned" by the "self," another chunk in the hierarchy. The model of reality based on the data scanned at one interval is the portion of experience that is "conscious." It may not be clear how such speculation can be put to experimental analysis, but it is consistent with the rest of our story about higher order relations between brain, behavior, and experience.]

Perhaps the most important feature of a "possible world" must be its stability, or constancy, an aspect of perception emphasized by Gestalt psychologists (Koffka, 1935). For example, we perceive a coin to be the same even when it moves or we move, despite the coin's shifting retinal image. Neural information about the coin is actually in flux all the time, even when the external situation is more or less fixed. In fact all neural analysis of environmental events is, in this sense, based on "uncertain" data about the environment, because the information from the external world is transformed into a statistical rather than deterministic neural code, at least as far as one can tell from observations of trains of responses by nerve cells to environmental stimuli (cf. Bullock, Orklund, & Grinnell, 1977, p. 236, who show that the "statistical" code is reliable in important ways). This changing information must be represented at some level in the hierarchy as transformed into events occurring in a stable, or constant, "real world," and such constancy is one remarkable outcome of neural activity in the brain.

In the human species, the most remarkable of the constancies created by the brain may be the constancy of the self as observer. For us, the self is the firm, permanent object to which external events are referred. There is integrity of the body image, and only rarely (in the absence of neuropathology) is there a serious question of what is and is not part of the self (Schilder, 1950). The self is constant in time as well as space: We change as we age, of course, and yet we "know" that we remain the same. This and other intuitions about the self are so strong that it is difficult to imagine a creature with information processing capacity comparable to ours, equal to us in intelligence, as it were (Jerison, 1982, 1985a), that has a differently constructed self. However, if we accept the constructed nature of the self, and the likelihood that it is this kind of construction that is one of the benefits of (and explanations for) an enlarged brain, we should consider the possibility that it might be on such a dimension of a model of reality that other large brained species might have evolved significantly. Unless there were remarkably parallel evolution, it is also on such a dimension that dolphins are most likely to be dramatically different from us, because they are likely to use their processing capacity in species-typical ways, just as so much of the processing capacity of the human brain is used in controlling species-typical human language.

The maintenance of constancies, both of the self and of less esoteric features of experienced reality, may be likened to the problem of pattern recognition in computer science, and this adds force to the identification of such adaptations as an explanation for encephalization. Pattern recognition is unusually difficult even for the largest computers (Dewdney, 1984). Very large amounts of processing capacity are required, and there is no reason to assume that this is less true for natural systems, such as brains, than for computers (see, e.g., Marr's [1980] computational model for visual pattern perception). I have argued that it is this kind of processing, which provides great benefits in the form of information about the environment, that explains the costly evolutionary "investment" by higher vertebrates in additional nervous tissue (Jerison, 1973, 1983, 1985a; cf. Oakley, 1983).

There are surely different possible worlds that would be consistent with the same neural data about the external world. In imagining the world built by a species with unusual sensory adaptations, living in an exotic environment, and having an unusually enlarged brain, there are different constraints on speculation than in the analysis of smaller brained species that live in environments similar to our own. The "a priori categories" that organize experience in dolphins could be significantly different from the ones that Kant proposed as universal because he identified them in the human species. Although Kant was not especially concerned with the self, it is as fundamental as any category constructed by the brain, and the nature of self is surely significantly different in different species (cf. Humphrey, 1983).

THE DOLPHIN'S WORLD

From the chapters in this volume by C. Scott Johnson, by Nachtigall, and by Ridgway it is evident that the sensory world of dolphins is very different from that of humans. In addition to its use of echolocation, and the likelihood that it uses no olfactory information at all, the dolphin has unusual "conventional" distance senses of vision and hearing. Though typically mammalian in retinal structure, its visual system may be unique among mammals in apparently lacking uncrossed fibers in the optic chiasma. Its auditory sensitivity to high frequency sound is also unusual for so large an animal (cf. Masterton, Heffner, & Ravizza, 1969). The dolphin's *Umwelt* would be recognized as peculiar even if its brain were not so unusually large.

Yet these sensory features would not, by themselves, lead us to expect the kinds of unusual worlds that must be imagined to account for the large brain. The smallest mammalian brains have enough neural machinery for at least an adequate analysis of the most complex sensory information. As in our discussion of echolocation, we have to consider the enhancement of sensory data that may be performed by the brain, because we have to explain, or at least acknowledge, the additional neural processing machinery available to the dolphin. Although the analysis of the dolphin's world must begin with a review of the sensory information available to dolphins, it must conclude by considering possible perceptual and cognitive enhancements of this information.

Sensory Information

Detailed analysis of delphinid sensory systems is presented in other chapters. I am concerned primarily with the distance senses because of their special significance for information about the external world, and with internal senses, especially the vestibular and kinaesthetic system, which contribute to information about the self. I will not consider "unenhanced" information from the latter group of senses, however, because I have no clues about significant differences between their functions in man and dolphin that suggest interesting speculations about how proprioception may be enhanced in large-brained species. The following seem to be the major contrasts in the distance senses.

The auditory spectrum of dolphins is broader than our own by several octaves in the higher frequencies, but the major unusual feature of their auditory system is its role in echolocation, as discussed earlier. Echolocation could contribute an unusual dimension to the dolphin's world, beyond elementary information about events at a distance. As a sensorimotor adaptation, echolocation has some features that are similar to human language. These are discussed later to suggest possible dimensions of enhancement of information from echolocation.

Somaesthesis in dolphins is not unusual by human standards. Lacking prehensile limbs and opportunities to feel details of their environment, dolphins live in a tactile world that is unlikely to be richer than ours. They are apparently not unusually sensitive to deformations of the skin of the torso that may be introduced by energy transmitted through the water, although such an adaptation would be useful for an aquatic species.

The dolphin's visual world may be comparable to that of prey species, such as deer and rabbits, in covering a 360° field (cf. Marler & Hamilton, 1966), with little or no overlap between the visual fields of the two eyes. The absence of uncrossed chiasmal fibers (a normal condition in birds) suggests perhaps more independence in the control and use of data from the two eyes than occurs in other mammals. Dolphins live in a scotopic visual world, as it were, limited by a retina that is comparable to that of most mammals rather than the cone-rich retina that evolved in primates. (The complete decussation at the optic chiasma also suggests a neurological dimension of difference that may be worth considering. There may be more independent specialization of the two cerebral hemispheres than occurs in the human species [cf. Ridgway, this volume], though, as in the human species, the callosal system probably insures that the representation of the external world is unified.)

The apparent absence of olfactory data in the dolphin's world is an oddity that may not impress us sufficiently, because we are primates. All anthropoid and hominoid primates have reduced olfactory bulbs, and humans are extreme even for primates (Jerison, 1973, pp. 221–224, 245–253). We almost certainly do not use olfactory data in ways typical of most mammals, in which the olfactory system is a major sensory system (Eisenberg & Kleiman, 1972). Despite its peripheral reduction in humans and other primates, the central "olfactory" system (essentially, the limbic system, as defined by gross phylogenetic comparisons) in primates is essentially normal or only slightly undersized for mammals, and this system supports adaptations to handle a domain of data that may be thought of as enhanced olfactory information about the external world.

We no longer relate these rhinencephalic functions, classically considered to have evolved from olfactory projection systems, to olfaction, because the processing is so remote from our usual notions of smell (Ebbesson, 1980). The functions of this "olfactory brain" are a model for thinking about enhancements. Its work is usually described as controlling emotion and motivation as well as cognitive functions of memory, mapping, and some aspects of human language. These functions are, therefore, examples of enhanced "smell," in a sense, and they are not even remotely related to our intuitions about smell. The absence of peripheral olfactory inputs combined with reasonably well developed central rhinencephalic processing capacity in paleocortical tissue (Jacobs, McFarland, & Morgane, 1979), suggests the possibility that there have been as unusual enhancements of this system in dolphins (and all cetaceans) as there have been in humans.

In the balance, the dolphin's *sensed* (unenhanced, as it were) external world does not seem unusually difficult to refer to a human perspective. The dolphin's sensory data could be used for a model of reality that is mappable on our own experienced real world. The evidence is in these sentences. We can, after all, describe the dolphin's sensory world, even that based on echolocation, in human terms and with human language using imagery from events in our everyday lives.

There are additional criteria for an analysis of *Umwelt* in dolphins that are available in features of their external environment, because the dolphin's constructed world is presumably an adaptation to the requirements for knowing that environment. A special feature of an aquatic world in human perspective is the absence of a stable platform of the sort provided by land for terrestrial species. This negative point should be kept in mind, because the ground on which we stand and the special role of gravity in adaptations of land mammals are so central biologically and yet play so unremarked a role in human awareness. Our intuitions may fail when we try to imagine perceptual adaptations in species in which these features are either absent or radically different from ours, because we tend to be unaware of our own adaptations.

Information about gravity is likely to be important in dolphins to aid orientation by providing data about body position relative to the surface of the ocean, the horizon, and so on. Although there is no land to serve as a fixed platform in the dolphin's world, orientation in space is likely to be even more critical in their lives than in ours, because theirs is a world with more spatial degrees of freedom than ours. (The analogy can be to devices to simulate 0-g environments, which are used for training astronauts. These are giant swings with six "degrees of freedom" that permit the trainee to control rotation about the body's axes as well as linear movement.) It is more like the zero gravity world of space flight than the ordinary terrestrial world of everyday life. It is interesting that zero gravity in space has apparently raised no unique perceptual problems among astronauts. The few scattered reports of vertigo and nausea, perhaps related to conflicting visual and proprioceptive cues, are problems that arise occasionally in normal environments. Human sensory capacities are not strained by zero gravity.

As in the case of echolocation discussed earlier, the expectation about each sensory system is that it would enter easily into the polysensory resources used by a brain in the construction of reality. Seemingly exotic sensory adaptations can be accommodated without requiring massive additional amounts of neural tissue for their support.

An aquatic world seems exotic, but it is appropriate to recall that about half of the world's vertebrate species (bony and cartilaginous fish) are adapted for life in that world. Some fish have truly exotic sensory adaptations, including electric senses (Bullock, 1982), yet none are highly encephalized; most are well below the mammalian grade (Jerison, 1985a, 1985b). They provide sufficient evidence, if any were required, that a life in aquatic niches can be supported by relatively little brain tissue. The special features of the dolphin's world that are related to its enlarged brain must involve unusual enhancements of sensory information rather than the information in elementary form. These could be the construction of special spatial and temporal reference axes, of geographical maps that extend beyond immediate sense data, of the self, or unsuspected adaptations for which there is no analog in human experience, that improve the way sensory information is used.

Behaviorism and the Analysis of Sensory Enhancements

In the analysis of "unenhanced" sensory activity the goal is to determine stimulus-response relationships. When stimuli or responses are on dimensions that we do not experience, their discovery may make for elegant science, but it is really enough to measure or describe the data. That was the achievement, for example, in the analysis of the response of insects to polarized light, the elaborate story of the dance of the bees, and the response of fish to electric fields. Such analyses are major successes of behavioral biology. Yet we may recognize that private experience, like overt behavior, is also a phenomenon of nature, and should be wary of a rigid behaviorism that excludes experience from "natural philosophy." The behaviorist ideal can distort the analysis of experience by placing it under inappropriate constraints.

We understand an animal's experience by imagining it as our own, were we restricted to the sensory information available to the animal (cf. Griffin, 1976; Humphrey, 1983; von Uexküll, 1934/1957; Walker, 1983). That was the approach taken earlier in this chapter in the analysis of echolocation. The analogy was between acoustic data about echoes and photic data from very rapidly painted arrays of pixels on a television screen. Transformed by the optical system of the eye and stimulating the retina, the pixels generate patterns of neural activity in the optic nerve that are analyzed by the central visual nervous system. A visual scene is experienced as part of the neural response to the sequence of dots on a television screen, and an analogous spatial experience might be generated by the sequence of neural activity in the auditory system generated by the data for echolocation. The information could be comparable to that available to the visual system, except that it is provided by a different sensory channel. One might "see" the same scene if the dots consisted of units of information processed by a fast auditory apparatus, such as the one involved in echolocation.

The questions then become, what does one "see" when alternative channels or different processing networks are used? These questions are answered by reconstructing *Umwelten* of other species. In view of the difficulty in answering this kind of "mind/brain" question for the human species, even for the familiar channels and networks of the visual system (see Marr, 1980), we may be forgiven some reluctance about offering precise answers for dolphins. In fact, a precise answer is not really necessary. It may matter little for the description of perception if the experience associated with a stimulus-response function differs in different species. The description of "behavior" (i.e., the input-output function) without considering the experience is likely to be sufficient for most scientific purposes. We need not put ourselves into the mind of a bee to appreciate von Frisch's (1950) discoveries about their "language."

Unfortunately, in addition to omitting the analysis of a significant experiential component of perception, this standard also limits possibilities of applying our second constraint on speculations, namely, that we posit functions known to require large amounts of brain tissue. It is conceivable that dolphins analyze sensory information available to them in very unusual ways and live in extremely odd worlds by human criteria. We can be sure that this is the case for visual worlds, in which we have to imagine a possible world in which the self is at the center of a hemisphere and "knows" a 360° world. We recognize that this world must differ from that constructed from the (120°) proscenium stage of human experience. And yet it is possible to convey a picture of that world, exotic as it is; it is the way we describe the visual world of many other mammals, such as horses, cattle, and rabbits, as mentioned before (Marler & Hamilton, 1966). Our human verbal (or even pictorial) description is not especially good, but it is good enough to convey some notion of this feature of the worlds of other animals.

However, describing these "worlds" is only the beginning of our problem. Horses and sheep and rabbits are "average" or less than average in brain size compared to other mammals. Difficult though a 360° visual field may be for the imagination of a (primate) species that lives in a 120° world, the construction of a hemisphere of existence is apparently not an especially difficult problem for a mammalian brain, assuming, as I have in this chapter, and as most of us do, that such a construction of an experienced world is a normal result of processing sensory information by mammals. Its construction would not account for encephalization beyond an average grade and could not explain any of the enlargement of the dolphin's brain.

Among the sensorimotor adaptations of dolphins, echolocation may be unusual in the way the sensory-motor interaction occurs, but all "sensory" data have motor components. For example, proprioceptive feedback from the eye muscles is necessary for normal vision; vestibular inputs about head position and movement are essential components of visual and auditory spatial localization. Exotic as it is, echolocation is another adaptation of that sort. I am not concerned with the adaptation per se (see C. Scott Johnson, this volume) but with its possible enhancements.

Let us review some formal and structural relations between echolocation and the human language system that make the possible enhancements of data from echolocation especially interesting. Like echolocation, human language is based on the intimate interaction between motor and sensory component systems (see Liberman, Cooper, Shankweiler, & Studdert-Kennedy, 1967). The clinical distinction between motor and sensory aphasia and the fine distinctions that can be made among the pathologies (Benson, 1979) are evidence that this feature of language can be dissected by disease. I have already reviewed one notion of "enhancement" in the case of the olfactory system. For another case of what an enhancement may be like, note that speech and language are enhancements of auditory-vocal neural information, and we should contrast the information in language with that in nonlinguistic vocalizations. The information in language is semantic and grammatical (Liberman, 1974) and is unimaginable from the analysis of acoustic data in the speech signal. Enhancements of echolocation that might occur in dolphins could be quite different from and may be equally unimaginable from the use of echolocation in the detection and identification of targets.

A hint about a possibly unique feature of the dolphin's world that could be an enhancement of echolocation, may be available in one nonlinguistic feature of language in our own *Umwelt*. I have been impressed by the cognitive role of language, which is recognized, but underemphasized, perhaps because of the obvious importance of language as an adaptation for communication. Experiments on the interaction between consciousness, language, and perception (Marcel, 1983a, 1983b) prove that language contributes to the construction of our perceptual world. But human language is more than that. As a communication system that is also a cognitive system (i.e., part of the "reality" building system) it may build perceptual worlds for one individual from "sense data" provided by other individuals. Something analogous could occur in dolphins.

Human Language as a Model of "Sensory Enhancement"

It seems strange to think of language as a *sensory* enhancement. Yet, if sensory data are the basis of our knowledge of reality, the "basis" is clearly enhanced by language. Language is a double medium, which supports both cognition and communication. It is so much a means of communication that language and communication have been treated as synonyms. This is surely the intent when calling rule-governed communication in honey bees a language. But human language is also involved in the construction of a perceptual world. Bartlett's (1932) famous experiments on the way words affect one's memories of objects, Vygotsky's (1934/1962) analysis of the close relation of thought to language, and cross-cultural studies pioneered by Sapir (1949) and Whorf (1956) in which the varieties of experience could be linked to the vocabularies available for their description, all demonstrate the place of human language in the structure of the perceptual world in man.

A uniquely human experience (species-typical for *Homo sapiens*) may arise from our use of a cognitive system as a communication system. I have argued (Jerison, 1973, 1982) that this was a kind of evolutionary accident and that this bimodal system (language) first evolved as an adaptation in response to selection pressures for geographical mapping of an extended range. The adaptation may have occurred as the solution by a primate species of a major navigational and range-maintenance problem that arose when it invaded a social predator's niche. Its auditory-vocal system, which is typically well-developed as a communication system in simian primates, supplemented an olfactory and scent-marking apparatus that is normally used by mammals to map an area.

If language began to evolve in that way it would have required enhancements of sensory systems for knowing the external world. It is in this sense a cognitive system, that is, a system that contributes to the reality constructed by a brain and which, in experience, contributes to one's knowledge of the external world. In its later evolution, human language obviously became a specialized adaptation for communication as well, and much more elaborate than typical primate communication systems. If one communicates with a cognitive system, as one does when one uses language, the *data* communicated are part of one's reality, a part constructed by a "sensory" language system. The data in the message could contribute to the reality constructed by the brain in the same way as information from one's own retina or cochlea. When I talk to you with words I send you data that are also elements of my reality as constructed by my brain. When you hear my words you receive data in a form that can be transformed directly into the reality that your brain builds. If the visual system worked in this way we would be able to share one another's visual experiences directly, because we would have access to the neural data and visual code of one another's visual system.

This may be the genuinely unique feature of language. When we talk we share realities, and that may occur in only a limited way in communication in other animal species (cf. Smith, this volume). More normal is a dog's signaling another dog, for example, by the complex set of sign stimuli that include baring its teeth, piloerection and other skeletal and autonomic displays that are unmistakable even to human observers. The message for another dog is, in effect, a command to retreat. We can also communicate in this way, and may do so when we blush, flinch, smile, laugh and so on, using "body" languages. But when we talk we share what is on our minds, or better, following the argument just presented, we share our minds. When we read we share past states of the mind of the writer, and when we write we invite any reader to share our thoughts. As an audience at a movie, we may join collectively in living a few lives in the cleverly created worlds of the writer, director, editor and actors as we experience the pleasures and pains of a "participant-observer." Language is a medium for sharing consciousness.

It requires only slight changes in wording to suggest something analogous in dolphins, but the extension of the argument to dolphins can be even more interesting. As I present it I want to emphasize that the suggestions are about analogies and not identities in the dolphin's world. There is no reason to treat communication among dolphins as based on a natural language that is at all like the human, species-typical, grammatical and syntactic language, even though it now seems clear that dolphins, like chimpanzees, can learn to communicate with signs and rules taken from human language (Herman, Richards, & Wolz, 1984; Herman, this volume). This analysis is concerned primarily with the concept or construct of self and the place of this construct in an animal's *Umwelt*. The construct is related to enhanced auditory-vocal (i.e., language) mechanisms in humans and may be related to enhanced echolocation in dolphins.

Human Language and Self-Consciousness

Our immediate experience of the external world is anchored in the complementary experience that we are each unique in our privately known realities. The experience has linguistic dimensions, as we have just seen, which contribute to our private knowledge but add a feature that makes the knowledge less private. We recognize that when we read a book or watch a film our experiences may be very similar to those of other people. When we converse or read or go to a movie, or when we lose ourselves in an audience at the movies or at a ball game, we may be less completely individual. We become members of a group or crowd. The fundamental experience remains private, of course, an activity of a self, which, under analysis, is recognizable as a brain-construction that does the experiencing and observing.

There is an obvious benefit from the construction of this kind of self, for example, to reduce possible confusion of parts of the body, such as a paw or tail, with objects that are not part of the self. It is amusing to see a kitten or puppy fail this test, but failure is so unusual that we may, perhaps mistakenly, call it play. It is easier to assume that when a full range of cues is available, most mammals know self from not-self; the distinction is maintained so strongly that only orang and chimpanzee have, thus far, been able to learn to recognize their mirror images (patently not-self by location) as somehow related to the self (Gallup, 1979). In nature, the ability to construct a reality and a self from the neural code is adaptive, because it enables animals to know what is to be protected and preserved. Humphrey (1978) has pointed out the adaptive value of a self-consciousness in which an animal may use a capacity to imagine itself in the role of another animal to predict the behavior of the other animal.

By self-consciousness we normally mean more than the simple distinction between self and not-self. We mean the awareness of the self as knower and the awareness of knowing as part of reality. I suggest that the evolution of this self-consciousness was a by-product of the evolution of human language, an adaptation to resolve an unusual problem about the nature of the external world that can arise when experiences can be based on data from the language "sense." Those experiences could be generated by others: a speaker to whom one is listening or the author of a book that one is reading. How are they to be distinguished from experiences generated by data about the external world received from one's own conventional senses? If it is true that a reality is constructed from available sensory data, "reality" should be as real when the information is exclusively linguistic as when it is exclusively auditory or exclusively visual. When a scene is constructed in one's imagination on the basis of words in a book, is there some danger that the scene will be mistaken for reality? There would be, if no additional constructions were available. We may find the external world odd when we are temporarily deprived of part of the normal sensory data about it, e.g., if we are deafened or blinded, but we do not lose the sense that it is real.

This is not a trivial problem. Confusions do occur in distinguishing among realities constructed by the brain. Most of us have known such confusions when our dreams have been sufficiently vivid, but they are serious and abiding problems in the psychoses. "Hearing voices" is a recognized symptom in diagnosis, and the psychotic's private world may be more real for him than any other.

I suggest that the human solution of these problems included the evolution of self-consciousness as a perceptual and cognitive function: to know that one knows and to recognize that knowledge may come from sources other than one's eyes and ears, e.g. from dreams and books. Such self-consciousness, according to this view, is a by-product of the evolution of species-typical human language, rather than a general feature of the evolution of consciousness in mammals as awareness of the external world (cf. Humphrey, 1978, 1983).

The conventional system that evolved in connection with the evolution of language was the human auditory-vocal system, and these speculations on the evolution of self and self-consciousness describe further elaborations of the system. I think they are reasonable speculations, consistent with available data. "Enhancement" of the auditory-vocal system in human evolution included, according to this analysis, the evolution of language and the evolution of self consciousness. This can be a model of how unusual an enhancement of a sensorimotor system may be: how remote the enhanced capacities may be from the elementary capacities.

The human self is a central feature of our experience. So central is it that we enjoy solipsistic speculations about whether others are real or not, and even whether the external world is real, because we recognize intuitively that the self is a knower and that knowledge of the external world is funneled through that self. Fundamental knowledge is of the self, as it were; everything else is inference. The distinction between self and not-self is a "given" of experience, and part of that fundamental knowledge. It takes special evidence: neurological symptoms like hemi-neglect and phantom limbs, philosophical discussions of the place of pared versus unpared finger nails in one's concept of self, and so forth, to make us recognize that the boundary between self and not-self is not quite absolute.

The evidence on dolphins, as I read it, does not force one to assume that individuation in this species evolved in the same way as in humans, especially if the human concept of self includes species-typical components that are related to the evolution of human language. What sort of self/nonself dichotomy would make sense in a large-brained nonlinguistic echolocating marine mammal? More generally, what sorts of things (if the self is one such thing) are proper objects in the dolphin's world?

Enhancements in Dolphins: Auditory and Visual Objects

I undertake this speculation emphasizing two bits of evidence as points of departure. There is, first, the synchronous swimming and other unusual group behavior at institutions like Sea World, in which the behavioral capacities of dolphins are displayed in performance for an audience. There is extensive information on related behaviors in the field, which is part of the lore of cetacean ethology (see chapters by Bradbury and by Johnson and Norris, this volume). Second, and especially relevant for the way sensory information enters the perceptual world of dolphins, is Herman's (1980) impressive report of a dolphin's "behavioral capacity" in discrimination learning based on visual versus auditory information. I begin with Herman's results.

His dolphin learned to discriminate visual forms only with difficulty, and was erratic in using these as guides to the "correct response" in a standard setup. It had no problem with comparable tasks based on auditory cues, which were sometimes learned in a single trial, and its memory for and its ability to discriminate sounds were comparable or even superior to those of its human testers. The limitation in the visual tasks was not due to a sensory incapacity, because the tasks could be learned if they were first taught with the help of auditory cues. This may tell us something about when and how a dolphin knows that an object is an object.

For the dolphin an object is apparently more of an object when it is heard than when it is seen (cf. Wood, 1953). This odd situation is almost the opposite of the human experience in which auditory "objects" may be difficult to identify; even familiar sounds may be identifiable only after much training. (Consider the difficulties of identifying bird calls, and the effort bird watchers devote to learning the calls.) Words and simple melodies (whatever "simple" means in this case) may be the only really natural auditory objects for us. Words are the only acoustically complex signals that are easily identifiable auditory objects for most of us, although this is true only for the words in our own language. Other complex sounds are random sounds, and are apparently more difficult for us than for dolphins to identify.

The human brain may be better organized to impose structure on visual data than on auditory data, and in the dolphins the reverse may be true. The analysis of visual form has been explained as the work of a computational system that is inherent in the structure of the visual system (Marr, 1980). As we have learned more about the auditory system in primates, it has become clear that it, too, can impose structure on auditory data, especially for "natural" sounds (e.g., Eimas, 1985; Heffner & Heffner, 1984). In any event, the dolphin's auditory capacity is apparently sufficient to supply the necessary structure to auditory patterns that are not especially natural but are easy for human experimenters to generate in the laboratory. There is plasticity in their auditory world (but not in their visual world), which appears to be comparable to the plasticity that enables us to recognize almost any oddly shaped objects we *see* in our external environment.

Enhancements in Dolphins: The Self as an Object

The possibility that a dolphin's objects are most real when based on auditory data has interesting implications for the kind of self that might be constructed by dolphins, especially when echolocation is recognized as a sensorimotor mode that can construct auditory objects. Echolocation shares an unusual structural feature with human language, namely, that its contribution to the reality that is presumably built by the brain depends on a signal generated by the animal, as well as its echo, and the signal could be generated by another animal as well as by the self. Fenton (1980) points out that bats intercept vocal signals of the type used by other echolocating bats, and various social interactions appear to depend on this ability. It is reasonable to assume that dolphins can do the same.

Although Fenton emphasizes the social interactions of bats that are based on echolocation, his suggestions are primarily about agonistic interactions and the discovery of foraging areas, and he points out that the interactions lead to problems as well as advantages for individual animals. The problems are related to competition, with advantages to the winning competitor but costs to the loser. There may be no costs and only benefits when the data are used cooperatively (as they can be by foraging bats when resources are plentiful).

Agonistic and foraging behaviors are important for dolphins as they are for all animals, but the interesting speculations are on the experience rather than behavior of dolphins. It is appropriate to minimize our entities (applying Lloyd Morgan's canon or Occam's Razor) when analyzing the small-brained bat's world, and to assume as simple as possible a set of experiences in bat species to be correlated with the behaviors. In large-brained dolphins, on the other hand, we must propose possible enhancements of the data from echolocation. Because of the nature of echolocation, some of the enhancement may be comparable to the human experience of self. Let us consider how such experiences might be constructed from data based on echolocation, and what it may mean for objects to be more natural if they are auditory rather than visual.

In the construction of a reality from echolocation, dolphins could share "raw" sensory information with one another, which would be even more unusual than the way we share the enhanced sensory data provided by language. (They might, of course, also share enhanced sensory data analogously to the way we do when we communicate with language.) Their situation could be like the one mentioned earlier: the direct experience of another's vision of the external world that would be possible if we could share neural data in the visual system. Intercepted echolocation data could generate objects that are experienced in more nearly the same way by different individuals than ever occurs in communal human experiences when we are passive observers of the same external environment. Since the data are in the auditory domain the "objects" that they generate would be as real as human seen-objects rather than heard-"objects," that are so difficult for us to imagine. They could be vivid natural objects in the dolphin's world. Although it is difficult to speculate on possible enhancements of this cognitive capacity, a possibility of a "social," or "communal," cognition is worth exploring.

Enhancements in Dolphins: "Communal" Cognition

A perceptual world constructed from shared raw data would permit unusual group cohesion and a different kind of individuation. We might imagine such a world as an extreme variant of the world we know in the movie theater, a world generated by a film maker, which we can experience communally, though passively, with others in the audience. The dolphin's social world could be an active rather than purely passive communal world. It would not be impossible to have shared elementary decision making in such a world as well as shared responses. For example, if the neural work underlying the kind of decision making that occurs in performance on signal detection tasks (Green & Swets, 1966) involved circuits in the echolocation system, the processes underlying decisions might be shared by several dolphins as a group when facing the same task. The dolphin's would indeed be an unusual world, because the perception itself would be "known" directly (just as we "know" when we detect a signal, unaware of the decision-making) as a communal event in which several different animals participate. The idea of an "individual" would have to be redefined if judgments could be made in this way. A communal experience might actually change the boundaries of the self to include several individuals.

If the perceptual world of dolphins were as unusual as just described it should produce surprising features in their behavior. Behaviors that have been observed have been explained in less fanciful ways, however, but "less fanciful" really means no more than an explanation of an observation consistent with one's experiences, and in the case of the phenomenon of "self" in other animals, it is difficult to avoid being anthropomorphic, because our own is the only self that we have experienced.

A recent analysis of complex behavior in the field (Conner & Norris, 1982) argued that dolphins are reciprocal altruists as defined by sociobiologists, that is, that they do favors for one another, "expecting" to benefit from this because of the reciprocity. This was based on many examples of higher order social behaviors that have been observed in the field. Such altruism might need a label other than "reciprocal" if the "individual" (at least during the altruistic episode) was not one animal but a group of dolphins sharing communally in the experience as well as the behavior.

Their many synchronized activities displayed at public performances makes dolphins fascinating to watch, and such behavior is seen in the field as well. Sociality seems to be built into these animals. John Lilly, who has been one of the most experienced, thoughtful and imaginative of the scientists who have studied these animals, makes a special point of the importance of establishing a social bond with dolphins as experimental subjects (Lilly, 1975). This is echoed by the expert trainers who prepare elaborate public exhibitions, and is recognized by all scientists who have worked closely with the animals. It is well known that social bonds between experimenter and animal subject are important in many contexts (Lorenz, 1977), and especially so with highly encephalized mammals such as apes (Premack & Woodruff, 1978). It is not necessary to assume the existence of an unusual perceptual world such as that just described as a possibility in dolphins to account for these social interactions, but the behaviors in dolphins, such as reciprocal altruism, are easy to understand in terms of a communal *Umwelt*.

Behavioral tests designed to explore the speculation would be based on the assumption that dolphins share a preceptual code, analogous in some ways to human language. These would not be conventional cognitive tests of learning capacities or of abilities to see relations, nor would they use all of the conventional controls. One control to avoid would be any interference with acoustic signalling and echolocation, because that would interfere with the natural perceptual code. It would disrupt the construction of the hypothesized communal self.

Conventional tests are usually anthropomorphic in the perspective of this speculation, because they assume a concept of self in other animals that is similar to the one organized by human brains. Natural and universal as that self may appear to us, accepting this appearance as reality perpetuates Kant's error of assuming that our experience is an unfailing guide to the nature of the external world. Our experience is a guide to the nature of our experience. We do not expect the physicist's world to be an intuitively sensible one and can tolerate strange models of the universe that make better sense of experimental data than is available from our intuition. Models of behavior all involve the identification of individuals as behaving units, and I have suggested that we may be misled by our perception of our own species-typical self when we assume things about analogous constructs in the perceptual worlds of other animals.

Emotion and Motivation in the Dolphin's World

To go slightly beyond my assignment, there are a few additional features of the dolphin's *Umwelt* that should be considered that are not usually labeled perceptual. These were touched on briefly earlier when the problem of bonding between experimenter and subject was raised. It is a difficult issue to discuss, because the data are even fuzzier than those considered thus far. In examining the perceptual world we have, at least, the well-established methods of sensory physiology and comparative neurology at our disposal. There is nothing like this available for the study of attachment among individuals, important as that issue is for all social animals. I raise the issue because of the major discovery reported by Morgane (this volume) about the microscopic organization of the dolphin's neocortex and related discoveries summarized a few years ago by Bullock and Gurevich (1979) on gross differences between dolphins and almost all other mammals in the extent of lamination in the cerebral cortex.

Neocortical structures in dolphins seem to be organized as if they were paleocortical. It is difficult to integrate such organization with the facts of cortical localization that are presently available (Ridgway, this volume), yet it is important to incorporate this anatomical perspective in one's speculations.

There are two points that I will raise. First, recognizing structural similarities between "neocortex" in dolphins and paleocortical structures in other mammals, it may be that there are functional similarities as well. Further, recognizing that paleocortical systems in rats, cats, and monkeys are important in autonomic, emotional and motivational activities, it may be that higher brain functions in dolphins are more strongly represented on those dimensions (or in those domains) than are comparable human functions. Social bonding might involve deeper and, in a sense, more primitive attachments in dolphins than we usually see in humans (cf. Ainsworth, Blehar, Waters, & Wall, 1978). Reinforcement as a variable in experiments on learning might be unusual in dolphins, if their cortical systems have unusual motivational properties.

Second, can information processing capacity as represented by the quantity of neural machinery be accepted as a generally useful measure despite this unusual structural organization of the dolphin's brain? The question is whether it makes sense to recognize an equality in encephalization between man and dolphin despite the fact that the human neocortex is layered and the dolphin's is less so, and that the dolphin's cortex is so peculiarly organized with respect to the cell types described by Morgane. For the present, it may be heuristic to continue to accept simple quantitative measures and to disregard the differences in organization. It is consistent with evolutionary thinking that the processing done by a brain will be appropriate to the analytic problems that it must solve. For example, a bird's forebrain areas that are functionally equivalent to the mammalian visual cortex are structurally peculiar. They are nonlayered and are similar in appearance to the basal ganglia in mammals, and yet birds are primate-like in their capacities to use visual information. There is no clue about other differences between birds and mammals that might be related to this gross difference in the structural organization of their brains. The peculiarly arranged dolphin cortex might handle the same kinds and amounts of neural information as is handled by the normally layered neocortex of other mammals, but the best guess is that fundamental differences in processing will be discovered that are correlated with the structural differences.

SUMMARY AND CONCLUSIONS

In these speculations I have treated experienced reality as a construction of the brain and the self as part of experienced reality. This implies that our idea of self may be a species-typical feature of our perceptual world. Among the implications of this view in a reconstruction of the *Umwelt* of dolphins is that although something analogous to self as we know it may occur in dolphins its expression is likely to be different from ours. The self as an object can presumably be made only by large amounts of brain tissue, as required by the "second constraint" mentioned at the beginning of this chapter. The self is the center and point of reference in the perceptual world.

When knowledge of the external world is based on echolocation, the sensory data as enhanced in a large-brained species may generate an especially unusual self. Information from echolocation can be sensed at the same time by several individuals, and if dolphins were to construct their realities from such data the perceptual worlds of a group of dolphins would be much more nearly the same than ever occurs in human groups. I suggested the analogy to the way we would know the external world if we could share neural data actually processed in the visual system. In this sense a group of dolphins could occasionally share an immediate experience of "self" in their perceptual worlds.

There is no reason to assume that individual dolphins do not distinguish themselves from other individuals or cannot distinguish between self and notself. But if their reality is built partly from the analysis of data generated by echolocation, the analysis, enhanced, could at least occasionally take the form of a communal model of reality rather than the kind of model that our brain generates and which we know as *private* experience. An extended self could be constructed (and experienced) by a group of several animals. It is hard to imagine that an individual animal would not be identified as such, especially in view of the ubiquitousness of signature calls among the vocal signals of cetaceans. But the signature call could also be an element in a more extended self that included several individuals. The basis of the extended, communal self would be the presence of identical patterns of activity at the hierarchical level of "objects" in a particular "real world" as constructed from echolocation data in the different brains.

There are, of course, many implications for an understanding of behavior if the self is not always a unique and fixed reference point for the external world. My intention was to consider this possibility, and I conclude that it should not be rejected for dolphins.

REFERENCES

Ainsworth, M. D. S., Blehar, M. C., Waters, E., & Wall, S. (1978) *Patterns of attachment: A psychological study of the strange situation.* Hillsdale, NJ: Lawrence Erlbaum Associates.

Bartlett, F. C. (1932). *Remembering.* Cambridge, England: Cambridge University Press.

Benson, D. F. (1979). *Aphasia, alexia, and agraphia.* New York, Edinburgh, and London: Churchill Livingstone Inc.

Bullier, J. (1983). Les cartes du cerveau. *La Recherche, 14*(No. 148), 1202–1214.

Bullock, T. H. (1982). Electroreception. *Annual Review of Neuroscience, 5,* 121–170.

Bullock, T. H., & Gurevich, V. S. (1979). Soviet literature on the nervous system and psychobiology of cetaceans. *International Review of Neurobiology, 21,* 47–127.

Bullock, T. H., Orklund, R., & Grinell, A. (1977). *Introduction to nervous systems.* San Francisco: W. H. Freeman.

Busnel, R.-G., & Fish, J. F. (Eds.). (1980). *Animal sonar systems.* New York: Plenum Press.

Carterette, E. C., & Friedman, M. P. (1974). *Handbook of perception, Volume 2: Psychophysical judgment and measurement.* New York: Academic Press.

Conner, R. C., & Norris, K. S. (1982). Are dolphins reciprocal altruists? *American Naturalist, 119,* 358–374.

Craik, K. J. W. (1943). *The nature of explanation.* London and New York: Cambridge University Press (reprinted in 1967, with postscript).

Dewdney, A. K. (1984). Computer recreations. *Scientific American, 251*(3), 22–34.

Diamond, I. T. (1979). The subdivisions of the neocortex: A proposal to revise the traditional view of sensory, motor, and association areas. *Progress in Psychobiology and Physiological Psychology, 8,* 1–43.

Ebbesson, S. O. E. (Ed.). (1980). *Comparative neurology of the telecephalon.* New York: Plenum.

Eccles, J. C. (1973). The cerebellum as a computer: Patterns in space and time. *Journal of Physiology, 229,* 1–32.

Eimas, P. D. (1985). The perception of speech in early infancy. *Scientific American, 252*(1), 46–58.

Eisenberg, J. F. (1981). *The mammalian radiations.* Chicago: University of Chicago Press.

Eisenberg, J. F., & Kleiman, D. (1972). Olfactory communication in mammals. *Annual Review of Ecology and Systematics, 3,* 1–31.

Erulkar, S. C. (1972). Comparative aspects of spatial localization of sound. *Physiological Review, 52,* 237–360.

Fenton, M. B. (1980). Adaptiveness and ecology of echolocation in terrestrial (aerial) systems. In R.-G. Busnel & J. F. Fish, (Eds.), *Animal sonar systems* (pp. 427–446). New York: Plunum Press.

Fraenkel, G. S., & Gunn, D. L. (1940). *The orientation of animals: Kineses, taxes and compass reactions.* Oxford: The Clarendon Press. (Reprinted. New York: Dover Books, 1961)

Gallup, G. G., Jr. (1979). Self-awareness in primates. *American Scientist, 67,* 417–421.

Gould, J. L. (1980). Sun compensation by bees. *Science, 207,* 545–547.

Green, D. M., & Swets, J. S. (1966). *Signal detection theory and psychophysics.* New York: Wiley.

Griffin, D. R. (1976). *The question of animal awareness.* New York: Rockefeller University Press.

Heffner, H. E., & Heffner, R. S. (1984). Temporal lobe lesions and perception of species-typical vocalizations by macaques. *Science, 226,* 75–76.

Herman, L. M. (1980). Cognitive characteristics of dolphins. In L. M. Herman (Ed.), *Cetacean behavior: Mechanisms and functions* (pp. 363–429). New York: Wiley.

Herman, L. M., Richards, D. G., & Wolz, J. P. (1984). Comprehension of sentences by bottlenosed dolphins. *Cognition, 16,* 129–219.

Humphrey, N. K. (1978). Nature's psychologists. *New Scientist, 78,* 900–903.

Humphrey, N. K. (1983). *Consciousness regained.* Oxford: Oxford University Press.

Jacobs, M. S., McFarland, W. L., & Morgane, P. J. (1979). The anatomy of the brain of the bottlenose dolphin (*Tursiops truncatus*). Rhinic lobe (rhinencephalon): The archicortex. *Brain Research Bulletin, 4*(Suppl.1), 1–108.

Jerison, H. J. (1973). *Evolution of the brain and intelligence.* New York: Academic Press.

Jerison, H. J. (1982). The evolution of biological intelligence. In R. J. Sternberg (Ed.). *Handbook of human intelligence* (pp. 723–791). New York & London: Cambridge University Press.

Jerison, H. J. (1983). The evolution of the mammalian brain as an information processing system. In J. F. Eisenberg & D. G. Kleiman (Ed.), *Advances in the study of mammalian behavior* (pp. 113–146). Special Publication No. 7, American Society of Mammalogists.

Jerison, H. J. (1985a). Animal intelligence as encephalization. *Philosophical Transactions of the Royal Society* (London), *B308,* 21–35.

Jerison, H. J. (1985b). Issues in brain evolution. *Oxford Surveys in Evolutionary Biology, 2,* (102–134).

Jones, E. G., & Powell, T. P. S. (1970). An anatomical study of converging sensory pathways within the cerebral cortex of the monkey. *Brain, 93,* 793–820.

Kant, I. (1934). *Critique of pure reason* (2nd ed.). (J. M. D. Meiklejohn, Trans., with an Introduction by A. D. Lindsay). London: J. M. Dent & Sons Ltd., Everyman's Library. (Original work published 1787)

Koffka, K. (1935). *Principles of Gestalt psychology.* New York: Harcourt.

Kosslyn, S. M. (1980). *Image and mind.* Cambridge, MA: Harvard University Press.

Liberman, A. M. (1974). The specialization of the language hemisphere. In F. O. Schmitt & F. G. Warden (Eds.), *The neurosciences: Third study program* (pp. 43–56). Cambridge, MA: MIT Press.

Liberman, A. M., Cooper, F. S., Shankweiler, D. P., & Studdert-Kennedy, M. (1967). Perception of the speech code. *Psychological Review, 74,* 431–461.

Lilly, J. C. (1975). *Lilly on dolphins.* Garden City, NY: Doubleday/Anchor Press.

Lorenz, K. (1977). *Behind the mirror: A search for a natural history of human knowledge* (R. Taylor, Trans.). New York and London: Harcourt Brace Jovanovich. (Original work published 1973)

Marcel, A. J. (1983a). Conscious and unconscious perception: Experiments on visual masking and word recognition. *Cognitive Psychology, 15,* 197–237.

Marcel, A. J. (1983b). Conscious and unconscious perception: An approach to the relations between phenomenal experience and perceptual processes. *Cognitive Psychology, 15,* 238–300.

Marler, P., & Hamilton, W. J. III. (1966). *Mechanisms of animal behavior.* New York: Wiley.

Marr, D. (1980). Visual information processing: the structure and creation of visual representations. *Philosophical Transaction of the Royal Society* (London), *B290,* 199–218.

Masterton, R. B., Heffner, H. E., & Ravizza, R. J. (1969). The evolution of human hearing. *Journal of the Acoustical Society of America, 45,* 966–985.

Merzenich, M. M., & Kaas, J. H. (1980). Principles of organization of sensory-perceptual systems in mammals. *Progress in Psychobiology and Physiological Psychology, 9,* 1–42.

Mountcastle, V. B. (1978). An organizing principle for cerebral function: The unit module and the distributed system. In G. M. Edelman & V. B. Mountcastle (Eds.), *The mindful brain* (pp. 7–50). Cambridge, MA: MIT Press.

Oakely, D. A. (1983). The varieties of memory: A phylogenetic approach. In A. Mayes (Ed.), *Memory in animals and humans* (pp. 20–81). Wokingham, England: Van Nostrand Reinhold.

Pavio, A. (1978). The relationship between verbal and perceptual codes. In E. C. Carterette & M. P. Friedman (Eds.), *Handbook of perception* (Vol. 8., pp. 375–397). New York: Academic Press.

Pirlot, P., & Stephan, H. (1970). Encephalization in Chiroptera. *Canadian Journal of Zoology, 48,* 433–444.

Premack, D., & Woodruff, G. (1978). Does the chimpanzee have a theory of mind? *Behavioral and Brain Sciences, 4,* 515–526.

Sapir, E. (1949). *Selected writings of Edward Sapir in language, culture and personality.* (D. G. Mandelbaum, Ed.) Berkeley: University of California Press.

Schilder, P. (1950). *The image and appearance of the human body.* New York: International Universities Press.

Schnitzler, H-U., & Ostwald, J. (1983). Adaptations for the detection of fluttering insects by echolocation in horseshoe bats. In J.-P. Ewert, R. R. Capranica, & D. J. Ingle (Eds.), *Advances in vertebrate neuroethology* (pp. 801–827). New York and London: Plenum Press.

Schusterman, R. J. (1980). Behavioral methodology in echolocation by marine animals. In R.-G. Busnel & J. F. Fish (Eds.), *Animal sonar systems* (pp. 11–41). New York: Plenum Press.

Simon, H. A. (1974). How big is a chunk? *Science, 183,* 482–488.

Suga, N., Niwa, H., & Taniguchi, I. (1983). Representation of biosonar information in the auditory cortex of the mustached bat, with emphasis on representation of target velocity information. In J.-P. Ewert, R. R. Capranica, & D. J. Ingle (Eds.), *Advances in vertebrate neuroethology* (pp. 829–867). New York and London: Plenum Press.

von Frisch, K. (1950). *Bees: Their chemical senses, vision, and language.* Ithaca, NY: Cornell University Press.

Von Neumann, J. (1958). *The computer and the brain.* New Haven: Yale University Press.

von Uexküll, J. (1920). *Theoretical biology.* New York: Harcourt Brace.

von Uexküll, J. (1957). A stroll through the worlds of animals and men. In C. H. Schiller (Ed. and Trans.), *Instinctive behavior: The development of a modern concept* (pp. 5–80). New York: International Universities Press. (Original work titled "Streifzüge durch die Umwelten von Teiren und Menschen," published 1934)

Vygotsky, L. S. (1962). *Language and thought.* (E. Hanfmann & G. Vakar, Trans.). Cambridge, MA: MIT Press. (Original work published 1934)

Walker, S. (1983). *Animal thought.* London: Routledge & Kegan Paul.

Welker, W. I. (Ed.). (1976). Neocortical mapping studies. *Brain, Behavior and Evolution, 13* (Whole No. 4), 241–343.

Whorf, B. L. (1956). *Language, thought and reality* (edited with an introduction by B. J. Carroll). Cambridge, MA: MIT Press.

Wood, F. G. (1953). Underwater sound production and concurrent behavior of captive porpoises, *Tursiops truncatus* and *Stenella pagiodon. Bulletin of Marine Science of the Gulf and Caribbean, 3,* 120–133.

Wood, F. G., & Evans, W. E. (1980). Adaptiveness and ecology of echolocation in toothed whales. In R.-G. Busnel & J. F. Fish (Eds.), *Animal sonar systems* (pp. 381–425). New York: Plenum Press.

7

How Can You Tell if an Animal is Intelligent?

E. W. Menzel, Jr.
State University of New York at Stony Brook

"Darwin revolutionized our study of nature by taking the actual variation among actual things as central to the reality, not as an annoying disturbance to be wished away. That revolution is not yet completed. Biology remains in many ways obdurately Platonic. . . . (For example,) Neurobiologists want to know how the brain works, but they don't say whose brain. Presumably when you've seen one brain you have seen them all" (Lewontin, 1983).

FOLK TAXONOMY

Trying to arrive at an airtight definition of intelligence is as thankless a job as trying to define Life or Man. The worst pitfall here, so far as most biologists are concerned, is Platonic essentialism (Mayr, 1982). Let me give two brief illustrations. According to Diogenes Laertius:

> Plato had defined Man as an animal, biped and featherless, and was applauded. Diogenes plucked a fowl and brought it into the lecture-room with the words, 'Here is Plato's man.' In consequence of which there was added to the definition, 'having broad nails.' (1970, p. 43).
>
> As Plato was conversing about Ideas and using the nouns 'tablehood' and 'cuphood,' (Diogenes) said, 'Table and cup I see; but your tablehood and cuphood, Plato, I can nowise see.' 'That's readily accounted for,' said Plato, 'for you have the eyes to see the visible table and cup; but not the understanding by which ideal tablehood and cuphood are discerned.' (1970, p. 55).

Are the ghosts of Plato and Diogenes dead? I do not think so, at least when I read the current debates about vultures that in some sense are "tool users," rats that in some sense "reason," and apes and dolphins that in some sense acquire "human langauge." It would, of course, be unfair to accuse current investigators (as Plato has been accused today) of providing us only with a taxonomy of our own verbal concepts rather than with a taxonomy of living beings or of mentality; but I do agree with Popper (1972) that in science debates about terminology and the definitions of concepts are to be avoided, and that insofar as possible one's attention should always be focused instead on natural phenomena and what they signify.

As I see it, where one draws the line between intelligent beings and nonintelligent ones, or between various subclasses of intelligent beings, rests above all on one's perception of kinship and (even more explicitly) upon empathy. This way of putting the problem renders it amenable to a Darwinian analysis; but at the same time, perception of kinship (especially in man) is not a fixed quantity but is highly influenced by one's own experiences and by social traditions and precedents, and the sufficiency of neo-Darwinian principles alone is highly questionable (Sahlins, 1976; Slobodkin, 1976). It seems to me that one necessary step toward developing a true taxonomy of intelligence will be to set aside our scientific chauvinism toward the "folk taxonomies" of the rest of humanity, and to see what we can learn from them. (See here Blurton Jones, & Konner, 1976; Cole, Gay, Glick, & Sharp, 1971; Cole & Scribner, 1974.) To what degree do they correlate with the morphological taxonomies of classical biology? Are the rankings of various species that we have in the past come up with from our "standardized" tests of intelligence really that different from what a 5-year-old child might surmise from an afternoon at the zoo? Classical taxonomists would not think the latter question absurd or insulting to their own discipline, and it would be most interesting to see more formal analyses conducted to discover the sorts of cues that human judges use in making their judgments as to the relative intelligence of other species (cf. Hediger, 1968; Lorenz, 1971).

The poet, Robert Frost, once uncovered a tiny and (to him) unfamiliar insect and was just about to kill it when he noticed its apparent fear reactions toward him, and restrained himself. Said he, "I have a mind myself and recognize/ Mind when I meet with it in any guise." I suspect that a majority of people— including zoologists and comparative psychologists—share this sentiment and belief; where we differ from one another is in precisely where we would "draw the lines" between different classes of beings, what decision rules and criteria we employ, and what judgments we would be inclined to render should the case be genuinely in doubt by these rules and criteria. The poet's statement is important not because it solves the question of how we can tell whether animals are intelligent (which it obviously doesn't solve) but because it cuts the Gordian knot of essentialistic philosophising and returns us to commonsense. To fall back on my original analogy, few citizens of ancient Athens and few laypersons today would have any difficulty in telling humans from other species or estimating other kinship relations with fair accuracy—it is the philosophers and scientists who make it sound like an impossible problem. It is not in fact far fetched to say that almost any animal faced with almost any novel object faces a "taxonomic" problem that is quite analogous to Robert Frost's problem (Lorenz, 1971; Menzel & Johnson, 1976; Simpson, 1961; cf. also Green & Marler, 1979); our job, as students of intelligence, is in effect to identify and classify how they in turn identify and classify the things that are important to them, and how they then act upon these decisions.

How do we get from "knowing that" to "knowing how" and, insofar as possible, avoid the Scylla of animism and anthropomorphism on the one hand and the Charybdis of Cartesian mechanism on the other hand? That is the question. It seems to me that Lloyd Morgan's Canon of parsimony is useful largely as a corrective to the "Type 1 errors" that almost all modern undergraduates have already picked up before commencing their formal training in behavioral science, and that a majority of behavioral scientists (including Lloyd Morgan) retained throughout their lives in earlier eras. What about "Type 2 errors," however? The appropriate canons and decision rules for dealing with them have yet to be satisfactorily formulated—at least within the domain of animal psychology.

INTELLIGENCE WITHIN THE DOMAIN OF BEHAVIORAL SCIENCE

Even the most adamant of antimentalists do not very often hesitate to say that they can directly see "real behavior" on the part of their animals, rather than (say) merely the moment-to-moment spatial positions of various "stimuli" which they infer to constitute an "animal" that is "moving" in such a way that it seems to be "chasing" and "hitting at" its "conspecific." From the perspective of behavioral science the leap from this to saying that one can sometimes directly see the difference between a relatively intelligent performance and a relatively stupid performance is a large one; but from the perspective of a physical scientist the leap would seem a very small one, for either statement assumes an unmeasurably greater quantity of intellect (or whatever you wish to call it) than one would ever attribute to anything other than a live animal, unless one were speaking facetiously or by way of pure animistic metaphor (Gibson, 1979; Köhler, 1925, 1929; Menzel, 1979).

Just where cold, hard, neutral objective facts leave off and the biases of the human observer begin is a moot point; in my opinion, the role of the observer cannot be discounted in any science, and the goal of "total objectivity" is a metaphysical delusion. Stated otherwise, intelligence as most current investigators view it "is not an entity, nor even a dimension in a person, but rather an evaluation of a behavior sequence (or the average of many such) from the point of view of its adaptive adequacy. What constitutes intelligence depends on what the situation demands'' (Tuddenham, as cited by Hodos, 1982). Such evaluations are, of course, customarily those of outside human observers. But regardless of who makes them they are provisional guesses or working estimates which might have to be revised in the light of further information. For excellent reviews of the concept of "biological intelligence," see Hodos (1982) and Jerison (1982).

QUANTITY VS. QUALITY

Undoubtedly the strongest single stimulus to research on animal intelligence was Darwin's doctrine of "mental continuity," which held (among other things) that the differences between species were matters of degree rather than of kind. Taken in its extreme form by some investigators, and viewed as a self-sufficient principle, this doctrine in turn led to the conception of intelligence as a unitary, general, quantitative "trait" which all living individual organisms (or at least all animals) possessed in some degree. A primary goal of comparative psychologists was to rank species along this presumed continuum, and to compare their ranking with taxonomists' "phylogenetic ranking." Within the domain of human intelligence testing, closely analogous reasoning was used in some of the earliest research, but the difficulties became obvious much sooner than was the case in comparative psychology. Today, both the concept of unitary general intelligence and the notion of a linear "phylogenetic scale" are, at least officially, all but unanimously rejected by scientists—but this is not to say that they are not still used every day in unofficial discourse, and reflected in the way we treat animals. (The National Institutes of Health guidelines for the humane treatment of animals coincidentally apply almost exclusively to "warm-blooded" vertebrates, and even the most ardent of Animal Rights activists have not thus far agitated on the behalf of cockroaches, endoparasites, or bacteria.)

Actually, qualitative considerations have always entered into the logic of intelligence testing; what has changed is our recognition of their importance, and our recognition that they are, if anything, more consistent with Darwin's views (or at least with neo-Darwinian thinking) than the foregoing logic. Since the time of Binet human intelligence tests have been devices for assessing individuals that are drawn from the same population, and the pitfalls of cross-cultural comparisons have been (at least in principle) well known. What, however, constitutes "the same population" or a population that is homogeous enough to enable one to accurately estimate the relative degree of intelligence of different individuals? Whether one is a comparative psychologist or a human mental tester, this question revolves around the issue of how well individual X is adapted to *its* environment, not how well it responds to environmental pressures that are appropriate for the observer himself (e.g., Gould, 1981; Hodos, 1982; Hodos & Campbell, 1969).

But how far can we push this logic? Most comparative psychologists and ethologists today would say that comparisons of the intelligence of closely related animal populations are more meaningful than comparisons of animals with more remote common ancestry; and, analogously, assuming that one is dealing with species that are capable of learning and of establishing social traditions, comparisons of individuals with similar experiences will be more meaningful than comparisons of individuals with dissimilar experiences. To cut a long story short, just as there is very good reason to scale the quantitative scores of an individual according to the norms for his or her taxonomic status, age group, society, and so forth, there is good reason to recognize the indisputable fact that no two individuals in any larger aggregate are identical in all respects that might "contaminate" an assessment of their relative degrees of intelligence. (As Mayr puts it, "he who does not understand the uniqueness of individuals is unable to understand the working of natural selection" (1982, p. 47).) Thus, one could well conclude that all individuals may be assumed *a priori* to be of precisely equal intelligence—the differences in their quantitative scores being attributable to qualitative differences in the problems they have faced to date, the strategies they have somehow or other come up with for solving those problems, and the way in which the so-called intelligence test is "loaded" for or against them. (For an even more radical statement—to the effect that nonhuman vertebrates have yet to be shown to differ from one another intellectually, either quantitatively or qualitatively—see MacPhail, 1985. And for an excellent recent review of the concepts of mental continuity and discontinuity, see Demarest, 1983.)

To be sure this is an overstatement and an assumption, not an empirical "fact." But precisely the same is true of the belief that individuals differ merely in degree, not in kind. To argue over which position is right and which is false is about like arguing over whether the differences between night and day are qualitative or quantitative. It seems to me that the "qualitative" position is just another way of saying what students of optimal foraging theory (for reviews, see Kamil & Sargent, 1981), if not most neo-Darwinians, have been saying for the past decade. The emphasis is, quite simply, shifted from judgments as to the short-run "adaptive adequacy" of the subject's behavior in a physicalistically "standardized" test situation to the assumption that in the long run every individual will, insofar as possible, behave in such a way as to maximize its inclusive biological fitness, and that apparent short-run lack of "adaptive adequacy" must be assessed in the light of how the specific test situation in question deviates from those situations to which the individual (or its ancestors) has heretofore been adapted and the precise significance of the particular behavior in question within its overall behavioral organization or its "adaptive behavioral complex."

Obviously, we are talking here about biological adaptation in its broadest sense, not "intelligence" as it is ordinarily thought of. But how would one sharply separate the two without getting embroiled in any number of largely unresolvable issues, most particularly the "heredity vs environment" issue? The distinction is, of course, an important and meaningful one—as long as one does not try to make it any sharper than our knowledge regarding such issues warrants. Perhaps, also, it rests as much as anything on the fundamentally different sorts of questions that different investigators ask. Students of intelligence, if not most psychologists in general, have by tradition been concerned with trying to isolate particular sorts of hypothetical internal processes, and to study them as such. Students of adaptation, on the other hand, are concerned above all with how problems are solved. They would not discount any strategy that animals might employ here as irrelevant to the conceptualization of "animal intelligence" as they see this topic simply because it is different from the strategies that we ourselves would employ and that a psychologist might dismiss as "nonintellectual" or even "cheating." Let me, however, try to be even more specific.

SOME WAYS OF STUDYING ANIMAL INTELLIGENCE

In practice the study of animal intelligence has been approached in at least five different ways:

1. *Ecologically* speaking, the central question is how particular species (or societies, or individuals) go about making their living in the world at large. What sorts of problems do they face, what strategies do they use to solve these problems, and how do they cope with novelty and change?

2. *Philosophically* speaking, the issue is whether they comprend what they are doing. Do they apprehend or understand the relationships between novel presented facts in such a way as to guide their actions appropriately; do they fill in certain blanks of information for themselves; do they ever go beyond the information given; is there any glimmer of symbolic activity as opposed to innately "given" sign stimuli, or "mere" conditioned responses?

3. *Psychometrically,* the question is how they rank relative to one another on "standardized" tests that we have some reason to believe can discriminate more intelligent species from less intelligent ones. Such research saw its heyday before the 1960s, when the concepts of unitary "general intelligence" and of any simple linear taxonomic ordering of species were called into serious question. The vast majority of the tests that were used were tests of learning (or, more precisely, speed of learning, as measured by the number of "trials" the subjects required to reach the investigator's criterion of good performance); when classical conditioning or "simple" discrimination learning failed to yield any clear ordering of species, investigators went on to "higher order" tasks such as learning set formation or reversal learning. Fortunately or unfortunately, these tasks have not yielded any simple ordering either.

4. *Anthropocentrically,* the question is whether other animals do what we ourselves do. Can they, for example, count, use or make tools, speak in sen-

tences, lie, imitate one another, or recognize themselves in a mirror? Does a maturing gorilla or monkey go through the same "stages" of intellectual development that have been posited for human children by (say) Jean Piaget; and what is the "most advanced" stage they achieve?

Many of the most illustrious students of animal psychology have followed either this approach or the last one (which might, in the last analysis, be difficult to distinguish from it). As Harry Harlow put it quite explicitly, "Throughout my entire academic life I had never suffered for research ideas, since I simply stole the research ideas from human studies or human problems. I always believed that I should never do anything with monkeys that would not have significance with man. . . . *I firmly believe that one should never study problems in monkeys that cannot be solved in man.* What direction my research might have taken had this not been true, I have no idea" (Harlow & Mears, 1979, p. 1; italics added).

Given such a rationale, it should surely come as no surprise that our own species will tend to rank at the top of the tests that were thus selected—regardless of whatever this might or might not have to do with "intelligence" as a Martian psychologist might see it. In other words, what is actually being studied is other species' relative resemblances to humans. This is, of course, a more straightforward empirical task than trying to identify intelligent performances in the abstract; and I know of no definition of intelligence that is not "loaded" in favor of humans, if not of members of one's own society; so I do not object to it in principle. I do believe, however, that the aims of such studies should be more clearly labelled for what they are, and that one should be equally explicit that who "should" rank at the top of this scale is being assumed beforehand, rather than being considered an open empirical question.

5. *Technologically,* the question is whether or not it would be possible to "shape" seemingly intelligent performances in animals who otherwise show no great proclivity for them, or, for that matter, to create a machine that can do the same thing. Studies of this sort may be undertaken either for theoretical reasons or with the "applied" goal of devising prosthetic devises or training techniques for otherwise handicapped people.

To answer any one of the above five questions we must, either explicitly or implicitly, contrast or compare the particular animal under consideration against some other being, either actual or hypothetical. Thus, most obviously and importantly, it is unlikely that the animal's performance would be called intelligent if it were not judged "significantly different" from that of a being whose entire repertoire is predictable from known Newtonian laws alone or from the so-called laws of Brownian motion (i.e., "chance"). Everyday inanimate objects are, in other words, ordinarily taken by custom as the ultimate standard of nonintelligence or zero intelligence (whatever that is). Additional standards of comparison may of course be necessary, and they may be assumed to entail either zero intelligence (e.g., any animal whose actions presumably entail nothing more than "genetically determined fixed action patterns," any robot devisable by man) or the acme of intelligence (e.g., humans) or efficient adaptation (e.g., an optimal foraging theorist's specification of what would constitute optimal performance). Which such standard of comparison is most appropriate, whether or not it is clearly enough understood in its own right to be of any great use, and whether or not the assumptions that underlie its usage are empirically warranted depend largely upon the particular problem that one is investigating, and upon the point of view of the investigator.

"SIMILARITY" IS A MULTIDIMENSIONAL, NOT A UNIDIMENSIONAL, CONCEPT

Given that judgments regarding intelligence imply some sort of comparative judgment, a further problem arises: By what criterion is the similarity or the difference between our chosen animal and our chosen standard of comparison to be assessed? Here I would draw a sharp distinction between studies of artificial intelligence and radical behaviorists on the one hand and studies of "natural intelligence" on the other hand. The former studies are almost by definition concerned largely with analogical similarity, which is to say that a sufficient demonstration that two beings (e.g., a computer and a human being, a pigeon and a chimpanzee) are "doing fundamentally the same thing" would be to show that an otherwise completely uninformed human judge, who is shown only a formal data transcript that describes the moment-to-moment performances of the two beings in question, could not reliably tell whose data was whose. For most ethologists and comparative psychologists, such a criterion of similarity is insufficient, pre-Darwinian and nonfundamental. Similarity of presumed ontogenetic and (especially) phylogenetic origins, and similarity of presumed internal biological mechanisms strike me as far more important; and any study that fails to consider these criteria is simply irrelevant to the problem of natural intelligence as I see it.

In saying this I am not passing judgment on the relative merits of different sorts of investigations; I am simply saying that they might involve totally different criteria of similarity, and that these criteria are logically independent of one another and have no necessary bearing on one another. Thus, for example, it is very amusing, and instructive in some respects, to learn that one can build a robot (Walter, 1961) and shape a pigeon (Epstein et al., 1981, 1984) to do things that seem analogically similar to the activities of chimpanzees (cf. Gallup, 1977; Köhler, 1925) and human children; but unless one confuses problems of artificial intelligence with problems of natural intelligence it is not in the least obvious what such a demonstration tells us about how the latter activities themselves originated or what internal mechanisms they involve or how they are best characterized. Obviously, the fact that my teachers could somehow or other get me to solve one problem in calculus does not prove that I am the intellectual peer of

Newton and Leibnitz, and that these latter individuals not only did not invent the calculus, but acquired it in "fundamentally" the same fashion that I did. Or—to return to the point from which we commenced this discussion—in what sense is Diogenes' plucked fowl "really" a featherless biped?

HOW HAVE OUR VIEWS OF ANIMAL INTELLIGENCE CHANGED OVER THE PAST TWO OR THREE DECADES?

Here I shall be talking principally about primate research (for more detailed reviews, see Dewsbury, 1984; Fobes & King, 1982). And the first thing to be noted is that whereas up until about the mid 1960s well over half of all of the research that was conducted by behavioral scientists on nonhuman primates could, at least euphemistically, be called "intelligence testing" (see, for example, the reviews by Harlow, 1951; Schrier, Harlow, & Stollnitz, 1965; Yerkes, 1943), by today it is doubtful that more than 10% of the articles that come out each year can be so characterized. On the negative side, this can probably be traced to the demise of the concepts of unitary general intelligence and of the so-called *scala naturae* (Hodos & Campbell, 1969)—and of the notion that the key to understanding adaptive behavior of any sort is to study the ability of individuals to learn new problems (preferably of a sort, moreover, that they would not encounter in everyday life, and for which they are not already "prepared"). On the positive side, it can be traced not only to the "invasion" of behavioral primatology by zoologists and anthropologists, but also to an increasing respect on the part of psychologists themselves for "Darwinian" and "naturalistic" problems and methods. Let me, however, be more specific.

Prior to the 1960s only a handful of primate field studies had been conducted, and their impact on the thinking of laboratory researchers had been almost unnoticeable. By today, they are not only common but are a major source of research ideas even for investigators who have no direct interest in conducting field research themselves. How animals perform on puzzles of our own devising might, in other words, still be of some interest insofar as this might help to explain how they solve the sorts of problems they might face in their native habitats, but fewer and fewer investigators would assume it to be of intrinsic interest without the latter sort of rationalization. (Curiously enough, only a handful of primate field researchers have to date performed experiments of any sort, let alone experimental studies that are explicitly devoted to problem solving or learning. Hopefully, this situation will be remedied in the future.)

The problems that are studied today are far more apt to be concerned with "social" as opposed to "nonsocial" behavior, and hardly anyone still describes communication or social learning or social intelligence as if it were nothing more than a special case of (e.g.) classical or instrumental conditioning, the only distinction being that the "stimulus objects" in question are other animals rather than inanimate objects. (Studies of communication are far more apt to be introduced and discussed with references to ethologists or linguists, if not a "put down" of the theories that dominated psychology a few decades ago.) A principal justification for this shift in research emphasis has been that primates are, after all, social animals. For recent reviews of primate social intelligence, see Kummer (1982) and Mason (1982).

In their methodology, even experimental studies have come to place increasing reliance on observational techniques and on using as one's dependent variables behaviors that are already in the animal's repertoire before one's study begins, rather than using more arbitrary measures that entail special training. The importance of this change can scarcely be overestimated, and the most outstanding single illustration comes from studies of human neonates. Many textbooks in developmental psychology go so far as to say that more has been learned about the "real" sensory, learning, intellectual, and communicative capacities of preverbal infants in the past 2 decades than in the entire prior history of such research, and that this breakthrough is either directly or indirectly attributable to the methods introduced by Fantz (1964), which followed the above rule. (They seldom if ever add in this connection, however, that Fantz's work on human infants was a straightforward extension of a study that he had previously conducted on a newborn chimpanzee under the guidance of Henry Nissen [Fantz, 1958], and that this study in turn was devised on the basis of his work on chickens [Fantz, 1957] in the laboratory of Eckhard Hess. Nor are they very likely to note, when they are discussing chimpanzee research, that the Gardners [1971] very explicitly used a very analogous logic in selecting manual rather than vocal behaviors of chimpanzees as the basis for their attempt to teach chimpanzees a human language, and that the results of their project and others in the same vein might necessitate an analogous revision in our assessment of the capacities of these non-verbal animals. Human infants can obviously think well before they have acquired vocal language; but chimpanzees . . . or chickens. . . ? Here psychology's patron saint is still Descartes rather than Darwin.)

Studies of the ontogenesis of behavior remain as important as ever, but they are much less dominated by the so-called nature-nurture issue and by a search for some single, species-general principle of behavioral modification than was the case in the past. Such studies are more likely, also, to be conducted in a relatively "natural" social setting than to entail the rearing of individual animals in isolation. In all of these respects, the old controversies between ethologists and psychologists are largely a thing of the past.

Perhaps as an after-reaction to the grandiose learning theories of earlier eras (to whose downfall primate researchers, and especially Harry Harlow, contributed very substantially), some investigators would go so far as to say flatly that "there cannot be any grand universal theories of behavior; the nature of the data, primarily the diversity of species, forces on . . . (us) a greater respect for facts and for the diversity of life than for attempts to explain them in a simple way'' (Blurton Jones & Konner, 1976, p. 346). Even they, however, would consider themselves remiss if they were not quite familiar with the modernized synthetic theory of natural selection; and there can be little doubt that, overall, more research today in behavioral primatology is guided by this theory than by all other theories put together, or that it is the leading contender for a "grand universal theory of behavior,'' or at least the cornerstone to it. (This does not, of course, imply that neo-Darwinians are not a very heteogeneous lot, and do not disagree with one another on many details.) Thus far, it has been applied much less to problems of learning and intelligence than to other topics, such as social organization, but this situation is changing (see, for example, Lumsden & Wilson, 1981; Maynard Smith, 1984). Of particular importance here, of course, will be studies in which the investigator's theorizing is not post hoc, but entails some relatively precise and empirically testable predictions as to what animals should do in any given situation if they are indeed behaving "optimally" (cf. Kamil & Sargent, 1981; Milton, 1981; Sibly & McFarland, 1976; Slobodkin & Rapoport, 1976). I for one have for many years questioned the belief of early investigators of animal intelligence that they could specify the so-called environmental demands of a given situation, or what constitutes a "correct vs incorrect" response on the part of their animals; but it is conceivable that this problem might be resolvable on nonarbitrary and solidly biological grounds after all.

To my knowledge, very few students of primate psychology have ever considered themselves foes of cognitivism, especially if they have worked with these animals for more than a few years, so the so-called cognitive revolution of the past decade or so, while it is certainly apparent in primatology, has involved less change than might be the case with most other species. The biggest change I can see is that one can now say in print things that one would have saved for lunchtable debates and exchanges of stories, and that fewer of one's colleagues are likely to jump down one's throat for such behavior.

Given that Darwin (see Smith, 1978) and Lorenz (1971) themselves had plenty to say about mentalistic and cognitive issues, I do not see "cognitive ethology'' as a brand-new discipline either. (Especially when he is talking about primates, Lorenz's theoretical position is very similar to Köhler's, and he himself has said as much repeatedly.) At the same time, neither primate cognitive ethology nor its psychological counterparts are, in my opinion, a simple return to the past. Some of the concepts invoked might sound the same as those used before the turn of the century, but the problem situations studied and the experimental and recording techniques used (i.e., the data-base from which cognition is inferred) are very different, as are the investigators' concepts of phylogeny and of ecology. Furthermore, whereas investigators who worked before the era of behaviorism and so-called noncognitive ethology would have said that the study of behavior is of interest only insofar as it might shed some light on problems of mind and consciousness, it is doubtful that many students of primates would agree. I for one do not consider myself either a student of Mind in the abstract or of Behavior in the abstract, but a student of primates—or, to be more precise, chimpanzees (*Pan troglodytes*) and saddle-back tamarins (*Saguinus fuscicollis*). To paraphrase Darwin (as cited by Smith, 1978), mind and behavior are functions of body. You must have some stable function to argue from.

SUMMARY AND CONCLUSIONS

The classification of behaviors (or animals) as either "intelligent" or not, and the further classification of various subclasses of intelligence is, at least in principle, a straight-forward taxonomic problem. It is philosophers and scientists more than laypersons who have muddied the problem, for that fairly reliable judgments can be made, and that these judgments correlate to some degree with the morphological and ecological classifications of classical biology, would seem obvious to almost anyone who approaches the problem with a sufficiently broad base of observational data and with a sufficiently "naive" naturalistic orientation. This might, of course, be folk taxonomy rather than scientific taxonomy, and it is unquestionably colored by our perception of kinship and by our prejudices against nonkin; but is is probably as good a starting point as any for more systematic and objective analyses.

Among the many questionable dogmas which have impeded the analysis, probably the most prominent are these:

a. *Anthropocentricism*: All species are more or less like us, but of course all nonhumans are vastly "simpler" and less "sophisticated" than we are.

b. *Cartesianism*: The only mind I can know is my own; the best working attitude is to assume that other living beings (or at least nonhumans) are mindless robots.

c. "*Quantism*": Animals differ from one another in degree, not in kind. Qualitative differences are best understood as different "levels" in developmental or evolutionary advancement.

d. *Nominalism*: Intelligence is whatever it is that is being measured by the tests that are used by those who call themselves students of intelligence.

e. *Intellectualism*: To solve the problem of making a living in the world at large by such devices as "mere" instinct, "mere" conditioned responses or finding one's niche and sticking to it, rather than by reason, is a mark of biological inferiority.

f. *Essentialism*: A first and absolutely necessary step toward studying intelligence or any particular facet of it is to arrive at an airtight definition of its "essence"—ideally *before* watching one's animals.

g. *A-biologism*: Two individuals can be said to be doing "fundamentally the same thing" if a human judge, who can see only a formal transcript of their data, cannot tell whose data is whose.

h. *Scientism*: The judgments of laypersons are value-laden and subjective, but those of scientists are not.

A necessary step in clearing up this muddle is to clearly distinguish between several questions which have very often been entangled with one another. Can a given animal not only solve the sorts of problems it faces in everyday life but also come up with solutions that are (in the long run of biological adaptation if not in the short run, when the animal is first confronted with novelty or change) "functionally adequate" if not optimal? What sorts of behavioral strategies and internal mechanisms does it employ? How did these strategies and internal mechanisms originate, both developmentally and phylogenetically speaking? What is the full range of circumstances to which the animal could adapt itself? What IQ score should one give it according to human norms? The last of these questions in particular must be disassociated from the others, if not consigned to the domain of nonscience.

As I still have not answered the question that I posed in the title to this paper, let me be explicit. Quite possibly we can never know with dead certainty whether or not any given animal is "really" intelligent, let alone precisely how intelligent it is or to what degree it actually comprehends what it is doing or saying, as opposed to simply fooling us into thinking as much. (After any experiment is completed a radical skeptic can, after all, always come up with some still further consideration or doubt—or revise his or her definitions, as Plato did.) The same doubts could, however, be expressed even more pointedly regarding the validity of the judgments one might pass on one's colleagues and students; and this does not prevent many scientists from passing such judgments themselves and requesting others to do the same. I am also confident that if students of animal behavior had had no interest whatsoever in questions of intelligence it would be very unlikely that they would have been led to discover more than a fraction of the phenomena that have been discovered in the past few decades—which phenomena would have been viewed not merely as incredible but as inacessible to analysis by the adamant antimentalists of earlier eras. Philosophers might or might not be satisfied with such an answer, but those whose interests are first and foremost in elucidating "actual variation among actual things" should be.

REFERENCES

Blurton Jones, N. G., & Konner, M. J. (1976). !Kung knowledge of animal behavior (or: The Proper Study of Mankind is Animals). In R. B. Lee & I. DeVore (Eds.), *Kalahari hunter-gatherers* (pp. 325–348). Cambridge, MA: Harvard University Press.

Cole, M., Gay, J., Glick, J. A., & Sharp, D. W. (1971). *The cultural context of learning and thinking.* New York: Basic Books.

Cole, M., & Scribner, S. (1974). *Culture and thought.* New York: Wiley.

Demarest, J. (1983). The ideas of change, progress, and continuity in the comparative psychology of learning. In D. W. Rajecki (Ed.), *Comparing behavior: Studying man studying animals* (pp. 143–180). Hillsdale, NJ: Lawrence Erlbaum Associates.

Dewsbury, D. A. (1984). *Comparative psychology in the twentieth century.* Stroudsburg, PA: Hutchinson Ross.

Diogenes Laertius. (1970). *Lives of Eminent Philosophers,* Vol. 2. (Trans. By R. D. Hicks.) Cambridge, MA: Harvard University Press.

Epstein, R., Lanza, R. P., & Skinner, B. F. (1981). "Self-awareness" in the pigeon. *Science, 212,* 695–696.

Epstein, R., Kirshnit, C. E., Lanza, R. P., & Rubin, L. C. (1984). "Insight" in the pigeon: Antecedents and determinants of an intelligent performance. *Nature, 308,* 61–62.

Fantz, R. L. (1957). Form preferences in newly hatched chicks. *Journal of Physiological and Comparative Psychology, 50,* 422–430.

Fantz, R. L. (1958). Visual discrimination in a neonate chimpanzee. *Perceptual and Motor Skills, 8,* 59–66.

Fantz, R. L. (1964). Visual experience in infants: Decreased attention to familiar patterns relative to novel ones. *Science, 146,* 668–670.

Fobes, J. L., & King, J. E. (Eds.). (1982). *Primate behavior.* New York: Academic Press.

Gallup, G. G. (1977). Self-recognition in primates: A comparative approach to the bidirectional properties of consciousness. *American Psychologist, 32,* 329–338.

Gardner, B. T., & Gardner, R. A. (1971). Two-way communication with an infant chimpanzee. In A. M. Schrier & F. Stollnitz (Eds.), *Behavior of nonhuman primates,* Vol. 4 (pp. 117–184). New York: Academic Press.

Gibson, J. J. (1979). *The ecological approach to visual perception.* Boston: Houghton-Mifflin.

Gould, S. J. (1981). *The mismeasure of man.* New York: W. W. Norton.

Green, S., & Marler, P. (1979). The analysis of animal communication. In P. Marler & J. G. Vandenbergh (Eds.), *Handbook of behavioral neurobiology,* Vol. 3 (pp. 73–158). New York: Plenum.

Harlow, H. F. (1951). Primate learning. In C. P. Stone (Ed.), *Comparative psychology* (3d ed.). Englewood Cliffs, NJ: Prentice-Hall.

Harlow, H. F., & Mears, C. (1979). *The human model: Primate perspectives.* New York: Wiley.

Hediger, H. (1968). *The psychology and behavior of animals in zoos and circuses.* New York: Dover.

Hodos, W. (1982). Some perspectives on the evolution of intelligence and the brain. In D. R. Griffin (Ed.), *Animal mind—human mind* (pp. 33–56). Berlin: Dahlem Konferenzen Springer Verlag.

Hodos, W., & Campbell, C. B. G. (1969). Scala naturae: Why there is no theory in comparative psychology. *Psychological Review, 76,* 337–350.

Jerison, H. J. (1982). The evolution of biological intelligence. In R. J. Sternberg (Ed.), *Handbook of human intelligence* (pp. 723–791). Cambridge: Cambridge University Press.

Kamil, A. C., & Sargent, T. (Eds.). (1981). *Foraging behavior: Ecological, ethological and psychological approaches.* New York: Garland Press.

Köhler, W. (1925). *The mentality of apes (trans. E. Winters).* New York: Harcourt Brace.

Köhler, W. (1929). *Gestalt psychology.* New York: Liveright.

Kummer, H. (1982). Social knowledge in free-ranging primates. In D. R. Griffin (Ed.), *Animal mind—human mind* (pp. 113–130). Berlin: Dahlem Konferenzen Springer Verlag.

Lewontin, R. C. (1983). Darwin's real revolution. *New York Review of Books, 30*(10), 21–27.

Lorenz, K. Z. (1971). *Studies in animal and human behavior,* Vol. 2. Cambridge, MA: Harvard University Press.

Lumsden, C. J., & Wilson, E. O. (1981). *Genes, mind, and culture.* Cambridge, MA: Harvard University Press.

MacPhail, E. (1985). Vertebrate intelligence: the null hypothesis. *Philosophical Transactions of the Royal Society of London,* B308, 37–51.

Mason, W. A. (1982). Primate social intelligence: Contributions from the laboratory. In D. R. Griffin (Ed.), *Animal mind—human mind* (pp. 131–144). Berlin: Dahlem Konferenzen Springer Verlag.

Maynard Smith, J. (1984). Game theory and the evolution of behavior. *Behavioral and Brain Sciences, 7,* 95–125.

Mayr, E. (1982). *On the growth of biological thought.* Cambridge, MA: Harvard University Press.

Menzel, E. W. (1979). General discussion of the methodological problems involved in the study of social interaction. In M. E. Lamb, S. J. Suomi, & G. R. Stephenson (Eds.), *Social interaction analysis: Methodological issues* (pp. 291–310). Madison: University of Wisconsin Press.

Menzel, E. W., & Johnson, M. K. (1976). Communication and cognitive organization in humans and other animals. *Annals of the New York Academy of Sciences, 280,* 131–142.

Milton, K. (1981). Distribution patterns of tropical plant foods as an evolutionary stimulus to primate mental development. *American Anthropologist, 83,* 534–548.

Popper, K. R. (1972). *Objective knowledge.* London: Oxford University Press.

Sahlins, M. (1976). *The use and abuse of biology.* Ann Arbor: University of Michigan Press.

Schrier, A. M., Stollnitz, F., & Harlow, H. F. (Eds.). (1965). *Behavior of nonhuman primates* (2 vols). New York: Academic Press.

Sibly, R., & McFarland, D. (1976). On the fitness of behavior sequences. *American Naturalist, 110,* 601–617.

Simpson, G. G. (1961). *Principles of animal taxonomy.* New York: Columbia University Press.

Slobodkin, L. B. (1976). The peculiar evolutionary strategy of man. *Transactions of the Boston Colloquium of Philosophy of Science.*

Slobodkin L. B., & Rapoport, A. (1974). An optimal strategy of evolution. *Quarterly Review of Biology, 49,* 181–200.

Smith, C. U. M. (1978). Charles Darwin, the origin of consciousness, and panpsychism. *Journal of the history of biology, 11,* 245–267.

Walter, W. G. (1961). *The living brain.* Harmondsworth, Middlesex: Penguin Books.

Yerkes, R. M. (1943). *Chimpanzees: A laboratory colony.* New Haven: Yale University Press.

8

Describing Intelligence

Earl Hunt
The University of Washington

With becoming modesty, our species has named itself *"Homo sapiens sapiens."* What quality do we have that justifies this claim? Is the quality of intelligence also possessed by other species. . .or by machines? These questions cannot be answered until the terms in them are defined. The importance of definition is illustrated by the history of debates over human intelligence. Discussions of racial, cultural, and sexual differences in intelligence have often degenerated into emotional, poorly focused conflicts. The issues have not been settled in part because the questions have not been clearly stated. More recently we have seen the rise of a vocal "Animal Rights" movement. It is based on an interesting, albeit poorly articulated, set of concepts about the nature of the nonhuman mind and about the obligation of humans to other sentient beings. The debate between animal welfare advocates and biological scientists is difficult to carry forward because the two sides see the issues so differently. Failing a definition of what we are talking about, we are not likely to talk about it very sensibly.

Virtually all scientific studies of human, animal,[1] or for that matter, machine intelligence are carried on at two levels. The investigators always have a theory of the general nature of intelligence, but they seldom make this theory explicit. Nevertheless, the implicit theory is used to generate explicit situations for observing behavior. These are described in detail and the behavior that is observed then becomes "intelligence." Because different people may have different implicit theories, disagreements arise about the meaning of empirical findings,

---

[1] Throughout this paper I shall use the term "animal" to refer to species other than *H. sapiens*. I do so solely to avoid the term "infrahuman," which literally means "below human," and thus is humanist jargon.

although there is no confusion about the data. An excellent illustration of this point is the debate concerning the linguistic capabilities of chimpanzees (Ristau & Robbins, 1982). There is evidence that this ape can be taught to engage in elaborate communications with humans, using symbolic systems and training procedures that are entirely human inventions. The communications themselves are far more like human language than any of the communication behavior yet observed in chimpanzees in the wild. On the other hand, the communications certainly do not have the full syntactic or semantic power of human language. Are the apes using language? The answer is a matter of definition.

Intelligence can be defined comparatively, by focusing on those behaviors that differentiate individuals, all of whom are presumed to possess intelligence to varying degrees. The comparative approach has dominated the study of human intelligence, where it has produced useful results. Therefore it is worth looking at its strengths and weaknesses. An alternative approach, which I believe to be more suitable to the study of animal intelligence, is to define certain behavioral capabilities as being central to cognition, and then to study the extent to which a particular species has these capabilities. The rationale for such an absolute approach to intelligence is that a cognitive act is a computation. The complexity of the computation can be defined in terms of the complexity of the machine required to execute it. This is the basic philosophical position of Pylshyn (1984) in the newly developing field of "cognitive science." This paper presents a case for applying a computational approach to the study of animal intelligence, surely a topic in the biological sciences. First, though, some remarks are in order about the historically dominant comparative approach.

THE COMPARATIVE APPROACH

The comparative approach begins with the assumption that identifiably different individuals possess intelligence in different amounts. The first intelligence tests to be of practical use were elaborations of Binet and Simon's (1905) assumption that mental capacity develops ontologically, i.e., that adults, as a group, are more intelligent than children. Test items were developed by asking teachers what sorts of problems could be solved by children of different ages. A slight modification was introduced by the assumption that the extremes of "bright" and "not-so-bright" people can be identified within a particular age group. If so, then to develop an intelligence test one finds those mental behaviors that maximally discriminate between those who do and don't have intelligence. Many of our modern tests can be fairly characterized as statistically sophisticated variants of this conclusion. In the extreme case (which no one believes) statistical criteria rather than logical analyses determine test content. This is the sort of reasoning that lead Boring (1923) to assert that "intelligence is what the intelligence test measures". . .a statement that, if accepted, answers once and for all time any question about cetacean intelligence! Slightly less arrogantly, Neisser (1979) has proposed that intelligence be defined by the characteristics of a prototypically intelligent person. Neisser's remark is the quintessence of the comparative approach. But who is to identify the prototype?

Menzel (this volume) has pointed out that a strong variety of the comparative approach dominates our folk psychology of animal intelligence. Since we define us as being protypically intelligent, another animal is seen as being *prototypically* intelligent if it either is phylogenetically close to man, or it solves problems that we humans understand, perhaps in the manner that we humans solve them. These criteria may explain why the possibility of cetacean intelligence has excited so much public interest. A creature that is both phylogenetically and ecologically very different from *Homo sapiens* appears able to solve problems that humans set for it. The discordance between the dolphin's appearance and its problem solving (on our terms) needs to be explained.

There are two powerful arguments in favor of the comparative approach. The strongest one is pragmatic; the comparative approach tells you what to do. An excellent way to establish tests of competence is to find those measures that best contrast the competent and the incompetent. From the limited view of personnel classification, Binet's approach was exactly correct. From a scientific point of view, the comparative approach can be bootstrapped into an absolute theory of sort. Psychometricians in the 1920s and 1930s were able to use the statistical distribution of test scores to reject a unidimensional view of intelligence in favor of a description of human intelligence as a multidimensional space, in which the dimensions defined basic abilities, such as verbal or spatial reasoning (Carroll, 1982). The comparative approach is also useful in scientific studies because it provides behavior to be explained. Assume that intelligence is, indeed, what the test measures. The next step is to find out what that is, by breaking the behavior on intelligence tests down into its components, and by understanding individual differences in those components (Sternberg, 1977).

To a limited extent the benefits of the comparative approach can be applied to questions about animal mental competence. Just as one might document phylogenetically related changes in, say, courtship behavior, it may be reasonable to document phylogenetically related changes in cognitive capacities. Rumbaugh and Pate's (1984) report of learning capacities in primates provides a good example. At a practical level cognitive abilities may determine the relative usefulness of two species for human purposes, even though both have the requisite physical capacities. There are few proposals for seeing-eye sheep, or for training fish to retrieve objects that humans drop in the water. Studies directed at either scientific or practical goals could provide the data for a comparative analysis of animal intelligence, somewhat akin to the psychometric analysis of human abilities. The picture would be a limited one, as is the psychometric picture. Why?

The comparative approach depends upon the identification of the prototypically intelligent. (*Homo sapiens sapiens* sees no problem here!) There must also be agreement on the rules of comparison. Shoe size differentiates younger children from older ones, but Binet did not consider shoe size as a measure of intelligence. If this example seems silly, consider the case of "personality" measures that are studied apart from intelligence, although personality variables are clearly contributors to mental performance. The way in which they contribute does not fit into our intuitions about the nature of thought. In other words, the comparative approach itself contains an implicit absolute theory of cognition. People who do not share the same theory may disagree both as to who has intelligence and as to how it may be measured.

Further problems of the comparative approach are illustrated by its failure in cross-cultural studies of cognition. Specialists in cognitive anthropology have argued that the intellectual experiences posed by different cultures are so different that a framework that is appropriate for interindividual comparisons in one culture may simply not be relevant in another (Berry, 1981; Laboratory of Comparative Human Cognition, 1982). To take a specific example, Berry (1981) has pointed out that hunter-gatherer and agricultural cultures simply face different problems, and must encourage different mental skills.

Menzel (this volume) makes a similar claim about the weakness of comparative definitions of intelligence in cross-species research. From a biological perspective an animal's mental behavior is adaptive if it improves the animal's reproductive fitness, broadly defined. Success is to be defined by considering how an animal deals with its environment, and not how it might deal with ours.

The view just expressed, whether about people or animals, is usually called a contextual view of intelligence (Sternberg, 1984). While it is an appealing counterweight to an extreme comparative view, it too has weaknesses for both human and animal research. "Intelligence" cannot be defined as any behavioral capacity that is adaptive; this is simply too broad a view. Furthermore, this approach removes intelligence from the status of an individual property. A particular species (or individual) could have its "Intelligence" changed because some outside agent changed the environment. Is it reasonable to argue that the gorilla (*Gorilla gorilla*) is less intelligent than the rhesus monkey (*Macaca mulatta*) because the gorilla is less able to share ranges with humans?

THE ABSOLUTE APPROACH

The alternative to a comparative theory is an absolute theory of cognition. An absolute theory must be based on assumptions about the process of thought rather than upon observations of the outcome of thought. Such a theory is beginning to emerge in the writings of a variety of psychologists, philosophers, linguists, and computer scientists who see all these disciplines as special cases of studies in "cognitive science."

The cognitive science view is that thinking involves the manipulation of an internal representation of the external world (Johnson-Laird, 1980). This statement turns out to be a starting point rather than a definition, for it can be applied to behavior that no one wants to call thinking. When humans kick their legs in response to a tap below the knee (the patellar reflex), the movement is based on a manipulation of an internal representation, for the blow on the knee does not transmit mechanical forces to the leg in the direction of the kick. Indeed, the mechanical forces are in the opposite direction. In executing the patellar reflex the nervous system acts as an electro-mechanical relay system, about as intellectual as the circuit that is used to switch on a room light.

To avoid having to define reflex action as thinking, let us add the restriction that a sentient being is "thinking" if the internal manipulations that occur in response to a physically present stimulus are influenced in part by the being's past experience. The restriction differentiates Einstein's patellar reflex from his creation of the theory of relativity. However, the expanded definition does include a wide range of behaviors as "thinking." It would certainly include the response of a computer to its input. . .since the general purpose computer will not respond at all until it has "experienced" a program. . .and it would force us to say that a honey bee is thinking when the bee expresses its memory of the location of flowers by its dance inside the hive (Griffin, 1981).

Should we be bothered by a definition that allows for thinking in machine and insect? Only if we wish to take the humanist position that thinking can only be done by beings like us. A less humanist alternative is to describe the intelligence of a being by stating a model of his, hers, or its capacities to represent the external environment and to manipulate that representation. Descriptions of mental capacity at this level are symbolic descriptions of what the sentient being does. The problem is to find a consistent, useful notation for describing cognitive behavior rather than to search for the "true" description. In the case of animal intelligence we hope that the same notation will be applicable to a wide variety of species. If this is the case, it should be possible to describe the mental competencies of different species in the same language. "Intelligence" then becomes "the topics that can be discussed in the theoretical language." Cross-species (or cross-cultural) comparative statements are possible. However these statements can go well beyond the statement that "species X is more intelligent than species Y."

Truth does become an issue in exploring the brain-mind relation. The thought processes of a sentient being are only understood completely when we know both the symbolic computations the being can perform and the physical mechanisms that realize the computations. It may be too much for our own minds to grasp all of these issues at once. Furthermore, it does not follow that questions about the mind would disappear if all questions about the physical properties of the brain were answered. Knowledge of the action of LSD at the neurochemical level does not explain the effect of the drug on perception, nor does an explanation of transistors prove very useful in understanding a computer's operating system. Most descriptions of intelligence will be presented at the level of abstract symbol systems. But what does this mean?

The following sections present some of the major topics of thought, as viewed in cognitive science, and discuss their application to the study of animal cognitive behavior.

THE INTERNAL REPRESENTATION OF OBJECTS

In order to model a being's thinking, one must know the mental world that the being lives in. What aspects of the external world are carried over into the internal representation? The formal statement of what it means for one system to represent another can be quite involved. As a loose, nontechnical guide, objects in the external world can be characterized by their values on dimensions of variation. The dimensions provide a first level of coding of external objects into internal representations. To know a thinker's mind we must first know what these dimensions are. What aspects of the flower-tree cavity system appear in the internal representations of worker honey bees? What aspects of the ocean are coded in the dolphin mind?

An animal (or a machine) cannot use a dimension to code the environment unless the animal can discriminate between objects that differ along the dimension in question. Determining the limits of an animal's sensory capacities is a straightforward experimental project (proving that people know that a particular discriminatory capability exists). What is more difficult to discover is how an animal makes use of its sensory capabilities. Discrimination studies show what dimensions an animal can discriminate, but do not tell us how the animal uses its powers of discrimination to order the world. A bit of the latter information can be obtained by the use of a data analytic technique known as multidimensional scaling (MDS), that was originally developed to study human representations of objects. The basis of the method will be described briefly, and a sketch of its use in research on animals is given. A more complete description of MDS can be found in Schiffman, Reynolds, and Young (1981).

MDS is based on the fact that the locations of objects in an n-dimensional space can (usually) be inferred from knowledge of the pairwise distances between each point. The recovery of geographic positions is a frequently used example. Figure 8.1 shows the two-dimensional locations of several U.S. cities, as obtained by Schiffman et al.'s MDS analysis of the relative airline distances between cities.[2] To allow an evaluation of the solution the true positions of the cities are shown, based on an analysis using actual distances. Comparing the solutions shows that a great deal of information can be obtained using judgments of perceived relative similarity. These are fairly easy to get.

Color perception in humans provides a second example that is more psychological and makes less demands on the original data. Humans will judge red to be

---

[2]Seattle was arbitrarily placed at its correct position in order to coordinate the two displays.

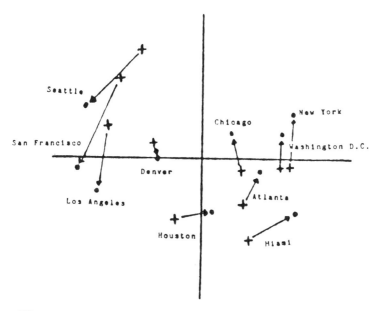

FIG. 8.1. A Multidimensional Scaling "Map" of United States cities. The pluses indicate the positions derived from an analysis of relative airline distances. The arrowheads indicate the locations of the cities as determined by an analysis of actual airline distances. The latter locations correspond closely to the positions indicated on a standard map.

more similar to yellow than it is to green, blue to be more similar to green than to yellow or red, violet more similar to blue than to green and, finally, red to be more similar to violet than to green. The only way that these judgments can be satisfied by a Eucliden representation is to arrange the colors in a two-dimensional "elliptical" figure. This is true even though the colors vary along a single physical dimension, wavelength. Because we are people, we know this. The discovery of the human color wheel by a nonhuman MDS user would probably be considered a major scientific accomplishment. Furthermore, the discovery could be made by knowing only the relative closeness of stimulus A to stimuli B and C, e.g., red to green or yellow.

The MDS procedure has been applied to studies of animal cognition. Sands, Lincoln and Wright (1982) trained a rhesus monkey to perform a "same-different" matching task. First picture A would be exposed, then picture B. The animal was trained to move a lever in one direction for "same" pictures and in the other for "different" pictures. After the animal had learned the procedure throughly the testing phase was initiated. The stimuli were pictures that fell into one of five classes; monkey faces, human faces, trees, fruits, or flowers. Sands et al. used the relative frequency of "same" responses as ordinal measures of the closeness of pictures. Note that this measure is defined on picture pairs, not on class pairs. However, the grouping of pictures into classes should be apparent when the pictures are located in the appropriate multidimensional space.

Figure 8.2 presents the results from one of Sands et al.'s (1982) subjects. The grouping of items into classes is apparent. Based on these results, one has to be encouraged about the application of the MDS technique to the study of intelligence in other mammals. The animal under investigation must be capable of performing the "same-different" discrimination. This is certainly within the capacities of some marine mammals, for they can be trained to do the more difficult "match-to-sample" procedure (Herman, 1980). An alteration of the paradigm might provide a somewhat finer ordinal measure of similarity than that used by Sands et al. (1982) In the normal match-to-sample paradigm a target object, A, is shown and then removed. The animal is then shown a pair of test objects, A and B, one of which is identical to the target. The animal is trained to choose this object. In the modified test paradigm an animal would be shown a target, A, followed by two distinct test objects, B and C. The animal's choice of test object would be a relative similarity judgment. In fact, if this experiment were conducted with humans the procedure would be referred to as the "method of triads" procedure, a standard tool in psychometric scaling.

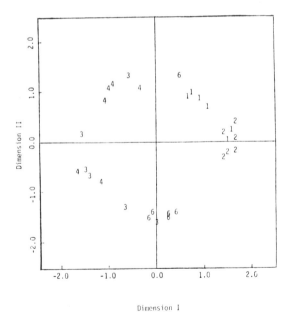

FIG. 8.2.   Location of various objects determined by multidimensional scaling of rhesus monkey's responses. Number 1 designates pictures of humans, 2 monkeys, 3 trees, 4 fruit, and 6 flowers. Adapted from Sands et al., 1982.

There are a number of technical problems that would need to be overcome. For instance, the animal would probably have to be highly overtrained in the standard paradigm to ensure that there was any response at all in the modified paradigm. A schedule of reinforcement would have to be found that would keep the animal responding without inadvertently rewarding choices ("similarity judgments") along a particular stimulus dimension. These problems do not appear to be insurmountable. Assuming that they could be solved, the technique of MDS ought to be of considerable use in understanding even how such alien species as the cetaceans order their world. Elaborations of the MDS procedure permit systematic comparison of the internal spaces of related species, in different ecological niches, or of unrelated species in the same niche. The results should be useful to anyone who wants to know what conceptual categorizations are made by different animals in different places.

CLASSIFICATION BEHAVIOR

An important aspect of cognition is the ability to react to objects as members of sets. This is essential if previously acquired responses are to be extrapolated to new situations, for the new situation must be classified. Coyotes do not repeatedly encounter the same rodents, but they manage to behave appropriately. Any description of a being's cognition must include a statement of the classification rules that it is capable of using.

Perhaps the simplest classification rule is the "nearest neighbor" rule: Upon encountering an unknown object treat it as belonging to the class of the previously encountered object that it most resembles. The nearest neighbor rule places all the computational burden on memory. Mathematical models of nerve nets have been proposed that could realize the nearest neighbor rule (Anderson, 1977). Because these models are so simple, one might think that the rule itself is a naive one. This is not so; complex behavior can be produced by it. In fact, if the classifier has an infinitely large memory and infinite experience the nearest neighbor rule approaches maximum likelihood classification (Cover & Hart, 1967). The principal objections to nearest neighbor classification as a model of biological computations are that the rule deteriorates if memory is not perfect and that the rule does not produce an abstract description of the characteristics of class. Whether or not this is an issue in dealing with nonhumans is problematical.

Prototype classification is an amplification of the nearest neighbor rule. The classifier stores a record of an "ideal" instance for each of its categories. When a new object is encountered it is classified as being a member of the class associated with the closest prototype. (The rule can be elaborated to allow for the absolute frequency of members of different classes.) There is a good deal of evidence that humans often utilize prototype classification (Smith & Medin, 1981). Prototype classification rules are simpler to execute than nearest neighbor rules, for the classifying device need only record the prototypes instead of having to retain an explicit memory of all examples. On the other hand, a classifying device that uses prototype rules must contain some mechanism for acquiring prototypes and for updating them as a result of experience. While prototypes could conceivably be implanted genetically, classification using prototypes would not qualify as thinking as defined here, for the mental behavior would not be determined by past experience. On the other hand, classification based on genetic prototypes might be part of a sequence of actions that, as a whole, would fit the definition of thinking.

It is not easy to discriminate between prototype and nearest neighbor classification rules, for the behavior dictated by the rules may be much the same. The key distinction is between responses to new objects that resemble the prototype and responses to atypical objects that have been experienced previously. According to a prototype rule the new objects should be easy to classify and the atypical objects hard to classify. A classifier using the nearest neighbor rule would classify the experienced, atypical objects rapidly, but would have to search the description space in order to find the nearest neighbor of the new, typical objects.

A considerable literature has developed on the construction of appropriate tests of human classification rules. The basic idea is to present a learner with a sequence of items that could be classified by two different rules, then present a choice situation in which the rules conflict. The learner's preference for one rule or another can be inferred from the choice that is made. To take a somewhat whimsical example, imagine that you were trying to guess people's political preferences from their demographic characteristics. Suppose further that up to day X all the Republicans you meet are over 6 feet tall and over 35-years-old. Similarly, all the Democrats are under 35-years-of-age and under 6 feet tall. On day X you are presented with two people, one of whom is 6 feet 2 inches and 28-years-old, while the other is 5 feet 10 inches and 39-years-old. Who is the Republican? Your answer would reveal your preference for classification rules.

While the example is whimsical, a logically analogous experiment could easily be conducted with animals. The subject would first learn to discriminate between objects in a situation in which either of two rules might be used. On the crucial test trial the animal would be presented with a stimulus pair that discriminated between the rules. The rule the animal actually had learned could be inferred from its choice behavior. For example, this technique could be used to distinguish between cetacean's relative preference for echo location and visual cues.

A still more abstract classification procedure involves the creation of explicit boundaries between regions of the description space, and the assignment of all points within each region to the same class. Linear boundaries are those that are created by linear functions of the dimensions of the space. This is the sort of classification that is created by the familiar discriminant analysis procedure of statistics. Simpler examples abound in the scientific literature. For instance,

Jerison (1973) classified animals as "big brained" if their brain weight exceeded that expected on the basis of their body weight multiplied by a constant of proportionality. Geometrically, Jerison established a boundary line,

$$\text{brain weight} - k \text{ (body weight)} = 0$$

in the two-dimensional space defined by brain weight and body weight. Large brained species lay on one side of the space and small brained species on the other side. (In practice, one would also consider the distance from the boundary, but this would unduly complicate the example.)

Linear classification rules are attractive as models of biological cognition because they can be implemented by a plausible "simplified nerve net" consisting of threshold devices. An example is shown in Fig. 8.3. The device assigns weights to an object's values on each dimension in the description space, and determines whether the sum of the weighted values exceeds a threshold. There are simple learning algorithms for adjusting the weights, so that the device will eventually "learn" any classification rule that it is capable of executing. Put another way, a linear device can be designed to execute any arbitrarily chosen linear threshold rule. Furthermore, one linear device can be "taught" to become another. Now suppose that one begins with a linear classification rule and a device that does not compute the rule. Objects are presented, one at a time, and the system is told if its classifications are correct. A simple learning mechanism can use this information to change the initial device into a linear threshold device that executes the correct classification rule.

Linear threshold devices can obviously be applied to the classification of objects represented as points in a Euclidean descriptive space, but a Euclidean description is not a necessary precondition for the use of linear classification. Minsky and Papert (1969) introduced the idea of a "retina" consisting of n binary points, and a set of features $\{g\}$, each of which defines logical predicates upon the retina. In their terminology a primitive stimulus is described at its first level by a vector x of n binary values, indicating whether or not a particular sensor is "on" or "off" when the stimulus is present. The primitive stimulus is

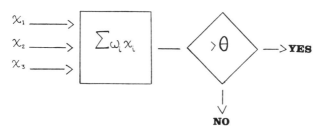

FIG. 8.3.   The schematic diagram of a linear discriminating device. Primitive inputs to a summing device are weighted, and the device produces an output if the summed weights exceed a fixed threshold.

then transformed by the feature detectors, to provide a vector of features, $(g(x))$, each of which is either "on" or "off" (i.e., has value one or zero) depending on the presence or absence of the feature in the stimulus. Linear classification procedures can then be applied to the collection of stimulus features, by considering whether there exists a vector of weights, w, such that

$$f(x) = w \ g \ (x)$$

exceeds a threshold value.

Minsky and Papert showed that linear threshold devices are limited in the range of the logical classification rules that they can compute. For instance, linear classification rules can be constructed to execute the rule

"Class 1 members have feature a and feature b"

or the rule

"Class 1 members have feature a or feature b,"

but there is no linear classification device that can express the rule

"Class 1 members have the feature a or the feature b, but not both."

There is similarly no way to express "Class 1 objects have an odd number of features of type a" as a linear classification rule. Limitations on geometric classifications are even more telling. If the "retina" is interpreted as a set of contiguous points on a surface. . .a reasonable interpretation for the eye. . .linear threshold devices are not sufficient to execute certain rules based upon topological invariants that, intuitively, a human could use to discriminate classes of plane figures.

The limitations of threshold devices have been cited widely as showing that these devices are inadequate models for human classification behavior. But are they good models for the classification behavior of different nonhuman species? Answering this question would require a systematic, but feasible, study of the performance of different species on problems that either can or cannot be classified by linear threshold devices. The theoretical investigation need not stop there. A literature is beginning to develop on the behavior of "expanded" linear threshold devices (Hinton & Anderson, 1981). These can be thought of as networks of linear threshold units that communicate with each other. Thus the effective stimulus to any one unit will be: (a) a description of the external stimulus, and (b) information about how other units in the network are reacting to the current and previous stimuli. While the mathematical descriptions of the behavior of these complex devices have not been developed in great detail, a start has been made (Anderson, 1977; Grossberg, 1980; Hinton & Anderson, 1981; McClelland, 1979). The usual motivation for this work is either to model the behavior of an abstract, and hence unobservable, neural system or to model the behavior of humans. One can envisage an intermediate research program based upon studies of animal cognition. The goal would be to establish the least expansion of a linear threshold device required to model the classification behavior of the species being studied.

PROBLEM SOLVING

Let us define a "state" as the internal representation of a possible external situation. A state refers to a representation held in (working) memory, as the representation of a particular situation, rather than the "timeless knowledge" held in permanent memory. By contrast, the rules defining object descriptions and set memberships would be part of (semantic) permanent memory. A problem exists when a thinker has a state and a goal. The goal can be thought of as a restriction on states, so that a particular state satisfies a goal if the goal's restrictions are met by the state description. For example, if the goal is to obtain food and the current state is that the animal is eating, the goal is satisfied. Problem solving is conceived of as the task of finding a series of actions that will change the current state into a state satisfying the goal restrictions. Problem solving is carried out by manipulating internal representations, thus avoiding the costly and potentially dangerous alternative of solving a problem by poking about in the real world.

The actions of a particular problem solver (man, animal, or machine) may be modeled by stating the rules that are followed as the problem solver passes from one internal state to another. The machine itself is a model of thinking. What the thinker knows is modeled by the knowledge embodied in the rules. How the thinker's brain uses knowledge is embodied in the model of how the rules are selected and executed. The latter model raises questions concerning mind-brain relations as well as questions about the actions of the mind.

In most cognitive science research on problem solving, rules are stated as *Production Systems*. This is a notational device in which the basic element is a condition-action pair called a *production*. Each production states that action f can be executed under condition x to produce condition y. Since productions are statements about how states are changed into new states, they implicitly define a theory of causality.[3]

---

[3]There is a logical distinction between a theory of causality, and awareness of that theory. My argument is that a sentient being embodies a theory of causality in the external world if the being's behavior can be described by rules that map from one internal representation to another, and that have interpretations in the external world. This is not the same as arguing that the being is consciously aware of having a theory of causality. For this to be the case the being must be able to distinguish between internal representations that do or do not include the "causal" rules as descriptors of the being's own internal representation.

A frequently used example of production system modeling is the analysis of some observations in Kohler's (1927) account of problem solving in the chimpanzee. Since cognitive scientists are somewhat cavalier about family and species distinctions, this has become known as the ''monkey and banana'' problem.

Imagine that a hungry monkey is in a cage that contains a box and a bunch of bananas. The problem is that the bananas are hanging from the roof of the cage, beyond the monkey's reach. The monkey's internal world is represented by the following set of statements.

The monkey is at the center of the floor.

The bananas are at the center of the roof.

The box is at the corner of the floor.

The monkey is hungry.

The animal is also assumed to have knowledge about the effects of actions. This knowledge is expressed by five rules.

1. If the monkey is at point x on the floor, moving from point x to another point, y, also on the floor, places the monkey at point y.
2. If the monkey and the box are at point x on the floor, pushing the box to point y on the floor moves the monkey and box to point y.
3. If the monkey and the box are on the floor at point x, climbing the box places the monkey on the roof at point x.
4. If the monkey is at point x and there is an object y at point x, object y can be grasped.
5. If object y is a food and y can be grasped, y can be eaten.

The animal also needs four rules about more general situations. One provides motivation for problem solving; the others are rules about problem solving itself.

6. If the monkey is hungry and x is a food, establish the goal of eating x.
7. If x is a goal and if action a, taken under condition y, would produce x, then set as a goal the production of condition y.
8. If x is a goal and if action a, taken under condition y, would produce x, and if condition y exists, then take action a, eliminate x as a goal, and assert that x exists or has been accomplished.
9. If there are two rules R1 and R2, and if the conditions required to execute R1 are a proper subset of the conditions required to execute R2, then rule R2 should be followed instead of R1 whenever the conditions for executing both rules are satisfied.

Rule 9 is very important. It ensures that if two actions could be taken the one with the more restrictive domain will be preferred. In this particular example rule 9 ensures that the monkey will act whenever possible.

Now consider the steps in solving the monkey and banana problem.

1. Rule 6 is activated because the monkey is hungry and a banana is food. The goal is to eat a banana.

2. Since the goal is to eat a banana a condition for eating the banana must be satisfied. Rule 7 and rule 5 combine to establish subgoal 1; grasp a banana.

3. Subgoal 1 and rule 4 are combined by rule 7, to establish subgoal 2; move the monkey to the center of the roof. (At this point and throughout the rules for dealing with partially satisfied subgoals will not be considered. They would be required here because the condition for grasping a banana is that the monkey and the banana both be at the center of the roof, and the banana already is.)

4. Subgoal 2 and rule 3 are combined by rule 7, establishing the new subgoal 3; move the box to the center of the floor. (The monkey is already there.)

5. Subgoal 3 and rule 2 are combined by rule 7. This establishes a new subgoal 4; move the monkey to the corner of the floor.

6. The conditions for moving the monkey to the corner of the floor exist. Rule 9 ensures that rule 8 has priority over rule 7, so the monkey is moved to the corner, (Rule 1) satisfying subgoal 4.

7. The conditions for rule 2, pushing the box, now exist. By rule 8 the box is pushed, and subgoal 3 is satisfied.

8. The conditions for rule 3, climbing the box, are satisfied. The monkey climbs the box, satisfying subgoal 2. The monkey is at the roof.

9. The conditions for rule 4, grasping the banana, are satisfied. The banana is grasped, fulfilling subgoal 1.

10. The monkey can now eat the banana (Rule 5). The goal has been satisfied.

It is important to note precisely what the computational model of animal thinking has claimed. It was asserted that the animal's internal representation of the situation contained information equivalent to propositions such as "A banana is a food," but no claim was made that the animal could comprehend these statements to the point of translating them into an internal or external statement, as a human presumably could. The rules used to deal with the problem representation fell into two broad classes; rules about problem-specific behaviors (boxes, pushing, climbing, and bananas) and rules about general problem solving activity (rules 7, 8, and 9). The general problem-solving rules allow the animal to put together previously acquired behavior sequences. A demonstration that the animal could not solve the problem without having prior specific training in the component behavior sequences, therefore, is *not* evidence against the existence of general problem solving rules. (Even in humans, very few problems are solved by completely novel methods.) The important demonstration is that the animal can use a sequence of previously acquired rules without going through a period of trial and error combination.

When one offers a computational model to explain behavior there is an implicit assumption that the animal being modeled possesses a physical information processing system that can support the required computations. The account of the monkey and banana problem assumes that the animal has a working memory capable of representing information about the state of the world and a permanent memory that can serve as a repository for problem-solving rules. Further, the computational model assumes that the animal's brain contains a sophisticated pattern recognition system that can match the contents of working memory to the condition part of the rules stored in permanent memory. These assumptions seem necessary to explain even simple forms of human problem solving (J. R. Anderson, 1983). What is claimed here is that the cognitive behavior exhibited by other species also requires a computational explanation. It may be that the models required for these explanations, and the information processing architecture needed to support them, will turn out to be very different from the models and architecture required to analyze human thought. Presumably there will be some correlation between the features of models required to explain the behavior of different species and the phylogenetic origins of the species whose behavior is to be explained. Let us speculate about where such an approach may be useful.

Herman, Richards, and Wolz (1984) and Schusterman and Krieger (1984) report that two quite different marine mammals, bottle-nosed dolphins and sea lions (*Zalophus californianus*), can be trained to solve problems that involve interpreting and carrying out simple commands, such as "touch the ball with the tail." From the subject's point of view, there were two stages to the problem: command comprehension and problem solution. It would be possible to develop a production system "program," similar to that just described for the monkey and banana problem, to mimic the animal's behavior in each domain. Such a program should contain an account of characteristic errors as well as an account of correct behavior. Indeed, providing an analysis of the error producing "bugs" in the animal's program is likely to be even more informative than producing a program that mimics correct behavior. Comparing the programs required to model each animal's behavior would provide a detailed analysis of the relative cognitive capabilities of each species.

Constructing a production system model forces the theorist to provide an explicit description of how an animal's (or a person's) separate mental capacities interact to produce rational behavior. A second advantage of modeling modeling is that it forces a theoretician to develop ideas about how different cognitive capabilities fit together. For instance, a good deal has already been said about classification behavior. The act of creating problem-solving models shows how essential classification is. Each step in problem solving is a classification step, for the problem solver must decide which of several rules to apply. A theorist must explain what classification rules can be executed by the animal under study. Similar remarks can be made about the knowledge that a theorist may assume an animal has. The model only knows a rule if an explicit production has been provided to it. A theorist also has to be specific about the sorts of "mental responses" that are permitted as an animal explores its internal world. Clearly a problem solver needs to be able to reason about the consequences of physical actions, such as pushing and climbing. To what extent must models of an animal's behavior include very general rules about problem solving, such as those illustrated in the example? Would it be possible to characterize the problem-solving capabilities of different species in terms of the complexity of their general problem-solving rules?

In order to explore possible states of the world, a thinker must execute computations upon an internal representation. How are the qualities in the external world modeled inside an animal's head? To illustrate, many scientific models use operations on real numbers to represent operations on physical objects. The representation is adequate, because there is a correspondence between physical operations and arithmetical operations, e.g., between the concatenation of weights and addition. Now consider a more psychological example. What internal operations can be applied to human representation of visual space? The following "thought experiment" illustrates the issue. Visualize an expensive power boat, such as might be found in an exclusive marina. Focus your attention on the stern. Then answer one of the following two questions:

(a) Is the bridge open or enclosed?
(b) Is the anchor hanging down from the side of the bow, or is it resting on the deck?

Obviously there are no right or wrong answers to these questions; it depends on the boat you imagined. The interesting fact is that if your attention was focused on the stern, question (b) will be answered more quickly than question (a). The converse is true if you first focus your attention on the bowspirit. Kosslyn (1980) has used evidence such as this to infer that people contain an internal operation on images whose properties correspond to many of the physical properties of visual scanning.

Animals may well image, and this could be an important part of their cognition. Inasmuch as verbal reports of images are unlikely to be obtained (!), a more behavioral procedure is needed. One potentially useful paradigm is based on the idea that a thinker can recognize an equivalence between an object, x, and a transformation, f(x), of an object if and only if the being can compute the inverse of the transformation. To be specific, humans can clearly "compute" the equivalent of translations and rotations of rigid objects in three dimensional space, because we can read typescript presented at various angles with respect to the line of sight. Several experimental studies have shown that the time that is required to rotate a visual object mentally (e.g., reading a distorted R) is a linear function of the angle through which the rotation must be carried (Cooper & Shepard, 1973). One could imagine similar studies being conducted to determine the capacities that animals have for translation and rotation. Other transforms could be studied as well, even using other modalities. To illustrate, humans can recognize the same tune, played in different keys. Can dolphins?

Rotation is an example of a transformation whose purpose is probably to bring a perceived object to its canonical form, so that it can be recognized. Other transformations may have the effect of recoding the current situation into a description that is easier to work with, either because it is more directly connected to the pattern part of the thinker's pattern-action rules, or because the thinker's internal imaging capabilities are more suited to a particular code. A good illustration of this is the human tendency to recode visually presented words into an internal auditory code (Conrad, 1963). There is some evidence for similar recoding in animals. A particularly good example is Herman's (1980) report that a dolphin had great difficulty solving a problem involving memory for visual stimuli, but that the animal could solve the problem if it was first taught to associate the visual stimuli with acoustic "labels." It seems a reasonable inference to assume that the animal: (a) was more capable of memory for sounds than visual stimuli. . .a fact that had been previously established, and (b) that the animal had the ability to transform stimuli from one internal code to another. Such an ability fits in well with the notion that an explanation of thinking should be stated in terms of pattern-action transformation, for recodings are simply particular types of transformations.

The cognitive science approach places great emphasis upon goal-oriented problem solving. There is nothing teleological about this position. In terms of the psychology of the 1940s and 1950s, what is being emphasized is the stimulus property of the goal. No thinker reacts to an external situation; the reaction is to an internal representation of the external situation, and the goal. . .as a stimulus. . .is part of that representation. Therefore the capacity to react to overt stimulus situations conditional upon the thinker's goal state is an essential part of problem solving. (The old proverb about leading horses to water acknowledges the cognitive capacity of horses.) More generally, in establishing the cognitive capabilities of an animal an explicit statement must be made about how goals, as stimuli, exert control over the execution of the pattern-action rules assumed to exist in the animal's mind.

There is a behavioral indicator of goal-oriented problem solving. Can the thinker react to the same situation in different ways, depending on its current goal structure? A demonstration that it can is positive but not sufficient evidence for goal-oriented behavior. A more rigorous test requires a demonstration of novel problem solving behavior. Suppose that a problem solver learns that response R1, in situation A, leads to consequent state B. Suppose further that the problem solver has also been shown that in state B response R2 will lead to goal state C. If the problem solver is placed in state A, and requires C, will the sequence of responses R1. . .R2 be emitted? As a further test, suppose that response R1' to A leads to B', and response R2' to B' produces C', a goal state distinct from goal state C. If the problem solver is placed in state A, will it respond with R1 or R1', depending upon its goals at the time? If so, the problem solver has displayed a rudimentary bit of goal directed thinking.

Animal observations can be used to illustrate the principle. Schusterman and Krieger (1984) report that a sea lion correctly responded to the command "touch with tail" when the object to be touched was out of the tank. The animal had previously been trained to "touch with tail" objects that were in the water. Since the action of tail-touching involves different muscle groups on land and in the water, the sea lion's response can be offered as an example of goal-directed thinking rather than an example of "mechanical" responding to stimuli.

Finally, but most importantly, thinking substitutes reactions to a computed internal environment for the possibly dangerous task of poking about in the real world. This means that the thinker must be able to uncouple itself from sensory stimulation while it examines its internal world. How much uncoupling is possible, and how much advisable? This question leads into the study of attention. To what extent can the being attend to its internal computations, regardless of the state of the external world? There are many examples of selective attention in studies of human intelligence. For example, people are slower to react to a probe signal when they are busy memorizing information (Lansman & Hunt, 1982). Obviously the ability to shut out the world can be overdone. Daydreaming undoubtedly contributes to automobile accidents. The basic point remains. Humans, by definition the most intelligent species, split their attention between the internal and external world. Otherwise internal thought processes would be driven by the flux of events in the external world. In fact, people who lack this ability. . .notably hyperactive children. . .are poor problem solvers. To what extent do animals show an ability to uncouple themselves from their perceptual world? Can the decoupling be related in any systematic way to their problem solving performance? A variety of experimental paradigms have been developed to study the control of attention in humans. Most involve studies of how attention to one stimulus diverts attention from others. Many of the paradigms could be adopted for the study of animals.

CONCLUDING COMMENTS

Philosophically, most scientists would argue that there is continuity between human and animal thought. What has been proposed here is that continuity be treated as a practical reality rather than a philosophic position. Many of the same paradigms and theoretical models used to explain human thought can be applied to the study of animal cognition. Why not do so? If there are laws of cognition itself these laws apply to all species.

There are two objections to a cognitive science approach to intelligence. The behaviorist position is that there are only a few laws governing behavior, that these laws are primarily concerned with learning, and that the linkage between the laws of learning and complex behavior are quite tight. It follows that the laws can be uncovered by studying unnatural, laboratory behavior of cognitively simple animals and then generalizing these laws to the free behavior of other species. The argument is not without merits. At some level, all behavior must be controlled by the same laws of learning. More pragmatically, the well-documented feats of behavior modification that have been obtained by generalizing laboratory laws of operant conditioning are certainly impressive. Is it possible that computational models of the sort proposed here are unnecessary mentalisms that could be derived from more basic laws without undue complications?

The answer to this question is probably "No." Serious attempts to derive cognition from more basic laws conclude by so complicating those laws that the cognitive science position is itself approximated. Consider B. F. Skinner's (1966) comments on problem solving. Skinner stated that problem solving occurs when behavior is emitted in order to set up a situation in which other, goal-acquiring behavior can be emitted. How is this different from the characterization of goal-oriented problem solving presented above? Skinner had to account for the emission of actions in terms of the stimuli that triggered them. He argued that problem solvers produce their own discriminative stimuli and react to them. In what way is this different from saying that internally generated goals and class-name symbols are part of the internal representation of a problem? The difference between Skinner and cognitive science may be more a difference in notation than a philosophical dispute.

Attacking the extreme behavioral position is a bit like setting up a straw man, for there are few extreme behaviorists among students of animal behavior today. Menzel's (this volume) views on animal intelligence include subtler objections to the cognitive science approach. Menzel lists several "dogmas" that he believes have hindered research on animal thought. The first is that belief that there is a continuity between human and animal intelligence. Menzel believes that there are qualitative differences in the mental competences of various species. Menzel believes that the continuity dogma was implicit in the traditional psychometric view that intelligence is a quantity that can be possessed to a greater or lesser degree. Cognitive science assumes that the expression of mental competence is determined by the possession of cognitive rules and the mechanisms required to execute them. The rules and mechanisms may be present to a greater or lesser degree. Since the rules and mechanisms present may make qualitative changes in behavior, the sort of continuity that the cognitive science approach sees between humans and other species is not necessarily expressable as a unidimensional intelligence. It is not clear that Menzel would object to the cognitive science interpretation of a neo-Darwinian approach to intelligence.

Two other dogma do appear to apply to cognitive science theories. Menzel defined *essentialism* as the belief that before animal behavior is examined one should first develop a precise idea of what is meant by intelligence. A closely related dogma is that an *a-biological* approach to intelligence is possible. Menzel objected to the logic of concluding that two organisms are "thinking in the same way" if their behavior can be described by the same computational model. The reason Menzel objected to the conclusion is that it does not consider the possibility that the behavior may have evolved in response to different environmental demands, and may be supported by different brain structures. To take a particularly cogent example, some apes and some cetaceans appear surprisingly adept at solving communication problems that humans choose to pose to them. Suppose it were to be shown that the same computational model could simulate the behavior of both the primates and the cetaceans. Would it be reasonable to say that these animals "think the same way"? They have very different brains.

Cognitive science does accept the essentialism dogma. There is no point to the discipline unless there are laws of thought *in general* that apply to all sentient beings. Some of the concepts that have been presented here represent an attempt to state these laws. Cognitive science specialists really believe that one has to talk about goal structures, working memory, and rule selection in order to talk about thinking. We do not plead guilty to Menzel's charge of essentialism because we do not think it is a crime.

Cognitive science is not necessarily a-biological. Cognitive science provides methods for a rational analysis of the computational mechanisms required to execute particular types of mental behavior. One can then investigate the role of physical structures in realizing these representations. For example, analysis would determine the variations of behavior that would be influenced if a particular computational module were or were not present (Fodor, 1983). One can then ask if the behaviors observed in the presence or absence of a brain system correspond to the behavior that would be predicted by computational modules with and without a particular module. Coltheart (1984) analysis of the effects of brain injuries upon reading is an outstanding case study of such an investigation. Coltheart chose amongst various computational models of reading by an analysis of how specific disorders arose following brain injuries to humans. The logic of Coltheart's analysis could be extended to studies of animal intelligence. For instance, one could envisage a program of research in which alterations in delphinid and primate problem solving abilities were induced by experimental brain lesions. Such a program of studies would probably be impractical on economic grounds, and would certainly introduce a serious ethical issue,[4] but these objections are irrelevant to the logic behind the study. Perhaps a more

---

[4]In proposing an experimental study of the effects of lesions on animal cognition one is simultaneously proposing that the (nonhuman) subjects have intelligence to some degree and that it is ethical to remove that intelligence. Biological scientists are not at all clear in their own thinking about this issue. Literally thousands of psychologists (including myself) have altered the brains of rats and mice, and are not at all bothered by moral issues. A proposal to conduct experimental brain surgery on any of the well studied communicating primates or delphinids would meet with vehement objections by the scientists responsible for the animals. I do not think that the objections would be motivated by economic considerations.

practical line of research would be to make simultaneous comparisons of the naturally occurring brain structures of related species and of the computational models required to simulate their cognitive abilities. Either example makes the same point. Cognitive science is not irrelevant to biological science; it is complementary.

The complementarity is needed. This essay will have been more than a success if it contributes to only one experiment in which computational analyses are applied to the very real question of animal intelligence.

ACKNOWLEDGMENT

The preparation of this paper was supported by the Office of Naval Research, Contract N00014-80-C-0631. The views expressed are those of the author and are not necessarily endorsed by the Office of Naval Research or the Department of the Navy. I am happy to acknowledge helpful discussions with Michael Beecher and Elizabeth Loftus, and comments on the paper by Nina DeLange and Colene McKee. Naturally, the views expressed are my own and do not represent the opinions of my colleagues or, of course, of the Office of Naval Research.

REFERENCES

Anderson, J. R. (1983). *The architecture of cognition.* Cambridge, MA: Harvard University Press.

Anderson, J. A. (1977). Neural models with cognitive implications. In D. La Berge, D., & S. Samuels (Eds.), *Basic Processes in Reading: Perception and Comprehension* Hillsdale, NJ: Lawrence Erlbaum Associates.

Berry, J. (1981). Cultural systems and cognitive sytles. In M. P. Friedman, J. P. Das, & N. O'Connor (Eds.), *Intelligence and learning.* New York: Plenum Press.

Binet, A., & Simon, T. (1905). The development of intelligence in children. *L'annee Psychologique, 12,* 163–244.

Boring, E. C. (1923). Intelligence as the tests test it. *The New Republic,* June 6, 35–37.

Carroll, J. B. (1982). The measurement of intelligence. In R. J. Sternberg (Ed.), *Handbook of human intelligence.* Cambridge: Cambridge University Press.

Coltheart, M. (1984, July). *Cognitive neuropsychology.* Paper read at Attention and Performance Conference, Eugene, OR.

Conrad, R. (1963). Acoustic confusions and memory span for words. *Nature, 197,* 1029–1030.

Cooper, L., & Shepard, R. (1973). Chronometric studies of the rotation of mental images. In W. Chase (Ed.), *Visual information processing.* New York: Academic Press.

Cover, T., & Hart, P. (1967). Nearest neighbor pattern classification. *IEEE Transactions on Information Theory, IT-3,* 21–27.

Fodor, J. (1983). *Modularity of the mind.* Cambridge, MA: MIT Press.

Garcia, J. (1974). In Hankins, W. G., & Rusiniak, K. W. "Behavioral regulation of the mileu interne in rat and man." *Science, 185,* 824–831.

Griffin, D. R. "The question of animal awareness." (1976) Rockefeller University Press.

Grossberg, S. B. (1980). How does the brain build a cognitive code? *Psychology Review 87,* 1–51.

Henley, N. (1969). A psychological study of the semantics of animal tears. *Journal of Verbal Learning and Verbal Behavior, 8,* 176–184.

Herman, L. M., Richards, D. G., & Wolz, J. P. (1984). Comprehension of sentences by bottlenosed dolphins. *Cognition, 16*(2), 129–219.

Herman, L. M. (1980). Cognitive characteristics of dolphins. In L. M. Herman (Ed.), *Cetacean behavior: Mechanisms and functions* New York: Wiley.

Hinton, G. E., & Anderson, J. A. (1981). *Parallel models of associative memory.* Hillsdale, NJ: Lawrence Erlbaum Associates.

Jerison, H. J. (1973). *Evolution of the brain and intelligence.* New York: Academic Press.

Johnson-Laird, P. N. (1980). Mental models in cognitive science. *Cognitive Science, 4,* 71–114.

Kohler, W. (1959). *The mentality of apes.* New York: Vintage Books. Translated from the second revised edition by Ella Winter.

Kosslyn, S. L. (1980). *Images and mind.* Cambridge, MA: Harvard University Press.

Krumhansl, C. L. (1979). The psychological representation of musical pitch in a tonal context. *Cognitive Psychology, 11,* 346–374.

Lansman, M., & Hunt, E. B. (1982). Individual differences in secondary task performance. *Memory & Cognition. 10, 1,* 10–24.

Laboratory of Comparative Human Cognition.(1982). Culture and intelligence. In R. J. Sternberg (Ed.), *Handbook of human intelligence.* Cambridge: Cambridge University Press.

Lawrence, D. H., & DeRivera, J. (1954). Evidence for relational transposition. *J. Comp. Physiol. Psychol., 47,* 465–471.

McClelland, J. L. (1979). On the time relations of mental processes: An examination of systems of processes in cascade. *Psychol. Rev., 80,* 287–330.

Minsky, M., & Papert, S. (1969). *Perceptions.* Cambridge, MA: MIT Press.

Neisser, C. (1979). The concept of intelligence. In R. J. Sternberg & D. Detterman (Eds.), *Human intelligence.* Norwood NJ: Ablex.

Plyshyn, Z. (1984). *Computation and cognition.* Cambridge, MA: Branford Press.

Risteau, C. A., & Robbins, P. (1982). Language in the great apes: A critical review. In J. S. Rosenblatt, P. A. Hinge, C. Beer, & M. C. Busnel (Eds.), *Advances in the study of behavior* (Vol. 12). New York: Academic Press.

Rumbaugh, D. G., & Pate, J. L. (1984). The evolution of cognition in primates: A comparative perspective. In H. L. Roitblat, T. G. Bever, & H. S. Terrace (Eds.), *Animal Cognition.* Hillsdale, NJ: Lawrence Erlbaum Associates.

Sands, S. F., Lincoln, C. E., & Wright, A. A. (1982). Pictorial similarity judgments and the organization of visual memory in the rhesus monkey. *JEP: General.* Vol. *111,* No. 4. 369–389.

Schiffman, S. S., Reynolds, M. L., & Young, F. W. (1981). *Introduction to multidimensional Scaling: Theory, methods, and applications.* New York: Academic Press.

Schusterman, R. J., & Krieger, K. (1984). California sea lions are capable of semantic comprehension. *Psychological Record, 34,* 3–23.

Skinner, B. F. (1966). The operant analysis of problem solving. In B. Kleinmuntz, (Ed.), *Problem solving: Research, method, and theory.* Norwood, NJ: Ablex.

Smith, E. E. & Medin, D. L. (1981). *Categories and concerns.* Cambridge, MA: Harvard University Press.

Sternberg, R. J. (1977). *Intelligence, information processing, and analogical reasoning.* Hillsdale, NJ: Lawrence Erlbaum Associates.

Sternberg, R. J. (1984). Toward a triarchic theory of human intelligence. *The behavioral and brain sciences.* 7(2), 269–315.

9 Suggestions for Research on Ethological and Comparative Cognition

Theodore Holmes Bullock
University of California, San Diego

INTRODUCTION

Three widely divergent views on the comparison of cognitive capacities, especially intelligence, are current. One is that these capacities develop, in evolution as in ontogeny, from very modest levels in primitive taxa to very high levels in some of the advanced taxa, though not in a linearly progressive or ladder-like way. A second applies to the vertebrates and asserts that evidence at hand does not justify recognizing any general difference in intelligence among the classes from fish to mammals or among the orders of mammals, except for the human species, which stands out from all others. The third view is that cognition and especially intelligence in different species is so different in quality that it cannot be compared in degree.

The comparative study of cognitive capacities in various species of animals is not only intellectually important but socially urgent. The term cognition is used here in its broad sense, not confined to thinking or excluding emotion; in particular this essay is concerned with conscious feelings and affective states, thinking and intelligence—in all degrees. In many societies the public concern over suffering believed to be experienced by nonhuman species, especially that inflicted by human activities, has reached a high pitch. Yet the knowledge base of reasonably established information permitting assessments of the suffering, worry or other consciously experienced feelings, the self awareness, the insight and capacity for rational processes of even the best known laboratory and domestic species is so meager that major disagreements exist in the broad conclusions to be drawn.

There is a tendency, even among careful scientists, to speak in terms of *whether or not* a given animal has a mental life, thoughts, consciousness or awareness of being aware—implying that these features are present or not present, all or none. This may be a reaction to the behaviorist-reductionist extreme. It is curious that this is often the only extreme warned against, and no danger is seen in the extreme of assuming all or none conscious awareness, prior to adequate evidence! It is therefore not trivial today to underline the probability, on zoological, psychological and neurological grounds, that these capacities are present in *widely varying degree* among animal species, classes and phyla.

At the same time we should recognize the probability that some features, even though called by the same general name, such as intelligence, are in some important respects *qualitatively* different in various taxa. (However, only those qualitative differences are relevant here which render the cognitive achievements not comparable as achievements; differences in mechanism are to be expected without preventing assessment of the result.) If such qualitative differences in cognitive features were found to be too great and if it were true of too many of the cognitive features of organisms, we could only compare species by ranking the qualities according to our estimate of their stage of evolutionary advancement. It would still not be impossible to grade the taxa or to apply words such as "better," or "more advanced," but it would be more subjective than if we can assay *quantitatively* the level of development of an operationally (not mechanistically) defined feature, such as intelligence or curiosity.

It may well turn out that species differences in *relative development* of each of an array of capacities, qualities, and dispositions really appear valid and account adequately for many of the observed behavioral characteristics of species, including their apparently qualitative differences. By analogy, in spite of apparent qualitative differences in morphological, physiological, and behavioral features, we are usually able to compare and arrange them in order, from more primitive to more derived, for example to make phylogenetic dendrograms (albeit with difficulty, especially in some groups of animals). If it is true that given taxa can be compared as to their relative development on an interesting set of dimensions, there is still ample room for *evolutionary saltations* leading to novelties in cognitive features, or emergents which are barely foreshadowed in ancestral groups.

This emphasis on the *multiplicity of distinct features* of each species, cognitive as well as morphological or other, is congruent with the position of Fodor (1983) on the "modularity of mind," though it does not take sides in the sense of embracing or asserting fully independent, equivalent modules. It means that the whole behavior and cognitive life of an animal is not to be characterized in a word or a few words or an intelligence quotient, but is a composite of distinct and only partly linked, evolving characters, the behavioral characters probably as diverse and numerous as the morphological, physiological and chemical characters. This is, at the least, an heuristic way of thinking because it dictates many quantifiable, objective measures, each clearly relevant but none pretending to be *the* measure of intelligence or mind or consciousness. It is certainly compatible with Barlow's (1983) view of intelligence although emphasizing the multiplicity of measures required. Even a jumping spider might pass one test, say skill in guesswork, with high marks. It agrees with Bunge's (1980) claim that the mind-body problem belongs in the hands of scientific biologists. However, I would not say, with Hoyle (1983) that the primary hope for this question is from neurophysiology, but rather from ethology and psychophysics.

PURPOSE

The purpose of this essay is to suggest some of the research strategies that might lead to new insights, and to make a series of claims about what can in fact be done—imperfectly and with difficulty but with some validity—which could go a long way toward enlarging our information base for judgments about cognitive capacities of various species. It is a call for comparisons among taxa—which are rare in the burgeoning literature on comparative cognition; a call for ethological study of cognition or cognitive ethology. It is intended otherwise to echo, support, and extend the approach exemplified by Herman (1980) and to be appended as a commentary on the body of literature, including the following, among others (Darwin, 1882; Romanes, 1883; Hinde, 1970, 1983; Griffin, 1976, 1982, 1984; Dawkins, 1976, 1980; Rozin, 1976; Humphrey, 1976, 1983; Gibson, 1977; Rosch & Lloyd, 1978; Hulse, Fowler, & Honig 1978; Fantino & Logan, 1979; Sebeok & Umiker-Sebeok, 1980; Reynolds, 1981; MacPhail, 1982; Sternberg, 1982; Kalat, 1983; Walker, 1983; Crook, 1983; Rajecki, 1983; Kitchell et al., 1983; Roitblat, Bever, & Terrace, 1984; Smith, 1984; Burghardt, 1984). It is not a comment on our moral imperatives or on animal rights but is aimed at the evaluation of the sentience of each species, which many people, including the author, regard as one important factor in the recognition of rights and moral imperatives.

Tactically it is of the first importance that we should try to evaluate each characteristic under study in a quantitative or semiquantitative way, in comparison to other species (more than one or two others, to reduce the likelihood of chance correlations). If a given species is relatively aggressive or curious or hunts in packs, these features can, with enough effort and ingenuity, be evaluated on some scale, relative to closely related and to more distant species. I would like to emphasize the importance of building into our research protocols this kind of evaluation, even for subtle and high level features such as the degree of prominence in a given species of declarative learning versus procedural learning—as has been done recently in human patients after related lesions (Weingartner, et al., 1983).

Strategically it is of the first importance that we should at least begin a listing of candidate *distinguishable cognitive features,* the sum of which might approximate a characterization, not only of the given species but of a broad range of taxa. Such a list would not only serve as an agenda, it would provide a basis for the daily challenge of explaining to students and lay people the problem of assessing, for example, cetacean cognition.

LIST OF MEASURABLE VARIABLES

In what follows I venture a preliminary and tentative list of categories, intended to stimulate others, more knowledgeable than I in behavioral science, to refine, correct, and enlarge the list, toward the goal of devising estimators for the degree of expression of each item in each of a range of species. Many items in the list have, of course, been studied extensively in one or a few species and have a body of literature. A few references as examples are Bitterman (1965), Glickman and Stroges (1966), Simpson (1976), Chevalier-Skolnikoff (1976), Delius and Habers (1978), Desmond (1979), Beck (1980), Herman (1980), Chevalier-Skolnikoff, Galdikas, and Skolnikoff (1982), Holland and Delius (1982), Moynihan and Rodaniche (1982), Panksepp (1982), Schmid and Hake (1983), Weingartner, Grafman, Boutelle, Kaye, and Martin (1983), Wilkie (1983), Marin, Glenn, and Rafal (1983), Blough (1983), Epstein, Kirshnit, Lanza, and Rubin (1984).

The list of candidate features of cognition is intentionally long, although that runs the risk of discouraging the reader, since many items are patently difficult to manage. In our present state of badly needing a large body of verifiable data, to break out of the still surviving tendency to judge animal cognition by one or a few, impressive or favorite characters, it is worthwhile to aim for a time at expanding the list in hopes of discerning enough feasible measures, before selecting a contracted subset that might overlook something clever. Many items are suggested by human characteristics and may be undetectable except in the highest nonhuman species. Each presents a challenge in respect to devising means for grading the expression of some aspect of that capacity.

The status of items as members of a numbered list does not imply any equivalence in scope, neurological mechanism or ecological significance, but merely in being a potentially quantifiable aspect of behavior, possibly graded in evolution. Many are in need of dissection into distinguishable facets. It can be hoped that some will prove to be so correlated as to justify a shorter list of independent components of cognition.

1.   I begin with items roughly related in measuring the degree of flexibility in **interacting with the environment.**

1.1.   Desire for *novelty;* graded for example by the number of different forms and modalities of reinforcement for which the animal will perform. A potentially rich measure should be used, for example counting how many levers, or manipulanda (chosen to be appropriate for the species) the animal will bring under control if it has an excess of them and each one gives it a different reinforcement (e.g., water, food, shelter, view out, acoustic or video stimuli such as radio or TV stations, step down or up in temperature, light, etc., access to toys, or to conspecifics, each novelty falling back toward a ground state with a certain time constant). This is an example of the kind of countable measure that should be sought for each of the following items. In some cases it will be a challenge to ingenuity and require a good knowledge of the ethology of the species concerned to do this.

1.2.   Desire for strong and *complex sensation;* effort expended to create unusual sensory experiences. Is the human unique in seeking sensations such as hot baths, deliberately prepared and spiced foods, artifacts made to look at (not as signals to others)? As in each category, the evaluation should include an estimate of the degree of development of this proclivity.

1.3.   *Object manipulation;* duration and diversity of movements in handling objects; use of objects as tools—graded as to the degree of adaptability. Is this really two or more distinct items? Perhaps tools to solve immediate problems and things to twiddle should be separated.

1.4.   *Stereotypy* vs adaptability to different conditions, for example in food procurement, locomotion, orientation, navigation and similar spheres of behavior—each a potentially independent measure.

1.5.   *Rule following* in obeying learned commands, graded as to the sophistication of the rules generally obeyed. The same might be done quite independently for locomotor rules in maze running, for social rules in playing games, for grammatical rules in sentence commands, and rules in other contexts.

1.6.   *Exploration,* graded as to boldness, or inquisitiveness in a new situation.

1.7.   *Play,* graded in respect to diversity, to frequency and to the trouble invested in it, especially in adults.

2.   The next group measure aspects of **social interactions.**

2.1.   Tendency to *mimic* has been proposed by Griffin (1984), among others. I would insist on its being graded as to the complexity, flexibility or stereotypy of the mimicry.

2.2.   *Observation-learning;* graded by the readiness to acquire a variety of habits by watching.

2.3.   *Sharing;* graded by the degree of prominence or the level of attainment.

2.4.   *Aggressivity* under specified conditions might be a candidate if it is graded, e.g. by the degree expressed in young males, during the breeding season, ranked by stereotypy, range and adaptability.

2.5.   *Repertoire* in courtship, and in other definable categories of behavior may be useful if graded for example in diversity, adaptability, or in time spent in gaining access to that option.

2.6.   Spontaneous signalling about the *non-self,* e.g. about the human investigator, weather, tomorrow, absent family.

2.7.   Relative *prominence of learned* superimposed on innate behavior, for example in courtship, agonistic and other defined spheres of behavior.

2.8.   Degree of *dependence on teaching* and social tradition in the care of the young, in vocal and visual communication, in nest building, territory defense or other categories of activity.

If the problems of feasibility and difficulty of measurement loom in the reader's mind, read on; we will remark on them shortly!

3.   The third group of measures concern the sophistication of **communication.**

3.1.   *Number of signals* used naturally; perhaps especially the increment in number with experience and age.

3.2.   Number of *elements* used in defined sequences of distinct signals, such as our *sentences,* especially when spontaneously used in the interindividual interactive mode. It is important to grade them in complexity of syntax.

3.3.   *Sentence comprehension,* in the receiving mode, graded for example by the number of total elements or of subsets like qualifiers of nouns, or graded in the delay before the animal is permitted to execute a symbolized command, or in the amount of distraction required to reduce performance.

3.4.   Use of *writing and rhyme,* with evidence of intention. I must include these even if they are believed to be peculiar to the human species. The list should contain the faculties in which humans excel, as well as those in which other species excel.

4.   The fourth group represent somewhat **higher levels** of cognitive range, performance and affect. No doubt they are increasingly difficult to measure, but the essence of comparative cognition is to embrace all levels, particularly the most cognitive, in order to consider their qualitative and quantitative development in different taxa.

4.1.   Range and variety of learned, referential, *arbitrary symbols* that can be taught; e.g., nouns, verbs, qualifiers, contingencies, concepts ("same," "different," "taller," "shorter").

4.2.   Range of types of *game learning,* e.g., discrimination of attributes, or of sequences, match to sample, delayed discrimination, delayed match, improvement in habit reversal, playing against odds for remotely possible rewards.

4.3.   *Concept learning,* such as threeness, fourness; oddity-nonoddity, with graded complexity; transfer index for each kind of reversal. There is much room for ingenuity in devising tests suited to the species.

4.4. *Dynamic range of emotions;* from ecstasy to agony, from anxiety to terror, under isolated and under social conditions. Though related, this is not the same as the next item.

4.5. *Variety of emotional responses* and spontaneous moods: the number of distinguishable emotions, their subtlety and adaptability, the degree of complexity of situations eliciting emotion, complexity of mixed emotions, motivations or "hang-ups."

4.6. Higher parameters of motivation, beyond elementary drives, such as evidence of *planning* for less proximate rewards or avoiding more remote hazards.

The broad category of *problem solving* has been distributed among a number of the foregoing, in recognition of its heterogeneous nature.

This, or an improved list might be considered a partial agenda for describing each taxon, even each sex and age, toward assembling a picture of its cognitive capacities relative to other animals. It is intended to emphasize the qualitative **range** of characters and the quantitative possibilities for multiple **measures** under each item. It becomes clear that most of the numbered items should be subdivided. The longer the list and the more discrete, operational and measurable the items, the better will be the representation of the species. It makes obvious that the time is past when one could simply say, "See, this species shows altruism," or "That species can tell lies," without adding an estimation of the degree, the complexity, the variety of forms. This will be a particularly difficult habit to break, so I give it special emphasis. Treating species as cognitively equivalent in respect to characters such as, for example, mimicry, or tool use without a serious effort to estimate degrees is a flaw found even in recent arguments (Griffin, 1984). I believe a revision of this or a similar list would be a major contribution to the goal of rational recognition of animal capabilities and to the field of comparative cognition.

Comparisons between species are sometimes disappointing, for example if laborious measurements have been made on two species of dolphins and they are not very different. Two things should be said about this. First, it would be well wherever possible to make comparisons among more than two species of distinguishably different biology in respect to some relevant ecology or ethology. It is generally more meaningful to assert that species A lies between B and C in this or that respect, than merely to say that A is below B. Second, comparisons are usually more interpretable between species of at least different families if not orders.

A major concession is called for, to my mind, namely to admit that the experienced investigator can to some degree grade the cognitive demand or the sophistication of many of the tests or qualities, and that this ordering, although partly subjective and certainly refineable by debate among experts, has some significance. Similarly, in grading the performance of an animal, whereas many capacities or proclivities can be objectively quantified, with ingenuity, for others, subjective grades are both necessary and valuable, if made by observers who have established their credentials, specifically as reliable ethologists of the particular taxon.

5.   The following items, operationally **difficult, higher forms of cognition,** though presenting problems even for qualified observers, are examples of dimensions where deliberate estimates would be a real contribution, even if given simply as low, medium and high levels, relative to human norms.

5.1.   Range and subtlety of *prevarication*. We can not be satisfied with "Species A can tell lies."

5.2.   Range, magnitude and remoteness of targets of *charity*, or other forms of altruism requiring, as we experience it, deliberate planning.

5.3.   Variety, subtlety and incidence of *humor*.

5.4.   Variety, subtlety and incidence of *music*.

5.5.   Variety, subtlety and incidence of organized *teamwork* in relatively sophisticated activities such as making music, team sports, cooperative acting (playing roles), group governance involving politics, group accumulation of collections of aesthetic or historic objects.

COMMENTS ON THE LIST

One of the strong propositions of this essay is that just such difficult domains as the last five belong in the list of research desiderata, when we consider the more advanced species. The full range of human qualities and institutions should be systematically explored, making efforts, even if largely subjective, by cautious experts, to compare their development, importance, role and level in the non-human species of interest, relative to ours. It might be objected that this list is anthropocentric, as though that condemns it. Certainly it is, by design. The intention is to choose human qualities just as much as those distinctive of other species and to look, not merely for some hint or trace of them, but for the degree of development. It is precisely when we are asking about higher forms of cognition that human capacities are heuristic sources of ideas for estimators. I agree with Griffin (1976) that we can and should make innovative efforts to assess the mental life of other species, that we are different in degree and owe it to each other to attempt fearlessly to evaluate all the facets, particularly the highest ones. I agree that complexity is a slippery character but I cannot consider the "fishing" for termites by assassin bugs equally "as suggestive of thought as the chimpanzee's use of a termite probe" (Griffin 1984) any more than the chimpanzee's use of a stick is equal in creativity of thinking to that of a 5-year-old child, perhaps even a 3-year-old.

A major category that I have not explicitly included in the list, although implicitly distributed among several items, is that suggested by the proposition that the essence of intelligence is less a matter of reasoning ability than of knowing a lot about the world, that is of **acquired knowledge** (Waldrop, 1984). It is not listed simply because I find it even more difficult than the last group of items to design a cross-species, comparable way to estimate. No doubt some experienced ethologists develop an impression as to the specific information about the local habitat and social group that must be acquired by members of the species they study. However, it is more difficult to see how such observers could convey their estimates in a form permitting comparison with the estimates of others; this means the estimate would only be useable if the same observer became equally familiar with several taxa.

In line with my concept of good science, I now attempt to make explicit my guess as to the way it will turn out. This might represent a bias and if it is enunciated, it is more likely to be controlled for in the design of measurements. It is a mistake, on this view, to pretend that by not so guessing we are less likely to allow bias to contaminate our findings. After being properly impressed with the instances of nonhuman species telling lies, laughing, noticing their own features in mirrors, saving drowning victims, and using four- or five-word sentences, I think we will enter a phase of quantitation and that evidence will converge from many kinds of tests that even the species believed to be the most advanced in mental faculties, including apes and cetaceans, will have to be regarded as very far short of the human condition. If there is indeed an enormous unoccupied gap, even allowing for the possibility that different cognitive capacities can evolve considerably out of proportion, in different taxa, it would compel much more caution than is usual in attributing even to the chimpanzee and dolphin anything like a human degree of self awareness, or of worry or suffering, to say nothing of complex language or conceptualization.

Of the three views outlined in the first paragraph, I expect the first to be most generally recognized, namely that higher cognitive capacities including whatever is meant by intelligence, conscious awareness and the ability to suffer are not unique to the human nor equally developed in all species, or in all nonhuman species, but are graded, as they are in development of the child. I would not say that the cognitive states of adults of various species are identical to those of stages of human development but that the cognition of jellyfish, earthworms, ants, carp, alligators, and baboons is graduated in that order. This conclusion is based on their ethology—to be sure inadequately known, and the anatomical and physiological advancement of the brain, also inadequately though extensively known. It leaves open for discussion how great is the difference in each case and for each aspect of cognition. It recognizes that evolution is not a ladder, that some amphibians may be less advanced than some fish, and octopus may be more advanced than some fish, that qualitative differences may restrict such statements to pretty gross contrasts between taxa that are quite clearly distinct in overall advancement. Nevertheless, if we could agree to it, the consequences of this simple conclusion would be significant. For example, we would not expect all vertebrates, from hagfish to chimpanzees, to be treated alike, as some of our present guidelines do.

The mere fact that such evaluations will be controversial does not excuse neglecting to put them forward in the scientific literature, where the rules of the game of debate and criticism are powerful tools. The best science is not limited to the most objective methods and hardest facts but adds to them extrapolations, judgments, and inductions. The late physical chemist Blaine Ramsey repeatedly expounded the importance of "enthusiastic tentativeness". Experienced observers using the methods of science can surely arrive at an approximation, with some validity, of the relative sophistication of communication by jungle drums and by a Shakespearean actor. Physicians routinely judge levels of consciousness, dividing it into a number of grades. Music teachers grade capacities in their domain—not fully agreeing with each other, but achieving some verifiability.

My hope is that at such conferences in the future we will not confine ourselves, each to his own animal and hard data, to the exclusion of fresh attempts to sum up estimates on comparisons of cognitive capacities. In order to show preliminary progress in the intrinsically exciting field of comparative cognition, and in particular in the task of recognizing the rightful place of dolphins, more workers are needed who will take up this challenge. Instead of confining arguments to one or two characters at a time, the broader, ethological experts will venture approximations as to several items from a longer list, some of them estimated objectively and others subjectively. It may be too much to expect 25 items or even 10 at first, but it is important to deal with as many as possible. At least we can see each hard won datum as part of a large agenda that has the potential of yielding reasonably scientific answers. If we do this with enthusiastic tentativeness and without excessive emotional attachment to our preliminary conclusions, this branch of science may be under way.

SUMMARY

Comparative cognition is badly in need of an expanded base of information on the capacities of a variety of taxa, both for its intrinsic intellectual interest and because of urgent social pressures.

It is argued that the mental life, thought processes, consciousness and intelligence of nonhuman species are not all or none but graded over a very wide dynamic range in evolution as in ontogeny. The position is supported that these major domains of cognition are made up of a number of partly independent constituents. Although many constituents of general cognitive complexes like intelligence are qualitatively different among species, thereby presenting some serious difficulties, it is argued that some significant comparisons of achievements are possible.

A list of some thirty items in five categories is offered, representing potentially quantifiable aspects of these constituents, confined to overt behavioral endpoints. This long range agenda derives many items from the most distinctively human characteristics since a major part of the comparative challenge is to assess the degree of similarity or difference with respect to the human species. It is claimed that even the more subtle and high level features can, with ingenuity, be estimated in a semiquantitative way. It is also asserted that subjective judgments on more difficult features, by ethologists who have qualified themselves for the given species are not without value and should be debated and refined by the game rules of scientific literature. The importance is emphasized (i) of quantitation of each trait (ii) of graded estimators of widely different level and (iii) of multiple measures.

REFERENCES

Barlow, H. B. (1983). Intelligence, guesswork, language. *Nature, 304,* 207–209.

Beck, B. B. (1980). *Animal tool behavior.* New York: Garland.

Bitterman, M. E. (1965). The evolution of intelligence. *Scientific American, 212,* 92–100.

Blough, D. S. (1983). Pigeon perception of letters of the alphabet. *Science, 218,* 397–398.

Bunge, M. (1980). *The mind-body problem.* Oxford: Pergamon.

Burghardt, G. M. (1984). On the origins of play. In P. K. Smith (Ed.), *Play in animals and humans,* Oxford, Basil Blackwell.

Chevalier-Skolnikoff, S. (1976). The ontogeny of primate intelligence and its implications for communicative potential: A preliminary report. *Annals of the New York Academy of Sciences, 280,* 173–211.

Chevalier-Skolnikoff, S., Galdikas, B. M. F., & Skolnikoff, A. Z. (1982). The adaptive significance of higher intelligence in wild orang-utans: A preliminary report. *Journal of Human Evolution, 11,* 639–652.

Crook, J. H. (1983). On attributing consciousness to animals. *Nature, 303,* 11–14.

Darwin, C. (1882). Notes in G. J. Romanes, *Animal intelligence.* London: Kegan Paul Trench. International Scientific Series 41.

Dawkins, R. (1976). Hierarchical organisation: A candidate principle for ethology. In P. P. G. Bateson & R. A. Hinde (Eds.), *Growing points in ethology* (pp. 7–54). Cambridge: Cambridge University Press.

Dawkins, M. S. (1980). *Animal suffering. The science of animal welfare.* New York: Chapman & Hall.

Delius, J. D., & Habers G. (1978). Symmetry: Can pigeons conceptualize it? *Behavioral Biology, 22,* 336–342.

Desmond, A. J. (1979). *The ape's reflexion.* London: Blond & Briggs.

Epstein, R., Kirshnit, C. E., Lanza R. P., & Rubin L. C. (1984). ''Insight'' in the pigeon: Antecedents and determinants of an intelligent performance. *Nature, 308,* 61–62.

Fantino, E. J., & Logan, C. A. (1979). *The experimental analysis of behavior: a biological perspective.* San Francisco: Freeman.

Fodor, J. A. (1983). *Modularity of mind.* Cambridge, MA: MIT Press.

Gibson, K. R. (1977). Brain structure and intelligence in macaques and human infants from a Piagetian perspective. In S. Chevalier-Skolnikoff & F. E. Poirier (Eds.), *Primate bio-social development* (pp. 113–158). New York: Garland.

Glickman, S., & Stroges, R. W. (1966). Curiosity in zoo animals. *Behaviour, 26,* 151–188.

Griffin, D. R. (1976). *The question of animal awareness. Evolutionary continuity of mental experience.* New York: Rockefeller University Press.

Griffin, D. R. (1982). *Animal mind, human mind.* Berlin: Dahlem Konferenzen.

Griffin, D. R. (1984). Animal thinking. *American Scientist, 72,* 456–464.

Herman, L. M. (1980). Cognitive characteristics of dolphins. In L. M. Herman (Ed.), *Cetacean behavior: Mechanisms and functions.* New York: Wiley.

Hinde, R. A. (1970). *Animal behaviour.* 2nd edit. New York: McGraw-Hill.

Hinde, R. A. (1983). *Ethology.* New York: Oxford University Press.

Holland V. D., & Delius J. D. (1982). Rotational invariance in visual pattern recognition by pigeons and humans. *Science, 218,* 804–806.

Hoyle, G. (1983). Review of The mind-body problem, by Mario Bunge. *Journal of Neurobiology, 14,* 337–338.

Hulse, S. H., Fowler H., & Honig, W. K. (1978). *Cognitive processes in animal behavior.* Hillsdale, NJ: Lawrence Erlbaum Associates.

Humphrey, N. K. (1976). The social function of intellect. In P. P. G. Bateson & R. A. Hinde (Eds.), *Growing points in ethology* (pp. 303–318). Cambridge: Cambridge University Press.

Humphrey, N. K. (1983). *Consciousness regained: Chapters in the development of mind.* Oxford: Oxford University Press.

Kalat, J. W. (1983). Evolutionary thinking in the history of the comparative psychology of learning. *Neuroscience and Biobehavioral Reviews, 7,* 309–314.

Kitchell, R. L., Erickson, H. I., Carstens, E., & Davis, L. E. (1983). *Animal pain, perception and alleviation.* Bethesda, MD: American Physiological Society.

Marin, O. S. M., Glenn C. G., & Rafal R. D. (1983). Visual problem solving in the absence of lexical semantics: Evidence from dementia. *Brain & Cognition, 2,* 285–311.

Macphail, E. M. (1982). *Brain and intelligence in vertebrates.* Oxford: Clarendon Press.

Moynihan, M., & Rodaniche A. F. (1982). The behavior and natural history of the Caribbean reef squid *Sepioteuthis sepioidea* with a consideration of social, signal, and defensive patterns for difficult and dangerous environments. *Journal of Comparative Ethology,* suppl. *25,* 1–150.

Panksepp, J. (1982). Toward a psychobiological theory of emotions. *Behavioral and Brain Sciences, 5,* 407–467.

Rajecki, D. W. (1983). *Comparing behavior: Studying man studying animals.* Hillsdale, NJ: Lawrence Erlbaum Associates.

Reynolds, P. C. (1981). *On the evolution of human behavior: The argument from animals to man.* Berkeley: University of California Press.

Roitblat, H. L., Bever, T. G., & Terrace H. S. (1984). *Animal cognition* Hillsdale, NJ: Lawrence Erlbaum Associates.

Romanes, G. J. (1883). *Mental evolution in animals. With a posthumous essay on instinct by Charles Darwin* (pp. 355–384). London: Kegan Paul Trench.

Rosch, E., & Lloyd, B. B. (1978). *Cognition and categorization.* Hillsdale, NJ: Lawrence Erlbaum Associates.

Rozin, P. (1976). The evolution of intelligence and access to the cognitive unconscious. *Progress in Psychobiology and Physiological Psychology, 6,* 245–280.

Schmid, T. L., & Hake D. F. (1983). Fast acquisition of cooperation and trust: A two-stage view of trusting behavior. *Journal of the Experimental Analysis of Behavior, 40,* 179–192.

Sebeok, T. A., & Umiker-Sebeok, J. (1980). *Speaking of apes.* New York: Plenum.

Simpson, M. J. A. (1976). *The study of animal play*. In P. P. G. Bateson & R. A. Hinde (Eds.), *Growing points in ethology* (pp. 385–400). Cambridge: Cambridge University Press.

Smith, P, K. (1984). *Play in animals and humans*. Oxford: Basil Blackwell.

Sternberg, R. J. (1982). *Handbook of human intelligence*. Cambridge: Cambridge University Press.

Waldrop, M. M. (1984). The necessity of knowledge. *Science, 223,* 1279–1282.

Walker, S. F. (1983). *Animal thought*. London: Routledge and Kegan Paul.

Weingartner, H., Grafman, J., Boutelle, W., Kaye W., & Martin P. R. (1983). Forms of memory failure. *Science, 221,* 380–382.

Wilkie, D. M. (1983). Pigeon's spatial memory: III. Effect of distractors on delayed matching of key locations. *Journal of the Experimental Analysis of Behavior, 40,* 143–152.

10 Cognition and Language Competencies of Bottlenosed Dolphins

Louis M. Herman
*Kewalo Basin Marine Mammal Laboratory
and Social Science Research Institute,
University of Hawaii*

INTRODUCTION

Like any biological trait, cognitive characteristics may vary widely across species. A fundamental task for comparative psychologists and cognitive ethologists (see Griffin, 1981) is to describe these characteristics for any species of interest. The goals of the description are to understand the general and specific structures and processes of cognition, the dimensions of cognition, its continuities and discontinuities across species, how the described cognitive characteristics for given species may relate to the ecological and social pressures of that species' natural world, and what pressures may select for the evolution of particular cognitive traits.

The bottlenosed dolphin (*Tursiops truncatus*) is a compelling subject for study of animal cognition. The absolute and relative size of the bottlenosed dolphin brain, as well as its architecture and apparent complexity (Flanigan, 1972; Morgane, 1978; Morgane & Jacobs, 1972; but see Morgane, this volume), suggest exceptional information-processing power. Jerison (1973) has proposed that information-processing power, or biological intelligence, is indexed by the degree of encephalization of the brain—the "residual" mass of the brain not accounted for by body size nor mapped onto the control of basic biological functions. It is therefore noteworthy that encephalization in the bottlenosed dolphin may be comparable to that of living species of higher primates including humans (Jerison, 1978). Nevertheless, in the final analysis, intellectual *performance,* rather than structural criteria, defines the quality of a brain. This chapter reviews current knowledge of intellectual performance and related cognitive characteristics in bottlenosed dolphins, as obtained through laboratory studies.

221

A basic philosophy underlying my approach to the study of the cognitive characteristics of bottlenosed dolphins (or of any species) is that the quality and range of intellectual performance demonstrable is in part a function of the intensity and breadth of long-term education received. This is apparent for the human species and it is reasonable to grant as much to many other animals. Exposing animals to flexible, changing, and challenging training regimes that build a repertoire of skills and knowledge may reveal cognitive potential that is masked by more traditional behavioral approaches that use static training procedures or animals that are relatively naive educationally.

Within this philosophy, the following questions have guided many of the studies of dolphin cognition by myself and my colleagues over the past 15 years; the questions constitute a capsule summary of our research goals. While answers to these questions may be slow in coming, they can be revealing of the cognitive potential and the cognitive world of the dolphin. Answers to a given question may also uncover new questions, suggest better ways to frame older questions, or provide new solutions to old questions.

a. What are the capabilities, specializations, and limitations in cognition of the bottlenosed dolphin?

b. What underlying processes and structures may account for the described cognitive characteristics?

c. How do the cognitive characteristics of the dolphin relate to its biological, ecological, and social systems and constraints?[1]

d. Can cognitive performance be extended beyond the demonstrable needs of these systems?

e. How do the cognitive characteristics of the dolphin compare with and relate to those of selected other species?

f. What general theories and models of cognition, its function and its evolution, can be derived from the analyses of cognitive characteristics and cognitive processes across the different species?

The remainder of this chapter summarizes some of our major findings bearing on these questions. Included is a synoptic account of the capabilities and constraints of dolphins for processing and manipulating auditory and visual materials. The specializations, range, and limitations of memory, and the ability to acquire new knowledge and procedures, are considered as a function of these two major sensory modalities. Our recent work on the ability of dolphins to understand the semantic and syntactic features of artificial acoustic and gestural languages is also reviewed. Several topics related to language processing are dis-

---

[1]The word "dolphin," when used alone, refers to the bottlenosed dolphin, *Tursiops* sp.

cussed, including the ability to understand references to things remote in space or time, to report about objects, as well as to respond to them, and to interchange symbol and referent. The types of coding that may be used in some of the language tasks is discussed. Selected findings from studies by others of dolphins, or other animal species, are also considered.

PROCESSING AUDITORY AND VISUAL INFORMATION

Specializations in Auditory Information Processing

The remarkable development of the dolphin's peripheral and central auditory systems provides a major interface for extracting information from the underwater world. It seems likely that the cognitive structures for classifying, storing, organizing, interpreting, and manipulating auditory information are highly developed. The results of our laboratory studies support this contention. These studies have shown that the dolphin is capable of high levels of performance in a variety of complex auditory learning and memory tasks.

For example, a bottlenosed dolphin named Kea was given a series of two-choice auditory discrimination problems, each problem using new sounds. There was progressive improvement in Kea's speed of learning each problem, until an asymptotic level of one-trial learning was reached, and maintained for nearly 87% of 111 successive, unique two-choice auditory discriminations (Herman & Arbeit, 1973). A parametric analysis of performance as a function of sound characteristics revealed that sounds from a broad range of frequencies, modulation parameters, and complexity were handled well. Rapidly-pulsed tones were the most difficult, while frequency modulated tones proved easiest. Frequency modulation is characteristic of many of the whistle-like sounds produced by the dolphin (Herman & Tavolga, 1980), and the dolphin is also remarkably efficient in detecting the presence of sine-wave frequency modulation in sounds (Herman & Arbeit, 1972; Thompson & Herman, 1975).

In a study described in Herman (1980), we explored Kea's ability to learn to reverse her responses to pairs of sounds. After Kea had learned to respond to one sound of a pair for reward, a response to the alternative sound was rewarded instead. Five different pairs of sounds were given, each pair reversed a minimum of four times. The efficiency in learning to reverse increased progressively across successive problems; during the last of the five problems, there was a maximum of only one error at each of the four successive reversals. This reversal learning technique formed part of the procedures for the Herman and Arbeit (1973) study already described; apparently, Kea's experience with the multiple two-choice auditory discrimination problems transferred positively and immediately to the reversal learning procedure. In an earlier, preliminary study of this type with the dolphins Kea and Nana, Beach and Herman (1972) found little evidence of such transfer. In that study, however, the stimulus presentation methods likely caused some masking of sounds and perhaps some ambiguity in the association of sound and reward. These methodological difficulties were corrected in the subsequent Herman and Arbeit (1973) study.

We tested Kea's memory for sounds in a number of experiments using a delayed matching-to-sample format. Basically, we briefly (e.g., 2 sec) presented Kea with a "sample" sound of an arbitrary waveform, within a frequency range of 1 to 140 kHz, and then tested her ability to recognize that sound in a later test. Kea faithfully remembered the sample sound, even after delays of several minutes (Herman & Gordon, 1974; Herman & Thompson, 1982). The limits on performance appeared more a function of emotional disruption caused by the long within-trial delays, than a true constraint on memory.

In the Herman and Gordon (1974) study, new sample sounds, not previously heard by Kea, were used in each delayed matching test. This study tested Kea's ability to encode and remember any of a variety of sound attributes, as well as her ability to form and apply the general concept of "match the sample." A total of 346 novel matching problems were given: performance was variable during the first 171 problems but then increased dramatically over the remaining 175, during which there were only three first-trial errors in matching (98.3% correct first-trial matches). During this latter set of problems, the delays (time elapsed before the dolphin was given the opportunity to respond) sometimes reached 90 or 120 sec.

In other auditory delayed matching procedures given Kea, we found relatively little susceptibility of memory to proactive or retroactive interference (Herman, 1975), or to variations in sample duration or quality (reviewed in Herman, 1980). These studies used a small set of familiar sounds rather than a large set of novel sample sounds. Herman and Thompson (1982) showed that symbolic matching could be carried out about as well as identity matching, although the former task was initially difficult to learn. Kea could also reliably indicate whether a single alternative sound was or was *not* a match for the sample (called "probe" or "Yes/No" matching). Thompson and Herman (1977), and additional work reported in Herman (1980), showed that Kea could reliably report whether a probe sound was or was not a match for *any* sound in lists of up to eight different sounds. Although the more recently a sound appeared in the list, the better it was remembered, sounds that occurred as early as four or five items before the end of the list were still remembered at better than chance levels.

In summary, the work on auditory short-term memory has shown that a dolphin can faithfully register and maintain new auditory information, update old information, represent one form of information by another, and buffer multiple items in parallel for short intervals. The paradigms used to test these memory abilities also demonstrated the dolphin's ability to learn a variety of rules for problem solution. The high levels of correct responding achieved buttress the earlier findings of efficiency in learning to solve multiple discrimination problems and successive discrimination reversals. These problems all shared a common requirement: the discovery and application of rules for guiding errorless responding to the particular class of problem studied.

Most work on complex auditory learning in the dolphin has been restricted to the passive hearing system. However, complex problems can also be solved through the active sonar system. Nachitgall (1980) summarized work showing a dolphin's ability to classify ensonified objects by any of a variety of physical features, and Nachtigall and Patterson (1980) described the ability of a bottlenosed dolphin to learn the concept of "same-different," and to apply that concept appropriately to a small set of target pairs that it ensonified while blindfolded.

The dolphin's ability to develop and apply general rules was also exhibited in studies of vocal learning. In a recent study (Richards, Wolz, & Herman, 1984; Richards, this volume) we taught the dolphin Akeakamai to listen to computer-generated whistle-like sounds broadcast into her tank through an underwater speaker, and then to imitate those sounds by "whistling" into an adjacent hydrophone. The dolphin attempted to vocally imitate any new sound broadcast into the tank, indicating that she had learned not specific imitations but a general concept of mimic. Later, the dolphin was taught to use some of these same imitated sounds to vocally label any of six different objects she was shown. The ability for vocal mimicry, demonstrated in the Richards et al. study, parallels the dolphin's motor mimicry talents as evidenced in other reports, including an ability to imitate the motor behaviors of other species as well as its own species (see review in Herman, 1980). I know of no other nonhuman species for which capabilities for *both* vocal and motor mimicry have been demonstrated.

Visual Information Processing

Historically, the visual system of the dolphin has been an enigma. Until recently, little was known of the capabilities of the system; on the basis of optical calculations alone, early workers believed cetacean vision to be grossly ineffective in air (e.g., Walls, 1942), perpetuating the more general idea that vision may be of little consequence in the life of the dolphin (or whale). Cetaceans were thought of as strict auditory specialists, dependent primarily on passive hearing and, for odontocete species, on active sonar-ranging, as well.

Nevertheless, simple observations of dolphins reveal what appears to be elegant visual control of behaviors. In dolphinariums, performing animals execute precise leaps to a suspended object or watch for and act on subtle visual cues from a trainer. In the wild, the vivid coloration patterns on some dolphins, e.g., the white-sided dolphin, *Lagenorhynchus obliquidens,* or the common dolphin,

Delphinus delphis, suggests a social function that is visually mediated. Madsen and Herman (1980) hypothesized and described many functions of vision in the ecological and social world of dolphins.

Herman, Peacock, Yunker, and Madsen (1975), working with a bottlenosed dolphin named Puka, demonstrated that her visual resolution capabilities were well developed, both for the more common underwater viewing condition and for in-air viewing. The measured acuities, while not of primate caliber, were similar to those described for many terrestrial mammals, e.g., cat or dog. The acuities also approached values reported for California sea lions and a harbor seal (Schusterman, 1972). The acuities of the dolphin varied with viewing distance but seemed well adapted to the viewing medium: Underwater, acuity was best at near viewing distances (1 m or less) while in air it was best at far viewing distances (2.5 m or greater). Anatomical studies of the dolphin retina reveal a well-developed network of receptor cells, some of which appear to be specialized adaptations (Dawson, 1980; Dral, 1977). The eye is well adapted for the chemical, physical, and photic characteristics of the underwater medium and operates efficiently under bright or dim illumination (Madsen & Herman, 1980). Given these measured acuities and visual characteristics it is easy to see that vision may play a more important role in the life of cetaceans than has been previously supposed.

A review of some limitations in processing visual information, as found in our early work, may be instructive. This early work focused on visual learning tasks in which the visual materials were simple, two-dimensional geometric forms, or identical forms differing in brightness. We also experimented with a variety of real-world three-dimensional objects, such as balls, hats, boxes, and other oddly-shaped items. We used these visual materials as we had previously used auditory materials: In two-choice discrimination tasks or in matching tasks. Although the dolphin we studied, Puka, could learn to discriminate among these various visual items (albeit with difficulty) and could at times continue to respond reliably to one of two paired objects, when we tried anything more complex performance became unreliable and erratic. Successive visual reversals, for example, were characterized by a frustrating variation of performance, from nearly errorless reversals at times to chance levels at other times (Herman, 1980). Similarly, a Pacific bottlenosed dolphin named Wela could not learn to apply the "win-stay, lose-shift" strategy efficiently to successive two-choice visual discrimination problems (Herman, Beach, Pepper, & Stalling, 1969). The difficulties in learning these visual tasks sharply contrast with the ease with which analogous tasks are learned in the auditory mode.

Paul Forestell, Ron Antinoja, and I later attempted to teach visual matching to Puka. We met with no success until we hit upon the idea of giving the visual items auditory "names" (Herman, 1980). Assigning names to each of two different brightnesses resulted in the dolphin being able to match the correct alternative target to the sample target, even when the names were no longer offered. We later extended the problem to include delays between the sample target and the alternative targets. The dolphin performed reliably in this delayed matching problem, even when delays were stretched to 30 sec. By naming the targets we may have offered a way for the dolphin to represent the visual information as an auditory code, thereby allowing it to process the task through its auditory centers. Alternatively, through the use of auditory materials, we may have instructed the dolphin in the principles of the task, which it then applied successfully to the visual materials. Differentiating between these alternatives is an important task that we plan to undertake in future research.

Chun (1978) also reported difficulty in teaching a bottlenosed dolphin visual matching problems in which the stimuli were simple two-dimensional geometric forms. Chun succeeded in training the dolphin in simultaneous matching, in which both the sample and the two alternative targets were present at once, but was unable to show any transfer of training to new simultaneous matching problems. Transfer to new problems occurs easily in auditory matching (Herman & Gordon, 1974). Chun's results thus support our findings of limitations in the complex processing of simple visual form and brightness stimuli.

While some of these visual processing limitations can be overcome through techniques encouraging auditory recoding, an effect I called "release from constraint," it was not until we began our studies of comprehension of auditory and gestural languages that we realized that the limitations in visual processing were not general. In consequence, it is no longer tenable to undervalue the visual system, or to refer to the dolphin as a strict auditory specialist.

LANGUAGE COMPREHENSION

Sentence Understanding

Our studies of language learning focused on sentence understanding. We asked whether dolphins could learn to understand instructions conveyed by imperative sentences expressed within the grammar of artificial languages. We were particularly interested in the understanding of novel sentences—combinations of words not experienced previously—and sentences in which meaning depended in part on word order. A defining attribute of human language competency is the ability to produce and understand novel sentences. Sentences have both semantic and syntactic features; both features contribute to the interpretation of a sentence.

Sentence-processing ability was not demonstrated convincingly in studies with apes (e.g., Fouts, Chown, Kimball, & Couch, 1976b; Gardner & Gardner, 1969, 1971; Miles, 1978; Patterson, 1978; Premack, 1971, 1976; Rumbaugh, 1977), because of flaws or insufficiencies in procedures, in controls for non-linguistic cues, and in data analysis, reporting, and interpretation (e.g., see critiques by Petitto & Seidenberg, 1979; Terrace, 1979, 1981; Terrace, Petitto,

Sanders, & Bever, 1979; Seidenberg & Petitto, 1979; Ristau & Robbins, 1982). The critics have challenged claims of novel sentence production or of grammatical competency of apes. In fairness, however, virtually no effort was made by the original investigators to incorporate syntactic structure as information in the languages taught to apes. Instead, structure was treated as an emergent property, one that should appear spontaneously with increasing language practice and proficiency. Because novel sentence production cannot be planned for, most of the data on novelty are anecdotal. In at least some cases, alleged novelty has been reinterpreted as resulting from prompts by the trainers (Terrace et al., 1979).

Comprehension Versus Production

The bulk of the language work with apes emphasized the production of language, rather than its comprehension. As we (Herman, 1980; Herman, Richards, & Wolz, 1984) and others (Savage-Rumbaugh, Pate, Lawson, Smith, & Rosenbaum, 1983; Seidenberg & Petitto, 1981) have noted, there has been an implicit assumption in much of the work with apes that production automatically implied comprehension. Savage-Rumbaugh and her colleagues (Savage-Rumbaugh & Rumbaugh, 1978; Savage-Rumbaugh, Rumbaugh, Smith, & Lawson, 1980) have shown that apes that used symbols to produce requests for foods or other items did not necessarily understand those same symbols in the receptive mode. Specific, extensive training was required to establish "wordness" in a symbol, such that it functioned referentially in both language production and comprehension.

General Approach

Our early progress in studying the dolphin's ability to understand sentences expressed within the grammar of simple artificial languages was summarized in Herman (1980). Later methods and results were extensively described and updated in Herman et al. (1984). In this later work, carried out together with Douglas Richards and James Wolz, imperative sentences were constructed which directed two dolphins to carry out named actions relative to named objects and their named modifiers. One dolphin, Phoenix, was specialized in an acoustic language in which the words were sounds generated by a computer and broadcast into Phoenix's tank through an underwater speaker. The second dolphin, Akeakamai, was tutored in a visual language in which the words were the gestures of a trainer's arms and hands, analogous to sign languages used with the deaf or taught to apes. For both languages, a set of syntactic rules governed the combination of words into sentences of from two to five words in length. In the acoustic language words ranged from .5 to 1.5 sec in duration and were separated from other words in a sentence by .25-sec silent intervals. Signs in the gestural language were given rapidly with little pause between signs; the more experienced signers transitioned smoothly between signs. Signing rates and "crispness" varied somewhat across different trainers, but had no apparent effect on comprehension by the dolphin. A recent study at our laboratory (Shyan, 1985) indicates that Akeakamai attends to specific salient features of a sign, such as sign location or motion, that apparently transcend the idiosyncrasies of individual signers.

Tables 10.1 and 10.2 give, respectively, the vocabulary and the set of syntactic rules for each language. The classes of words used were agent, object, action, modifier, and simple function words; the specific words within each class are as shown in Table 10.1. Our main interest was not in developing a large vocabulary, but in choosing words that could be recombined in many ways with other words, according to the syntactic rules, to create a large number of unique semantic propositions (sentences).

Table 10.2 shows that the rules for two-word sentences, and for the simpler three-word sentences, were the same across both languages. The rules then diverged sharply for three-word and longer relational sentences, e.g., OBJECT-A FETCH OBJECT-B (acoustic language) versus OBJECT-B OBJECT-A FETCH (gestural language). In both examples the sentences may be glossed as "Take Object-A to Object-B." The relational sentences in the acoustic language may be parsed accurately in a straightforward left-to-right sequence, in the order of appearance of words. In the gestural language, however, the grammatical function of the first object word cannot be assigned until the second word appears. Hence, in this inverse grammar the dolphin cannot operate on the symbols as they occur, responding to each word successively as in a simple, linear chain. Instead, the response to the first word in the sequence must be reserved until the grammatical function of that word as direct or indirect object is resolved by the succeeding word. Successful performance with the inverse grammar cannot be explained satisfactorily by simple linear S-R associative-chaining models (cf. Terrace, 1983). The different grammars, linear and inverse, were chosen to allow a greater generalization of findings than could be obtained with a single, arbitrarily-chosen grammar, and to test whether a grammar need be of a linear form to be processed successfully by the dolphin.

Findings on Sentence Understanding

Sentence understanding was defined as the ability to carry out the instructions conveyed by the sentences, and was measured by the accuracy and reliability of response. The overall results showed that the dolphins were able to understand all of the sentence forms given by the syntactic rules (Table 10.2). Summarized below are some specific results for particular conceptual or linguistic categories into which the sentences can be grouped.

TABLE 10.1.
Comprehension Vocabulary of Phoenix (Pho) and Akeakamai (Ake);
If Only One Dolphin Understands a Listed Word it is Followed by the
Name of that Dolphin.

Objects

Tank Fixtures	Relocatable Objects[a]	Transferable Objects[b]
GATE (divides portion of tank; can be opened or shut) (Pho)	SPEAKER (underwater)	BALL
	WATER (jetted from hose)	HOOP
WINDOW (any of four underwater windows)	PHOENIX (dolphin as object) (Ake)	PIPE (length of rigid plastic pipe)
PANEL (metal panel attached underwater to side of tank) (Pho)	AKEAKAMAI (dolphin as object) (Pho)	FISH (used as object or as reward)
CHANNEL (channels connecting two tanks)		PERSON (any body part or whole person in or out of water)
		FRISBEE
		SURFBOARD
		BASKET
		NET

Actions

Take Direct Object Only	Take Direct and Indirect Object
TAIL-TOUCH (touch with flukes)	FETCH (take one named object to another named object)
PECTORAL-TOUCH (touch with pectoral fin)	IN (place one named object in or on another named object)
MOUTH (grasp with mouth)	
(G0) OVER	
(GO) UNDER	
(G0) THROUGH	
TOSS (throw object using rostrum movement)	
SPIT (squirt water from mouth at object)	

Agents
PHOENIX or AKEAKAMAI (prefix for each sentence; calls dolphin named to her station; indicates to dolphin which is to receive fish reward)

Modifiers
RIGHT or LEFT (used before object name to refer to object at that position) (Ake)
SURFACE or BOTTOM (used before object name to refer to object at that location) (Pho)

Function Words
ERASE (used in place of action to cancel the preceding words—requires the dolphin to remain at station or to return immediately)
YES (used after correctly executed instruction)
NO (sometimes used after incorrectly executed instruction—can cause emotional behavior)

[a]Objects whose locations may be changed by trainers.
[b]Objects that may be moved by dolphins—all names represent classes of objects with multiple exemplars.

TABLE 10.2.
Syntactic Rules for Acoustical Language for Phoenix (Pho)
and Gestural Language for Akeakamai (Ake).

Rule	Examples
2-word	
DO + A (Pho, Ake)	WINDOW TAIL-TOUCH; BASKET TOSS
	PHOENIX OVER (An instruction to Akeakamai)
	AKEAKAMAI UNDER (An instruction to Phoenix)
3-word modifier sentences	
M + DO + A (Pho, Ake)	LEFT PERSON MOUTH; RIGHT FISH PEC-TOUCH
	SURFACE PIPE SPIT; BOTTOM HOOP THRU
3-word relational sentences	
DO + R + IO (Pho)	SURFBOARD FETCH SPEAKER; ªHOOP FETCH PIPE
	ªFRISBEE IN BASKET
IO + DO + R (Ake)	SPEAKER SURFBOARD FETCH; ªPIPE HOOP FETCH
	ªBASKET FRISBEE IN
4-word modifer plus relational sentences	
M + DO + R + IO (Pho)	BOTTOM HOOP FETCH PANEL
	ªSURFACE FRISBEE IN NET
DO + R + M + IO (Pho)	ªBASKET FETCH SURFACE PIPE
	HOOP IN SURFBOARD
IO + M + DO + R (Ake)	SPEAKER LEFT HOOP FETCH
	ªBALL RIGHT NET IN
M + IO + DO + R (Ake)	ªRIGHT BASKET PIPE FETCH
	LEFT WATER BALL IN
5-word modifer and relational sentences	
M + DO + R + M + IO (Pho)	ªSURFACE PIPE FETCH BOTTOM HOOP
	ªBOTTOM PIPE IN SURFACE HOOP
M + IO + R + M + DO (Ake)	ªRIGHT HOOP LEFT PIPE FETCH
	ªLEFT HOOP LEFT BASKET IN

Notes. DO = Direct Object; IO = Indirect Object; M = Modifer; A = Action (nonrelational); R = Action (relational).
Also, the word ERASE may be substituted for any A or R term, and acts to cancel all previous words.
ªReversal of order of direct and indirect objects and/or of modifier alters or reverses meaning.

Lexically novel sentences. These were sentences constructed by inserting new lexical items into familiar syntactic slots. To take the simplest case, two-word lexically novel sentences, a dolphin may have learned the words HOOP and THROUGH, and the two-word sentence HOOP THROUGH (= "swim through the hoop") by specific training. It is then taught the word GATE, by requiring it to orient toward the gate in the tank on hearing GATE. The novel sentence GATE THROUGH (= "swim through the gate") is then constructed by inserting the new word GATE in the syntactic slot for object names in the two-word sentence form Object + Action. By immediately swimming through the gate, in the absence of any cue other than that provided by the sentence, the dolphin demonstrates its understanding of a novel combination of words expressed within a familiar syntactic form, that is, of lexical novelty. To test for understanding, the novel sentence was embedded within a list of familiar sentences and the entire list was then given the dolphin under carefully controlled, unbiased testing procedures that guarded against sequence constraints, context constraints, or other nonlinguistic cues that might guide responses (see Herman et al., 1984). The response of a dolphin to each sentence in the list was judged by an observer who had no knowledge of what sentence was given.

Table 10.3 summarizes performance on 214 lexically novel sentences given Akeakamai and on 191 novel sentences given Phoenix, under the described procedures. The novel sentences were drawn from all of the syntactic forms shown in Table 10.2. Table 10.3 shows that Akeakamai responded wholly correctly to 65.4% of her sentences and Phoenix to 67.5%. These performance levels greatly exceeded chance levels which were on the order of 4% or less (Herman et al., 1984). The criterion for scoring a response as correct was that the

TABLE 10.3.
Results of Novel Sentence Testing.

Sentence Type	Total Novel Sentences	Sentence Errors	Percent Correct	Element Error[a]					Mult. Error[b]
				M	DO	A	M	IO	
A: PHOENIX									
DO+A	24	7	70.8	—	6	1	—	—	0
M+DO+A	15	2	86.7	2	0	0	—	—	0
DO+R+IO	45	17	62.2	—	3	3	—	11	0
M+DO+R+IO	48	14	70.8	5	3	2	—	7	1
DO+R+M+IO	29	10	65.5	—	1	1	5	5	2
M+DO+R+M+IO	30	12	60.0	1	2	1	77	5	4
ALL	191	62	67.5	8.6	7.9	4.2	20.3	18.4	7
B: AKEAKAMAI									
DO+A	17	6	64.7	—	6	1	—	—	1
M+DO+A	58	15	74.1	8	6	5	—	—	4
IO+DO+R	50	22	56.0	—	7	2	—	21	7
IO+M+DO+R	51	21	58.8	9	3	3	—	13	6
M+IO+DO+R	38	10	73.7	—	2	5	3	5	3
ALL	214	74	65.4	17.7	11.2	7.5	7.9	18.1	21

Note. M = Modifier; DO = Direct Object; A = Action (not FETCH or IN); R = relational acti (FETCH or IN); IO = Indirect Object.

[a]Number of errors in each semantic category except for ALL which gives the percentage of err calculated by dividing the total of errors in that category by the number of sentences containing that catege and multiplying by 100.

[b]Indicates the number of sentences on which errors occurred to more than one semantic element.

instruction be carried out wholly accurately. In the majority of cases, errors, when they occurred, were to only a single semantic element of a sentence: the wrong modifier might be chosen, or the wrong object, but infrequently both.

Structurally novel sentences. These were new sentence types (new syntactic forms) that the dolphins had not experienced previously. Structural novelty can be achieved by adding a new syntactic slot to an existing structural form, or by more complex changes. Only a few examples of structural novelty were tested. Correct responding to new syntactic slots was shown by both dolphins: Both responded correctly to the first occasion that new four-word sentence forms were given. These forms combined the syntactic features of the two types of three-word sentences shown in Table 10.2; that is, for the first time modifiers were used before the direct object or before the indirect object in four-word relational-type sentences. Phoenix also responded correctly, in the majority of cases, to a new sentence form having linked action words, FETCH THROUGH and FETCH UNDER. Thus, in contrast to a sentence FRISBEE FETCH HOOP, which re-quires Phoenix to take the frisbee to the hoop and to pause there, FRISBEE FETCH THROUGH HOOP requires that she swim completely through the hoop while carrying the frisbee. Additionally, Phoenix gave appropriate responses to newly conjoined sentences. Conjoined sentences are discussed in more detail in a later section.

Akeakamai's responses to some anomalous sentences provide further evi-dence for successful processing of structurally novel sentences. In particular, she responded appropriately to meaningful segments within otherwise longer anoma-lous strings of words. For example, she responded to the three-word anomalous string PIPE NET SPIT by ignoring the first word, PIPE, which occupied the syntactic slot normally given to an indirect object, and responding instead to the last two words, a legitimate Object + Action sequence, by swimming to the net and spitting at it.

The entire three-word string is anomalous because two object names in a row must be followed by the relational words FETCH or IN (see below), or by the function word ERASE, a word that cancels all previous words in the current string.

Relational sentences. These sentences expressed a relationship between two objects, requiring either a transport of one object to another (FETCH) or the placing of one object inside of or on top of another (IN). Akeakamai successfully responded to the new relational term, IN, the first time it was used in a sentence. While she had had previous experience with sentence forms employing the relational term FETCH, IN had never before been used in a sentence. Instead, it had been presented only as a single word, to direct Akeakamai to take any object of her choice and place it in, or on, any other object of her choice. She was given the single word IN with many different objects present so that no bias devloped in her choices. Subsequently, in the context of a series of otherwise familiar sentences of a variety of forms, and with all of the objects in her vocabulary present, she was given her first IN sentence, BASKET HOOP IN. She swam directly to the hoop, carried it to the basket, lifted it above the surface of the water, and dropped it into the basket, thereby carrying out the instruction correctly.

During a series of carefully controlled tests of responses to all of the various types of sentences that could be constructed in the languages, including relational forms, Akeakamai responded wholly correctly to 66% of 128 three- and four-word relational sentences given her; in similar tests Phoenix responded wholly correctly to 81% of the 234 three-, four-, and five-word relational sentences given her. Both novel and familiar sentences were given. As noted earlier, relational sentences were constructed differently for the two dolphins (Table 10.2). Akeakamai, given an inverse grammar, performed less well on the relational sentences than did Phoenix, given a linear left-to-right grammar. However, during these same tests, Akeakamai's performance on nonrelational two- and three-word sentences (95% wholly correct responses) was somewhat better than Phoenix's (93% wholly correct responses). It appears, therefore, that the inverse grammar of Akeakamai's relational sentences is more difficult than is the linear grammar in Phoenix's relational sentences. This agrees with intuition, since the inverse grammar requires that the dolphin remember the indirect object while receiving information about the direct object and conducting a search for that object. In contrast, the linear grammar allows the dolphin to carry out the instruction in the same order as the words are given, permitting some search for the direct object before the indirect object is named. While we should not be surprised that increased processing demands retard performance, we should not lose sight of the fact that performance on the inverse grammar was well above the calculated chance level of approximately 4%. In conclusion, then, both types of grammar were processed successfully by the dolphins, in analogy to the human capability for processing diverse forms of grammar in different natural languages.

Sentences in which changes in word order produced changes in sentence meaning. These sentence types included semantically reversible sentences in which the objects could exchange their functions as direct or indirect object, and sentences in which the location of the modifier in the sentence changed the object modified. Both types occurred in the context of relational sentences. However, not all relational sentences are semantically reversible or can accept a change in modifier position. For example, the sentence HOOP FETCH PIPE (= "take the hoop to the pipe") can be semantically reversed to PIPE FETCH HOOP, because both the hoop and the pipe can be transported by the dolphin. In contrast, HOOP FETCH GATE is not reversible because the gate is a permanent fixture in the tank and cannot be moved by the dolphin. Similarly, while we may use the modifiers BOTTOM and SURFACE to refer to a basket lying on the bottom (BOTTOM BASKET) versus one that is floating (SURFACE BASKET), we cannot use such modifiers before the word GATE. in any event, both dolphins demonstrated their understanding of the effect of word order on meaning by responding correctly to the majority of the semantically reversible sentences given them. During the controlled tests mentioned above, Phoenix was given a total of 128 semantically reversible sentences, both familiar and novel, and responded correctly to 77% Akeakamai responded correctly to 59% of the 69 semantically reversible sentences that she was given. Importantly, while a dolphin might choose an incorrect direct or indirect object, she almost never reversed the role of the two, by taking the designated indirect object to the designated direct object. Such reversal of role occurred only once for Phoenix over her 128 sentences, and never appeared for Akeakamai during her 69 sentences. Hence, syntactic information strongly controlled the responses of both dolphins.

Conjoined sentences. These sentences joined together two simple two-word Object + Action sentences to form a compound instruction, Object A + Action 1 + Object A + Action 2. For example, in response to the sequence PIPE TAIL-TOUCH PIPE OVER, Phoenix swam to the pipe, touched it with her tail, and then jumped over it. A total of 15 such conjoined sentences were given as probes, without any specific training or previous reinforcement history. Video-tape analyses showed that Phoenix carried out the two indicated actions in 11 of the 15 cases; in all but one of these 11 cases, the actions were carried out in the order specified by the instruction. For three of the remaining four cases of the total of 15, only a single action was carried out. In the fourth of these cases, Phoenix executed what appeared to be an integrated response to the two actions TAIL-TOUCH and UNDER, by inverting as she normally does when swimming under an object but then touching the designated object (a basket) with her tail. Conjoined sentences are one way to demonstrate that the dolphins can understand sentence forms for which there was no specific training. Conjoined sentences also relate to the linguistic concept of recursion: In principle, the conjunction allows for the construction of infinitely long sentences. Natural languages are recursive in the sense that by conjoining or embedding clauses, sentence length can be extended indefinitely. Hence, we cannot possibly learn all of the properly formed sentences of a language individually; instead, the rules for sentence construction, which are finite, can be learned (implicitly) and used together with the lexicon to generate and understand an infinite number of sentences. The demonstration that a dolphin can understand a recursive feature is thus an important additional performance capability to consider when evaluating the sentence processing ability of this species.

Displacement and Reporting

Additional research with the dolphins focused on the linguistic concept of displacement (cf. Hockett, 1960) and on the ability to *report about* objects instead of *responding to* objects.

Displacement. Displacment is one of Hockett's (1960) ''design features'' of human language, and may be a feature of natural communication among some animal groups as well (e.g., bees and some nonhuman primates, Thorpe, 1972). Hockett described displacement as a linguistic reference to objects or events remote in time or space. The displaced referents in studies of natural communication among animals are objects of biological or ecological importance to the animals, such as food locations and awareness of predators. A demonstration that animals can understand references to arbitrary objects not immediately present takes on a different character, however.

The displacement studies I carried out together with Douglas Richards and James Wolz were within the framework of our language comprehension approach. We gave two-word Object + Action sentences to the dolphins Phoenix and Akeakamai, instructing them to carry out named actions to named objects, but no objects were present in the tank at the time of instruction (also, the No paddle was absent—see the following section on reporting). After a delay, up to seven different objects were flung into the tank at once from several locations around the dolphins' tank. The dolphin being tested could now respond to the earlier two-word sentence. The accuracy of response indexed the ability to understand an instruction referencing objects (temporarily) remote in time and space and, of course, to remember that instruction over time. The initial study examined response accuracy when seven different objects were introduced immediately after presentation of a two-word sentence that referred to one of those objects. Each dolphin was given a total of 43 different two-word sentences, and each responded correctly to 35 (81.4%).

Using the dolphin Akeakamai, we subsequently studied the effects of increasing the delay between the end of the instruction and the introduction of the objects. A total or 75 two-word sentences were given Akeakamai; the delay before introduction of any objects was either 0, 7, 15, or 30 sec. There was also a control condition in which the objects were introduced just prior to the start of an instruction. Each delay condition, as well as the control condition, was tested 15 times. Akeakamai made no errors at all on the control condition or on the zero-sec delay condition. She made one error each at the 7- and the 15-sec delays, and five errors at the 30-sec delay. Overall, she responded correctly to 68 (91%) of the 75 sentences.

These displacement procedures showed that semantic reference could be made to objects remote in time and space, and that there was relatively little loss in memory for the instruction, within the limits of the delays tested. By way of comparison, Ronald Schusterman (personal communication) reported that his California sea lions had greater difficulty with displacement paradigms than did our dolphins. For example, even in relatively large pools, the longest search time in which the sea lions correctly identified the object signified was about 15 sec, and usually the sea lion forgot which action to take.

Reporting. In the reporting procedure (Herman & Forestell, 1985) we tested Akeakamai's ability to indicate whether or not an object was present in her tank, without her necessarily taking any action to that object. For this purpose we introduced an interrogative sign to Akeakamai and used it in place of an action word in a two-word sequence. Thus, the sequence BALL QUESTION, signed to Akeakamai, is glossed as "Is there a ball in the tank?" Two paddles were available for response. A press by Akeakamai of a paddle to her left indicated negation ("No"), while a press of a paddle to her right indicated affirmation ("Yes").

Two types of sequences were given: Object + Question and Object + Action. For the first type of sequence, the correct response was to press the Yes paddle if the object named was indeed present, or to press the No paddle if it was absent. For the second type of sequence the correct response was to carry out the named action to the named object if that object was present, or to press the No paddle if the object named was absent. All four combinations of sequence type and object present or absent were studied in an experiment in which from one to three objects were present in the tank at once. The four combinations were presented in a balanced sequence. The objects present in the tank were chosen from a pool of six different objects (BALL, PIPE, HOOP, NET, BASKET and FRISBEE). The results were as follows: With one object present in the tank responses were 91% correct. With two objects present, performance dropped to 82%, and with three objects it fell further to 71%. Since there were three general categories of response that could be made—press the No paddle, press the Yes paddle, or take an action to the object named—a conservative estimate of chance performance is 33%. However, errors can also occur within the last category, respond to the object named, if the dolphin chooses an incorrect object or takes an inappropriate action. By all criteria, however, performance was well above chance. The lowered performance with more objects may have indicated that Akeakamai was attempting to remember the objects introduced into the tank, rather than verifying their presence or absence after the question. Her rapid responding, without obvious search, was further evidence for this strategy.

The combined results of the displacement and reporting procedures revealed the ability of the dolphin to understand references to objects not within its immediate perceptual field. Both procedures also support the idea that object names had acquired strong referential qualities. In natural languages, words stand as surrogates for their referents, enabling the symbolic representation and manipulation of objects and events. Elsewhere in this volume, Savage-Rumbaugh discusses the concept of linguistic reference in detail. In Savage-Rumbaugh's studies of language acquisition in apes, linguistic reference emerges only under special procedures that emphasize the use of the words in varied contexts. Context variation was a standard feature of all of our procedures with the dolphins, as discussed below.

Generalization and Representation of Meaning

Context variation. The context in which the language instructions were given was deliberately varied, in order that the understanding of the languages by the dolphins be as general as possible. Variations included the use of different trainers, different training stations, haphazard distribution of objects in the tank, different numbers of paired objects of the same name (paired objects allow for the use of modifiers), which particular objects were paired, and unpredictable sequences of sentences at a given session.

In one study, carried out with Gary Bradshaw and John Gory, we shifted the location of Akeakamai from one tank to another (the two 15.3-m-diameter tanks housing the dolphins are connected by a pair of 3-m long, 1.3-m wide channels). Additionally, objects were located either in the same tank as Akeakamai, or in the opposite tank, or were divided between tanks. There were thus six unique conditions representing all two-way combinations of dolphin in Tank A or Tank B and objects in Tank A, Tank B, or divided between tanks. Each of the six conditions appeared once during a session of 30 trials, for five consecutive trials. The ordering of conditions was counterbalanced over successive sessions. Akeakamai's performance in response to two-word sentences measured her ability to understand references to objects whose locations varied considerably and which often were at a considerable distance from the dolphin and hidden from her view. The results were that performance was equally good whether the objects were in the same tank as the dolphin (96.6% correct responses), in the opposite tank (96.6% correct responses), or split between tanks (95.0% correct responses). Over the course of the experiment Akeakamai came to restrict her searches, beginning with the first trial of a new condition, to the appropriate tank or tanks in which the objects were located. These various procedures and results highlighted Akeakamai's ability to understand, within a broad range of situational contexts, the referents of the sentences given her.

Semantic generalization. Initially, a new word was taught in a limited context, using a particular exemplar for a new object name, or restricting new actions to particular objects. However, once learned in this limited context, the range of use of names was greatly extended. Both dolphins easily generalized a name from a given exemplar of a class of objects to other objects in that class. For example, HOOP was taught in reference to a particular large, octagonal plastic hoop and generalized immediately to square hoops, round hoops, larger or smaller hoops, hoops of thicker pipe than that used originally, dark hoops as well as light hoops, and hoops that sank to the bottom as well as those that floated.

Similarly, the generalization of action words was a general feature of the dolphins' performance. An action learned with reference to a particular named object was almost always immediately performed correctly to another named object. Also, the dolphins spontaneously manipulated objects in order to make the required action possible. For example, if required to leap over an object that was adjacent to the tank wall, the dolphins first moved the object away from the wall and then leaped over it. Phoenix, in order to swim through a hoop that way lying flat on the tank bottom, raised the hoop to the vertical position and then darted through, before the hoop again sank. Likewise, in response to an instruction to toss an object that was lying on the bottom (e.g., BOTTOM FRISBEE TOSS), the object was first brought to the surface and then tossed. The dolphins learned either that it was difficult to toss an object that was beneath the surface, or else that that behavior was not rewarded since trainers could not discriminate an underwater toss.

These examples of generalization, as well as many others we have observed, add to information discussed in the displacement and reporting sections suggesting that the names used in the languages had acquired referential properties, symbolically representing the objects and events in the real world. Nevertheless, from time to time we have observed confusions between objects that were not previously confused, as well as relatively enduring confusions between other objects. This has occurred for both Phoenix and Akeakamai, so that the problem transcends particular animals, particular languages, or the sensory modality used for a language. Some of these problems may indicate sign confusions; others may be representational confusions in which there is difficulty in maintaining discriminations between objects that are placed in similar functional or attribute categories by the dolphins. Further research into the perceptual categories developed by the dolphins may help to clarify the nature of these problems as well as provide further insight into coding schemes used by the dolphin.

Coding processes.   We have recently begun investigations of the codes the dolphins may use to represent objects. It was mentioned that Akeakamai's inverse grammar appears to impose a greater memory burden than does Phoenix's linear grammar. The results in Table 10.3 illustrate that Akeakamai made more errors in selecting the designated indirect object than did Phoenix, although their direct object error rates were almost identical. A more detailed analysis of Akeakamai's indirect object errors revealed that such errors occurred mainly when the indirect object was itself a transportable object, e.g., HOOP or FRISBEE, rather than a semipermanent nontransportable object such as WATER or PERSON. Our observations suggested that the probability of making an error to a transportable indirect object increased if Akeakamai had difficulty in locating the direct object, even if she eventually found it. To check on whether latency of response to the direct object might influence error rate to the indirect object, Gary Bradshaw, John Gory, Paul Forestell, and I carried out a study in which the direct objects were placed at one of two distances, "near" or "far," from Akeakamai's instruction station. We then measured latency of response to the direct object specified in the sentence and observed error rates to the indirect object. For transportable indirect objects, the results showed a clear latency effect: Longer search times for the direct object produced higher error rates to the indirect object, regardless of whether the direct objects were positioned near or far. The slope of the curve relating errors to latency was steep and suggested that after 4 to 6 sec error probability was high. No such latency effect was found for nontransportable indirect objects.

Our preliminary view, pending further research, is that these effects represent the use of different coding schemes for the two classes of indirect object. To respond correctly to a named object the dolphin must both identify the object referred to and locate it in the tank. The locations of the nontransportable indirect objects are well known by the dolphin; if a nontransportable indirect object is used in a sentence, the dolphin can immediately organize a response to the known location and maintain that response decision in working memory. In contrast, if the location were uncertain, as it is for objects that float freely about the tank, the dolphin must maintain a representation of the object itself or of the sign for the object. These two coding situations may be conceptualized, respectively, as prospective and retrospective coding (Honig & Thompson, 1982), the latter being a representation of the stimulus to which a response is to be made, and the former a representation of the response scheme itself. Response uncertainty is resolved by prospective coding, but not by retrospective coding. Honig and Thompson (1982) suggested that prospective coding is more stable than retrospective coding, in that "animals remember anticipated outcomes and responses more readily than stimuli" (p. 279). The problem faced by the dolphin in carrying out the instructions specified in relational sentences is to remember the named indirect object while identifying and searching for the named direct object. It appears that this task is facilitated if the dolphin can encode the indirect object prospectively, organize its response in advance in terms of which indirect object and where to respond, while retrospectively remembering the specified direct object. This theory of coding, if valid, provides an interesting window into some of the processes of representation in the mind of the dolphin, as well as being a potentially useful model for guiding our future research.

Interchangeability of sign and referent.   A powerful indicant of referentiality is the ability for signs and their referents to exchange roles in sentences. Gary Bradshaw, John Gory, James Wolz, and I tested this idea by showing Phoenix an object in her language, and then presenting an acoustic action name through the underwater speaker. Together, the shown object and the action name constituted a two-word Object + Action sentence.

The object was shown briefly (ca. 2 sec) in air to Phoenix, withdrawn, and then the action name was played. Immediately thereafter, two alternative objects were introduced at once into the tank, one object to Phoenix's left and the other to her right. Phoenix's task was to choose the alternative matching the previously shown object (the "sample") and to carry out the indicated action to that object. To train the task, we played the name of an object through the underwater speaker while showing that object, and then played an action name after the alternatives were introduced. Phoenix responded to the named object appropriately. The proportion of trials on which the object name was used was progressively decreased until Phoenix came to respond appropriately on the basis of the shown object alone. Transfer tests were then made to two named and four unnamed objects, none of which were previously used in training this task. Object names or other auditory cues were not used. During these transfer tests a new object was paired with all old objects; on half the pairings the new object was shown (new object was S+) and on half the old object was shown (new object was S−). These pairings were interleaved among pairings of old objects. Phoenix responded at 93% correct or better to all pairings involving new objects. Moreover, she was correct on the very first transfer trial for five of the six new objects when the new object was S+, and on four of the first six transfer trials when the new object was S−. These results underscored the interchangeability of sign and referent, and additionally demonstrated that Phoenix could process and integrate sentence information arriving from two different sensory modalities, object information through the visual mode and action information through the auditory mode.

DISCUSSION

Auditory and Visual Processing Capacities and Constraints

Results of a variety of laboratory learning and memory tasks demonstrate the dolphin's ability for manipulating auditory information complexly. The range of auditory problems and materials that can be handled is wide, although some limitation in processing pulsed signals was seen. Possibly, this limitation may be more a discrimination problem, peculiar to the materials we used, than a conceptual problem.

Auditory information obtained through either passive listening or active echolocation is amenable to complex cognitive manipulation, although there have been only a limited number of tests of cognitive skills in the active mode. Still fewer tests have been made of cognitive capacities or constraints in producing sound. The study by Richards et al. (1984) is an exception and showed that a generalized vocal rule ("mimic") could be learned, and that real-world objects could be vocally labeled. Overall, the positive findings on the ability to process and manipulate auditory materials complexly is in keeping with expectations based on the extensive auditory and sound production specializations of the dolphin, and concomitant developments in auditory cortex.

Limitations were found in the ability to form generalized rules about relationships between simple visual forms or brightnesses. Paradoxically, these limitations were absent for the more complex visual stimuli produced by the manual gestures of a trainer. Gestures provide information as an unfolding visual pattern over time. The key may be to consider the bottlenosed dolphin not as an auditory specialist, but as a specialist in processing temporally structured events, regardless of their mode of arrival. Sounds are temporal structures, as are gestures apprehended through vision. Sounds and gestures thus have a common attribute of temporal patterning that seems to be easily accessed and manipulated by the dolphin. The underwater visual world of the dolphin, and of most other marine vertebrates, is more one of movement apprehension than of form apprehension. It is therefore not surprising that the dolphin eye appears to have specializations for movement detection (Dawson, 1980). It is important, however, that movement information be integrated into some meaningful percept; this is what the dolphin brain appears especially proficient at doing.

Our finding that associating sounds with simple visual brightness stimuli can make a previously insoluble visual matching problem solvable for the dolphin suggests that these visual stimuli, in their auditory representation, were routed through centers for processing temporal patterns. These findings suggest more generally that some of the limitations of animals in carrying out complex manipulations on information arriving through "secondary" modalities is in routing that information to *appropriate* higher centers. Transforming the information into the code of a "dominant" modality—e.g., expressing visually apprehended objects by their auditory "name" codes—can unlock that constraint and, in theory, allow access to more advanced processing centers. Focus must be placed on the apprehension and learning of patterned information by other animals if we are to understand the basic nature and import of this skill (cf. D'Amato & Salmon, 1982, 1984b).

Forming and Generalizing Rules

There is by now extensive evidence of the ability of the dolphin to form and use generalized rules when solving laboratory problems. These rules are generalized in the sense that they guide responses to a whole class of problems rather than to a single problem. Premack (1976) referred to these as second-order rules—rules that specify relationships about relationships—and found that they are easily acquired by chimpanzees. The index of a generalized rule is its immediate or efficient transfer to new problems of the class within which the rule is learned. While generalized rules are certainly within the grasp of animals other than primates and cetaceans, it is important to document the range of rules that a species may acquire, the degree of abstractness of rules learned, the ease with which rule learning occurs in general, the flexibility with which rules may be changed as the situation changes, and the degree to which the rules that may be learned are independent of biological predispositions or constraints of the species. The bottlenosed dolphin has been shown capable of readily forming and using rules governing stimulus-reward relationships, matching and nonmatching relationships, sameness-difference relationships, as well as rules for imitation. Additionally, within the language tasks, rules governing sentence structure were mastered and applied in a flexible way. These various rules range from relatively concrete to relatively abstract and were often easily learned. The language rules, in particular, were highly abstract, and difficult to relate to any natural biological predisposition of the species. The same dolphin typically was taught a variety of rules, which could be maintained separately and used within the appropriate context.

Memory

Short-term memory in the dolphin is well developed. In an earlier summary of results from a series of auditory delayed matching studies, Herman (1980) concluded that the auditory short-term memory of the dolphin was impressively faithful over time for a variety of auditory materials. This conclusion is still warranted. The performance of the dolphin on its auditory delayed matching tasks was very similar in form and level to the performance of nonhuman primates tested on analogous visual delayed matching tests. The performance similarity was maintained over a wide range of variables studied, including types of materials to be remembered, duration of presentation of the sample, introduction of interfering conditions, and use of different types of alternative choices. After the procedures for "release from constraint," described above, were applied, a dolphin was also capable of visual delayed matching. The materials to be remembered in these matching tasks had neither intrinsic nor learned meaning. In contrast, the language tasks that we have used subsequently dealt with lexical items of learned meaning organized into sentences. An instruction given within the language system was retained well in short-term memory. For example, Akeakamai was able to carry out instructions contained in two-word imperative Object + Action sentences, conveyed to her gesturally, after delays of up to 30 sec, the longest delays tested.

Coding

The dolphin appears able to utilize either prospective or retrospective forms of coding in memory. It may immediately organize a response for later execution (prospective coding), or it may continue to remember the stimulus until able to organize and carry out a response to it (retrospective coding). Thompson and

Herman (1981) discussed these forms of coding in analyses of the dolphin's responses in delayed discrimination versus delayed matching tests. In this chapter I have pointed to the apparent use of these coding forms in the more difficult language tasks involving relational terms. Either code may be used to remember the indirect object of a relational sentence, but the prospective code is hypothesized to be more stable and to facilitate correct responding.

Some Comparative Perspectives on Capacities and Constraints

Many species appear to have limitations on their ability to perform complex cognitive tasks when information arrives through a "secondary" sensory modality. The nonhuman primate is able to carry out many complex tasks when information relevant to that task arrives through the visual system, but not when it arrives through the auditory system (e.g., D'Amato, 1973; Wegener, 1964). Albino rats are able to form learning sets using olfactory, but not visual information (Jennings & Keefer, 1969). These and other biological constraints on learning have been discussed extensively in the literature (e.g., Bolles, 1973; Hinde & Stevenson-Hinde, 1973; Seligman, 1970). It seems as if information from some sensory systems cannot or does not access relevant higher centers concerned with the acquisition, storage, integration, and utilization of new knowledge and procedures. It is not clear why there are such constraints, but the phenomenon provides an interesting topic for speculation about brain specializations.

When comparing cognitive characteristics across species account must be taken of the limitations in information processing imposed by different sensory systems, or of different specializations within a sensory system. The auditory information processing system of the dolphin can justifiably be described as a major interface with the real world. A strong convergence in cognitive abilities takes place between dolphin and nonhuman primate (mainly, the macaque species, which have been studied the most) when tasks for the dolphin are processed through the auditory system and tasks for the primate through the visual system. For example, high levels of performance have been obtained for both dolphin and primate on delayed matching, multiple reversal, and multiple discrimination tasks (reviewed in Herman, 1980). In all cases, there was rapid transfer to new problems within a task.

Constraints in learning also appear to run in parallel across dolphin and primate. We noted that the dolphin has difficulty in learning some complex tasks (e.g., matching-to-sample) when the stimuli are simple visual forms or brightnesses. We eventually succeeded in training visual matching, however, by temporarily pairing the visual stimuli with sounds. Until recently (Colombo & D'Amato, 1985) monkeys had not been shown capable of auditory matching, although much effort has been expended in attempts to teach the task (D'Amato, 1973). Other constraints on auditory learning by monkeys (and apes) are given by D'Amato and Salmon (1984a; 1984b) and by Davenport (1977).

Studies of delayed matching in pigeons suggest that performance may differ in level, and even in kind, from that reported for monkey or dolphin. Unlike monkey or dolphin, the matching performance of the pigeon falls to near chance levels after delays of only 5 to 10 sec, and decreasing the duration of the sample stimulus markedly retards pigeon performance but not monkey or dolphin performance (Roberts & Grant, 1976). In keeping with the dominance of the visual modality in most birds, the delayed matching work with pigeons has used visual stimuli. Pigeons have not yet been shown capable of auditory matching, although they are capable of auditory-visual symbolic matching (Kraemer & Roberts, 1984).

The serial probe-recognition procedures used by Thompson and Herman (1977) were adapted by Sands and Wright (1980) for study of rhesus monkeys, except that lists of photographs (projected color slides) of real-world objects were shown the monkeys. Lists as long as 20 items were used. The monkeys showed a strong recency effect, as did the dolphins, but additionally showed good retention of early list items (primacy effect). Items in the middle of the list suffered the most. Performance was considerably higher on lists comprised of three trial-unique stimuli than on lists restricted to subsets of three highly familiar stimuli. Later work reported in Wright, Santiago, Sands, and Urcuioli (1984) showed that the length of delay before the probe trial influenced the emergence of primacy and recency effects. Possibly, the primacy effect also reflects the meaningfulness of the items used, enabling the monkeys to buttress early items by referencing them to stored knowledge. Middle items suffer because of storage interference from earlier items and from retrieval interference from later items. The sounds used with the dolphin studied by Thompson and Herman (1977) were chosen to be arbitrary and, presumably, had little semantic value for the dolphin. Semantic value is an important variable in human memory for lists, and should not be neglected in assessments and discussions of animal memory.

Pigeons have not generally shown capabilities for remembering multiple list items much above chance levels (e.g., MacPhail, 1980). However, Wright et al. (1984) reported success in teaching this task to pigeons. Acquisition depended on a fixed list length (three items). Unlike the monkeys trained in this same study by Wright et al., pigeons were unable to perform well with variable list lengths, or with long lists, and did not adopt some of the efficient strategies used by the monkeys. Santiago and Wright (1984) additionally pointed to some differences in the time parameters affecting the appearance of a primacy effect in monkey and pigeon. Pigeon and monkey both showed a primacy and a recency effect at 0- or 2-sec probe delays, but the monkey additionally showed the two effects at 10-sec delays. In our work with the dolphin, we studied both 1- and 4-sec delays, but found only a recency effect. This represents a still unresolved performance difference between the dolphin and either of these other species.

Honig and Thompson (1982) recently reviewed the literature on serial probe recognition and concluded that both dolphin and monkey appear to scan through the remembered list before reaching a decision and making a response. This "retrospective" strategy is different from the "prospective" strategy observed in tests of memory for single items. In the latter case, both monkey and dolphin appear to organize a response immediately, based on the particular stimulus that appeared, and to remember that response over the delay. I would emphasize the conclusion about different strategies. Intelligent systems, if they are to justify the term intelligent, must be organized flexibly to allow for the strategic selection of responses and, indeed, for strategy innovation.

Language Competency

Although the artificial languages applied to the dolphins did not approach the complexity of a natural language, they did preserve some important features of natural language. The lexicon of the artificial languages was open and new words could be added to the vocabulary as desired; the symbols for words were arbitrary and generally not iconic; the words could be combined, and recombined, according to the dictates of a set of syntactic rules, into a very large number (ca. 1500 to 2000) of uniquely meaningful sentences. Also, tacit knowledge of the syntactic rules underlying the language was necessary for a correct interpretation of the grammatical function of the lexical items in a sentence.

Processing of semantic and syntactic features. Results from the language comprehension tasks showed that the dolphins processed both the semantic and syntactic features of the sentences given them in arriving at an interpretation of the underlying instruction. The language work with apes, which has emphasized the production of language rather than its comprehension, has failed to yield convincing evidence of sensitivity of apes to syntactic structure (Ristau & Robbins, 1982; Seidenberg & Petitto, 1979; Terrace, 1979). Unlike our work, the ape language investigators, aside from Premack (1971, 1976), did not teach the role of syntactic constraints in sentence generation or interpretation, so it is not surprising that there was little evidence for its emergence. Premack (1971, 1976) reported on the chimp Sarah's ability to understand the function of word order in imperative sentences such as "(put) red on green" versus "(put) green on red." These sentences instructed Sarah to carry out the indicated actions on available colored objects. The interpretation of Sarah's good performance is problematical because generally only two objects were available as alternatives, there was no contrasting preposition (e.g., "under" in addition to "on"), and there were constraining context cues present. Terrace (1979) suggested that Sarah could have learned the task by attending to the first color word alone, and putting that colored object on top of whatever other object was present.

Using a gestural language, Schusterman and Krieger (1984) have recently applied our language comprehension approach to two California sea lions, with good success. The sea lions showed semantic comprehension of gestural strings constructed as Modifier + Object + Action. Two modifiers were conjoined to increase string length and complexity. There are, as yet, no strings in which word order affects meaning. Hence, the ability of the sea lions to process syntactic information remains to be tested. Such testing would be an important contribution to our understanding of the ability of different animals to process the structural features of imposed grammars.

Different syntactic rules can be learned. The syntactic structure for the relational sentences given the dolphins differed across the acoustic and gestural languages. The variation was deliberately introduced to study whether different structures might be learned by the dolphins and whether the structure need be a linear left-to-right ordering of words in which the order of appearance of words and the order of operation on those words were the same. The results indicated that both the linear and the inverse grammatical forms could be learned by dolphins, although the inverse form appeared to be the more difficult. The findings with the inverse grammatical form argue against explanations of the dolphin's performance being necessarily based on a simple linearly organized chain of responses. Instead, later occurring information frequently controlled responses to earlier occurring information. In natural languages it is common to recast interpretations of earlier words on the basis of later, nonadjacent terms. Several different tests of the inverse form, including responses to the canceling term ERASE, and to certain anomalous strings discussed earlier, revealed the dolphin's ability to interpret the function of an early word in a sentence on the basis of a later-appearing word or words.

Understanding of novel sentences. The dolphins' understanding of novel sentences and of novel structure was one of the more important findings on language understanding. Here, the advantage of the comprehension approach is apparent: The experimenter can introduce novel material under controlled conditions and contexts that allow for documentation and for objective interpretation of the data. In contrast, the conditions and context in which novel sign combinations were produced by apes were often difficult to specify or record, and interpretations are therefore open to question. It is also unclear whether an ape that produced a novel combination of signs would understand that same combination in the receptive mode. As was stressed earlier, production does not necessarily, perhaps usually in the case of the apes, imply comprehension. For the dolphins, one might also caution that an ability to comprehend does not necessarily imply that the same animals could produce language. It may yet be shown that receptive and productive processes are sufficiently distinct for animals that transfer from one mode to the other is difficult, at best (cf. Savage-Rumbaugh et al., 1983).

Object labeling and reporting. Our work on object labeling using self-produced vocalizations, and our studies of reporting, are modest first steps into the exploration of production. The procedure for training vocal labeling was a straightforward application of associative techniques. We have no information on whether or not the labels acquired the referential quality of names (cf. Savage-Rumbaugh, Rumbaugh, & Boysen, 1980; Savage-Rumbaugh et al., 1983). The reporting procedure used a binary "Yes/No" system for response that in principle is often used with animals. For example, in some psychophysical procedures an animal may be asked to respond when it sees a stimulus ("Yes"), and to withhold response when it does not ("No"). Yes/No procedures have also been used in delayed matching-to-sample tests (e.g., Herman & Thompson, 1982). The major conceptual departure of our reporting procedure is in asking questions within a language format about the *referents* of the lexical items (or stimuli), rather than about the lexical items (or stimuli) themselves. In the future, we hope to use the reporting procedure to pose binary questions to the dolphin about more abstract topics than the objects to which the signs refer, e.g., are you at the particular location in the tank named in the question, did you just carry out the particular action named in the question (cf. Shimp, 1976), did the other dolphin carry out the named action?

Modality independence. The successful use of both visual and acoustic information in the language tasks given the dolphins is not paralleled in the language work with apes. The emphasis of the current generation of language work with apes has been on the visual medium, in response to earlier unsuccessful attempts to teach apes vocal languages (Hayes, 1951; Kellogg & Kellogg, 1933). Possibly, an acoustic language might be used successfully in the comprehension mode with apes, but this remains to be fully tested (but cf. Fouts, Chown, & Goodin 1976a; Patterson, 1978). For the dolphins, the successful use of two different language mediums implies that the cognitive skills underlying the demonstrated competencies are very general and not specialized with respect to either the auditory or visual systems. This modal independence may reflect the shared attribute of sounds and gestures as temporal patterns, and that the perception and integration of temporal patterns is a specialization of the dolphin brain.

ACKNOWLEDGMENTS

Preparation of this chapter was supported by Grant BNS 8109653 from the National Science Foundation to L. M. Herman, and by grants from the Center for Field Research to L. M. Herman and J. P. Wolz. Additional support was through Contract N00014-85-K-0210 from the Office of Naval Research to L. M. Herman. I thank Douglas Richards, Gary Bradshaw, and James Wolz, who initially were postdoctoral appointees, for their collaboration in the language comprehension studies reported here. Paul Forestell, a long-term associate, collaborated on many of the earlier studies, as well as on the more recent ones. I also thank graduate students John Gory, Esme Hoban, and Melissa Shyan for their continued assistance in the language studies. John Hovancik assisted in portions of the data analysis for the "reporting" study. Finally, there has been able support from many undergraduate students, research interns, and volunteers, too numerous to list here, whose contributions made the work possible.

REFERENCES

Beach, F. A., & Herman, L. M. (1972). Preliminary studies of auditory problem solving and intertask transfer by the bottlenosed dolphin. *Psychological Reports, 22,* 49–62.

Bolles, R. C. (1973). The comparative psychology of learning: The selective association principle and some problems with "general" laws of learning. In G. Bermant (Ed.), *Perspectives on animal behavior.* Glenview, IL: Scott-Foresman.

Chun, N. K. W. (1978). *Aerial visual shape discrimination and matching-to-sample problem solving ability of an Atlantic bottlenose dolphin.* Report Number NOSC TR 236, Naval Ocean Systems Center, San Diego, CA.

Colombo, M., & D'Amato, M. R. (1985 March). *Auditory matching-to-sample in monkeys.* Paper presented at the meeting of the Eastern Psychological Association, Boston.

D'Amato, M. R. (1973). Delayed matching and short-term memory in monkeys. In G. H. Bower (Ed.), *The psychology of learning and motivation: Advances in research and theory.* New York: Academic.

D'Amato, M. R., & Salmon, D. P. (1982). Tune discrimination in monkeys (*Cebus apella*) and in rats. *Animal Learning and Behavior, 10,* 126–134.

D'Amato, M. R., & Salmon, D. P. (1984a). Processing of complex auditory stimuli (tunes) by rats and monkeys (*Cebus apella*). *Animal Learning and Behavior, 12,* 184–194.

D'Amato, M. R., & Salmon, D. P. (1984b). Cognitive processes in cebus monkeys. In H. L. Roitblat, T. G. Bever, & H. S. Terrace (Eds.), *Animal cognition.* Hillsdale, NJ: Lawrence Erlbaum Associates.

Davenport, R. K. (1977). Cross-modal perception: A basis for language? In D. M. Rumbaugh (Ed.), *Language learning by a chimpanzee: The Lana Project.* New York: Academic.

Dawson, W. W. (1980). The cetacean eye. In L. M. Herman (Ed.), *Cetacean behavior: Mechanisms and functions.* New York: Wiley-Interscience.

Dral, A. D. G. (1977). On the retinal anatomy of Cetacea (mainly *Tursiops truncatus*). In R. J. Harrison (Ed.), *Functional anatomy of marine mammals.* New York: Academic.

Flanigan, N. J. (1972). The central nervous system. In S. H. Ridgway (Ed.), *Mammals of the sea: Biology and medicine.* Springfield, IL: Thomas.

Fouts, R. S., Chown, W., & Goodin, L. T. (1976a). Transfer of signed responses in American sign language from vocal English stimuli to physical object stimuli by a chimpanzee (*Pan*). *Learning and Motivation, 7,* 458–475.

Fouts, R. S., Chown, W., Kimball, G., & Couch, J. (1976b). *Comprehension and production of American sign language by a chimpanzee (Pan).* Paper presented at the XXI International Congress of Psychology, Paris, July 18–25.

Gardner, R. A., & Gardner, B. T. (1969). Teaching sign language to a chimpanzee. *Science, 165,* 664–667.

Gardner, B. T., & Gardner, R. A. (1971). Two-way communication with an infant chimpanzee. In A. M. Schrier & F. Stollnitz (Eds.), *Behavior of Nonhuman Primates, Vol. 4.* New York: Academic.

Griffin, D. R. (1981). *The question of animal awareness: Evolutionary continuity of mental experience.* New York: Rockefeller University Press.

Hayes, C. (1951). *The ape in our house.* New York: Harper.

Herman, L. M. (1975). Interference and auditory short-term memory in the bottlenosed dolphin. *Animal Learning and Behavior, 3,* 43–48.

Herman, L. M. (1980). Cognitive characteristics of dolphins. In L. M. Herman (Ed.), *Cetacean behavior: Mechanisms and functions.* New York: Wiley-Interscience.

Herman, L. M., & Arbeit, W. R. (1972). Frequency difference limens in the bottlenose dolphin: 1-70 KC/S. *Journal of Auditory Research, 2,* 109–120.

Herman, L. M., & Arbeit, W. R. (1973). Stimulus control and auditory discrimination learning sets in the bottlenose dolphin. *Journal of the Experimental Analysis of Behavior, 19,* 379–394.

Herman, L. M., Beach, F. A. III, Pepper, R. L., & Stalling, R. B. (1969). Learning set performance in the bottlenosed dolphin. *Psychonomic Science, 14,* 98–99.

Herman, L. M., & Forestell, P. H. (1985). Reporting presence or absence of named objects by a language-trained dolphin. *Neuroscience and Biobehavioral Reviews.*

Herman, L. M., & Gordon, J. A. (1974). Auditory delayed matching in the bottlenose dolphin. *Journal of the Experimental Analysis of Behavior, 21,* 19–26.

Herman, L. M., Peacock, M. F., Yunker, M. P., & Madsen, C. J. (1975). Bottlenosed dolphin: Double-slit pupil yields equivalent aerial and underwater acuity. *Science, 139,* 650–652.

Herman, L. M., Richards, D. G., & Wolz, J. P. (1984). Comprehension of sentences by bottlenosed dolphins. *Cognition, 16,* 129–219.

Herman, L. M., & Tavolga, W. N. (1980). The communication systems of cetaceans. In L. M. Herman (Ed.), *Cetacean behavior: Mechanisms and functions.* New York: Wiley-Interscience.

Herman, L. M., & Thompson, R. K. R. (1982). Symbolic, identity, and probe delayed matching of sounds by the bottlenosed dolphin. *Animal Learning and Behavior, 10,* 22–34.

Hinde, R. A., & Stevenson-Hinde, J. (Eds.). (1973). *Constraints on learning: Limitations and predispositions.* New York: Academic.

Hockett, C. F. (1960). Logical considerations in the study of animal communication. In W. E. Lanyon & W. N. Tavolga (Eds.), *Animal sounds and communication.* Washington, D.C.: American Institute of Biological Sciences, Pub. No. 7.

Honig, W. K., & Thompson, R. K. R. (1982). Retrospective and prospective processing in animal working memory. In G. H. Bower (Ed.), *The Psychology of Learning and Motivation* (Vol 16). New York: Academic.

Jennings, J. W., & Keefer, L. H. (1969). Olfactory learning set in two varieties of domestic rat. *Psychological Reports, 24,* 3–15.

Jerison, H. J. (1973). *Evolution of the brain and intelligence.* New York: Academic.

Jerison, H. J. (1978). Brain and intelligence in whales. In S. Frost (Ed.), *Whales and whaling, Vol. 2.* Canberra: Australian Government Printing Service.

Kellogg, W. N., & Kellogg, L. A. (1933). *The ape and the child.* New York: McGraw-Hill.

Kraemer, P. J., & Roberts, W. A. (1984). Short-term memory for visual and auditory stimuli in pigeons. *Animal Learning & Behavior, 8,* 10–16.

Madsen, C. J., & Herman, L. M. (1980). Social and ecological correlates of cetacean vision and visual appearance. In L. M. Herman (Ed.), *Cetacean behavior: Mechanisms and functions.* New York: Wiley-Interscience.

MacPhail, E. M. (1980). Short-term visual recognition memory in pigeons. *Quarterly Journal of Experimental Psychology, 32,* 531–538.

Miles, H. L. (1978). Language acquisition in apes and children. In F. C. C. Peng (Ed.), *Sign language acquisition in man and ape: New dimensions in comparative psycholinguistics.* Boulder, CO: Westview Press.

Morgane, P. J. (1978). Whole brains and their meaning for intelligence. In S. Frost (Ed.), *Whales and whaling, Vol. 2.* Canberra: Australian Government Printing Service.

Morgane, P. J., & Jacobs, N. S. (1972). Comparative anatomy of the cetacean nervous system. In R. J. Harrison (Ed.), *Functional anatomy of marine mammals.* New York: Academic.

Nachtigall, P. E. (1980). Odontocete echolocation performance on object size, shape and material. In R.-G. Busnel (Ed.), *Animal sonar systems.* New York: Plenum.

Nachtigall, P. E., & Patterson, S. (1980). Training of a sameness/difference task in the investigation of concept formation in echolocating *Tursiops truncatus*. In J. Pearson & J. Barry (Eds.), *Proceedings of the International Marine Animal Trainer Association Conference, October 28– 31, 1980*. Boston: New England Aquarium.

Patterson, F. G. (1978). The gestures of a gorilla: Language acquisition in another pongid. *Brain and Language, 5*, 72–97.

Petitto, L. A., & Seidenberg, M. S. (1979). On the evidence for linguistic abilities in signing apes. *Brain and Language, 8*, 162–183.

Premack, D. (1971). On the assessment of language competence in the chimpanzee. In A. M. Schrier & F. Stollnitz (Eds.), *Behavior of nonhuman primates, Vol. 4* (pp 186–228). New York: Academic Press.

Premack, D. (1976). *Intelligence in ape and man*. Hillsdale, NJ: Lawrence Erlbaum Associates.

Richards, D. G., Wolz, J. P., & Herman, L. M. (1984). Vocal mimicry of computer-generated sounds and vocal labeling of objects by a bottlenosed dolphin *(Tursiops truncatus)*. *Journal of Comparative Psychology, 98*, 10–28.

Ristau, C. A., & Robbins, D. (1982). Language in the great apes: A critical review. In J. F. Rosenblatt, R. B. Hinde, C. Beer & M.-C. Busnel (Eds.), *Advances in the study of behavior. Vol. 12.* New York: Academic Press.

Roberts, W. A., & Grant, D. S. (1976). Studies of short-term memory in the pigeon using the delayed matching-to-sample procedure. In D. L. Medin, W. A. Roberts, & R. T. Davis (Eds.), *Processes of animal memory.* Hillsdale, NJ: Lawrence Erlbaum Associates.

Rumbaugh, D. M. (1977). *Language learning by a chimpanzee: The Lana project.* New York: Academic.

Sands, S. F., & Wright, A. A. (1980). Primate memory: Retention of serial list items by a rhesus monkey. *Science, 209*, 938–940.

Santiago, H. C., & Wright, A. A. (1984). Pigeon memory: Same/Different concept learning, serial probe recognition acquistion, and probe delay effects on the serial-position function. *Journal of Experimental Psychology: Animal Behavior Processes, 10*, 498–512.

Savage-Rumbaugh, E. S., Pate, J. L., Lawson, J., Smith, S. T., & Rosenbaum, S. (1983). Can a chimpanzee make a statement? *Journal of Experimental Psychology: General, 112*, 457–492.

Savage-Rumbaugh, E. S., & Rumbaugh, D. M. (1978). Symbolization, language, and chimpanzees: A theoretical reevaluation based on initial language acquisition processes in four young *Pan troglodytes. Brain and Language, 6*, 265–300.

Savage-Rumbaugh, E. S., Rumbaugh, D. M., & Boysen, S. (1980). Do apes use language? *American Scientist, 68*, 49–61.

Savage-Rumbaugh, E. S., Rumbaugh, D., Smith, S. T., & Lawson, J. (1980). Reference: The linguistic essential. *Science, 210*, 922–925.

Schusterman, R. (1972). Visual acuity in pinnipeds. In H. Winn & B. Olla (Eds.), *Behavior of Marine Animals, Vol. 2.* New York: Plenum.

Schusterman, R. J., & Krieger, K. (1984). California sea lions are capable of semantic comprehension. *The Psychological Record, 34*, 3–23.

Seidenberg, M. S., & Petitto, L. A. (1979). Signing behavior in apes: A critical review. *Cognition, 7*, 177–215.

Seidenberg, M. S., & Petitto, L. A. (1981). Ape signing: Problems of method and interpretations. In T. A. Sebeok & R. Rosenthal (Eds.), *The clever Hans phenomenon: Communication with horses, whales, apes and people.* New York: New York Academy of Sciences.

Seligman, M. E. P. (1970). On the generality of the laws of learning. *Psychological Review, 77*, 406–418.

Shimp, C. P. (1976). Short-term memory in the pigeon: Relative recency. *Journal of the Experimental Analysis of Behavior, 25*, 55–61.

Shyan, M. R. (1985). *Determinants of perception of gestural signs in an artificial language by bottlenosed dolphins and humans.* Unpublished doctoral dissertation. University of Hawaii, Honolulu.

Terrace, H. S. (1979, August). Is problem solving language? *Journal of the Experimental Analysis of Behavior, 31,* 161–175.

Terrace, H. S. (1981). A report to an academy. In T. A. Sebeok & R. Rosenthal (Eds.), *The clever Hans phenomenon: Communication with horses, whales, apes, and people.* New York: New York Academy of Sciences.

Terrace, H. S. (1983). Simultaneous chaining: The problem it poses for traditional chaining theory. In M. L. Commons, A. R. Wagner, & R. J. Herrnstein (Eds.), *Harvard Symposium in the Quantitative Analysis of Behavior.* Cambridge, MA: Ballinger.

Terrace, H. S., Petitto, L. A., Sanders, R. J., & Bever, T. G. (1979). Can an ape create a sentence? *Science, 206,* 891–902.

Thompson, R. K. R., & Herman, L. M. (1975). Underwater frequency discrimination in the bottlenosed dolphin (1-140kHz). *Journal of the Acoustical Society of America, 57,* 943–948.

Thompson, R. K. R., & Herman, L. M. (1977). Memory for lists of sounds by the bottlenosed dolphin: Convergence of memory processes with humans? *Science, 195,* 501–503.

Thompson, R. K. R., & Herman, L. M. (1981). Auditory delayed discriminations by the dolphin: Nonequivalence with delayed-matching performance. *Animal Learning and Behavior, 9,* 9–15.

Thorpe, W. H. (1972). The comparison of vocal communication in animals and man. In R. A. Hinde (Ed.), *Non-verbal communication.* London: Cambridge University Press.

Walls, G. (1942). *The vertebrate eye and its adaptive radiation.* New York: McGraw-Hill.

Wegener, J. G. (1964). Auditory discrimination behavior of normal monkeys. *Journal of Auditory Research, 4,* 81–106.

Wright, A. A., Santiago, H. C., Sands, S. F., & Urcuioli, P. J. (1984). Pigeon and monkey serial probe recognition: Acquisition, strategies, and serial position effects. In H. L. Roitblat, T. G. Bever, & H. S. Terrace (Eds.), *Animal cognition.* Hillsdale, NJ: Lawrence Erlbaum Associates.

11 Reinforcement Training as Interspecies Communication

Karen Pryor
Commissioner, Marine Mammal Commission, Washington, D.C.

DOLPHIN DOMESTICATION

Most of the large mammals that are trained to perform useful work for man, whether horse or dog, camel or yak, were brought into captivity and successfully domesticated by the dawn of recorded history. The dolphin, therefore, is a very recent addition to the roster of man's animal partners. We may think of dolphins primarily as performers, like circus animals, However, beginning in the early 1960s, dolphins have also become established as at least semi-domesticated animals, capable of performing useful tasks in their natural environment, the ocean. For example, at the United States Naval Ocean Systems Centers in San Diego and in Hawaii, dolphins have been trained to carry burdens and (as have sea lions) to seek, locate, and aid in the recovery of underwater objects.

Dolphins differ, however, from horses, dogs, and most other domestic animals, not only in being aquatic but in the methods by which they are trained. The training of behavior in terrestrial domestic animals is almost always accomplished by means of negative reinforcement, coercion, and restraint; and it is enforced with punishment. The ox moves forward to avoid the goad, and thus pulls the wagon. The dog must obey the leash, the horse the bridle. The sheep which will not move with the other sheep will be barked at or even bitten by the dog, and the dog which does not chase sheep when told to will be beaten by the shepherd. The dolphin, however, is not easily trained by these negative methods. You cannot use a leash or a bridle or even your fist on an animal which just swims away. The dolphin thus has become one of the few large mammals with

253

which we have had extensive experience in the shaping of behavior primarily, and indeed in most cases almost exclusively, by the use of positive reinforcement.

Although a few dolphins were kept as aquarium specimens as early as the 1860s, routine maintenance of dolphins in captivity first occurred just before World War II (for a history of dolphins in captivity, see Defran & Pryor, 1980.) Thus techniques for the maintenance and training of dolphins were being developed during roughly the same decades in which experimental psychologists were reaching an understanding of the laws of operant conditioning, and the ways in which behavior could be modified by using positive reinforcement—the area of research associated most prominently with B. F. Skinner.

Several behavioral psychologists, students or colleagues of Skinner, were closely involved with the development of dolphin training techniques in the early decades of dolphin use and research. Keller Breland, under the auspices of a visionary Naval research director, William B. McLean, was instrumental in the development of the Navy's dolphin research programs and in the uses of operant techniques for both basic and applied research with dolphins by Navy scientists. R. N. Turner, working with Kenneth Norris at Marineland of the Pacific, developed reinforcement training techniques for some of the first dolphin sonar research, and was the original source of operant conditioning techniques for innovative work at Sea Life Park and the Oceanic Institute in the 1960s. Kent Burgess provided a sound scientific grounding for the training program at Sea World during its early years. Many contributions to methodology have since been made by trainers at these and other organizations (Schusterman, 1980; Turner, 1964).

POSITIVE REINFORCEMENT TRAINING
AND COGNITION

In traditional force-training of domestic animals, the subject typically is not given choices (other than the implied choice, "Obey, or else!") For example if one asks a horse pulling a wagon to turn left, one wants only that behavior, and no other: not a right turn or an increase in speed, and certainly not some self-initiated behavior such as standing on the hind legs or jumping in the air. However the training of dolphins by positive reinforcement techniques often gives the animal freedom to demonstrate whatever capabilities it may have. During the training process the animal is at liberty to initiate its own behavior, as well as interactions with the trainer, in a way that is almost impossible in the restrictive circumstances of traditional training of domestic animals (or, for that matter, in the "whip-and-chair" aversive training traditionally used with circus animals). To a certain extent it is this circumstance, rather than some intrinsic characteristic of the dolphin, which has given the public and scientists alike such respect for the animal's cognitive abilities: We get more chances to observe cognitive processes in these animals than in most others.

Reinforcement training is interactive: What the trainer does depends on what the animal does. The trainer can, and often does, develop behavior without making any attempt to prompt or cue the animal, but instead by watching, reacting, and reinforcing behavior that does occur. Thus the animal discovers that various actions of its own may result in reinforcement. One might say that as the trainer is developing behavior, the animal in effect is training the trainer to give fish.

Opportunity is thus provided for an animal to utilize cognitive skills. A well-known example is the much-anthologized "creative porpoise" experiment at Sea Life Park in which a rough-toothed dolphin (*Steno bredanensis*) was taught to respond to the criterion, "Only behavior which has not previously been rewarded will now be reinforced." In each training session a behavior was selected for reinforcement which had not previously been a conditioned behavior. Within a few such sessions, the normal behavioral repertoire was exhausted. After a period of confusion, the animal began offering novel behaviors such as aerial flips, spitting, and swimming in corkscrew patterns, thus fulfilling the criterion—and demonstrating a capacity not only for complex learning but also for a certain amount of creativity (Pryor, Haag, & O'Reilly, 1969).

Another example of insightful behavior is the ability of some experienced animals to "check out" training criteria by running through a series of variations on a learned behavior. A false killer whale (*Pseudorca crassidens*) at Sea Life Park did this when trainers attempted to correct an error in a routine in the performance. Two whales had been trained to jump over a hurdle simultaneously in opposite directions; however one whale had taken to jumping late. When the trainers held a practice session and did not reinforce the late jumper, it "tested the premise" by a series of five jumps: (1) it made a perfect jump and was reinforced; (2) it made a late jump and was not reinforced; (3) it made a perfectly timed jump, but from the wrong side, traveling parallel to the other whale rather than in the opposite direction, an unprecedented event for which it had never been reinforced; (4) it made a correct jump that was just a little bit late, and received a very small reinforcement; and, finally, (5) it made a correct jump that was also perfectly timed, received a large number of fish, and performed correctly from then on (Pryor, 1981b).

Another not uncommon example of cognitive activity in trained dolphins is the deliberate wrong response. Ronald Schusterman has described an experiment in which a bottlenose dolphin (*Tursiops truncatus*) was being asked to make a series of choices, and after many correct responses, one day made a long series of completely wrong responses. The animal was being reinforced by fish dispensed from a feeding machine; examination revealed that the fish in the machine had dried out and become unpalatable. When the fish were replaced, the dolphin resumed making correct responses (Schusterman, personal communication).

Within the context of a positive reinforcement training session it is not just dolphins that can use the rules of the game to "train the trainer." During a project at the National Zoological Park in which I taught reinforcement training to a group of keepers (Pryor, 1981a), primate caretaker Melanie Bond was using food reinforcement to shape behavior in a chimpanzee. When the session was over, she moved to open the door and let the chimpanzee into its outside run, whereupon the animal reinforced this desirable behavior by handing her a piece of celery. During the same project, I was training a juvenile elephant to retrieve objects tossed into its pen. In the first session, the elephant quickly trained me to give it only the preferred reinforcement, sweet potatoes, from an assortment of food. When that was successful, it used the same methods—eye glances and trunk movements, primarily—to try to get me to unlock the cage door. I have seen similar grasping of both concept and opportunity in a wolf (Pryor, 1984). It is perhaps worth noting that this kind of event occurs frequently only in the training of those species which are commonly thought to be the most "intelligent," such as apes, dolphins, elephants, and some parrots.

Because these kinds of events take place within a training situation, they are often amenable to replication (the "creative porpoise" experiment described above was a replication of a serendipitous event that occurred during public performances). Thus reinforcement training constitutes an excellent tool for the investigation of animal cognition.

REINFORCEMENT TRAINING
AND INTRASPECIFIC SIGNALS

Another consequence of reinforcement training is that the animal may—in fact almost invariably does—direct its own intraspecific social signals at the trainer. Reinforcement training thus becomes a marvelous tool for the ethologist. Suppose one is looking at a tankful of dolphins, and a single animal leaps into the air and comes down sideways, a behavior known as breaching. In a tank of captive dolphins, one might be able to speculate about why the animal breached, based on past observations and the concurrent behavior of the other dolphins; but a great many observations might be needed to speculate correctly. Also, since breaching in dolphins appears to have several functions, from removal of remoras to driving of prey to various kinds of social signals, it might also take long observation to be able to state with some confidence what the function of a particular breach might be in a particular circumstance. Suppose, however, that I am engaged in a training session with a dolphin, shaping some particular behavior, and, either accidentally or deliberately, I fail to reinforce some action which previously has invariably resulted in the arrival of a fish. If the dolphin then leaps up in the air and comes down sidewise in such a way that it soaks me from head to toes—then I can say, from just that one experience, that at least in certain circumstances a breach is an aggressive or agonistic display, and a pretty good one, too.[1]

It is not just with dolphins that reinforcement training is a useful tool to the student of animal communication. While working at the National Zoo I saw several magnificient examples of animals directing intraspecific social displays to their keepers/trainers. Hyenas, for instance, are quite transformed by the throes of a greeting display: The tail goes in circles, the dorsal hair stands on end, the ears come up, the mouth opens, tongue hanging out, and the animal makes an incredible variety of sounds, giving the effect (to portray the behavior with an anthropomorphic metaphor) of a person exclaiming, "My dear, where have you *been,* I haven't seen you in ages, you look *wonderful,* well don't just stand there come *in,* tell me what's happening!" I have seen a polar bear respond to a reinforcement during a training session by bouncing down on its elbows and offering its trainer, on the other side of the bars, a clear-cut play invitation: a piece of communication which one might not expect to see in an adult of that species in a lifetime of watching. It is the context provided by the training situation that allows one to interpret behavior with considerable accuracy. As ethologist Konrad Lorenz has put it, one can use "the subtlety of conditioning not only as an end in itself . . . but as a tool to gain knowledge about the animal as a whole." (Lorenz, 1975.)

REINFORCEMENT TRAINING
AND HUMAN-ANIMAL COMMUNICATION

In this rich setting of mutual interaction and the mutual exchange of reinforcement (the animal's successful responses are the trainer's reinforcement) we can communicate a remarkably various and detailed set of information to the dolphin, as demonstrated by the performance of many research, display, and working animals all around the world. However the training context also gives the dolphins a fine opportunity to communicate with us, and thus to allow us fleeting but real glimpses of both the animal's state of affect and of cognitive processes in action. At Sea Life Park in Hawaii in about 1965 I was working with a newly captured rough-toothed dolphin, an unusual oceanic species about which little

---

[1]In this circumstance, familiar to most dolphin trainers, the training context not only illuminates the nature of the social signal, but also allows the signal to function as communication. For example, if the breaching animal is young or inexperienced, and especially if my failure to reinforce (thus putting the animal on an extinction schedule) was inadvertent, I would at once modify my own behavior and reinforce more liberally, in order to reduce the animal's distress lest it interfere with the progress of training.

was then known. I was beginning to initiate this individual into the rules of the training game by teaching it a few ways to earn a reinforcement. The first step, teaching the animal to associate the sound of a whistle (a conditioned reinforcer) with the arrival of a fish (a primary reinforcer) had been accomplished. Now, as I watched at tankside, the animal happened to lift its tail from the water. I blew the whistle, and tossed the animal a fish. Within a few minutes the animal was lifting its tail repeatedly, earning one fish after another.

Then the animal happened to make a noise, a little squeak. Unlike many other species of dolphins, rough-toothed dolphins rarely make audible sounds, and I had never heard this individual make a noise before; curious to hear more, I reinforced the emission of the sound. The animal made the sound several times and I reinforced the noise-making several times. I was surprised and pleased that a newly captured animal with so little training experience could learn to repeat a new behavior so readily.[2] Then the animal lifted its tail again, and I made a training mistake. I was more interested in the unusual noise-making, now, than in tail-lifting, which I felt sure I would have other opportunities to reinforce, as the animal did it often. So I did not respond to the tail-lift.

The animal became visibly upset. A very "green" animal, it had had no previous experience of failure to earn reinforcement in a training situation, and it rushed around the tank breaching and then went over to the far side of the tank and turned its back on me. "I don't want to play this game any more."

It took a few "free" fish to get the animal to participate again (a common trainer's device to stimulate the offering of behavior in an animal that is not responding, by making it clear that reinforcement continues to be available). In a few minutes, the animal was swimming around the tank, and again it offered the tail lift.

Now a clarification of the rules was needed, a signal that would define when tail lifting would be reinforced. I raised my hand, to act as a cue, and reinforced tail-lifting when my hand was up, but not when it was down, several times. In a few minutes the animal was exhibiting the correct behavior in the presence of the newly established cue (again, in my opinion, a rather impressive rate of learning in a novice subject).

Then the animal happened to make the noise again. I reinforced the noise, and immediately also lifted my hand so it would have the opportunity to get reinforced for tail-lifting too, which it did. The animal then initiated and carried out

---

[2]Usually, in reinforcing spontaneously occuring behavior in an inexperienced dolphin, one expects to have to reinforce the behavior several to many times, perhaps over a period of days, before the animal "realizes" what action is being reinforced, and offers the behavior repeatedly. Often one must condition two or three kinds of responses before the individual generalizes, i.e. becomes capable of immediately repeating any new response as soon as it is reinforced more than once. This animal had learned to offer not just one but two new behaviors, with high frequency, in its first real training session. At Sea Life Park we were to find that rough-toothed dolphins seem to be unusually good at acquiring and exhibiting such rule-governed behavior.

the sequence of "noise, conditioned reinforcement, signal for tail-lift, tail-lift, and reinforcement" several times. It then swam to the other side of the tank, but without apparent agitation, so I took advantage of the pause in the proceedings to put my arms in the water and rinse the fish juice off my hands.

As I was doing this, the dolphin came over, and with one flipper stroked my arm up and down, very vigorously, an affiliative signal frequently seen between dolphins but never, in my experience, from dolphin to person. In this context it might be loosely interpreted as "Okay, stupid, I understand what you mean now, and you're forgiven" (Pryor, 1974).

This kind of event, a real communication, can be an emotional experience for man and beast alike. When this individual, Malia, later to become a rather well-known research and performance animal, rubbed my arm, I was touched, and dumped all the rest of the fish into the tank. However, this and all similar anecdotes are not so much an indication of some quasi-human capabilities of an animal or a species, or of the sentimentality of porpoise trainers, but of the enormous potential of interactive training as a window into animal behavior *and* potentially into animal consciousness.

CONCLUSION

Traditional animal training can also develop a situation of rapport and communication between trainer and subject. Traditional training, however, of dogs or horses, say, requires the patient acquisition of physical skills, sometimes at considerable risk. Just learning to ride a horse involves more time and physical effort than most people care to spend, and that is nothing compared to the physical skills and risks involved in training a horse. Thus the "glimpses through the window" afforded to the traditional animal trainer are not available to most people; and those who are both traditional trainers and convincing communicators are few.

Here, slightly paraphrased, is a statement from a professional writer who is also a trainer:

> These are beautiful, marvelous creatures, whose responses and instincts work on a plane as different from humans as water and oil. . . . Insight into their senses and consciousness is like a half-opened door or a half-learned language; our comprehension is maddeningly balked by not having the right sorts of hearing, or sense of touch; or maybe good enough telepathy. The feeling of oneness I have sometimes had with them has been their gift to an inferior being; but maybe my passion to [find out what we can accomplish together] has been my gift to them. (Francis, 1976)

This paragraph was not written by a dolphin trainer, but by Dick Francis, a horse trainer and steeplechase jockey. The oneness he speaks of is the learned interaction of horse and rider in a race. It's a communication not available to many, and not particularly accessible to research. However, reinforcement training brings this particular window into the house of science. As the philosopher Gergory Bateson said, "Operant conditioning is a method of communication with an alien species" (Pryor, 1975). It is not merely a way of communicating our wishes to an animal, but a two-way system. It is, in fact, a game, rigorous in rules but admitting of spontaneity. We should not be misled by the effects of this sytem into thinking that dolphins are somehow more "intelligent" than they are, nor that all other animals are necessarily less. Instead we should perhaps give more serious attention to the possibilities of the training context as an investigative tool in the study of animal awareness and cognition.

REFERENCES

Defran, R. H., & Pryor, K. (1980). Social behavior and training of eleven species of cetaceans in captivity. L. Herman (Ed.), In *Cetacean behavior: Mechanisms and functions*. New York: Wiley-Interscience.

Francis, D. (1979). *Whip hand*. New York: Harper & Row.

Lorenz, K. (1975). Foreword. In K. Pryor *Lads before the wind: Adventures in porpoise training*. New York: Harper & Row.

Pryor, K. W. (1974). Learning and behavior in whales and porpoises. *Naturwissenschaften, 60*, 137–143.

Pryor, K. W. (1975). *Lads before the wind: Adventures in porpoise training*. New York: Harper & Row.

Pryor, K. W. (1981a). The rhino likes violets. *Psychology Today*, April, 92–98.

Pryor, K. W. (1981b). Why porpoise trainers are not dolphin lovers: Real and false communication in the operant setting. *Annals of the New York Academy of Science, 304*, 137–143.

Pryor, K. (1984). *Don't shoot the dog!* New York: Simon & Schuster.

Pryor, K. W., Haag, R., & O'Reilly, J. (1969). The creative porpoise: Training for novel behavior. *The Journal of Experimental Analysis of Behavior, 12*, 653–661.

Turner, R. N. (1964). Methodological problems in the study of behavior. In W. N. Tavolga (Ed.), *Marine bio-acoustics*. Oxford: Pergamon Press.

Schusterman, R. (1980). Behavioral methodology in echolocation by marine mammals. In R. G. Busnel & J. F. Fish (Eds.), *Animal sonar systems*. New York: Plenum.

12 Dolphin Behavior and Cognition: Evolutionary and Ecological Aspects

J. F. Eisenberg
*The University of Florida,
Gainesville*

INTRODUCTION

I believe we are concerned in this symposium with complex social organizations and thus may disregard aggregations which show only limited coordination and integration. Integrated social organizations are characterized by the following attributes: The members have a complex system of communication; they often have a division of labor based on specialization for role; and the members show a cohesion or tendency to remain together. Some groups may show seasonal changes in composition. In highly social forms a member may be involved with the same set of adult companions for its entire life. Finally, there is a tendency for the group to be relatively impermeable to nonrelated conspecifics (Eisenberg, 1966).

THE SOCIAL ORGANIZATIONS OF MAMMALS

Because of the unique mode of neonatal nutrition in mammals, namely that only the female lactates and the young are nourished by milk, the bulk of parental care falls to females and often the most cohesive social unit in a mammal society is that composed of a mother and her young. In long-lived species this grouping can be expanded into a unit involving a mother and several age classes of young. Where daughters remain with mothers and males leave, a matriarchy may be formed. The only advance possible beyond this stage of sociality is the inclusion of an adult male in the group as a provisioner or protector of the female-neonatal grouping. This extended family forms the core of most cohesive mammalian social systems (Eisenberg, 1966; Wilson, 1975).

The formation of flocks, schools, herds, and colonies is not necessarily a result of pair bonding or the maternal neonatal relationship, but rather a formation from outside recruitment. It is in this instance that perhaps we can speak of a social drive that is divorced from sexuality and parental, care-giving behaviors.

An individual may pass through several grades of sociality in its life history; however, an animal adapted for a social life generally is found only in a social grouping except when dispersing. In summary, we can distinguish several grades of complexity in mammalian social organization:

1. solitary, except for mating or the rearing phase;
2. social life with a high tolerance for conspecifics of the same reproductive class:

(a) simple social systems without long-term cohesion that derive either from aggregations at resource areas or during migration,
(b) the reproductive social system with pronounced division of labor and interdependence with two subvariants, the mating interaction and the parental-young interaction; and, finally,
(c) complex social systems with pronounced division of labor and interdependence, cohesion, permanence; often rather impermeable to outside recruitment; and consisting of adults of both sexes.

When we eliminate the simpler social systems concerned with reproduction and care, then extended groupings generally have adaptive value because they either enhance antipredator behavior or result in an increased capacity for finding food. The form of social organization then can be molded by the selective forces of predation, and the manner in which food or other essential resources are dispersed in space and time (Eisenberg, 1981; Wilson, 1975).

SOCIAL ORGANIZATION AND ENCEPHALIZATION

Mammals do not form permanent neuter castes in so far as we know. That is, each individual at birth has the potential of becoming an independent, reproducing adult. Thus, no mammalian system converges toward those forms that are displayed by the social ants and termites with the possible exception of the naked mole rat *Heterocephalus glaber* (Jarvis, 1981). With this in mind it is possible to construct steps toward the evolution of complex social organizations and identify physiological and morphological attributes that are correlated with these stages.

If individuals of a species have a short life span, large litters, and rapid maturation of the young so that generational overlap is nearly impossible, then the young are placed in a situation with a decreased percentage in the amount of life span that can be spent in a social learning situation. Such species tend to have low encephalization quotients, and social structures tend to be simplified and confined to those social groupings concerned with mating and early parental care (Eisenberg, 1981; Jerison, 1983).

On the other hand, if there is a tendency for selection to favor overlapping generations it follows that an adult tends to have a longer life span, small litters, and a trend toward iteroparity in its reproductive strategy. If the resource base is predictable during the existence of a cohort, then on the average there is a decrease in percentage of life span spent in a social learning situation. This leads to an intermediate level of encephalization and a tendency toward simpler social structures. On the other hand, if the resource base is temporally uncertain and difficult to predict or spatially hyperdispersed, then selection tends to favor an increase in the percentage of the life span spent by the young in a social learning situation. This results in increased selection for larger relative brain size, an increase in the proportion of neocortex, which is expressed as a high encelphalization quotient (Eisenberg, 1981). The attainment of this level of neural organization demands the evolution of increased homeothermic capacity, a higher basal metabolic rate, and increased growth of the central nervous system (McNab & Eisenberg, in press).

At this latter stage of sociality, if there is no selection for a long-term phase of nonreproduction on the part of the young, there is little increase in social complexity but cohesive group formation is possible. On the other hand, if there is selection favoring a *temporary,* nonreproductive caste, and the young are incorporated into a helping capacity with respect to the reproductive members of the social group, then the stage is set for the complex, interdependent social grouping characterizing big brained, long lived, slow reproducing mammals. This latter cluster of interdependent characters typifies mammals that show extended interdependent social groupings, a high degree of coordination in movements, and a communication system that is subtle and expressive. Thus terrestrial mammals such as elephants, higher primates, and larger social carnivores all exhibit attributes in common with the delphinid cetaceans (Eisenberg, 1981). That the driving selection forces behind this are determined by resource dispersion and availability over time and space as well as methods of controlling predation by the group is not to be doubted (Wilson, 1975).

NATURAL SELECTION AND SOCIAL DYNAMICS

Once having characterized the various forms of social structures visible in nature and identified key selective forces that promote their appearance, one is left to consider the internal dynamics in social groupings. Most of the theory has been worked out in studies of terrestrial vertebrates, but it is certainly the case that the same principles apply to the delphinids and other cetaceans. It is only the difficulty of studying the aquatic cetaceans that retards progress in our knowledge of their behavior.

Several useful tools have been developed in recent years for the analysis of the dynamics of interindividual interaction. Through direct observation a behavioral inventory or ethogram can be developed. Once terms have been defined behavior can further be described by considering which age and sex class exhibit a given behavior pattern and with what frequency and to whom behaviors are directed within the social group. The application of the theory of games and optimum foraging strategies has allowed workers to formulate testable models. This modeling can be applied to analysis of conflict as well as competition resolution in foraging strategies (Alexander, 1974; Maynard-Smith, 1968).

Natural selection in the sense originally meant by Darwin acts so as to select for the fittest individuals, that is, those individuals that leave behind more adult offspring than the average (Darwin, 1859). What actually is selected is the genotype, although the bearer of the genotype is an individual. Fitness can be measured by the number of copies (i.e., individual carriers) of a given genotype that exist in a population. Since sexual reproduction implies that the unchanging carriers of hereditary traits are genes, and not the entire genotype, one can speak of a gene and use as a measure the number of copies of that gene within a given interbreeding population. Any action or behavior that increases this number also increases the fitness by definition. Genes for parental care will be selected for in species in which newborn infants are helpless without such care. The very existence of such genes implies their self-perpetuation in the progeny. Hamilton (1964) recognized that it is not only parents and children along a direct line of descent that share genes, but relatives not so directly connected. This concept was termed *inclusive fitness*. When acts benefit another individual (that is a relative) and demand a cost to the donor, the cost can be measured in terms of loss of fitness. This "altruistic trait" will only be selected for if the benefit to the recipient should exceed the cost to the donor by a factor which at least makes up for the distance in relatedness. This is *kin selection* as a general case of offspring selection.

Seemingly altruistic acts then can be explained as evolving through such means as kin slection or some form of delayed benefit such as reciprocal altruism. Types of altruism have been identified in mammalian societies. The origin of altruistic acts has been eloquently explored with the social insects and documented further in higher vertebrates such as the scrub jay, primates, social carnivores, elephants, and communal rodents (Bertram, 1983; Wilson, 1975).

All is not necessarily harmonious in social groupings. Usually priority of access to resources is controlled along a dominance axis, and nepotistic tendencies, that is the aiding of relatives, tend to further create asymmetries in the expression of social traits. The theory is at hand and needs to be tested; delphinids are a further challenge (given their aquatic environment) to explore principles expounded and developed by Bertram (1983), E. O. Wilson (1975),

Maynard-Smith (1968), Alexander (1974), and many others (see Bradbury, this volume).

HIGHER MENTAL PROCESSES AND COGNITION

The attainment of the interdependent system of large brain, long life, and social living raises the question: To what extent are these species capable of cognition? Cognition is a very slippery term. In Webster's Dictionary I find the following definitions: the process of knowing or perceiving; I turn to knowing and find (1) having knowledge, (2) shrewd, clever, (3) implying shrewd or secret understanding; and turning to perception (1) the awareness of objects, etc., to the senses, (2) the faculty of perceiving, (3) knowledge, that is gained by perceiving. Thus, *knowledge* becomes the word and the key. Therefore the definition for knowledge is (1) the fact or state of knowing, (2) ranges of information or understanding, (3) what is known by learning, (4) the body of facts accumulated by mankind.

At this point with the introduction of mankind I can begin to perceive a touch of Descartes (1952) and his formulation of the mind-body dualism wherein animals were considered as automatons not guided by a mind; and humans were considered to be creatures with a mind, free will, and attributes of reasoning. By the same token, this set the stage for considering animal communication to consist of expressions of specific motivational states in arousal, while human language was symbolic referring to objects in the external environment.

This view persists to this day in the works of Susanne K. Langer, who in 1971 wrote:

> All animal reaction is instinctive. Animal intelligence is the capability to find implementation for acts developed from the physiologically engendered instinctual repertoire. One may say that animal intelligence, where it exists, is exhibited in the pursuit of instinctive action; but instinctive behavior may be quite devoid of intelligence. (p. 319)

She concludes:

> What I have tried to show is how deep the division between beasts and men goes. Very deep indeed. But when we touch bottom, when we glimpse the beginning of man's great biological departure we come upon the ultimate unity—the common source of his and all other animal's impulses pressing for expression; the basic vital needs he still shares with the field mouse and the crow. (p. 330)

On the other side I note a formulation from Imanuel Kant (1949). In brief, humans can never know a thing as itself but only what we perceive it to be by means of our sense organs. Humans do experience, and we experience through sense organs and the processes of sense organ data reduction by the brain so that we form a world view, albeit this world view is limited. The construction of our nervous system and sense organs are laid down according to precise developmental rules and they are the foundation of all experience. Thus the structure of our neurosensory system defines in the sense of Kant what is a priori. Lorenz (1973) in his *Behind the Mirror* valiantly attempted to bridge this Kantian formulation with his own ideas of the adaptive modification of behavior. To quote from Lorenz (1965):

> If we conceive our intellect as the function of an organ (and there is no valid argument against this) our obvious answer to the question why its form of function is adapted to the real world is simply the following: our categories and forms of perception fixed prior to individual experience are adapted to the external world for exactly the same reason as the hoof of a horse is already adapted to the ground of the steppe before the horse is born and the fin of the fish is adapted to the water before the fish hatches. (p. 74)

In short, the mind and its functioning is as much a product of natural selection as is the capacity to learn, structure perceptions, and store and retrieve information (Lorenz, 1965). This view of the functioning mind as an evolved organ has been elaborated by Lumsden and Wilson (1981) by tying this view to the many theories developed by psychologists of how the mind functions and works.

Certain functional aspects of animal brains have been investigated through intricate experimentation. W. Köhler (1951) pioneered to demonstrate the reasoning ability of chimpanzees. E. C. Tolman (1958) was the first to propose that rats had the capacity to form cognitive maps that were organized at levels higher than simple reflexes. O. Köhler (1952) first propounded the concept that higher vertebrate brains seemed to function in a cognitive manner in his article "Thinking Without Words." Recently D. Griffin (1981) has explored the methodologies we might employ to determine the extent to which higher cognitive functions are representative in behavior patterns of higher vertebrates that do not necessarily have syntactic communication systems—in short, thinking without words.

Thus, we come around to the problem of communication, higher functional categories, and the structure of the brain. As John Robinson has noted "The syntactic rules of capuchin monkeys are not analogous to grammatical rules generating sentences." First, "the simple addition of meaning," as represented by the compound calls of the *Cebus*, "is a long way from the hierarchical complexity of grammar and speech." Second, "these syntactic rules are not open in their ability to include additional referents and further combine them together in an infinite number of ways." And, third, "both the simple and compound calls of *Cebus* monkeys have similar relations to their referents" (Robinson, 1984). Clearly, higher mammals and higher birds (in the sense of those that have high encephalization quotients) are capable of certain cognitive functions without the elaboration of a syntactical communication system on a par with humans. That the evolution of the human brain made a significant departure from the capacity of animals is not to be doubted, but the links and functional analogs are certainly worth elaborating on and investigating.

The basic problem is that cognition may be defined in a number of ways. Indeed, psychologists differ on the definition (Leeper, 1951). At issue is an operational definition. We recognize that even some human activities are reflexive (such as knee jerk reflex, etc.) and from detailed physiological studies of neural arcs we actually know the pathways of mediation for simple muscular contraction. We also know that some human activities, such as playing chess, involve considerable learning and are examples of a "higher mental process." A chess master may be able to glance at a board and with minimal reflection reproduce the position of the pieces when the board is no longer in front of him. The time for the act of perception is very brief and little if any conscious reflection on the chess master appears to be involved. We as humans would not dispute that the chess master is utilizing "higher mental processes"; however, conscious reflection does not seem to be involved. Now the problem before us is to demonstrate that infrahuman vertebrates have neural mechanisms that operate in a fashion analogous or homologous to the processes we observe as operative in our own conduct when we are engaged in "higher mental processes."

Griffin (1981) has offered us the challenge to investigate higher mental processes in infrahuman organisms. The problem is a difficult one, however, since our unique communication system, speech, does not permit easy access to the minds of our fellow species on this planet; we must use a roundabout method for demonstrating higher mental processes in infrahuman mammals. Indeed, so difficult is the problem that in 1976 I still clung to the belief that the semanticity of animal communication was a closed book for the ethologist (Eisenberg, 1976). I have reason for hope, however. I never doubted that "higher mental processes" were operative in the behavior of infrahuman animals. The efforts by E. C. Tolman, O. Köhler and W. Köhler had convinced me of that. I had given up on a "Cartesian" view of the universe as a total explanation but did not feel that a good starting point for the analysis of animal behavior was the position with a maximum number of a priori assumptions.

The pioneering positions taken by Lilly (1961) and Williams (1965) in the last 25 years have forced all of us to reevaluate. Marler (1983) and his coworkers have made a convincing case for the existence of some form of semanticity inherent in certain primate calls. The Gardners (1969), and Savage-Rumbaugh (this volume) have pioneered in the exploration of human to animal communication. Regardless of the theoretical position the challenge is there before us.

Schusterman and Krieger (1984), Herman (this volume) and Richards (this volume) have convincingly demonstrated that members of the order Cetacea and Pinnipedia can exhibit something like semantic behavior. Lilly (1961) and re-

TABLE 12.1.
Some Social and Cognitive Attributes of Mammals
with High Encephalization Values

Taxon	Object Manipulation	Concept Learning (Numbers)	Concept Memory	Repetoire Diversity	Use of Referentia	Vocal Mimicry	Dependency on Social Tradition	Authority*
Proboscidea								
Elephas maximus	3	2	3	4	?	2	4	Rensch & Altevogt, 1953
Pinnipedia								
Zalophus californicus	4	?	3	4	2	?	2	Schusterman & Krieger, 1984
Phoca hispida	2	?	?	3	?	3	?	Ralls et al. in press
Primates								
Macaca mulatta	4	?	3	4	2	1	3	Rumbaugh, 1975
Cercopithecus aethiops	4	?	3	4	2	1	3	Marler, 1983
Pan satyrus	4	3	4	4	4	1	4	Rumbaugh, 1975
Cetacea								
Tursiops truncatus	4	?	3	4	4	2	3	Herman, this volume

1 = little developed
4 = highly developed
? = unknown
*includes author's subjective estimates

cently Richards (this volume) have shown that dolphins can exhibit vocal mimicry. Clearly there are whole classes of "higher mental processes" that animals share with humans. Table 12.1 contains a listing of behaviors that may indicate either higher learning abilities, or if you like "cognitive" abilities for selected species of mammals. Note that although vocal mimicry is not uncommon in birds, it is rare in mammals and curiously absent in infrahuman primates. The demonstration of vocal mimicry in the harbor seal (*Phoca vitulina*) by Ralls, Fiorelli, and Gish (1985) is nothing short of sensational. Wemmer and Mishra (1982) have offered an elegant example of intraspecific vocal mimicry from the Asiatic elephant (*Elephas maximus*). These latter two examples do not necessarily indicate "higher mental processes" but they do indicate abilities heretofore unsuspected by ethologists.

Restricting myself to the class Mammalia I must admit to the following: Large, long-lived species with a low reproductive potential probably offer the best subjects for demonstrating "higher mental processes." They tend to have relatively large brains (for whatever that is worth) and seem to be less "hard wired" than their small-brained compatriots. If we could agree on a set of operational definitions we could very probably reach the goal that King Solomon achieved three thousand years before. He was so wise he could "speak also of beasts and of fowl and of creeping things and of fishes" (First Kings 4:33, as noted by Lorenz, 1952).

REFERENCES

Alexander, R. D. (1974). The evolution of social behavior. *Annual Review of Ecology and Systematics 5*, 325–383.

Bertram, B. C. (1983). Kin selection and altruism. In J. F. Eisenberg & D. G. Kleiman (Eds.), *Advances in the study of mammalian behavior* (pp. 721–737). Special Publication of the American Society of Mammalogists No. 7.

Darwin, C. (1859). *The origin of species*. New York: The Modern Library. (Reprint)

Darwin, C. (1872). *The descent of man*. New York: The Modern Library. (Reprint)

Descartes, R. (1952). *The meditations and selections from the principles* (translated by J. Veitch). La Salle, IL: Open Court Publishing Company.

Eisenberg, J. F. (1966). The social organizations of mammals. *Handbuch der Zoologie, 8 Band, Lieferung 39*.

Eisenberg, J. F. (1976). Communication and social integration in the black spider monkey, *Ateles fusciceps robustus*, and related species. *Smithsonian Contributions to Zoology*, No. *213*, 108 pp.

Eisenberg, J. F. (1981). *The mammalian radiations*. Chicago: University of Chicago Press.

Gardner, R. A., & Gardner, B. T. (1969). Teaching sign language to a chimpanzee. *Science, 165*, 644–672.

Griffin, D. R. (1981). *The question of animal awareness*. New York: Rockerfeller University Press.

Hamilton, W. D. (1964). The genetical evolution of social behavior. Parts I and II. *Journal of Theoretical Biology, 7*, 1–16, 17–52.

Jarvis, J. (1981). Eusociality in a mammal: Cooperative breeding in naked mole rat colonies. *Science, 212*, 571–573.

Jerison, H. (1983). The evolution of the mammalian brain as an information-processing system. In J. F. Eisenberg & D. G. Kleiman (Eds.), *Advances in the study of mammalian behavior* (pp. 113–146). *Special Publication of the American Society of Mammalogists # 7.*

Kant, I. (1949). *Kant's Prolegomena* (translated and edited by Paul Carus). Chicago: Open Court Publishing Company.

Köhler, W. (1951). *The mentality of apes* (translated by E. Winter). London: The Humanities Press.

Köhler, O. (1952). Vom unbenannten Denken. *Zoologischer Anzeiger,* Suppl. 16, 202–211.

Langer, S. (1971). The great shift: Instinct to intuition. In J. F. Eisenberg & W. S. Dillon (Eds.), *Man and beast: Comparative social behavior* (pp. 313–332). Washington, D.C.: Smithsonian Institution Press.

Leeper, R. (1951). Cognitive processes. In S. S. Stevens (Ed.), *Handbook of Experimental Psychology* (pp. 730–757). New York: Wiley.

Lilly, J. C. (1961). *Man and dolphin.* New York: Worlds of Science, Pyramid Publication.

Lorenz, K. Z. (1952). *King Solomon's Ring.* London: Methuen.

Lorenz, K. Z. (1965). *Evolution and modification of behavior.* Chicago: University of Chicago Press.

Lorenz, K. Z. (1973). *Behind the mirror* (translated by R. Raylor). New York: Harcourt, Brace, Jovanovich.

Lumsden, C. J., & Wilson, E. O. (1981). *Promethean fire.* Cambridge, MA: Harvard University Press.

Marler, P. (1983). Monkey calls: How are they perceived, What do they mean. In J. F. Eisenberg & D. G. Kleiman (Eds.), *Advances in the study of mammalian behavior* (pp. 343–356). *Special Publication of the American Society of Mammalogist # 7.*

Maynard-Smith, J. (1968). *Mathematical ideas in biology.* Cambridge: Cambridge University Press.

McNab, B. K., & Eisenberg, J. F. (in press). Brain size and its relation to rate of metabolism in mammals. *Oecologia.*

Ralls, K., Fiorelli, P., & Gish, S. (1985). Vocalizations and vocal imitation in captive harbor seals, *Phoca vitulina.* Canadian Journal of Zoology, *63,* 1050–1059.

Rensch, B., & Altevogt, R. (1953). Visuelles Lernvermogen eines Indischen Elefanten. *Zeitschrift für Tierpsychologie 10,* 119–134.

Robinson, J. (1984). Syntactic structures in the vocalizations of wedgecapped capuchin monkeys, *Cebus nigrivittatus. Behaviour.* 90:46–79.

Rumbaugh, D. M. (1975). The learning and symbolizing capacities of apes and monkeys. In R. H. Tuttle (Ed.), *Socioecology and psychology of primates* (pp. 353–401). The Hague: Mouton.

Schusterman, R., & Krieger, K. (1984). California sea lions are capable of semantic comprehension. *The Psychological Record, 34,* 3–23.

Tolman, E. C. (1958). *Behavior and psychological man.* Berkeley: University of California Press.

Webster's New World Dictionary. (1958). New York: World Publishing Company.

Wemmer, C., & Mishra, H. (1982). Observational learning by an Asiatic elephant of an unusual sound production method. *Mammalia, 46,* 556–557.

Williams, L. (1965). *Samba and the monkey mind.* London: Bodley Head.

Wilson, E. O. (1975). *Sociobiology, the new synthesis.* Cambridge, MA: Harvard University Press.

COMMUNICATION IN DOLPHINS

Jeanette A. Thomas

Life in the water governs many of the characteristics of cetacean communication and has resulted in the evolution of unique adaptations for signal production and reception in an aquatic environment. For example, sound travels about four-and-a-half times faster in water than in air and range is frequency dependent. Low-frequency sound of sufficient amplitude (e.g., that of large mysticetes), if not masked by ambient noise, may be detected hundreds of miles from the source. Odontocetes produce broadband and very high amplitude sounds associated with echolocation. Hearing abilities are similarly broadband, requiring that elaborate processing be used to interpret echolocation signals.

In contrast, odontocetes do not have a well-developed olfactory sense. Although *Tursiops* has perianal glands which could conceivably function in chemocommunication, they probably are not used to the same extent as in terrestrial mammals for communication. Chemical signals in a marine environment tend to diffuse rapidly and would not be appropriate for a site-specific signal.

Distinctive color patterns in toothed whales (e.g., *Orca, Phocoenoides, and Lagenorhynchus*) suggest that visual signals are used in communication. However, vision varies among cetaceans (it has been lost in some of the river dolphins), and its usefulness may be restricted to short distances. Visual abilities have probably evolved as a compromised system that can be used in both air and water.

271

Tactile communication is common in these hairless mammals, which use many areas of the body for contact. The aquatic environment is a good medium for detecting subtle pressure changes over the body that might relate to communication between individuals.

Studies of communication in wild dolphins are difficult because observing natural interactions between mobile animals at sea is impractical. Not only is it costly and opportunistic, but the context of signals is rarely, if ever, known. Captivity provides a good setting for studies of hearing, vision, or chemoreception in toothed whales. However, collections of captive cetaceans may not reflect a "normal" social group, so that studies on communication are limited because important signals in their repertoire may not be elicited. Given these difficulties, studying cognitive processes related to communication in dolphins is also frustrating, and many scientists compare cognitive and communicative abilities in dolphins to those in other, better studied, species of animals.

Because studies have documented well-developed echolocation abilities in toothed whales, dialects in whales such as killer whales and humpback whales, and vocal mimicry in dolphins, some researchers have assumed that cetaceans have well developed cognitive and communicative abilities. Perhaps because of their high vocalization rate, the ease of recording underwater vocalizations that propagate over long distances, and the fascinating nature of these sounds, most is known about vocal communication in dolphins. As a result, papers in this section of the book primarily address cognitive processes in vocal communication in dolphins. The paper by Douglas Richards presents a good example of "state of the art" research on vocal mimicry in relation to communication in dolphins. He addresses the topic of how cognitive processes allow a dolphin to alter its vocal behavior to mimic a man-made acoustic signal.

This section of the book, especially, draws on the results of studies that have examined cognitive and communicative abilities in other animals. Two of the papers compare cognitive processes in birds to those in dolphins. Irene Pepperberg describes impressive allospecific communicative abilities using human-based codes that can be comprehended by dolphins and parrots. W. John Smith describes the context-specific vocal communication of the eastern kingbird and acknowledges that, as in these birds, context may play an important role in cognitive processes in dolphins. Using a terrestrial mammal as a model, E. Sue Savage-Rumbaugh and William D. Hopkins point out the relationship between awareness or intentionality of communicative behavior and cognitive processes in primates.

Collectively, these chapters emphasize the variety of intricate communicative behaviors that several groups of animals have independently evolved which depend on elaborate cognitive processes. Cetaceans have evolved this ability in an aquatic environment and many differences may be attributed to adaptations or constraints that result from living in this medium.

13 Dolphin Vocal Mimicry and Vocal Object Labeling

Douglas G. Richards
Kewalo Basin Marine Mammal Laboratory,
University of Hawaii

INTRODUCTION

Dolphins and other members of the cetacean order are among the most vocal of the nonhuman mammals and exhibit remarkable development of the sound production and auditory mechanisms. This paper reports on the training of a bottlenosed dolphin (*Tursiops truncatus*) to mimic a wide variety of computer-generated sounds and to vocally label displayed real-world objects using some of these same sounds. The description of the training results is followed by a consideration of the implications of the mimicry and labeling ability for cognition in dolphins, particularly in regard to the relation of mimicry to cognitive complexity, and to the potential use of a vocal response mode for two-way communication in an artificial language. Finally, I discuss the implications of a laboratory demonstration of mimicry for studies of the natural communication behavior of dolphins.

The bottlenosed dolphin in captivity produces two broad categories of vocalizations: (a) narrow-band, frequency-varying, continuous tonal sounds referred to as ''whistles'' and (b) broad-band pulsed sounds expressed as trains of very short-duration clicks of varying rates (Evans, 1967; Lilly, 1962). The pulsed sounds are used for both communication and echolocation, and the whistles appear to be used primarily for communication (Herman & Tavolga, 1980). Descriptions of vocalizations emphasizing either the whistles or the pulsed sounds have led to contradictory hypotheses in the literature concerning the communication system of the dolphin. Some descriptions concentrating on the whistle vocalizations of dolphins in captivity have stressed the stereotyped, individually specific nature of these sounds. It has been reported that individually specific stereotyped whistles often comprise over 90% of the whistle repertoire of captive bottlenosed dolphins, with the degree of stereotype varying among different individuals (Burdin, Reznik, Skornyakov, & Chupakov, 1974; M. Caldwell & Caldwell, 1965, 1968). Such vocalizations would resemble the individually recognizable songs of some species of birds. Other workers have reported considerable variation in the whistles, in captivity or in the wild (Busnel & Dziedzic, 1966; Dreher, 1966; Dreher & Evans, 1964; Gish, 1979). A number of observations of apparent vocal mimicry have been made, though with no systematic investigation of the degree of vocal flexibility (Batteau & Markey, 1967; Caldwell & Caldwell, 1972; Evans, 1967; Lilly, 1962). The observed variability in the whistles, combined with the difficulty of identifying individual vocalizing dolphins in a group, has led to speculation that the whistles might be a complex, shared system, in which specific meanings could be assigned to specific whistles. The extreme view is that the shared system could approach or even exceed the complexity and functional capabilities of human language (Lilly, 1978). There is no behavioral evidence at this time to support the concept of an underlying grammatical system comparable to human language, although unsuccessful attempts have been made to induce dolphins to use their natural communication system to transmit arbitrary information (Bastian, 1966; Bastian, Wall, & Anderson, 1968).

The pulsed vocalizations, on the other hand, resemble the graded signals of most other mammals (Caldwell & Caldwell, 1967). The use of at least some of the sounds appears to follow the motivational-structural rules discussed by Morton (1982) for a variety of terrestrial species, in which vocalizations used in an aggressive context are relatively low in frequency, and harsh and broadband in tonal quality.

This paper considers only the whistle vocalizations. It is clear that the potential of the pulsed sounds for communication is also great, and mimicry of pulsed sounds as well as whistles has been observed though not yet investigated in detail (Caldwell & Caldwell, 1972; Gish, 1979; Herman, 1980).

Andrew (1962) cautioned against interpreting as vocal mimicry the elicitation of a species-typical vocalization by a sound that resembles it. Though this dichotomy between mimicry and phonoresponse is oversimplified, it is clearly difficult to investigate mimicry without some knowledge of the baseline repertoire of the subject. The definition by Thorpe (1963) of "true" imitation as the copying of an otherwise improbable act or utterance is the definition that is followed here. The criteria for mimicry were (a) the vocalization produced by the animal in response to a presented "model" sound must resemble that model, and (b) the model must not resemble sounds present in the established baseline pre-training repertoire of the animal. Resemblance was measured along the dimensions of frequency and time, and for a few sounds, relative amplitude. In this study we required vocal responses immediately following the model sound to facilitate training for mimicry and judgments of mimicry ability, but there is no necessary requirement for the response to follow the model immediately. The "mimicry" described as matching of "sonic bursts" by Lilly (Lilly, 1965; Lilly, Miller & Truby, 1968) does not satisfy these criteria, since the bursts produced consisted of the dolphin's own unmodified vocalizations. The anecdotes concerning mimicry of human speech presented neither baseline data nor criteria for comparison with the model sounds.

VOCAL MIMICRY

The study reported here involves a bottlenosed dolphin that had a pre-training whistle repertoire that was repetitive and highly stereotyped. Nevertheless, the dolphin was able to learn to mimic a variety of computer-generated model sounds with high fidelity and reliability. All of the sounds were imitated by the dolphin using its whistle mode of vocalization, and all were distinct from the unreinforced whistles characteristically produced by that dolphin prior to training. The following is a summary of a study reported in detail in Richards, Wolz, and Herman (1984). The goals were to determine the unreinforced baseline vocal repertoire of the dolphin subject; to explore the range of vocal talent of the dolphin in the mimicry task; to assess the reliability with which specific sounds could be imitated in repeated tests; and to examine the ability of the dolphin to develop a generalized concept of mimicry which might enable it to attempt to mimic novel sounds.

The bottlenose dolphin studied was an approximately five-year-old (subadult) female named Akeakamai, 2.17 m in length. She was collected in waters near Gulfport, Mississippi in June 1978, together with another female of like size named Phoenix. During the course of initial adaptation and subsequent training both dolphins were exposed to a wide variety of electronically generated sounds (Herman, Richards, & Wolz, 1984). In October 1979 we began training Akeakamai for vocal mimicry.

Before beginning mimicry training, we had unobtrusively collected 14 hours of "baseline" sound recordings of the two dolphins, over a period of time spanning their first 14 months at our facility. Monitoring of the whistles under conditions in which it was possible to identify the vocalizing individual allowed us to determine that the large majority of each dolphin's whistle vocalizations was an individually specific acoustical pattern. Approximately 90% of the whistles emitted fell into this category, the stereotyped "signature whistle" described by Caldwell and Caldwell (1965). Figure 13.1a shows the typical whistles of Akeakamai and Figure 13.1b shows the typical whistles of Phoenix. The rest consisted primarily of short chirps (Fig. 13.1c), whistles with characteristics resembling those of both dolphins (Fig. 13.1d), and occasional spontaneous mimicry of sounds used in other training (see Herman, 1980, for examples of spontaneous mimicry).

The model sounds used ranged between 4 and 20 kHz, were produced by computer-controlled Wavetek Model 154 programmable waveform generators, and were projected into the tank through a J-9 speaker obtained from the Naval

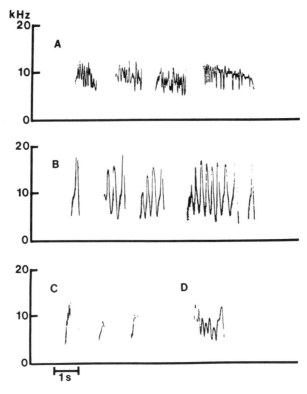

FIG. 13.1.   Spectrograms (Spectral Dynamics SD 350 spectrum analyzer, 50 Hz
resolution) of typical whistles recorded prior to training for mimicry. (A: Whistles
characteristic to Akeakamai, the subject of the experiments. B: Whistles characteristic to Phoenix, the companion dolphin. C: Short whistles of unknown origin.
D: Long whistles with characteristics similar to those of both dolphins. For clarity,
background noise and harmonics, resulting primarily from acoustics of the tank
and overloading of the input amplifier, have been removed from the figures.)
From Richards, Wolz, & Herman (1984). Vocal mimicry of computer-generated
sounds and vocal labeling of objects by a Bottlenosed Dolphin, *Tursiops truncatus*. Journal of Comparative Psychology, 98, 10–28. Copyright (1984) by the
American Psychological Association. Reprinted by permission of the publisher.

Research Laboratory. Responses were monitored visually on an oscilloscope
display produced by a frequency-to-voltage converter, and auditorily on a
speaker connected to the hydrophone in the tank. Most responses were tape
recorded for later analysis as necessary.

Training for mimicry involved reinforcement of successive approximations to
the desired imitation. Initial training proceeded according to a series of steps: (a)
the reinforcement (with food reward and social praise) of *any* whistle sound in
the presence of an acoustic signal to vocalize, (b) the reinforcement of only those

whistles that approximated the temporal duration of several computer sounds that were similar in structure to Akeakamai's most commonly produced whistle, and (c) the reinforcement of whistles that matched the base frequency and modulation parameters of arbitrary new sounds ("models") not resembling any whistles recorded during the baseline period. Following training on a few sounds, Akeakamai developed a generalized concept of mimic, such that she made an attempt to mimic any new sounds presented. Thereafter, much less shaping of approximations was necessary.

The important results of the mimicry training were as follows: (a) Akeakamai was able to mimic tonal sounds with frequencies between 4 and 20 kHz, with modulation rates between 0 Hz (unmodulated) and 11 Hz. Modulation wave-

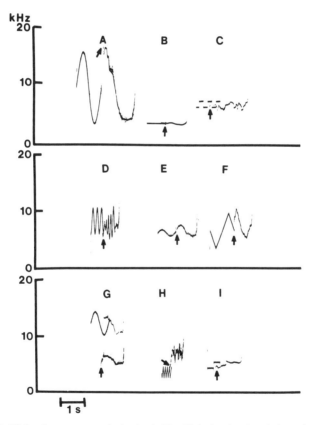

FIG. 13.2.   Spectrograms, obtained as in Fig. 13.1, showing the mimicry of nine selected computer-generated model sounds. (In each case the model sound is shown at the left. The arrow indicates the beginning of the mimicry, which often begins slightly before the end of the model sound.) From Richards et al., 1984. Copyright (1984) by the American Psychological Association. Reprinted by permission of the publisher.

forms included sine, triangle, and square waves (Fig. 13.2). (b) Akeakamai developed a generalized concept of mimic, such that she made an attempt to mimic any new sound presented. The concept went beyond the explicitly trained mimicry of frequency modulation. She spontaneously generalized to mimicry of amplitude modulation, and to mimicry of switching transients at the onset of some of the model sounds. (c) For sounds outside her preferred range, Akeakamai tended to transpose her mimicry up or down, often by an octave (Fig. 13.2g,h). (d) Akeakamai's mimicry of sounds with which she had experience was highly reliable—on a test involving random presentation of four sounds in her repertoire, she immediately followed presentation of the computer model sounds with mimicry on all 32 trials. See Richards et al. (1984) for complete figures.

LABELING OF OBJECTS

Following establishment of the mimic response, we tested the ability of the dolphin to produce, in response to visually displayed objects, particular sounds originally learned in imitation of computer models, effectively "labeling" the objects. Five objects were chosen for labeling training. These were a white volleyball ("Ball", Fig. 13.2d), a .5-m length of plastic (PVC) pipe ("Pipe", Fig. 13.2b), a square shaped PVC hoop, 40-cm per side ("Hoop", Fig. 13.2a), an ordinary plastic Frisbee ("Frisbee", Fig. 13.2e), and the dolphin's tankside trainer ("Person", Fig. 13.2c). The objects chosen were those used in a language comprehension study with this dolphin and the companion dolphin Phoenix (Herman et al., 1984; Herman, this volume). The model sounds associated with the objects were either identical to or similar to those computer sounds understood by Phoenix as "names" of these objects in the comprehension mode.

The first procedure tried for teaching labeling involved pairing the sound and object stimulus, and gradually fading the intensity of the sound to encourage transfer to the object as the eliciting stimulus for the mimicry. Akeakamai, however, had spontaneously generalized the concept of mimicry to include the amplitude as well as the frequency-time characteristics of the sound, as noted above. As a result, attenuation of the model sound resulted in Akeakamai correspondingly attenuating the intensity of her mimicry further and further until her response was no longer detectable by the monitoring equipment. While this was additional confirmation of the ability of a dolphin to generalize the concept of mimic, it was not a successful procedure for the training of object labeling.

In the second, successful, procedure, the model sound was always presented at full intensity, but the probability of its being presented on any given trial was systematically decreased over successive blocks of trials. Progress was rapid with this method, and Akeakamai learned to label each of the five objects in the absence of the model sound. In a test performed with the observer blind to the identity of the object presented, Akeakamai was correct in 152 out of 167 trials

(91%). All her errors were confusions between Person and Frisbee, the two most similar sounds. Akeakamai, though excellent at mimicry in the presence of the model sound, tended to drift in her rendition of the models when only the objects were presented. For the sounds Ball, Pipe, and Hoop there was little drift, but for Person and Frisbee she had difficulty maintaining the sound discrimination for long periods of time without occasional practice with the model sound. For both sounds her tendency was to superimpose an extra, rapid frequency modulation resembling some aspects of her signature whistle. There did not seem to be any confusion of the objects themselves, but only a tendency to drift in the quality of the rendition of the labels.

IMPLICATIONS OF MIMICRY
FOR COGNITION RESEARCH

The implications of mimicry for cognition research involve two interrelated questions. The first concerns the relation between the capability for mimicry and the capability for complex cognitive processing in the dolphin, and the second explores the use of the mimic/labeling response as a tool to expand the traditional methods available for the investigation of dolphin cognition. The use of the mimicry response mode as a tool to investigate cognition should help clarify the relation between mimicry and cognitive processing.

   Since the early observations of mimicry in dolphins (Lilly, 1962), the capacity for mimicry has been seen as linked to cognition, providing an additional line of behavioral evidence supporting the physical evidence of brain size to suggest that dolphins are of high intelligence. The rationale is that mimicry of another species involves production of behaviors which cannot possibly be ''innate'', and therefore must require greater cognitive abilities than those necessary for normal species-typical behaviors. In addition to the cognitive abilities, however, which may involve very selective tendencies to mimic, the motor abilities play a crucial role. Apes, for example, with their outstanding ability for motor mimicry of other primates (like humans), are not known to attempt to fly. From the point of view of a bird, apes would be poor mimics, since they can neither fly nor sing. Andrew (1962), apparently in response to Lilly's observations, specifically challenged the idea that vocal mimicry and intelligence are necessarily related. He pointed out that intelligent mammals such as the chimpanzee have very poor vocal mimicry ability, whereas some birds with very small brains have outstanding mimicry ability. He concluded that the ability to vocally mimic has evolved in many species in response to social factors—the need for acquisition during development of complex species-specific, group specific, or individual specific patterns of vocalization. With his concentration on rebutting the idea of a link between *vocal* mimicry and intelligence, however, Andrew missed the point that a flexible motor capability must initially be present in species-typical behavior in any modality (vocal, flight, terrestrial locomotion, etc.) before that modality can be used for mimicry. Comparisons of cognitive ability based on mimicry performance presuppose motor development adequate to express the cognitive ability.

Andrew's oversimplified dichotomy between vocal mimicry and simple call elicitation does not lead to any testable hypotheses regarding the relation of intelligence (or alternative terms such as versatile adaptability or cognitive complexity) to mimicry. Since the Andrew article, substantial evidence has accumulated, particularly through research on birds, that there is a continuum from simple call elicitation to versatile vocal mimicry. Species differ in repertoire size, duration of vocal plasticity, types of sounds imitated, eliciting stimuli, and other characteristics. It should be possible to examine each of the abilities involved in mimicry in regard to the cognitive resources it requires. Of particular importance is the necessity for experimental differentiation of precision of vocal motor control from cognitive ability. Many species of passerine birds are known for their great precision of motor control. They have the ability to consistently reproduce intricate details in conspecific song. Yet their repertoire may become fixed at an early age, and they may show little facility for imitating sounds not normally present in the species repertoire. On the other hand, great precision of motor control is not necessarily required for acquisition of a large and flexible repertoire, even language, as is demonstrated by some humans with cerebral palsy. It is necessary that the sounds be discriminable and fairly reproducible, but otherwise there is no requirement for precise imitation to allow mimicry to be used as a tool to investigate cognition.

I offer the following list of aspects of mimicry which could be used to explore cognitive abilities and separate cognition from motor control.

(a) Formation of a generalized concept of mimicry, as has been demonstrated by the dolphin in the experiment discussed here, is a key ability. It represents a major cognitive leap from the requirement of learning to imitate each new sound as a completely new problem, to formation of a learning set such that presentation of any new sound is understood as a request for mimicry.

(b) Emancipation of the context of mimicry to include elicitation by arbitrarily selected stimuli (the labeling experiment), and its extension, capacity for functional use of learned vocalizations, is an ability directly related to the potential for use of learned vocalizations in symbolic communication. The use of vocalizations as symbols might occur in the wild, e.g., the predator specific warning calls of vervet monkeys (Seyfarth, Cheney, & Marler, 1980), or it might be taught in the laboratory, e.g., the requests produced by a grey parrot (Pepperberg, 1981). A demonstration of symbolic use of vocalizations can lead to the investigation of the potential of animals to form referential concepts (see Savage-Rumbaugh, Rumbaugh & Boysen, 1980).

(c) Developmental constraints on vocal plasticity and learning can be studied from both cognitive and motor control aspects. Many birds, for example, retain fine motor control while losing most of their vocal plasticity and capability for learning new sounds. Even humans, who into adulthood are capable of extensive vocal mimicry, lose much of their ability to acquire fine variations in pronunciation, and continue to speak in regional or foreign accents despite extensive exposure to new accents. Precision of motor control can be separated from cognitive ability if the animal loses some of the capacity to acquire new sounds, while continuing to precisely reproduce previously learned sounds. The degree of versatile adaptability persisting into adulthood can be compared with that seen on other measures of behavioral flexibility. One interesting possible experiment would be a vocal version of the "creative" motor behavior study carried out by Pryor, Haag, and O'Reilly (1969). As a response measure, vocalizations have the advantage that they can be precisely quantified by spectrographic analysis— the original creativity experiment was stopped when the dolphin's capacity for creating new behaviors exceeded the human capacity for discriminating new from old behaviors.

(d) The initial situation in which the animal learns to mimic may offer additional clues to cognitive flexibility. For many species of birds, a close social relationship to the producer of the model sounds greatly facilitates acquisition of the repertoire. Experiments with tutor tapes, though they produce some learning, have often yielded inferior results when compared to those involving exposure to a live model, even of a different species. Food reward alone has also not been as effective as establishment of a close social relationship (Todt, 1975; Pepperberg, 1981). It is not yet clear how flexible the context for repertoire acquisition in the dolphin may be. There is certainly a predisposition to mimicry which can be greatly increased with both food reward and social praise, apparently without the requirement of simulation of a natural social situation. But, in the absence of data on the use of mimicry in natural communication, we do not know to what degree simulation of that natural situation might facilitate vocal learning.

(e) It would seem that repertoire size should be a good measure of cognitive ability, since possession of a large repertoire implies a certain memory capacity, as well as the capability to discriminate and reproduce sounds from memory. Considering the immense repertoires of some passerine birds, however, repertoire size alone, without some measure of flexibility of retrieval, is probably not a good measure of cognitive ability. Some studies on song patterning in birds with large repertories (e.g., Verner, 1975, on the long-billed marsh wren) reveal stereotyped, though complex, patterning, suggesting that the bird does not have great flexibility for retrieval of stored song patterns. A large repertoire, reproducible on demand as in the mimicry reliability test or in the absence of the model sound as in the labeling demonstration, might be a better indicator of cognitive processing ability. On the other hand, a small repertoire of discriminable sounds can limit the extent of the investigation of cognitive ability, as happened to some extent in the labeling experiment, making the question difficult to resolve.

(f) Range of soundtypes and internal complexity of sounds, aspects of mimicry frequently studied in birds, may reflect primarily the degree of fine motor control, rather than any complex cognitive abilities. A great diversity of sounds, however, combined with a large repertoire, allows flexibility in the use of the mimic response by the experimenter to investigate cognitive processing. The above list focuses on new cognitive questions raised by the existence of vocal mimicry. How might mimicry be used as a tool to expand traditional experimental methods for the study of animal cognition? Cognition experiments frequently involve a complex learning situation but require only a simple response from the animal, i.e., a simple go-no go or 2-choice response. This type of experiment can be a powerful tool for investigation of such phenomena as discrimination learning set (Herman & Arbeit, 1973), symbolic match-to-sample (Herman & Thompson, 1982), or short-term memory (Thompson & Herman, 1977). For all of these types of studies, a capability for mimicry allows a multi-choice response mode, adding a new dimension to animal cognition experiments. For example, recall as well as recognition could be tested for short-term memory. A list of sounds could be presented as in the Thompson and Herman study, but instead of the question requiring a yes/no classification of a probe sound as present or not present in the list, the dolphin could be required to repeat the list—length of list and length of delay could be varied. The results might be directly comparable with human experiments involving recall of lists of nonsense syllables.

Further Issues Related to the Use of Mimicry as a Response Mode for Two-way Communication

Like mimicry, artificial language can be a tool to investigate the complex cognitive abilities of the dolphin. As discussed in Herman et al. (1984) many features of human language can be demonstrated in the comprehension mode alone. But, as many linguists and others have pointed out, part of the essence of human language is a two-way communication. Use of a vocal response mode has been proposed by various researchers (Lilly, 1962; Batteau & Markey, 1967) as the most promising avenue toward two-way communication. But even a demonstration of extensive cognitive abilities through a mimicry paradigm still does not guarantee that a vocal response mode is appropriate for an artificial language project.

Both dolphin and human capabilities must be considered in relation to the requirements for effective two-way communication. Issues involving dolphin capabilities include the following:

(a) Precision of motor control and its relation to discriminable repertoire size are important determinants of the physical structure of the language. In the labeling experiment with Akeakamai, the confusion between the sounds for Person and Frisbee did not appear to involve conceptual difficulties, but was rather almost entirely related to maintenance of precise mimicry in the absence of the model sounds. The problems became worse when Water, a sound similar to both Person and Frisbee, was added to the repertoire. At this stage in training we chose to use sounds resembling each other partly because of the small repertoire available, and partly from the desire to look at retention of mimicry discrimination of similar sounds in the absence of the model. The problem never appeared with sounds having very different acoustical characteristics, such as Pipe, a pure tone. It is important to investigate the maximum number of discriminable sounds that can be retained from memory in the repertoire.

(b) A related question is the duration of long-term retention. For several of the sounds, Akeakamai produced virtually perfect mimicry following a gap of a year without training. For other sounds, however, the ones discussed above, her production drifted substantially even from session to session.

(c) Inter-individual variability must be investigated as well. While it is certainly possible to design a response mode for communication with a single individual, it would be far more useful to have a language that generalizes to the characteristics of many dolphins, allowing dolphin-dolphin communication, as well as dolphin-human communication. Akeakamai's principal problem with sounds was regression toward her signature whistle—the addition of spurious, rapid modulation resembling the characteristics of her most common whistle prior to training. As Akeakamai's signature whistle was rather rapidly modulated compared to the norm among dolphins, this difficulty with rapid modulation may not be a typical problem, but characteristic of this individual.

(d) Even if dolphins are able to acquire and retain a fairly large, shared repertoire of sounds, assignment of meanings to the sounds requires careful consideration. The use of individual sounds for single meanings is bound to limit the language in two ways. The first is the number of possible words. The use of unitary sounds for individual words will require discrimination of a number of sounds equaling the number of words in the language. In natural human languages, in contrast, words are composed of a limited number of phonemes—the "duality of patterning" universal of language (Hockett, 1960)—that can be combined to generate an infinite number of words. This is a much more efficient way to use a limited number of accurately produced sounds, but it requires the dolphin to be able to produce ordered sequences of sounds. That sequences can be produced was demonstrated with a very few sounds in the mimicry experiment (though not yet in the labeling paradigm), but not pursued (Fig. 13.2i). If words are composed of sequences of sounds ("phonemes" or "syllables"), then to continue in the production mode what has been demonstrated in the comprehension mode (see Herman, this volume) the dolphin must also learn to produce sequences of words (composed of sequences of sounds). If the dolphin is unable to reliably produce strings of sounds, a failure to investigate this sequencing ability independently of the language paradigm may lead to a confounding of vocal ability and language-like cognitive abilities. This could lead to the kind of negative conclusions familiar from early language projects involving apes (Hayes & Hayes, 1951) where a failure to learn to speak was equated with inferior language-related cognitive abilities. The problem was not with cognition, but rather with the response modality chosen.

(e) The duration of vocal plasticity, particularly if it is not related to general behavioral plasticity, may also be a key factor. An early loss of vocal plasticity might well dictate an intensive vocal training program for the dolphin at an early age, even before some higher cognitive abilities become apparent.

(f) It should be emphasized that thus far only whistles have been considered, primarily because of the ease of describing whistles and monitoring performance. Pulsed vocalizations may offer a far greater diversity of sounds, and may even be easier for the dolphin to manipulate, since they appear to be quite diverse even in dolphins with stereotyped signature whistles.

(g) And, as a final caveat about the use of sounds for productive language, there is always the possibility of interference with the natural communication system. Akeakamai's drift problem—regression to her signature whistles—is an example. It may also be difficult to assign new meanings to other stereotyped natural signals such as pulsed sounds denoting aggression or alarm.

The human capability to deal with dolphin vocalizations is the other factor affecting the utility of a vocal response mode. It is quite possible that the dolphin's sound production may exceed the ability of the human, and even the computer, for monitoring. The training of Akeakamai relied on a human observer to monitor the sounds; for simple whistles the task was not particularly difficult, but, as the vocabulary increased, discrimination within the fraction of a second needed for effective training became much harder. Real-time computer analysis is likely to suffer from similar time problems as the vocabulary increases, and from the additional requirement of programming equal to or better than human judgement. A technique involving sampling only the modulation waveform, however, may reduce the demands on the computer. If only modulated tonal sounds are used, it is not necessary to sample at twice the highest frequency (for example, 40 kHz for a maximum frequency of 20 kHz). Such a sampling rate puts severe demands on processor speed and memory size. Instead, for tonal sounds, the sounds can be preprocessed using a frequency-to-voltage converter similar to that used for the present training, with the voltage fed to the computer through an analog-to-digital converter, and sampled at twice the highest frequency in the modulation (in our case 22 Hz for 11 Hz modulation). This would greatly decrease the memory requirements and allow rapid processing of the small number of samples for pattern recognition. Unfortunately the method precludes use of harmonics or the complexities inherent in pulsed sounds. Though mimicry can be recognized in the spectrum analysis of pulsed sounds (W. Evans, pers. comm.), real-time recognition of large numbers of sounds may be very difficult, akin to recognition of human speech, but likely to require development of completely different algorithms. It is likely that there are still many surprises in dolphin vocal capabilities, and it would be premature at this time to lock in to a particular response mode without a great deal of further data.

It is especially important that exploration of the capabilities and constraints of a vocal response mode proceed simultaneously with development of computer hardware and software.

NATURAL COMMUNICATION

While a laboratory demonstration of mimicry does not say anything directly about communication in the wild, it does show the existence of a capability which suggests that the alternative views of dolphin communication suggested at the beginning of this paper are oversimplified. The dolphin studied initially possessed a stereotyped, individually characteristic whistle produced repetitively in a variety of circumstances. This whistle fit the concept of a signature whistle. At the same time, observations of the dolphin interacting with its companion in the tank suggested that considerable communication was taking place via graded pulsed vocalizations resembling typical mammalian communication. The mimicry results, while far from providing evidence for language, suggest that the whistle communication alone (not considering pulsed vocalizations or other communication modalities) has the potential for far greater complexity than the simple signature whistle concept allows. It is only possible to speculate at this time on the function of mimicry in the dolphin's social world. Graycar (1976) has shown the presence of regional dialects in dolphins, the formation of which would be facilitated by a capability for mimicry. The extension of vocal plasticity into adult life could allow for changes in the regional whistles in response to the fluid structure of dolphin groups. Gish (1979) has shown that dolphins connected by an intertank acoustical link occasionally mimic whistles. An ability to immediately mimic the whistles of an unfamiliar conspecific could serve to maintain the social relationships in fluid groups. In marsh wrens, Kroodsma (1979) has demonstrated that subordinate individuals tend to match (previously learned) song themes with dominant individuals. An ability to match novel vocalizations may serve a similar function in the fluid social organization of the dolphin. The substantial mimicry ability of the Indian hill mynah appears to be used for the purpose of mimicking neighboring individuals (Bertram, 1970). Likewise, the capacity for labeling has parallels in the labeling ability of an African grey parrot (Pepperberg, 1981 and this volume), in vervet monkeys (Seyfarth, Cheney & Marler, 1980), and of course in humans. The extent to which dolphins make use of this ability in the wild awaits further investigation. Certainly the cognitive abilities demonstrated thus far in the Kewalo project, including both mimicry and comprehension, suggest that dolphins may possess a natural communication system as complex or more complex than that of the higher monkeys and apes. Direct evidence for complex symbolic communication resembling human language would be difficult to obtain from simple observation, and would require extensive successful experimentation on the order of that attempted by Bastian (1966), in which it was hoped that the dolphins could be induced to communicate arbitrary information over an acoustic channel. At the least, a knowledge of the existence of a mimicry capability in captivity will alert field researchers to the potential for use of the whistles in natural communication.

ACKNOWLEDGMENTS

The dolphin studies were supported by grants to Louis M. Herman from the National Science Foundation (Grants BNS77-16882 and BNS81-09653) and from the Center for Field Research, Belmont, Massachusetts. The work was helped greatly by discussions with Louis M. Herman and James P. Wolz. James Wolz also assisted in some of the judgements of vocal mimicry. I also wish to thank the many graduate and undergraduate students who helped in the testing of the dolphins, including Amy Suzuki, Gordon Bauer, Joseph Mobley, and Melissa Shyan.

REFERENCES

Andrew, R. J. (1962). Evolution of intelligence and vocal mimicking. *Science, 137*, 585–589.

Bastian, J. (1967). The transmission of arbitrary environmental information between bottlenose dolphins. In R. G. Busnel (Ed.), *Animal sonar systems, Vol. II* (pp. 803–873). Jouy-en-Josas, France: Laboratoire de Physiologie Acoustique.

Bastian, J., Wall, C., & Anderson, C. L. (1968). Further investigation of the transmission of arbitrary environmental information between bottlenose dolphins. *Naval Undersea Warfare Center, TP 109*, San Diego, California, pp. 1–40.

Batteau, D. W., & Markey, P. R. (1967). Man/dolphin communication. *(Final Report, Contract N 00123-67-1103*. 15 Dec. 1966–13 Dec. 1967). China Lake, California, U.S. Naval Ordnance Test Station.

Bertram, B. (1970). The vocal behavior of the Indian hill mynah, *Gracula religiosa. Animal Behaviour*, Monograph *3*, 80–192.

Burdin, V. I., Reznik, A. M., Skornyakov, V. M., & Chupakov, A. G. (1974). Study of communicative signals in Black Sea dolphins. *Akusti Cheskiy Zhurnal, 20*, 518–525.

Busnel, R.-G., & Dziedzic, A. (1966). Acoustic signals of the pilot whale *Globicephala malaena* and of the porpoises *Delphinus delphis* and *Phocoena phocoena*. In K. S. Norris (Ed.), *Whales, dolphins, and porpoises* (pp. 607–646). Berkeley: University of California Press.

Caldwell, M. C., & Caldwell, D. K. (1965). Individualized whistle contours in bottlenosed dolphins, *Tursiops truncatus. Nature, 207*, 434–435.

Caldwell, M. C., & Caldwell, D. K. (1967). Intra-specific transfer of information via the pulsed sound in captive odontocete cetaceans. In R. G. Busnel (Ed.), *Animal Sonar systems, Vol. II* (pp. 879–936). Jouy-en-Josas, France: Laboratoire de Physiologie Acoustique.

Caldwell, D. K., & Caldwell, M. C. (1972). Vocal mimicry in the whistle mode in the Atlantic bottlenosed dolphin. *Cetology, 9*, 1–8.

Caldwell, M. C., & Caldwell, D. K. (1968). Vocalizations of naive captive dolphins in small groups. *Science, 159*, 1121–1123.

Dreher, J. J. (1966). Cetacean communication: Small-group experiment. In K. S. Norris (Ed.), *Whales, dolphins, and porpoises* (pp. 529–541). Berkeley: University of California Press.

Dreher, J. J., & Evans, W. E. (1964). Cetacean communication. In W. N. Tavolga (Ed.), *Marine bio-acoustics, Volume I* (pp. 373–393). Oxford: Pergamon Press.

Evans, W. E. (1967). Vocalization among marine mammals. In W. N. Tavolga (Ed.), *Marine bio-acoustics, Volume II* (pp. 159–186). Oxford: Pergamon Press.

Gish, S. L. (1979). *Quantitative analysis of two-way acoustic communication between captive Atlantic bottlenose dolphins (Tursiops truncatus* Montague). Unpublished doctoral dissertation, University of California, Santa Cruz.

Graycar, P. (1976). *Whistle dialects of the Atlantic bottlenosed dolphin, Tursiops truncatus.* Unpublished doctoral dissertation, Gainesville: University of Florida.

Hayes, K. J., & Hayes, C. (1951). The intellectual development of a home-raised chimpanzee. *Proceedings of the American Philosophical Society, 95,* 105–109.

Herman, L. M. (1980). Cognitive characteristics of dolphins. In L. M. Herman (Ed.), *Cetacean behavior: Mechanisms and functions* (pp. 363–429). New York: Wiley-Interscience.

Herman, L. M., & Arbeit, W. R. (1973). Stimulus control and auditory discrimination learning sets in the bottlenose dolphin. *Journal of the Experimental Analysis of Behavior, 19,* 379–394.

Herman, L. M., Richards, D. G., & Wolz, J. P. (1984). Comprehension of sentences by bottlenosed dolphins. *Cognition, 16,* 129–219.

Herman, L. M., & Tavolga, W. N. (1980). The communication systems of cetaceans. In L. M. Herman (Ed.), *Cetacean behavior: Mechanisms and functions* (pp. 149–209). New York: Wiley-Interscience.

Herman, L. M., & Thompson, R. K. R. (1982). Symbolic, identity and probe delayed matching of sounds by the bottlenosed dolphin. *Animal Learning and Behavior, 10,* 22–34.

Hockett, C. F. (1960). Logical considerations in the study of animal communication. In W. E. Lanyon & W. N. Tavolga (Eds.), *Animal sounds and communication* (pp. 392–430). Washington, D.C.: American Institute of Biological Sciences, Pub. No. 7.

Kroodsma, D. E. (1979). Vocal dueling among male marsh wrens: Evidence for ritualized expressions of dominance/subordinance. *Auk, 98,* 506–515.

Lilly, J. C. (1962). Vocal behavior of the bottlenosed dolphin. *Proceedings of the American Philosophical Society., 106,* 520–529.

Lilly, J. C. (1965). Vocal mimicry in *Tursiops.* Ability to match numbers and durations of human vocal bursts. *Science, 147,* 300–301.

Lilly, J. C. (1978). *Communication between man and dolphin.* New York: Crown Publishers.

Lilly, J. C., Miller, A. M., & Truby, H. M. (1968). Reprogramming of the sonic output of the dolphin: Sonic burst count matching. *Journal of the Acoustical Society of America, 43,* 1412–1424.

Morton, E. S. (1982). Grading, discreteness, redundancy and motivation-structural rules. In D. E. Kroodsma & E. H. Miller, (Eds.), *Acoustic communication in birds, Volume 1* (pp. 183–212). New York: Academic Press.

Pepperberg, I. M. (1981). Functional vocalizations by an African grey parrot (*Psittacus erithacus*). *Zeitschrift für Tierpsychologie, 55,* 139–160.

Pryor, K., Haag, R., & O'Reilly, J. (1969). The creative porpoise: Training for novel behavior. *Journal of the Experimental Analysis of Behavior, 12,* 653–661.

Richards, D. G., Wolz, J. P., & Herman, L. M. (1984). Vocal mimicry of computer-generated sounds and vocal labeling of objects by a bottlenosed dolphin, *Tursiops truncatus. Journal of Comparative Psychology, 98,* 10–28.

Savage-Rumbaugh, E. S., Rumbaugh, D. M., & Boysen, S. (1980). Do apes use language? *American Scientist, 68,* 49–61.

Seyfarth, R. M., Cheney, D. L., & Marler, P. (1980). Monkey responsiveness to different alarm calls: evidence of predator classification and semantic communication. *Science, 210,* 801–803.

Thompson, R. K. R., & Herman, L. M. (1977). Memory for lists of sounds by the bottlenosed dolphin: convergence of memory processes with humans? *Science, 195,* 501–503.

Thorpe, W. H. (1963). *Learning and instinct in animals*, (2nd. Ed.). Cambridge, MA: Harvard University Press.

Todt, D. (1975). Social learning of vocal patterns and modes of their application in gray parrots (*Psittacus erithacus*). *Zeitschrift für Tierpsychologie, 39*, 178–188.

Verner, J. (1975). Complex song repertoire of male Long-billed marsh wrens in eastern Washington. *Living Bird, 14*, 263–300.

14 Acquisition of Anomalous Communicatory Systems: Implications for Studies on Interspecies Communication

Irene M. Pepperberg
Northwestern University

Humans have long been fascinated by the possibility of interspecies communication. Their interest generally has centered on three groups of animals: great apes, certain marine mammals (dolphins and sea lions), and mimetic birds. Recently, this interest has engendered serious scientific inquiry, and studies designed to explore animal/human communication have been undertaken in several laboratories. Although techniques vary, all such projects employ a common approach: the human researchers endeavor to impose the constraints of anthropocentric communicative systems onto the animals' natural behaviors. Animal subjects in experimental laboratories have thus been taught the use of either human codes or artificial forms of communication based on rules presumed to underlie human systems (see Gardner & Gardner, 1978; Herman, 1980; Herman, Richards, & Woltz, 1984; Miles, 1983; Patterson, 1978; Pepperberg, 1979, 1981, 1983; Premack, 1976; Savage-Rumbaugh, Rumbaugh, & Boysen, 1980; Schusterman & Krieger, 1984). Despite, and possibly because of, the widespread use of this methodology, questions consistently arise as to: (1) the validity and implications of this approach; (2) how the desired communicative behaviors may most efficiently be inculcated; and (3) what the consequences and significance of results might be with respect to the broad concepts of cognition and communication.

INCULCATION OF HUMAN CODES—VALIDITY AND IMPLICATIONS

A question immediately arises as to the validity of the premise which underlies much of this work: that animals possess cognitive abilities and exhibit complex communicative codes intended for information transfer upon which researchers can "map" human communicative systems (see Marler, 1983; Premack, 1976). Although the advent of Watsonian-style behaviorism may often have led researchers to design their experiments so as to ignore, if not deny, "purpose" or "meaning" to the communicative actions of nonhuman subjects, various studies have recently provided evidence indicative of semantic, and possibly syntactic, components of communication in many unrelated species (see Beer, 1976, 1982; Griffin, 1981). Careful study has enabled researchers to decode the communicative behavior of honey bees (see Gould & Gould, 1982). Vervet monkeys appear to learn a signaling system which employs different vocalizations to denote different predators and which may possibly be used to define or mediate social relations (Cheney & Seyfarth, 1980, 1982; Seyfarth, Cheney, & Marler, 1980a, 1980b; Struhsaker, 1967). Owings (Leger & Owings, 1978; Leger, Owings, & Boal, 1979; Leger, Owings, & Gelfand, 1980; Owings & Virginia, 1978) and Robinson (1980, 1981) have demonstrated similar learned semantic use of variegated calls in ground squirrels; as in the vervets, the degree to which an alarm call is heeded is often related to which individual has done the signaling. Certain birds may use different songs in different contexts such as mate attraction versus territorial defense (Kroodsma, 1981; cf. Lein, 1972, 1978; see also Sonnenschein & Reyer, 1983), and significant vocal gradations representing individual variations in meaning appear to exist in what were once thought to be uniform "long calls" in gulls (Beer, 1975, 1976, 1982).

The next question must then be that if these natural systems *are* so advanced, why have certain researchers, instead of focusing on comprehending the existent codes, chosen to train their subjects to different ones? Quite possibly because studies of natural behaviors are not necessarily easier, and direct comparisons between such findings and human communication are difficult (see Beer, 1982). By using, in diverse species, codes based on a common (albeit human) system, complex cross-species comparison is facilitated, not just between humans and animals, but between various animal species. Researchers may still argue about what actually constitutes human language (see Rieber & Voyat, 1983) but, by training animal subjects to communicate with humans by means of a human-based code, the animals' behaviors can more easily be examined in order to determine occurrences of interspecies communication. And, by investigating the processes by which animals acquire these human-based codes, researchers may gain insight into developing procedures for teaching such codes to noncommunicative humans, and possibly begin to understand the developmental processes which underlie acquisition of these codes.

It is important to recognize, however, that animals in such research projects are acquiring what may best be defined as *anomalous* or *exceptional* communicatory systems. For the parrot, it is a system consisting predominantly of allospecific vocalizations; for apes, it is a system of allospecific physical signals, and for marine mammals, it is a combination of these modes. As there generally exists in nature a predilection for organisms selectively to learn *conspecific* signaling systems, what are the implications of teaching, and of such very diverse subjects acquiring, anomalous communicative competence? Insights into these questions may most readily come from an examination of findings from two other, rather disparate lines of research: studies on natural avian vocal ontogeny and investigations (primarily by Bandura, 1971a, 1971b, 1977) of the effects of human social modeling.

Researchers have discovered, particularly from studies on avian vocal behaviors, that constraints may exist in nature which act to limit communicative learning. Thus, while some birds have the capacity to incorporate into their repertoires numerous diverse acoustic patterns (Baldwin, 1914; Bertram, 1970; Brenowitz, 1982; Güttinger, 1974; Howard, 1974; F. N. Robinson, 1975; for reviews, see Dobkin, 1979; Krebs & Kroodsma, 1980), many are known to acquire only conspecific vocalizations, often during a specific, limited developmental period (Kroodsma, 1977, 1978; Marler & Peters, 1977, 1981, 1982a, 1982b; Thorpe, 1961). Nevertheless, in the presence of a live avian tutor that interacts with the subject in a referential manner, even those birds that adhere most strongly to traditional patterns can acquire "anomalous" or "exceptional" behaviors—allospecific song, allospecific syllables or phrases, or vocalizations acquired beyond the recognized sensitive period (e.g., see Baptista, 1972; Baptista & Morton, 1981; Baptista & Petrinovich, 1984; Baptista, Morton & Pereyra, 1981; Borror, 1977; Dobkin, 1979; Eberhardt & Baptista, 1977; Kroodsma, 1972, 1973; Petrinovich, Patterson, & Baptista, 1981; see also Kroodsma & Baylis, 1982; Kroodsma & Pickert, 1984a). Given the numerous parallels that have been drawn between the ontogeny of song and human language acquisition (Dooling & Searcy, 1981; Marler, 1973; Marler & Peters, 1977; Nottebohm, 1970, 1975, 1981; Payne, Thompson, Fiala, & Sweany, 1981; Shiovitz & Lemon, 1980; Thorpe, 1964), it is interesting to note that studies on the effects of social interaction (i.e., type and degree) on various human learning processes have reported results similar to those found for vocal learning in birds: In certain situations, live, referential, interactive tutors have been shown to stimulate in humans learning which otherwise might not have occurred (see Asher & Price, 1967; Bandura, 1971a, 1971b, 1977; Scarcella & Higa, 1982; Whitehurst, Ironsmith, & Goldfein, 1974). Because researchers in the field of interspecies communication have been strongly cautioned about the disadvantages and methodological problems occasioned by social interactions with their subjects, these findings on the efficacy of social modeling interactions for the acquisition of nontraditional behaviors bear close examination (Pepperberg, 1985).

INCULATION OF HUMAN CODES—SOCIAL AND REFERENTIAL ASPECTS

Research into the effects of social interactions on learned behaviors has been of particular interest to my own work, which involves teaching a similarly anomalous form of communication—referential English speech—to an African grey parrot (*Psittacus erithacus*). Although the grey parrot is well-known for its ability to reproduce allospecific vocal patterns, the subject of this study is the first to demonstrate referential, communicative use of such sounds (Pepperberg, 1979, 1981, 1983); interestingly, this project is also the first to make extensive use of live, interacting human tutors. The parrot now employs English vocalizations in order to request, refuse, identify, categorize, or quantify more than 50 items, including objects which vary somewhat from the training exemplars (Pepperberg, 1981, 1983). He has acquired functional use of "no" and phrases such as "Come here," "I want X," and "wanna go Y" in order to influence (albeit to a limited extent) the behaviors of his trainers and to alter his immediate environment. He is also beginning to use the phrases "What's this?", "What color?" and "What shape?" to initiate interactions (Pepperberg, 1983). More importantly, this subject has also demonstrated the ability to decode our questions reliably: when queried about the color *or* shape of objects which vary with respect to *both* color and shape (e.g., he may be asked the color of a green wooden triangle or the shape of a blue rawhide square), he is capable of determining which of the two categories (color or shape) is being targeted, deciding which instance of what category is correct (e.g., "green" rather than "yellow"), and producing the appropriate set of vocal labels ("green wood," "four-corner hide"; Pepperberg, 1983). Studies now under way suggest that, when presented with two objects which may vary with respect to color, shape, or material (e.g., a blue wooden triangle and a yellow wooden triangle), this subject can discriminate, and indicate vocally, which of the three variables are "same" or "different."

In studies by other researchers, which employed recordings of human vocalizations (rather than social, interactive models) or live but noninteractive human models (i.e., vocal repetitions by humans with no active, referential aspects), mimetic birds failed to acquire either meaningful communication or exhibit significant vocal learning (Gossette, 1969; Grosslight & Zaynor, 1967; Grosslight, Zaynor, & Lively, 1964; Mowrer, 1954, 1958). However, Todt (1975), using a procedure which involved two live, interacting human models to demonstrate the vocal behaviors to be acquired, had significant success in training African grey parrots to produce, if not comprehend, varied human vocalizations. (Interestingly, anecdotal reports of extensive learning of human vocalizations by psittacines through ostensibly nonreferential procedures inevitably describe strong social bonds between the avian subjects and their human tutors [Amsler, 1947; Boosey, 1947; Hensley, 1980].) Data on vocal learning in nonmimetic birds also suggest (1) that certain birds are likely to learn somewhat more from live tutors than from recordings (Payne, 1981; Todt, Hultsch, & Heike, 1979; Waser & Marler, 1977); (2) that certain species appear incapable of significant learning *without* live tutors (Price, 1979; Thielcke, 1970, 1972); and (3) that some birds will choose preferentially songs of live avian tutors over those presented via recordings (Kroodsma, 1978; Payne, 1981; Todt et al., 1979). A search through the human psychological literature also provides ample evidence for the efficacy of live, interactive human models for influencing the acquisition of targeted behaviors (see Bandura, 1977 for a review; Bandura, 1971a; Litvak, 1969; Rimm & Mahoney, 1969; Salzinger, 1980; Snow, 1979). Previous failures to inculcate "anomalous" communicative competence in mimetic birds (i.e., referential, interspecies vocalizations) might thus have been due not to any inherent limitations in the avian subjects, but rather to have been a consequence of inappropriate training procedures (see Pepperberg, 1981).

The hypotheses underlying my work, and the training processes that have been developed, have therefore been based not only on the natural vocal and cognitive abilities of psittacine birds, but on extensive studies on avian and human social learning. In our procedure, humans demonstrate to the parrot the types of interactive responses which are to be acquired. Briefly, one human acts as a trainer of a second human, asking questions, giving praise and rewarding appropriate answers, showing disapproval for inappropriate responses. Rewards consist of acquisition of the objects which are to be identified, so that there is the closest possible association between each object and each vocal label to be learned. The second human acts both as a model for the parrot's behavior and as a rival for the trainer's attention. Roles of trainer and model are frequently reversed in order to demonstrate the interactive nature of the communicative task; that is, that the questioner may also be questioned (a significant departure from Todt's protocol) and our subject is given the opportunity to participate directly in these exchanges (see Pepperberg, 1981 for details).

Correlation of the findings on the efficacy of referential social modeling as a facilitator for learned communicative behavior in avian subjects with the corpus of data from human psychological studies thus leads me to postulate a particular role for social interactions and referential training that may be applicable to all interspecies projects: that is, that acquisition of most forms of nontraditional (i.e., *anomalous* or *exceptional*) communication in animal species may closely parallel human disinhibitory or antiphobic learning behavior, the critical similarity being the need for live, interacting tutors to overcome any inherent predilections against such learning. If nontraditional communication is indeed viewed as an inhibited behavior (possibly governed by a restrictive innate template; see Marler, 1970) then, for animals as well as humans, live social interactions, in the presence of behavioral constraints, may be necessary to overcome inhibitions which may exist towards learning specific tasks (see Bandura & Menlove, 1968; Bandura, Blanchard, & Ritter, 1969; Brown, 1976; Litvak, 1969; Rimm & Mahoney, 1969; Whitehurst et al., 1974). In particular, recognition that findings on the efficacy of social interactions derive from human studies may allay any doubts as to the use of such training protocols with animal subjects, as long as necessary precautions are observed in test situations (see Rumbaugh & Gill, 1976).

The intent of these comparisons is not, however, to claim that nontraditional learning can occur only within the context of social interaction. Capacities for, and constraints on, acquisition of nontraditional behaviors are best viewed along a continuum; the extent and circumstances of nontraditional learning are likely to vary from species to species. The point here, however, is to highlight the effects of live tutors and social interactions on such behaviors. In some cases, a live tutor may simply be a more effective stimulus for learning (Kroodsma, 1982; Kroodsma & Pickert, 1984a).

The other important aspect to modeling theory is that of *referential* examples; that is, the use of "intrinsic" rather than "extrinsic" rewards. Many programs designed to develop communicatory skills rely on food rewards which neither directly relate to the task being taught nor vary with respect to the specific behavior being targeted (i.e., all correct identifications for food or non-food items, or responses to varied commands such as "Pick up X" or "Drop Y," are rewarded with acquisition of a single food). Human as well as animal subjects in such programs often fail to acquire the targeted skills or fail to extrapolate knowledge that has thus been acquired to situations in which the extrinsic rein-forcer is absent. For example, Fouts (1973; Fouts & Couch, 1976) has shown that those few chimpanzees who needed a reward of food for learning ASL signs even for nonfood items often tested poorly (20–60% as compared to a usual 90%) when such food reinforcement was absent. Correspondingly, training programs for autistic and echolalic children also tend to rely heavily on single-item food rewards (Risley & Wolf, 1968), which normally are absent in the "real" world (Richey, 1976; see also Courtright & Courtright, 1979). Lovaas (1977) has reported that children in such programs are often unable to generalize and fail to use speech in spontaneous and context-appropriate ways (see also de Villiers & de Villiers, 1978).

In contrast, throughout the project with the parrot, training procedures have been developed which focus instead on a selection of objects (e.g., toys), which themselves arouse the interest of the subject, and permit the closest possible association of object and vocal label to be learned (Pepperberg, 1978, 1979, 1981): that is, each correct vocal identification by the subject is rewarded by presentation of the object to which the targeted label refers. Saunders and Sailor (1979) provide preliminary evidence that use of a different specific reinforcer for each response to be taught may aid children in discriminating among responses to be learned, and that the ease of learning a labeling task is related to the degree to which the stimulus and reinforcer are directly linked (e.g., children learned more quickly to "Point to X" when the reward was the opportunity to play with X than when the reward was a cracker; see also Fulwiler & Fouts, 1976). Extrinsic food rewards (e.g., food for nonfood identification) might actually delay label acquisition by confounding the name of the exemplar to be learned with that of the unrelated food reward (see Greenfield, 1978; Miles, 1983; Pepperberg, 1978).

CONSEQUENCES OF ANOMALOUS
COMMUNICATIVE COMPETENCE

Several different experimental approaches have been employed in order to achieve two-way, allospecific communication with animals. I have briefly outlined my work with the African grey parrot. Savage-Rumbaugh (this volume) has described some very complex behaviors which demonstrate that chimpanzee subjects are capable of using an arbitrary symbolic code for communication not only with humans but also with one another. Herman (this volume) has presented evidence for accurate use of synthesized acoustic or gestural patterns for communication with dolphins: A reliable association appears to exist between a particular object or action and a particular sound or gesture. Such abilities are the earliest indications of reference; as Savage-Rumbaugh has pointed out (Savage-Rumbaugh et al., 1980), if properly extended, this ability can develop into comprehension of a symbol as a representation of an object. But what is the significance of these findings for issues of cognitive development and comparative behavior?

If we return for a moment to studies on song acquisition and avian neurophysiology and neuroanatomy, an interesting implication may emerge for studies on acquisition of allospecific communicative competence. That is, for certain birds, there appears to be some positive correlation between the size of the particular part of the brain known to be responsible for song storage and the size of the vocal repertoire; moreover, these two factors seem inversely related to the degree of selectivity in what the bird learns (see Kroodsma & Canady, 1982; Kroodsma & Pickert, 1984b; Nottebohm, 1981; Nottebohm, Kasparian, & Pandazis, 1981). Species capable of allospecific acquisition may thus be facile learners with significantly more extensive neural capacity for storage of such learned material. (Note, however, that functions important for vocal *learning* appear to be carried out in areas of the avian brain which are different from those responsible for song storage; see Bottjer, Miesner, & Arnold, 1984.) If parallels do indeed exist with other animals, the fact that such very diverse subjects as chimpanzees, dolphins and parrots appear similarly competent—even in the relatively limited communicative tasks researchers have so far designed—may suggest significant comparable cross-species neural cognitive ability. Evidence exists for advanced sensory and information processing and extensive cognitive development in dolphins. The literature abounds with similar material on the great apes, and related data exist for certain avian subjects. The communicative studies presented in this symposium suggest something more. That is, it may be irrelevant to wonder whether these subjects evince language-like behaviors because they are employing neural systems similar to those underlying human language (possibly as a consequence of some evolutionary "quirk"; see Malmi, 1976) or if they have acquired communicative codes which are superficially similar because of researchers' use of related training procedures. If complex, allospecific communicative abilities of comparable sophistication can be acquired by animals as disparate as the dolphin, the chimpanzee, and the parrot, does this not suggest that related cognitive characteristics, whatever their bases, may exist in many species?

It therefore becomes important to discuss how researchers may most efficiently expand their knowledge of their subjects' capabilities. (1) Investigators can, most simply, see how far a subject can proceed in cognitive/communicative tasks: Might an animal subject exhibit a behavioral (e.g., cognitive) plasticity, as evidenced by increased allospecific learning, far greater than heretofore expected? If scientists are indeed "mapping" a human communicative system on to an existent nonhuman cognitive base (see Premack, 1976), are the most effective procedures being employed? And what are the implications for studies on cognition if scientists, by teaching their animal subjects concepts foreign to a natural behavior, have actually taken brain capacity originally developed, for example, to avoid predators or search out food and channeled it to subserve novel behaviors (see Premack, 1983)? (2) Using new noninvasive diagnostic techniques, cross-species neurological correlates for similar tasks such as "labeling" might be explored: Are entirely different areas of the brain used for this same task in different species? What kinds of differences can exist at the cellular or chemical levels, or in the way brain areas are interconnected? How different (or similar) are the neurological bases? Are there cross-species differences in how aspects of the environment may be categorized?—e.g., is movement a more salient discriminant for a dolphin than for a parrot? If such differences do exist, would they reflect neurological variances? (3) Cyclic "sensitive" periods for learning occur in some song birds (Nottebohm, 1981); might such periods occur in apes and dolphins, and could they be based on variables that are susceptible to manipulation (Lenneberg, 1973; see Kroodsma & Pickert, 1980; 1984a, 1984b; Nottebohm, 1981)? That is, can the use of animal subjects as experimental models enable us to determine what may control the initiation of communicative behaviors? For example, might vocal learning in dolphins be connected to hormone levels as is the case with certain birds (see Nottebohm, 1981)? (4) Researchers often suspect hierarchies for cognitive abilities in animals—what might results of studies such as those described at this conference suggest either to support or refute such claims? (5) The effects of particular training methods, especially those related to observational learning, should be examined. Observational learning appears to be effective in birds and humans; to what degree might activities be designed to facilitate such behaviors in dolphins? If, as some researchers propose (see Crook, 1983; Humphrey, 1979), complex communication did indeed develop as a response to, and in order to mediate, complex social interactions, our subjects could provide surrogates on which to test further the predictions of human social modeling theory. (6) Finally, this work might simply lead to a better understanding of the natural abilities of various nonhuman subjects: Such studies might, for example, provide a basis for comparison of "wild" and "trained" behaviors and their cognitive bases and functions. Studies of "intelligent" behaviors might even suggest the kinds of abilities for which to search in the wild, and allow researchers to uncover capacities heretofore unsuspected.

The communicative and cognitive features which have been shown to exist in these very disparate subjects (at least at the basic levels) are similar enough to suggest that the underlying mechanisms involved in their development, whether or not physically or functionally homologous, are indeed analogous. Understanding any one system may provide useful insights into the understanding of any other, including possibly that of *Homo sapiens*. Experimental manipulation of the procedures and environments used in animal studies would be ethically unacceptable in work with humans; studies on nonhuman subjects may thus be the means to gain potentially instructive insights into determining the critical variables involved in all systems.

ACKNOWLEDGMENTS

Preparation of this paper was supported by a fellowship from the Harry Frank Guggenheim Foundation; my psittacid research was supported by NSF grants BNS 7912945, BNS 801432, and the Guggenheim Foundation. I thank Kimberley Goodrich, Robert Mitchell, Jan Ramer, Katherine Davidson, Mary Sandhage, Denise Dickson and Bruce Rosen for their assistance with my research, Drs. Diane Reiss and Jeanette Thomas for critical reviews of this manuscript, and Drs. Donald Kroodsma and Luis Baptista for stimulating discussions about their research on avian vocal abilities.

REFERENCES

Amsler, M. (1947). An almost human Grey parrot. *Aviculture Magazine, 53,* 68–69.
Asher, J. J., & Price, B. (1967). The learning strategy of total physical response: Some age differences. *Child Development, 38,* 1219–1227.
Baldwin, J. M. (1914). Deferred imitation in West African Grey parrots. *IXth Int'l Congress of Zoology,* Monaco, 536.
Bandura, A. (1971a). Psychotherapy based upon modeling principles. In A. E. Bergin & S. L. Garfield (Eds.), *Psychotherapy and behavioral change: An empirical analysis* (pp. 653–708). New York: Wiley.
Bandura, A. (1971b). Analysis of modeling processes. In A. Bandura (Ed.), *Psychological modeling* (pp. 1–62). Chicago: Aldine-Atherton.
Bandura, A. (1977). *Social modeling theory.* Chicago: Aldine-Atherton.
Bandura, A., & Menlove, F. L. (1968). Factors determining vicarious extinction of avoidance behavior through symbolic modeling. *Journal of Personality and Social Psychology, 8,* 99–108.
Bandura, A., Blanchard, E. B., & Ritter, B. (1969). The relative efficacy of desensitization and modeling approaches for inducing behavioral, affective, and attitudinal changes. *Journal of Personality and Social Psychology, 13,* 173–199.

Baptista, L. F. (1972). Wild house finch sings white-crowned sparrow song. *Zeitschrift für Tierpsychologie, 30,* 266–270.

Baptista, L. F., & Morton, M. L. (1981). Interspecific song acquisition by a white-crowned sparrow. *Auk, 98,* 383–385.

Baptista, L. F., & Petrinovich, L. (1984). Social interaction, sensitive phases and the song template hypothesis in the white-crowned sparrow. *Animal Behaviour, 32,* 172–181.

Baptista, L. F., Morton, M. L., & Pereyra, M. E. (1981). Interspecific song mimesis by a Lincoln sparrow. *Wilson Bulletin, 93,* 265–267.

Beer, C. G. (1975). Multiple functions and gull displays. In G. P. Baerends, C. G. Beer, & A. Manning (Eds.), *Function and evolution in behavior—Essays in honour of Professor Niko Tinbergen, F.R.S.* (pp. 16–54). London and New York: Oxford University Press.

Beer, C. G. (1976). Some complexities in the communication behavior of gulls. *Origins and evolution of language and speech. Annals of the New York Academy of Sciences, 280,* 413–432.

Beer, C. G. (1982). Conceptual issues in the study of communication. In D. E. Kroodsma & E. H. Miller (Eds.), *Acoustic communication in birds. Vol. 2: Song learning and its consequences* (pp. 279–310). New York: Academic Press.

Bertram, B. C. R. (1970). The vocal behavior of the Indian hill mynah, *Gracula religiosa. Animal Behaviour Monograph, 3,* 79–192.

Boosey, E. J. (1947). The African Grey parrot. *Aviculture Magazine, 53,* 39–40.

Borror, D. J. (1977). Rufous-sided towhees mimicking Carolina wren and field sparrow. *Wilson Bulletin, 89,* 477–480.

Bottjer, S. W., Miesner, E. A., & Arnold, A. P. (1984). Forebrain lesions disrupt development but not maintenance of song in passerine birds. *Science, 224,* 901–903.

Brenowitz, E. A. (1982). Aggressive response of red-winged blackbirds to mockingbird song imitation. *Auk, 99,* 584–586.

Brown, I. (1976). Role of referent concreteness in the acquisition of passive sentence comprehension through abstract modeling. *Journal of Experimental Child Psychology, 22,* 185–199.

Cheney, D. L., & Seyfarth, R. M. (1980). Vocal recognition in free ranging vervet monkeys. *Animal Behaviour, 28,* 362–367.

Cheney, D. L., & Seyfarth, R. M. (1982). How vervet monkeys perceive their grunts: field playback experiments. *Animal Behaviour, 30,* 739–751.

Courtright, J. A., & Courtright, I. C. (1979). Imitative modeling as a language intervention strategy: the effects of two mediating variables. *Journal of Speech and Hearing Research, 22,* 389–402.

Crook, J. H. (1983). On attributing consciousness to animals. *Nature, 303,* 11–14.

de Villiers, J. G., & de Villiers, P. A. (1978). *Language acquisition* (pp. 270–271). Cambridge, MA: Harvard University Press.

Dobkin, D. S. (1979). Functional and evolutionary relationships of vocal copying phenomenon in birds. *Zeitschrift für Tierpsychologie, 50,* 348–363.

Dooling, R. J., & Searcy, M. H. (1981). A comparison of auditory evoked potentials in two species of sparrow. *Physiological Psychology, 9,* 293–298.

Eberhardt, C., & Baptista, L. F. (1977). Intraspecific and interspecific song mimesis in California song sparrow. *Bird Banding, 48,* 193–205.

Fouts, R. S. (1973). Acquisition and testing of gestural signs in four young chimpanzees. *Science, 180,* 978–980.

Fouts, R. S., & Couch, T. B. (1976). Cultural evolution of learned language in chimpanzees. In M. E. Hahn & E. C. Simmel (Eds.), *Communicative behavior and evolution* (pp. 141–161). New York: Academic Press.

Fulwiler, R. L., & Fouts, R. S. (1976). Acquisition of American sign language by a non-communicating autistic child. *Journal of Autism and Child Schizophrenia, 6,* 43–51.

Gardner, B. T., & Gardner, F. A. (1978). Comparative psychology and language acquisition. *Psychology, the state of the art. Annals of the New York Academy of Sciences, 309,* 37–76.

Gossette, R. L. (1969). Personal communication to O. H. Mowrer, 1980: *Psychology of language and learning* (pp. 105–106). New York: Plenum Press.

Gould, J. L., & Gould, C. G. (1982). The insect mind: Physics or metaphysics? In D. R. Griffin (Ed.), *Animal mind-human mind* (pp. 269–298). Berlin and New York: Springer-Verlag.

Greenfield, P. M. (1978). Developmental processes in the language learning of child and chimp. *Behavioral and Brain Sciences, 4,* 573–574.

Griffin, D. R. (1981). *The question of animal awareness.* New York: The Rockefeller University Press.

Grosslight, J. H., & Zaynor, W. C. (1967). Verbal behavior in the mynah bird. In K. Salzinger & S. Salzinger (Eds.), *Research in verbal behavior and some neurophysiological implications* (pp. 5–19). New York: Academic Press.

Grosslight, J. H., Zaynor, W. C., & Lively, B. L. (1964). Speech as a stimulus for differential vocal behavior in the mynah bird (*Gracula religiosa*). *Psychonomic Science, 1,* 7–8.

Güttinger, H. R. (1974). Gesang des Grunlings (*Chloris chloris*). Lokale Unterschiede and Entwicklung bei Schallisolation. *Journal für Ornithologie, 115,* 321–337.

Hensley, G. (1980). Encounters with a hookbill—II. *American Cage Bird Magazine, 52,* 11–12, 59.

Herman, L. (1980). Cognitive characteristics of dolphins. In L. Herman (Ed.), *Cetacean behavior: Mechanisms and functions* (pp. 363–430). New York: Wiley-Interscience.

Herman, L., Richards, D., & Wolz, J. (1984). Comprehension of sentences by bottlenosed dolphins. *Cognition, 16,* 129–219.

Howard, R. D. (1974). The influence of sexual selection and interspecific competition on mockingbird song (*Mimus polyglottos*). *Evolution, 28,* 428–438.

Humphrey, N. (1979). Nature's psychologists. In B. Josephson & B. S. Ramchandra (Eds.), *Consciousness and the physical world* (pp. 57–75). New York: Pergamon.

Krebs, J. R., & Kroodsma, D. E. (1980). Repertoires and geographical variation in bird song. In J. S. Rosenblatt, R. A. Hinde, C. Beer, & M-C. Busnel (Eds.), *Advances in the study of behavior, Vol. 11* (pp. 143–177). New York: Academic Press.

Kroodsma, D. E. (1972). Variation in songs of vesper sparrows in Oregon. *Wilson Bulletin, 84,* 173–178.

Kroodsma, D. E. (1973). Coexistence of Bewick's wrens and house wrens in Oregon *Auk, 90,* 341–352.

Kroodsma, D. E. (1977). A re-evaluation of song development in the song sparrow. *Animal Behaviour, 25,* 390–399.

Kroodsma, D. E. (1978). Aspects of learning in the ontogeny of bird song: Where, from whom, when, how many, which, and how accurately? In G. M. Burghardt & M. Bekoff (Eds.), *The development of behavior: Comparative and evolutionary aspects* (pp. 215–230). New York: Garland Press.

Kroodsma, D. E. (1981). Geographical variations and functions of song types in warblers (*Parulidae*). *Auk, 98,* 743–751.

Kroodsma, D. E. (1982). Learning and the ontogeny of sound signals in birds. In D. E. Kroodsma & E. H. Miller (Eds.), *Acoustic communication in birds. Vol. 2: Song learning and its consequences* (pp. 1–23). New York: Academic Press.

Kroodsma, D. E., & Baylis, J. R. (1982). Appendix: A world survey of evidence for vocal learning in birds. In D. E. Kroodsma & E. H. Miller (Eds.), *Acoustic communication in birds. Vol. 2: Song learning and its consequences* (pp. 311–337). New York: Academic Press.

Kroodsma, D. E., & Canady, R. (1982). Population differences in repertoire size, neuroanatomy, and song development in the long-billed marsh wren. (From *American Ornithologists' Union National Meeting Abstract,* October, Chicago, Illinois).

Kroodsma, D. E., & Pickert, R. (1980). Environmentally dependent sensitive periods for avian vocal learning. *Nature, 288,* 477–479.

Kroodsma, D. E., & Pickert, R. (1984a) Sensitive phases for song learning: effects of social interaction and individual variation. *Animal Behaviour, 32*, 389–394.

Kroodsma, D. E., & Pickert, R. (1984b). Repertoire size, auditory templates, and selective vocal learning in songbirds. *Animal Behaviour, 32*, 395–399.

Leger, D. W., & Owings, D. H. (1978). Response to alarm calls by California ground squirrels: Effects of call structure and maternal status. *Behavioral Ecology Sociobiology, 3*, 177–186.

Leger, D. W., Owings, D. H., & Boal, L. M. (1979). Contextual information and differential responses to alarm whistles in California ground squirrels. *Zeitschrift für Tierpsychologie, 49*, 142–155.

Leger, D. W., Owings, D. H., & Gelfand, D. L. (1980). Single-note vocalizations of California ground squirrels: Graded signals and situation-specificity of predator and socially evoked calls. *Zeitschrift für Tierpsychologie, 52*, 227–246.

Lein, M. R. (1972). Territorial and courtship songs of birds. *Nature, 237*, 48–49.

Lein, M. R. (1978). Song variation in a population of chestnut-sided warblers (*Dendroica pensylvanica*): its nature and suggested significance. *Canadian Journal of Zoology, 56*, 1266–1283.

Lenneberg, E. H. (1973). Biological aspects of language. In G. A. Miller (Ed.), *Communication, language, and meaning* (pp. 49–60). New York: Basic Books.

Litvak, S. B. (1969). A comparison of two brief behavior group therapy techniques on the reduction of avoidance behavior. *Psychological Record, 19*, 329–334.

Lovaas, O. I. (1977). *The autistic child: Language development through behavior modification.* New York: Irvington.

Malmi, W. A. (1976). Chimpanzees and language evolution. *Origins and evolution of language and speech. Annals of the New York Academy of Sciences, 280*, 598–603.

Marler, P. (1970). A comparative approach to vocal learning: Song development in white-crowned sparrows. *Journal of Comparative and Physiological Psychology, 71*, 1–25.

Marler, P. (1973). Speech development and bird song: Are there any parallels? In G. A. Miller (Ed.), *Communication, language and meaning* (pp. 73–83). New York: Basic Books.

Marler, P. (1983). Monkey calls: How are they perceived and what do they mean? In J. F. Eisenberg & D. G. Kleiman (Eds.), *Advances in the study of mammalian behavior* (pp. 343–356). American Society of Mammalogists, Special Publication # 7.

Marler, P., & Peters, S. (1977). Selective vocal learning in a sparrow. *Science, 198*, 519–521.

Marler, P., & Peters, S. (1981). Sparrows learn adult song and more from memory. *Science, 213*, 780–782.

Marler, P., & Peters, S. (1982a). Structural changes in song ontogeny in the swamp sparrow, *Melospiza georgiana. Auk, 99*, 446–458.

Marler, P., & Peters, S. (1982b). Long term storage of birdsongs prior to production. *Animal Behaviour, 30*, 479–482.

Miles, H. L. (1983). Apes and language: the search for communicative competence. In J. de Luce & H. T. Wilder (Eds.), *Language in primates* (pp. 43–61). New York: Springer-Verlag.

Mowrer, O. H. (1954). A psychologist looks at language. *American Psychologist, 9*, 660–694.

Mowrer, O. H. (1958). Hearing and speaking: An analysis of language learning. *Journal of Speech and Hearing Disorders, 23*, 143–152.

Nottebohm, F. (1970). Ontogeny of bird song. *Science, 167*, 950–956.

Nottebohm, F. (1975). A zoologist's view of some language phenomena with particular emphasis on vocal learning. In E. H. Lenneberg & E. Lenneberg (Eds.), *Foundations of language development* (pp. 61–104). New York: Academic Press.

Nottebohm, F. (1981). A brain for all seasons: Cyclical anatomical changes in song control nuclei of the canary brain. *Science, 214*, 1368–1370.

Nottebohm, F., Kasparian, S., & Pandazis, C. (1981). Brain space for a learned task. *Brain Research, 213*, 99–109.

Owings, D. H., & Virginia, R. A. (1978). Alarm calls of California ground squirrels (*Spermophilus beecheyi*). *Zeitschrift für Tierpsychologie, 46*, 58–70.

Patterson, F. (1978). Linguistic capabilities of a lowland gorilla. In F. C. C. Peng (Ed.), *Sign language and language acquisition in man and ape* (pp. 161–201). Boulder, CO: Westview Press.

Payne, R. B. (1981). Song learning and social interaction in indigo buntings. *Animal Behaviour, 29*, 688–697.

Payne, R. B., Thompson, W. L., Fiala, K. L., & Sweany, L. L. (1981). Local song traditions in indigo buntings: Cultural transmission of behavior patterns across generations. *Behaviour, 77*(4), 199–221.

Pepperberg, I. M. (1978, March). Object identification by an African Grey parrot. (From Midwest Animal Behavior Society Meeting Abstract, W. Lafayette, IN.)

Pepperberg, I. M. (1979, June). Functional word use in an African Grey parrot. (From Animal Behavior Society Meeting Abstract, New Orleans.)

Pepperberg, I. M. (1981). Functional vocalizations by an African Grey parrot (*Psittacus erithacus*). *Zeitschrift für Tierpsychologie, 55*, 139–160.

Pepperberg, I. M. (1983). Cognition in the African Grey parrot: preliminary evidence for auditory/vocal comprehension of the class concept. *Animal Learning and Behavior, 11*, 179–185.

Pepperberg, I. M. (1985). Social modeling theory: A possible framework for understanding avian vocal learning. *Auk, 102*, 854–864.

Petrinovich, L., Patterson, T., & Baptista, L. F. (1981). Song dialects as barriers to dispersal: A reevaluation. *Evolution, 35*, 180–188.

Premack, D. (1976). *Intelligence in ape and man*. Hillsdale, NJ: Lawrence Erlbaum Associates.

Premack, D. (1983). The codes of man and beasts. *Behavioral and Brain Sciences, 6*, 125–167.

Price, P. H. (1979). Developmental determinants of structure in zebra finch song. *Journal of Comparative and Physiological Psychology, 93*, 260–277.

Richey, E. (1976). The language program. In E. R. Ritvo, B. J. Freeman, E. M. Ornitz, & P. E. Tanguay (Eds.), *Autism: Diagnosis, current research and management* (pp. 203–226). New York: Spectrum Publication.

Rieber, R. W., & Voyat, G. (1983). *Dialogues on the psychology of language and thought*. New York: Plenum Press.

Rimm, D. C., & Mahoney, M. J. (1969). The application of reinforcement and participant modeling procedures in the treatment of snake-phobic behavior. *Behaviour Research and Therapy, 1*, 369–376.

Risley, T., & Wolf, M. (1968). Establishing functional speech in echolalic children. In H. N. Sloane, Jr. & B. D. MacAuley (Eds.), *Operant procedures in remedial speech and language training* (pp. 157–184). Boston: Houghton-Mifflen.

Robinson, F. N. (1975). Vocal mimicry and the evolution of bird song. *Emu, 75*, 23–27.

Robinson, S. R. (1980). Antipredator behaviour and predator recognition in Belding's ground squirrels. *Animal Behaviour, 28*, 840–852.

Robinson, S. R. (1981). Alarm communication in Belding's ground squirrels. *Zeitschrift für Tierpsychologie, 59*, 150–168.

Rumbaugh, D. M., & Gill, T. V. (1976). The mastery of language—type skills by the chimpanzee (*Pan*). *Origins and evolution of language and speech. Annals of the New York Academy of Sciences, 280*, 562–578.

Salzinger, K. (1980). The concept of the behavioral mechanism in language. In O. H. Mowrer (Ed.), *Psychology of language and learning* (pp. 213–232). New York: Plenum Press.

Saunders, R., & Sailor, W. (1979). A comparison of the strategies of reinforcement in two-choice learning problems with severely retarded children. *American Association for the Education of the Severely (Profoundly) Handicapped Review, 4*, 323–334.

Savage-Rumbaugh, E. S., Rumbaugh, D. M., & Boysen, S. (1980). Do apes use language? *American Scientist, 68,* 49–61.

Scarcella, R. C., & Higa, C. A. (1982). Input and age differences in second language acquisition. In S. D. Krashen, R. C. Scarcella, & M. H. Long (Eds.), *Child-adult differences in second language acquisition* (pp. 175–201). Rowley, MA: Newbury House Publishers.

Schusterman, R., & Krieger, K. (1984). California sea lions are capable of semantic comprehension. *The Psychological Record, 34,* 3–23.

Seyfarth, R. M., Cheney, D. L., & Marler, P, (1980a). Vervet monkey alarm calls: Semantic communication in a free-ranging primate. *Animal Behaviour, 28,* 1070–1094.

Seyfarth, R. M., Cheney, D. L., & Marler, P. (1980b). Monkey responses to three different alarms: Evidence for predator classification and semantic communication. *Science, 210,* 801–803.

Shiovitz, K. A., & Lemon, R. E. (1980). Species identification of songs by indigo buntings as determined by responses to computer-generated sounds. *Behaviour, 74,* (III–IV), 167–199.

Snow, C. E. (1979). The role of social interaction. In W. A. Collins (Ed.), *Children's language and communication, Minnesota Symposium on Child Psychology, Vol. 12.* (pp. 157–182). Hillsdale, NJ: Lawrence Erlbaum Associates.

Sonnenschein, E., & Reyer, H-U. (1983). Mate-guarding and other functions of antiphonal duets in the slate-coloured Boubou (*Laniarius funebris*). *Zeitschrift für Tierpsychologie, 63,* 112–140.

Struhsaker, T. (1967). *Behavior and ecology of the Red Colobus monkeys.* Chicago: University of Chicago Press.

Thielcke, G. (1970). Die sozialen Funktionen der Vogelstimmen. *Vogelwarte, 25,* 204–229.

Thielcke, G. (1972). Waldbaumläufer (*Certhia familiaris*) ahmen artfremdes Signal nach und reagieren darauf. *Journal für Ornithologie, 113,* 287–295.

Thorpe, W. H. (1961). *Bird song.* Cambridge: Cambridge University Press.

Thorpe, W. H. (1964). *Learning and instinct in animals.* London: Methuen.

Todt, D. (1975). Social learning of vocal patterns and models of their applications in Grey parrots. *Zeitschrift für Tierpsychologie, 39,* 178–188.

Todt, D., Hultsch, H., & Heike, D. (1979). Conditions affecting song acquisition in nightingales (*Luscinia megarhynchos L*). *Zeitschrift für Tierpsychologie, 51,* 23–35.

Waser, M. S., & Marler, P. (1977). Song learning in canaries. *Journal of Comparative and Physiological Psychology, 91,* 1–7.

Whitehurst, G. J., Ironsmith, E. M., & Goldfein, M. (1974). Selective imitation of the passive construction through modeling. *Journal of Experimental Child Psychology, 17,* 288–302.

15

Awareness, Intentionality, and Acquired Communicative Behaviors: Dimensions of Intelligence

E. Sue Savage-Rumbaugh
Emory University
Georgia State University

William D. Hopkins
Georgia State University

INTRODUCTION

The Evolution of the Capacity to Acquire New Behaviors

Most animals, and certainly all vertebrates, enter their environment, equipped with a specific morphology, a somewhat less specific set of predisposed behavioral patterns or fixed action patters (FAPs), and a rather loosely predetermined capacity to learn alternative behaviors under situations when they have either an incomplete behavioral "program" or essentially no behavioral "program." Thus, it might be said that genetic makeup affects morphology most directly, ritualized action patterns somewhat less directly, and the "to be acquired" behaviors least of all. However, precisely because these *to be acquired behaviors* differ, even between conspecifics, they have not been viewed from the evolutionary perspective which has characterized the biological study of morphology and fixed actions patterns.

Psychologists, in studying acquired behaviors, essentially have ignored the sum and substance of the behaviors themselves, and focused instead on *laws* or *principles* of learning. Acquired behaviors have not been viewed as something that needs to or can be understood better, or even described, but rather as something that needs to be *accounted for* or *predicted* and thereby controlled. Consequently, studies of learning in the field of psychology skipped the phase of description which characterizes the initial phase of each scientific discipline. Behavior, in all its intricacy never was described adequately for any species. Unfortunately, the "laws" of learning, "principles of reinforcement," etc., which emerged from the behavioral psychologists caldron were thought to reflect

303

general principles of learning. With so little known about the range of acquired behaviors in animals, it generally was accepted that these laws did indeed *account for* and predict behavior.

Ethologists, attacked this position, pointing out that various animals came into the world equipped to learn very different things, and consequently seemed to acquire certain types of information rapidly and other types not at all.

Since psychologists have not viewed acquired behaviors as structures in their own right, they have produced no valid means of investigating the origins and evolution of intelligence. Consequently, intelligence, as an evolving entity, is notably absent from the emerging synthesis of the behavioral and biological sciences termed sociobiology. If we wonder why, we have only to note that none of the *laws* of learning have any relationship to evolution. That is they do not deal with the phenomenon of acquired behaviors from a perspective which reflects the view that these behaviors have, in any sense, evolved.

The Evolution of the Capacity to Learn Communicative Behaviors

To explain more clearly, let us now refine our focus from the general area of acquired behaviors or intelligence to the subset of behaviors classified as communicative—behaviors that have become specialized for interacting with other organisms—and to the most puzzling of all behaviors, those broadly characterized as intentional communications and narrowly characterized as language. Nearly every serious scholar who has addressed the topic of human communication, with the notable though disparate exceptions of D. Griffin (1976) and B. F. Skinner, (1957) has felt compelled to set language apart from all other forms of communication in the animal kingdom.

Some have attempted to objectify this imposed dichotomy between animal and human communication systems by dissecting human communication into its constituent features and then comparing the human and animal systems by searching for the presence or absence of each feature of the human systems across a wide variety of animal species (Hockett, 1959, 1960; Hockett & Altmann, 1968). According to Thorpe (1974), if all animal communication systems are considered together, all but 2 of the 16 design features proposed by Hockett can be observed in the animal communication systems; these being prevarication (the ability to lie or talk nonsense) and reflectiveness (the ability to communicate about the system itself).

Biologists, such as E. O. Wilson (1975), also seek a dividing line and find it in the number and variety of language units—"What is truly unique [about language] is the very large number of such words and the potential for creating new ones to denote any number of additional objects and concepts" (1975, p. 177). Wilson contrasts this human capacity with what he considers to be the "most sophisticated of all animal communication systems," the celebrated waggle dance of the honeybee. Wilson (1975) notes that in the honeybee, ''messages cannot be manipulated to provide new classes of information and that like all other forms of nonhuman communication studied so far, [the bee's system] is severely limited in comparison with the verbal language of human beings . . . the separate messages are not devised arbitrarily. The rules they follow are genetically fixed and always designate, with a one-to-one correspondence, a certain direction and distance'' (p. 177). The leap from insect to man is so great that it seems illogical that Wilson should have to conclude (after reviewing the literature) that the honeybee's communication system is ''like all other forms of nonhuman communication.'' Surely on the way from insect to man, communicative behaviors must have become more complex. If studies of the communication systems of other animals do not reveal increasing complexity, we submit that these studies reflect an inadequate approach to the phenomena. It is not reasonable to conclude that communicative systems have made few important advancements beyond the honeybee when brain size has increased a thousandfold. Nature is not so inefficient.

The Man-Ape Dichotomies

It seems that with the appearance of symbol using apes, the focus of the traditional dichotomy between animal and human communication systems was redrawn to focus on the comparison between language-trained apes and human beings. For many, this new comparison raised a host of theoretical questions regarding the degree of humanness that should be granted to apes and the degree to which it was appropriate to consider a trained language skill equivalent to a skill that human children acquired without special training. The fact that apes may imitate the symbol usage of their teachers was viewed as a severely limiting factor (Terrace, 1979) even though many linguists studying language acquisition in young children (Nelson, 1980) repeatedly noted that such imitation seemed to be a critical part of normal language acquisition.

We believe that in time, these dichotomies will crumble and we will look back on them as strangely antiquated views, held as the last comfortable bastian of defense against Darwinism. Human language will be recognized for what it is, a special means of conveying information about objects and events which are removed in space and time. It will be recognized as being overlaid upon and intermingled with the affective communication system. It will be viewed as totally contiguous with similar systems found in other species. Grammar will no longer be viewed as a unique property of human language, but will be understood as a temporal processing system. Grammatical units and syntactical rules, far from being determined by an innate language acquisition device will be seen as being derived from the perceptual characteristics of the organism. Syntactical rules will be seen as devices which permit quick encoding and decoding, thus facilitating rapid auditory communication in what is otherwise a slow sequential channel. This interpretation will be accepted when it becomes more apparent that there is a neurological basis for both awareness and intentionality in other life forms and, that these phenomena are, in humans, not the result of some special capacity, but simply the outcome of an ever increasing set of neurological networks whose job it is to monitor and adjust ongoing behaviors with reference to some anticipated goal.

These dichtomies will also crumble as more researchers adopt a biological perspective of intelligence and begin to ask ''what does this animal know?'' and ''how did it learn it?,'' as opposed to ''how can I predict and control its behavior?'' To determine what an animal knows, it is necessary to provide accurate descriptions of what it does and then devise environmental tests to determine whether or not one's characterizations are accurate (Olton, 1979). As we begin to build a picture of animal intelligence that is dramatically different from what we now have it will become necessary to deal with the heretofore closeted topics of awareness and intentionality in animals.

THE DIFFERENCE BETWEEN ACQUIRED AND INNATE PATTERNS

Although acquired patterns may replace or interface with FAPs, the neurological evidence seems to suggest that they operate differently. When FAPs occur between two conspecifics the flow of communication and the ensuing exchange of displays typically flows quite smoothly. There are a few misintrepretations and thus little opportunity to assess what effect, if any, the sender intends to produce upon the receiver (Smith, 1977). In fact, it appears that the participants engaged in FAPs have little sense of the *goal* of their behaviors and act as if each interlinked unit in the chain is designed to evoke the next unit. For example, in the flightless male cormorant, we find the FAP of bringing seaweed to his mate on the nest. This has been interpreted as an appeasement gesture and, indeed, if the seaweed is snatched away from the male as he approaches the nest, he will be attacked by the female (Eibl-Eibesfeldt, 1970). However, the fact that the male still approaches the female once he has started toward her, suggests that he does not understand the consequences of bringing seaweed.

When consequences are attached to acquired behaviors to produce an increased frequency of behavior, the animal emits behaviors that suggest that he has some appreciation of those consequences. For example, a chicken who has learned to put a small ball in a net (in imitation of basketball) will, if it drops the ball, search for it, instead of proceeding to the net without the ball (Breland & Breland, 1966). The chicken has learned that the ball is a necessary component for reinforcement and it monitors its retention of the ball. Perhaps if the seaweed repeatedly was taken from the cormorant, it would begin to monitor the presence or absence of seaweed. However, it is equally possible that no matter how many times the seaweed is taken from the cormorant, it will not learn to replace the stolen bunch before approaching the female. With all our "laws" of learning we have none that would allow us to predict whether the cormorant will learn to retrieve another bunch of seaweed and thus, we would have to conduct this experiment.

Thus, significant distinction between acquired behaviors and FAPs seems to lie in the fact that the organism shows some anticipation of the consequences of its behavior—when the behavior has been learned; however, when it is a FAP there is little evidence of such anticipation of consequences.

If we assume that fixed action patterns are altered by evolutionary forces across generations, then it seems reasonable that the consequences of these FAPs should remain hidden from the individual organism emitting the behavior. However, acquired behaviors affect the success of that individual directly and are altered within its immediate life span, thus some sentience of the consequences of the behavior must be monitored at the neurological level in order to effect such rapid behavioral change.

It is often pointed out by behavioral psychologists that human beings are not "aware of the consequences" of their behaviors and yet the behaviors are shaped quite effectively despite this lack of awareness. Often given is the example of the trick pinball machine, which gave points when users kicked it, cursed it, hit it, etc. These behaviors increased in frequency, although when asked to describe how they produced high scores, none of the users mentioned any of these behaviors. This example demonstrates that human beings cannot always construct a lawful verbal statement that reflects the relationship between their behaviors and the consequences. It deals with a complex situation wherein multiple cause-effect relationships are possible and the relevant ones are disguised purposefully from the pinball player. Under these conditions it is not surprising that the subject does not express a verbal awareness.

This example is very different from most conditioning studies in which the consequences of behavior are made extraordinarily evident and the animal so conditioned clearly displays behaviors that reveal expectancy of consequence. For example, a rat trained to press a lever to operate a vending mechanism on a fixed ratio schedule does not wait until he hears the vendor open, rather he approaches the vendor *before* it opens.

We suggest that the avoidance of terms such as *awareness* has caused psychologists to oversimplify what animals are able to learn and to overlook the significant distinction of knowledge of consequences which separates learned components of behavior from FAPs.

Let us return to the earlier comparison, offered by Wilson, (1975), between the language of the honeybee and the language of humans. Is it really the case that all other species have communicative patterns that are as preprogrammed and inflexible as that of the bee? For some constructive comparisons, let us look at some FAPs in wasps as contrasted with monkeys. The digger wasp displays the FAP of searching of its larvae cavity before depositing food (caterpillers) in the cavity for the larvae. It drags the caterpiller to the ege of the cavity, drops it near the entrance, enters the cavity, inspects it, reappears head first, and pulls the caterpillar inside. "If one removes the caterpillar to a place some distance from the nest while the wasp is inspecting the cavity, it will search for it until it has found the caterpillar, bring it back to the entrance and repeat the entire sequence" (Eibl-Eibesfeldt, 1970, p. 218). This behavior can be reelicited 30–40 times before the wasp will finally pull the caterpillar into the cavity without inspecting it.

Contrast this difficulty in dealing with the disruption of a fixed action pattern with that of the squirrel monkey mother described by Rumbaugh (1965). Maternal behavior in these monkeys is far more complex than the larval care patterns of the digger wasp, yet it is the infant who is responsible for maintaining contact, by clinging, as the mother moves about. The mother, in normal circumstances shows no tendency to emit behaviors designed to keep the infant with her, she leaps rapidly about with little regard for the difficulties the infant may experience as she moves. Yet, when an infant's arms are bound so that he cannot cling, the mother picks the intant up and carries it. To do so, she has to walk bipedally, and her movement is impeded considerably. Prior to picking the infant up, she places herself near the infant as if to facilitate clinging, but when clinging does not occur, the infant is carried. The mother has formed the generalized concept that "the baby is to stay with me" and thus, she alters her behavior accordingly. Apes have also been observed to adopt and carry cats, who neither cling nor emit appropriate vocal or facial-fixed action-releasing stimuli (Savage, Temerlin, & Linden, 1974. These behaviors have often been dismissed by psychologists and ethologists as merely examples of instinct gone awry. However, this is not the case. The cat may well *elicit* maternal behavior but the chimpanzee mother, must alter her normal maternal patterns significantly to cope with a cat. Furthermore, dolphins have been observed adopting dead fish and adapting appropriate swimming patterns to prevent the fish from sinking to the bottom. In these cases, trainers could not take the dead fish away until it had virtually disintegrated (Norris & Prescott, 1961; Thomas, personal communication). It is not likely that insects could accomplish such alterations. True enough, some social insects are tricked into caring for the offspring of another species, but to do so requires no alteration in their extant communicative behavioral program. Yet, both the ape and the cat are able to alter their normal modes of interacting to affect coordinated behavior. The fact that the ape or monkey, in contrast to the wasp, is able to alter its behaviors when conditions call forth a need, indicates that the ape, unlike the wasp, is capable of understanding at least a portion of the consequences of its actions. Thus the monkey mother who positions herself for clinging and is not clung to, reveals that she understands the intent of the positioning posture by picking up the infant and holding it to her ventrum. The wasp who repeatedly inspects the larval cavity reveals that it does not understand the function of the inspection behavior as it is compelled to needlessly repeat itself after being moved one step back in its fixed behavioral chain.

Moreover, not only are apes able, if the need arises to alter their caretaking patterns, it is also the case that communicative patterns are often found to differ between mother-infant pairs of the same species. For example, Chevalier-Skolnikoff (1974) observed that nine different signals for the initiation of mother-infant contact occurred in a captive group of *Macaca arctoides*. These signals differed from pair to pair with no pair using the same set of signals, and with the number of signals employed between pairs varying from 1 to 6.

We suspect that the lack of more frequent observations of learned communicative patterns is due to lack of familiarity with the species, observational difficulties, and a bias toward reporting "displays" that are highly obvious and similar across species.

AWARENESS AND INTENTIONAL INFORMATIVE COMMUNICATIVE ACTS

To be aware is, in one sense of this word, to be cognizant of sensation. In that sense we are always aware of bodily emotions and perceptions except when injury has interrupted neuronal processes. In this sense, animals also are surely aware of their ongoing behaviors and sensations. However, awareness in the human individual is also used to imply a knowledge of behavioral alternatives, a concomitant knowledge of having chosen one of these alternatives as opposed to another, and an ongoing conscious monitoring of the progress toward a chosen alternative—as when we chose a particular route to point B on a map and note the towns as we pass to determine if we are actually on the correct highway. With this conscious monitoring goes a readiness to engage in other routes should that one be perceived as ineffective. This sort of awareness is also surely within the capacity of higher mammals and is to be contrasted with that strange experience we have all had of driving to a familiar location while our *thoughts* were elsewhere. On arriving, it is not possible to remember what happened along the way and thus we say we were unaware of where we were going, even though we were negotiating all the decision points quite well.

More important however, is the fact that *awareness* as applied to the phenomena of human communication also implies something we would not attribute to animals—and this is the awareness that communicative acts are *behaviors about behaviors* (Crook, 1983). An easy way to visualize this distinction is to think of the prespeech conversational babbling of human youngsters. During such "conversational exchanges between mother and infant" there is a reciprocal exchange of roles and the intonation patterns of the infant typically follows that of the mother in a responsive manner. At this stage, the infant is not saying anything, but rather is producing intonation exchange as a behavior in its own right. Later though, the mother will comment that the infant now knows what he is saying. At this stage, the vocalizations may well still be unintelligible to a novice observer and to the mother herself, yet as a result of the surrounding behavioral context, they will be recognized as intentional communications, albeit rather poor in quality. At this stage, utterances alone no longer fulfill their own function—the infant will insist that specific sorts of action to be taken in response to them and thus, these utterances have become behaviors about behaviors.

Moreover, not only does the infant now distinguish between behaviors which are their own *raison d'être* and behaviors which are about other behaviors, let us call these "intentional informative communicative acts," he recognizes that these informative communicative acts are primarily about the behavior of other individuals. That is, they are produced for the purpose of altering the behaviors of others in specific ways—ways which are best characterized as suiting the goals of the infant. Typically, the goals of the adults about the infant, and goals of the infant himself are rather different. Adults enjoy observing the infant, exchanging highly organized linguistic information, completing complex tasks, planning for future occurrences, while the infant wants to be played with, wants to eat the cookie that is out of reach, wants to be carried about, etc. Intentional informative communicative acts are used by the infant to control and orient the adults behaviors away from their own goals and toward his goals.

Along with the appearance of such intentional communicative acts, comes the concomitant awareness that other individuals also produce behaviors about behaviors and that they make choices regarding which behavior to perform. Thus, they may or may not respond to the infants communicative acts or not. If they do not respond, the infant may perceive the lack of response as resulting from one of two events; either the other party did not understand or perceive the intentional informative communication—or the other party received the communication, but chose not to respond (typically this will be apparent to the youngster because the recipient will in fact acknowledge the receipt of the communication and indicate their unwillingness to comply).

With the emergence of intentional informative communicative acts (IICA) comes the attribution of a similar capacity to others and the monitoring of the effectiveness of one's own IICA's as separate from one's other behaviors. Generally, one can determine the effectiveness of one's own behavior by the ensuing events that affect the individual directly; however, IICAs must be monitored by judging a change in the behavior of another and determining whether or not that change corresponds with the change which the IICA was intended to accomplish. It is the monitoring of the IICAs which, in fact, enables us to discern that behaviors are indeed IICA's as opposed to their simpler counterpart, unintentional emotive acts, such as the food barks produced by chimpanzees while eating desirable foods. The food bark may be perceived as communication by other chimpanzees but it is not intentionally communicated; it is an expression of the internal emotional state.

Are Dolphins Capable of Intentional Communications?

Chimpanzees and human beings are both capable of intentional and unintentional communicative actions. When engaged in intentional communications, they monitor the effect of their messages and emit the message again, with alterations, if it was not effective (Savage-Rumbaugh, in press). Language, as we know it, could not exist without the capacity for intentional communication as all linguistic communications are, by definition, intentional. It is the capacity for intentional communication that allows the ape to acquire rudimentary human language skills. Even in the wild, apes use complex gestures to convey messages. They monitor the effectiveness of these gestures upon the recipients and modify their behavior accordingly. Monkeys may engage in similar monitoring, but the evidence is less clear. For example, there are no observations of monkeys spitting on zoo visitors, just to observe their consternation—yet such behavior is unbiquitous in chimpanzee colonies.

Are dolphins capable of utilizing intentional communicative acts to purposefully alter the behaviors of other dolphins? Do they monitor the effects of the signals they send out and change their behaviors accordingly?

To answer this question now would be premature because so little is known about dolphin behavior in both the wild and in the laboratory situation; but dolphins do seem to possess many of the behavioral and cognitive constructs observed in apes. For example, dolphins have been observed to squirt or splash water at strangers who come near their tank. After squirting the water the dolpin will raise itself out of the water to curiously observe what effect their behavior had on the stranger (Pryor, 1973; Savage-Rumbaugh, personal observation).

Although this behavior is not communicative, nonetheless, it seems to suggest that the dolphin is aware of the effect of its behavior on others. Pryor (1973) has reported cooperative behavior between a dolphin and a false killer whale who shared adjacent tanks but preferred to share the same tank. The dolphin developed the ability to jump over the partition and, subsequently, a large barricade was built to prevent this from happening because the animals were difficult to separate when together. The whale, with its superior strength, learned to move the barricade enough to allow the dolphin to jump in. The barricade displacement was blamed on human intervention until a trainer happened to observe this behavior one evening. It should be noted that both animals considered the behavior to be illicit and made no attempt to join each other unless there were no people around. Certainly, in this case, the dolpin and whale had to be "aware" of the ongoing events surrounding them, which enabled them to monitor when individuals were present and when they were absent.

Dolphins also have been reported to use "tools" on several occasions. Brown and Norris (1956) reported two dolphins trying to persuade a moray eel to play with them. When the eel retreated to a crevice to hide while one of the dolphins went and killed a scorpionfish, which has sharp dorsal spines, and returned with it in its mouth and began to poke at the eel, finally forcing the eel into the open. Similar tool usage has been well documented in the laboratory (Yerkes & Yerkes, 1929) and field (Goodall, 1964; Pitman, 1931) for the great apes. Herman and Tavolga (1980) have shown that dolphins are capable of receptively comprehending strings of sentences using an artificial language.

In order to better understand the cognitive capacities of dolphins, and to determine whether or not they are capable of complex intentional communications, we must continue to investigate their receptive capacities (Herman, this volume), and to attempt to provide them with a communication system that would tap their productive capacities.

The study of those communicative behaviors that reflect higher order intelligence is of special interest in the dolphin because of its great evolutionary diversity from ourselves. Ape and man separated only 4.5 million years ago, while we divergenced from dolphins at least 60 million years ago. Should dolphins prove to have some capacities for intentional communicative behavior, we would have strong support for the idea that intelligence is an entity whose existence transcends the anatomy of the bearer. Similarities between the intelligence of apes and that of dolphins, if they are found to exist, will help us to better understand the evolution of mind in our own species. The use of a productive communication system with dolphins would also allow us to explore avenues of dolphine intelligence not presently open to us; do they for example, have a sense of time, of math, of music, of ethics? These questions are only just now being posed with apes, they should also prove fascinating if addressed to dolphins.

ACKNOWLEDGMENT

This research supported by grants from the National Institute of Child Health and Human Development (HD-06016) and from the Division of Research Resources, National Institutes of Health (RR-00165). Research for reprints may be sent to E. Sue Savage-Rumbaugh, Yerkes Regional Primate Center, Emory University, Atlanta, GA. 30322.

REFERENCES

Breland, K., & Breland, M. (1966). *Animal behavior.* New York: Macmillan.
Brown, D. H., & Norris, K. S. (1956). Observations of captive and wild cetaceans. *Journal of Mammalogy, 37,* 311–326.

Chevalier-Skolnikoff, S. (1974). The ontogoney of communication in the stumptail macaque (*macaque arctoides*). In *Contributions to Primatology*, (vol. 2, pp. 1–174). Basel: Karger.

Crook, J. H. (1983). On attributing consciousness to animals. *Nature, 303*, 11–14.

Eibl-Eibesfeldt, I. (1970). *Ethology: The biology of behavior*. New York: Holt, Rhinehart & Winston.

Goodall, J. (1964). Tool using and aimed throwing in a community of free-living chimpanzees. *Nature, 201*, 1264–1266.

Griffin, D. R. (1976). *The question of animal awareness: Evolutionary continuity of mental experience*. New York: The Rockefeller University Press.

Herman, L. M., & Tavolga, W. N. (1980). The communication systems of cetaceans. In L. A. Herman (Ed.), *Cetacean behavior: Mechanisms and functions*. New York: Wiley.

Hockett, C. F. (1959). Animal "languages" and human language. In J. Spuhler (Ed.), *The evolution of man's capacity for culture*. Detroit, MI: Wayne State University Press.

Hockett, C. F. (1960). Logical considerations in the study of animal communication. In W. Lanyon & W. Tavolga (Eds.), *Animal sounds and communication*. Washington DC: American Institute of Biological Sciences.

Hockett, C. F., & Altmann, S. A. (1968). A note on design features. In T. A. Sebeok (Ed.), *Animal Communication*. Bloomington:Indiana University Press.

Kellogg, W. H. (1961). *Porpoises and sonar*. Chicago: University of Chicago Press.

Lilly, J. (1967). *Mind of the dolphin: A non-human intelligence*. Moonachie, NJ: Pyramid Publishing.

Lilly, J. C. (1978). *Communication between man and dolphin: The possibilities of talking with other species*. New York: Crown Publishers.

Nelson, K. (1980, June). *First words of chimp and child*. Paper presented at the Southeastern Psychological Associations Symposium on Apes and Language, Atlanta.

Norris, K. S., & Prescott, J. H. (1961). *Observations of Pacific cetaceans of California and Mexican waters. University of California. Publications in Zoology, 63*, 291–402.

Olton, D. S. (1979). Mazes, maps, and memory. *American Psychologist, 34*, 583–596.

Pitman, C. R. S. (1931). A game warden among his charges. In G. B. Schaller (Ed.), *The mountain gorilla*. Chicago: Chicago University Press.

Pryor, K. W. (1973). Behavior and learning in porpoises and whales. *Die Naturwissenschaften, 60*, 412–420.

Rumbaugh, D. M. (1965). Maternal care in relation to infant behavior in the squirrel monkey. *Psychological Reports, 16*(1), 171–176.

Savage-Rumbaugh, E. S. (in press). *Ape language: From conditioned response to symbol*. New York: Columbia University Press.

Savage, E. S., Temerlin, J. W., & Lemmon, W. B. (1974, July). The appearance of mothering behavior toward a kitten by a human-reared chimpanzee. Paper presented at 5th Congress of the International Primatological Society, Nagoya.

Skinner, B. F. (1957). *Verbal behavior*. New York: Appleton-Century-Crofts.

Smith, W. J. (1977). *The behavior of communicating: An ethological approach*. Cambridge, MA: Harvard University Press.

Terrace, H. S. (1979). *Nim*. New York: Academic Press.

Thorpe, W. H. (1974). *Animal nature and human nature*. Garden City, NY: Anchor Press/Doubleday.

Wilson, E. O. (1975). *Sociobiology: A new synthesis*. Cambridge, MA: Harvard University Press.

Yerkes, R. M., & Yerkes, A. M. (1929). *The great apes: A study of anthropoid life*. New Haven: Yale University Press.

16 Signaling Behavior: Contributions of Different Repertoires

W. John Smith
University of Pennsylvania

The communication of dolphins and other cetaceans is clearly elaborate. Nonetheless, it remains difficult to describe the basic components of their signaling behavior in ways that reveal how this elaboration is achieved.

Because dolphins are difficult to observe, it may be useful to seek guidance from comparative research on other kinds of animals. Cetacean communication is unlikely to be unique in all ways, even though the phylogenetic lineage is markedly distinctive. Whatever features of communication are so basic as to be shared by diverse kinds of mammals, and shared even with birds and other vertebrates, also should be characteristic of dolphins.

At the most basic level, comparisons among species suggest that the diversification of signaling behavior is organized within a number of repertoires. Each repertoire is a distinct class of specializations. Only in the first repertoire can a unit be a single act of an individual performer. These signaling acts—vocalizations, postures, ways of depositing pheromones, and so on—are the basis of the formalized communication of any species. The units of the other repertoires are performed by varying and combining the basic signaling acts or by interacting in rule-bound ways—the signal units then being joint productions of the participants.

The overall richness of dolphins' or any other species' communication depends both on the extent to which each of the repertoires is diversified and on the ways the repertoires can be combined during actual interactions. In this chapter I attempt to describe the distinctive characteristics of each kind of signaling repertoire, as we are beginning to understand them through research on various species of birds and mammals. A few tentative suggestions are offered for research on the communication of dolphins.

THE REPERTOIRE OF SIGNAL ACTS

The acts of signaling behavior that make up the first repertoire are the units with which we are casually the most familiar in many species, for example, the songs, chirps, and crest-raisings of birds; the arched-back posture of a halloween cat; the bitelike threats of so many species, for instance the bill-snaps of birds and the jaw-claps of dolphins; the urinating of dogs on communal scent posts; and the blushing, frowning, and laughing of humans. Different units are specialized for reception by different senses. Indeed, such signals sometimes are classified on the basis of appropriate sensory modalities, a form of categorization that is orthogonal to the distinctions among repertoires proposed in this chapter.

Many of these basic signal acts have been called "displays" by ethologists. While we can learn fairly easily to recognize them in many species, the sounds, postures, movements, ways of making contact, and other units of this repertoire have been difficult to describe for dolphins. This is partly because dolphins are hard to observe. At least for phonations, and perhaps for other kinds of units, this difficulty is complicated by the second repertoire, which is discussed below.

How much we know about these signal acts differs greatly among species, and much more study is needed. Nonetheless, some general characteristics are becoming apparent from comparative studies:

1. *Kinds of referents*—Most signal acts appear to be correlated conditionally and probabilistically with the performance of other behavior. This cooccurrence makes signals reliably informative or predictive of the other actions. We can say that the correlated activities are among the signals' referents. (This implies that they also are informative about the internal motivational and emotional states underlying these activities; the initial interpretations of ethologists were attempts to specify such states.)

Signal acts provide information about more than behavior. All identify their performers. Sounds give some information about the location of signalers. In addition, some signals correlate with environmental stimuli to which signalers are responding when they perform: predators (chatters of ground squirrels, see Owings & Leger 1980; vocalizations of vervets, see Seyfarth, Cheney & Marler, 1980; see also Smith, 1981), food (Dittus, 1984), or possibly the situations the signalers perceive (screams of rhesus monkeys, Gouzoules, Gouzoules, & Marler, 1984). The few things or situations that have been well documented as referents thus far involve signaling when the signaler or the referent is not near appropriate recipients of the information. That is, recipients are being enlisted from a distance to interact or to respond to some key thing that they cannot perceive directly. Conversely, if signaler and recipient are already interacting at close quarters, then most relevant information about the situation is usually available from sources contextual to a signal—although crucial stimuli, such as predators, may be more distant. At close quarters situational referents are probably less necessary than information about how a signaler may behave. It is unknown whether many signals inform about environmental things and situations. Current indications are that such referents may be relatively uncommon and provided by signals that also have behavioral referents.

2. *General features of the behavioral referents*—Surveys of the information made available about behavior by the signal units of diverse species appear to reveal widespread commonalities. That is, most displays of most species provide information about the same set of behavioral options. There are exceptions. Most species appear to have few or no exceptional displays, however.

Much of the information predicts behavior in broad classes, for example: interactional behavior, vacillating actions, or activities incompatible with other predicted behavior. Behavior that is more narrowly specified tends to be of three sorts: (a) urgent, as in attack and escape, requiring a correct response immediately; (b) infrequent but essential, for example, copulation; or (c) very frequent and fundamental to harmonious social life, requiring correct responses repeatedly. An example is the interactional activity of "associating," in an undemanding way, with another individual. Without signaling, association would be hard to maintain while animals are busily foraging in dense cover.

3. *Size of repertoire*—No species seems to have a very large repertoire of signal units, including all those specialized for reception by different sensory modalities. By conservative criteria, the total number may be no more than about 40 to 45 signal acts in any species' repertoire (Moynihan, 1970; Smith, 1969). By other criteria there may be twice that many, but by any criteria the number is not large.

The limited number of signal units may be responsible both for the small number of kinds of information that this repertoire makes available about behavior and for the commonality of information classes among species (Smith, 1969, 1977, chapter 7). Small repertoires force the evolution of context-dependent communication. They lead natural selection to favor those classes of information that work best in conjunction with information from common and basic contextual sources—information that is relevant and useful in diverse circumstances.

Communication, nonetheless, is not nearly as constrained as we might conclude from the characteristics of this first repertoire. It is greatly extended and enriched by performance of the other repertoires, acting in concert with the fundamental signal acts.

REPERTOIRE OF VARIATIONS OF SIGNAL FORM

The components of this second repertoire are not signal acts but ways of adjusting and modifying signal form. Few signal acts from the first repertoire are invariant. Variation, however, has at least two principal manifestations. Some features, often termed variable, get fixed for individual lifetimes as features that differ among populations, social groups, and individuals. Examples include local "dialects" of bird songs, pod-specific sets of pulsed calls of killer whales, and the "signature" whistle of dolphins. Because these become fixed aspects of an individual's signal units, they are appropriately considered with that first repertoire.

Other informative variation is evident among performances of the same signal act by the same individual. This is seen in readily reversible shifts in duration, amplitude, and often many other physical characteristics of the signal. These shifts are manifestations of this second repertoire.

Phonations of dolphins, both whistles and pulsed sounds, are highly variable. This makes them hard to characterize, because the contributions of the repertoires of acts and of classes of variation must be disentangled. So it is appropriate to ask what some of the classes of variation might be and to study the clues that comparative studies offer.

To illustrate the way variation alters signals in a regular, predictable manner, let me describe examples from my current research with a species of tyrannid flycatcher, the eastern kingbird (*Tyrannus tyrannus*). To elicit samples of one of the less-common calls I sometimes set a stuffed hawk or owl near a kingbird nest and record responses on video. Kingbirds vigorously defend their nests and will fly at the decoy repeatedly, sometimes striking it. Eventually they usually decapitate the decoy. An individual may set up a figure-eight flight pattern, diving past the decoy, rising, turning, and diving to pass again in the other direction, repeatedly.

The flying kingbird repeats a brief, rapidly frequency-modulated vocalization that sounds like "zit" (Fig. 16.1a). This is a distinctive unit within the species' signal repertoire. It is uttered in several kinds of aerial maneuvering and is not restricted just to attack behavior. As a provisional interpretation, "zit" appears to provide the information that abrupt maneuvering is probable or in progress (that is, the calling kingbird is flying and probably making abrupt course changes).

Although simple in form, "zit" units vary in amplitude, duration, and frequency range, and in being quavered or not. By comparing different forms of "zit" from these experiments with those uttered during attacks on free-moving, living predators and uttered in other circumstances, I expect to find patterns that will lead to an interpretation of much of the variation.

The form varies throughout the flight path of a figure-eight attack sequence in a more or less regular fashion. Duration and frequency spread are slightest at the farthest point from the decoy, near the top of the kingbird's climb. Longer "zits" with somewhat greater frequency range come in the start of the sloping attack dive, usually followed by a brief silence until the kingbird is about two to three body lengths from its immobile, unresponsive target. At this point the kingbird begins to roll and swerve. It breaks off from a collision course to detour

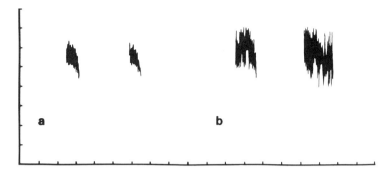

Fig. 16.1. "Zit" calls of *Tyrannus tyrannus*, traced from sonagrams made with a Kay 6061-B Sona-Graph using 300 Hz bandwidth. Abcissa: time, in tenths of seconds. Ordinate: frequency in kiloHertz. (a)Simple forms uttered in two separate events as a flying bird prepared to dive toward a stuffed predator. (b) Quavered variants uttered in two events as the diving bird abruptly veered from a collision course and passed close by the stuffed decoy.

close past its target. In the same field of videotape (i.e., the same 1/60 sec) in which this detour begins, the longest, most complex "zit" also begins (Fig. 1b). Superimposed on the rapidly frequency-modulated form is a much slower and very prominent frequency modulation, a "quaver."

Extreme quavering occurs only in those calls uttered during the veering detour around the decoy. Less extensive quavering, damping out, can mark those calls uttered as the kingbird passes the decoy and begins to climb, well before turning.

What excites me about quavering is not just that its correlates can be precisely described in an event such as this, but that the quavering variation is applied to other vocalizations. While "zit" is the only vocalization uttered in the figure-eight flight, a kingbird will utter a distinctly different vocal unit, "T-zee" (Fig. 16.2a), after its last pass as it flies to a perch, or in "loose" flying about without diving at a decoy or predator, and also from perch between bouts of attacks.

"T-zee" also is uttered in a much wider range of circumstances. The information it makes available is not the same as that provided by a "zit" call. Whatever else, "T-zee" provides information that a kingbird is choosing between flight (taking flight or continuing a flight already underway) and some unspecified alternative. "T-zee" appears to provide no information about maneuvering, which may or may not occur in these flights. "T-zee" and "zit" are thus two distinctly different units from the kingbird's basic signal repertoire.

One case in which a kingbird hit my stuffed decoy turned into an unexpected experiment. While the kingbird pulled up from its dive and began to turn for its next pass, the decoy keeled over and came to hang tail up from its perch. The kingbird saw this position only when lining up for its next dive. Probably it found the sight unique in its experience. It then called "T-zee" and flew level on a course that would have taken it about 5 meters above the decoy and on to one of

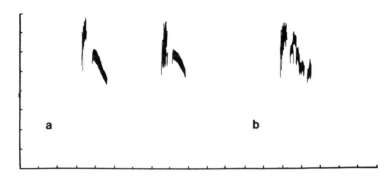

Fig. 16.2.   "T-zee" calls of *T. tyrannus,* traced from sonagrams made using a Kay 6061-B Sona-Graph with a bandwidth of 300 Hz. Abcissa: time, in tenths of seconds. Ordinate: frequency in kiloHertz. (a) The most common forms of this vocalization, the first uttered from perch while the bird looked at a stuffed predator set near its nest tree, and the second uttered in level flight as the bird passed above this decoy. (b) A quavered variant, uttered as the bird dove steeply toward the inverted decoy (see text) and, just before the end of the call, veered into level flight and passed above the decoy.

its perches. But as it drew near, it suddenly dove very steeply. Halfway through this dive it began a "T-zee." When the call was almost finished, the bird abruptly pulled out, flew past the decoy about a meter above it, and went on to a perch with further "T-zee" calls. The "T-zee" in the dive was quavered (Fig. 16.2b). None of the other calls was. (Note that most of the quavered "T-zee" was uttered before the kingbird began to pull out. Thus, the bird does not have to contort itself to produce a quaver; I have additional evidence that quavering is not a mechanical artifact.)

Among the diverse circumstances in which "T-zee" occurs is one in which a male sometimes utters it when following his mate on flights away from their nest. Typically he does not accompany her when she takes a break from incubating, but takes a perch overlooking the nest. Yet sometimes a male does follow his mate and forages with her. Once as I watched, a male left his perch, followed his mate, and began to utter "T-zee" calls as he flew past an adjacent tree where another limb provided a suitable guard perch. He suddenly turned approximately at right angles, flew to that perch, and called a few more times as she flew on; then he stayed and guarded. The "T-zee" uttered in that abrupt turn, but none of those before and after it, was quavered.

The events just discussed involve diverse behavior. Quavering of either of the two vocal signals provides no information about whether a kingbird will attack, withdraw, associate with a mate, or stay near a nest. The quavering *is* characteristic of a kingbird that, having been committed to one kind of behavior, is suddenly choosing another. Quavering seems, at this stage of the analyses, to provide information about the imminent likelihood of quitting some current activity.

Quavering is a means for adding information to two (and probably more) members of the eastern kingbird's basic signal repertoire. Further, quavering is widespread among species. It appears in the calls of many other species of tyrannid flycatchers during attacks on real and decoy predators. It also modifies vocalizations uttered by males approaching unreceptive mates (e.g., in the vermilion flycatcher, Smith, 1970a) or by neighbors in some phases of territorial encounters. Although much more common in flight than from perch, quavering can modify song-like performances of perched intruders in at least the black phoebe: the callers are immature birds who intrude yet consistently let themselves be driven out without fighting (Smith, 1970b). In all these vocalizations of different species, quavering seems to provide much the same information.

Quavered variants also occur in vocalizations of many other species of passerine and nonpasserine birds. I have examples of quavering, for instance, in calls uttered by young herring gulls as they veered from approaching a mob squabbling over food. And mammalian voices can quaver, although we need to determine if the phenomenon is truly comparable to that in birds. Caldwell and Caldwell (1977) and Norris (personal communication) mention quavered variants of dolphin whistling. (Could it be elicited experimentally? Perhaps dolphins offered food from a device that periodically does something frightening would become cautious. Then abrupt presentation of a novel stimulus might cause an approaching dolphin to veer. Would a quaver be superimposed on some sound? If so, it and the basic signal unit might both be rendered recognizable.) The term "quavered" also is used to describe human utterances, and I have begun to investigate the information it makes available. Even human quavering may provide at least roughly comparable information to that postulated for kingbirds and other flycatchers.

The point of this lengthy example is to show why form variations should be conceptualized as making up a kind of signaling repertoire distinct from that of signal acts. First, the procedure of quavering is applicable to more than one unit within a species' repertoire of signal acts, and it provides the same information wherever it is applied. Wide applicability need not characterize all other classes of form variation, but it does show that the classes can have a status independent of the acts they modify. Second, quavering variants are extremely widespread among species, again perhaps with little difference in the information they make available. This suggests that quavering behavior has a long evolutionary history, to a considerable extent independent of basic signal acts. If quavering has such a history, so too may other classes of variation.

There are many other classes of variation. Sounds can change in frequency, clarity and other tonal qualities, inflectional patterns (such as quavering), amplitude, duration, and in complexly patterned ways involving more than one of these. Other signaling, for example, visible or tactile, can be altered in many ways, including analogues to variations in sounds.

Because display units and procedures for varying their form are independent sources of information, they must be treated as separate repertoires of formalizations. Among other advantages, such treatment can resolve various issues that have troubled ethologists for some time. One such issue is how to recognize or define displays and determine their referents (see Beer, 1977, 1980 who asks: "what is a display?"). A second issue is how to deal with intergrading displays.

1. Displays and their referents. The referents of a display unit are determined by lumping all performances together, not distinguishing among the variants. This reveals what is common to all performances, that is, the information made available by the display unit itself (say, "zit" or "T-zee"). The procedure, of course, conceals what the variant forms contribute in particular instances; for example, it would indicate nothing about the contribution of quavering. The procedure is necessary in analyzing displays, but my use of it has confused some ethologists into believing that I assume variation in form provides no information. I have always maintained that consistent patterns of variation are informative (e.g., Smith, 1963, 1977: see especially pp. 177, 399–402, 408).

Beer argues that displays do not have fixed referents, that they make available different information in different events, particularly if combined differently with other displays. One of his examples is a compound display, the long call of the laughing gull. Although he does not interpret its referents, these appear to include interactional behavior: A long-calling laughing gull will, in appropriate conditions, interact variously with at least a mate, offspring, neighbor, or intruder. Beer describes two variants, one with the initial components louder than the next ones, the other with the initial components fainter. These must differ in the information they provide, because gull chicks respond differently in experiments playing back recorded examples. What Beer has discovered is part of the species' repertoire of procedures for varying its utterances—procedures that enable gull chicks to predict different interactional predispositions of a calling adult. Had he recognized that at least two repertoires of formalizations were in operation in any instance of uttering a long call, he would have had less trouble recognizing the long call as a unit. Variation in form no more negates the reality of signal units than it does of words (also signal units, of course, though very special ones). We regularly alter inflection, amplitude, frequency, and other characteristics as we use words for querying, emphasis, or with "emotional overtones," adding information to them while continuing to treat each word as a unit used in constructing phrases.

2. Intergrading of displays. Varying the forms of signals can lead them to intergrade, making it difficult to discriminate among display units. Nonarbitrary criteria with which researchers can delimit units are not always obvious (see Smith 1977, chapter 13). Part of the problem may be illusory, if researchers classify differently from the species employing these signals (who may bring categorical perception to bear). Even to the extent that it does occur, however, integradation in no way invalidates the display concept. It implies that rules for varying form may sometimes cause signal units to converge and that signalers may employ convergence when making available information characteristic of each of two signal units.

Where intergrading is abundant in a signal repertoire, some researchers have written as if display units do not exist. Morton (1977, 1982), for instance, considered intergrading of vocalizations used in close encounters as a facet of form variation. He suggested substituting what he calls a "motivational-structural code" for recognition of separate display units. He proposed that all sounds uttered in close encounters are produced by a motivational conflict of aggression and fear or, generalizing widely, approach and withdrawal. Low and harsh sounds he placed at the aggressive extreme of form, high and tonal at the fear or appeasement extreme, and chevron-shaped sounds (whose frequency rises then falls) he interpreted as being intermediate, revealing "interest" in a stimulus and indecision about what to do. His attempt to make sense of some widely occurring patterns of variation in sounds must be partly correct. Low or harsh sounds, at least, do appear correlated with attack behavior in many cases. Few cases have been studied intensively, however, and the proposed "code" may oversimplify considerably.

Nelson (1984, 1985), in one of the most carefully quantified analyses of continuously "graded" vocalizations, found mixed support for Morton's postulated dichotomy in vocalizations of pigeon guillemots. Attack correlated with their low-frequency variants, although withdrawal did not correlate significantly with higher-frequency calls. Withdrawal or local movements neither toward nor away from another participant in an interaction could be predicted from relatively short vocalizations (when not preceded by even briefer units), and both shorter and higher frequency sound were correlated with increased probability of local movements in each of four classes of vocalizations. The "motivational-structural" proposal rests on description that has been much less thoroughly analyzed than in Nelson's work and needs careful testing.

There are other problems with this proposal. For instance, approach, withdrawal, or interested, indecisive behavior can be seen in response to almost all stimuli that evoke signaling. Signaling aids in the prediction of such behavior, but it also often provides more precision, as well as information about kinds of activities that are missing from Morton's postulate (e.g., associating or other interacting, or choosing an incompatible alternative). Such information is made available not just by display units per se, but also by different categories of form variation. For instance, to interpret quavering simply in terms of approach, withdrawal, or indecisive interest is less accurate than the interpretation offered above (that there is imminent likelihood of quitting current behavior) and would miss the full value of the information made available by quavering. For another example, Green's study (1975) of the variable "coo" sounds of Japanese macaques reveals information about the extent of effort to be expended in interacting, the probability of responding to or soliciting interaction, and the probability of agitated or calm responses, in addition to prediction (common to all "coo" sounds) of indecisive behavior and a depressed probability of attacking. In an analysis of the information made available by graded visible signals (positions in which the tail is held) of *Cercopithecus aethiops* monkeys, Bernstein, Smith, Krensky, and Rosene (1978) found evidence for approach/withdrawal decisions but also could predict interactional behavior and alternatives.

Much of the information made available in any of these cases is common to all performances, whatever the momentary, variant form. It is not revealed by analyzing simply the significance of the differences among variants but comes from the display units themselves. That is, analysis of how variations in signal form affect the information being made available does not reveal all the information obtainable from any performance because it ignores what is contributed by signal units. Two repertoires of signaling specializations are contributing in any case in which signal form varies among repetitions.

REPERTOIRES OF PATTERNED COMBINATIONS OF SIGNAL UNITS

Signals are performed in combinations, simultaneously or in sequence with one another, as occasions demand. Some combinations, however, are specialized as units in their own right and are not simply concatenations fortuitously elicited by an event. As I have treated these issues in some detail elsewhere (Smith, 1977, pp. 405–25), the following account is brief.

Simultaneous combinations of signal units are common:vocalizations with visible signals, postures with movements, the whole array of features that makes up a human "facial expression." Those that are specialized as combinations, however, are difficult to distinguish from opportune concatenations. One procedure is to show that a combination makes available information that is not predictable from a knowledge only of the components. Dolphins can emit clicks and whistles simultaneously and perhaps combine some with postural or tactile signals. Whether any such combinations are formalized as such, that is, are assembled in accordance with rules for making combinations, is unknown.

Specialized combinations are more readily detectable in sequences. They appear as products of rules governing the intervals between signals and as grammars that make some orderings of signals occur and others not.

Black-tailed prairie dogs, for instance, regulate intervals between their bark vocalizations in accordance with simple rules (Smith et al., 1977). Intervals of equal duration provide the information that the signaler is sustaining the attentive behavior about which the barks themselves inform. Shortened intervals correlate with an increased probability of breaking off and withdrawing, and irregularly lengthened ones with an increased probability of interrupting vigilance with some other behavior (but not escape).

The effects of grammars can be evident when different signal acts are combined in sequences. Eastern phoebes, for instance, utter nonrandom sequences of two different vocal forms in sustained, rhythmic bouts of "singing" (Smith, 1969, 1977, chapter 3). Shifts in the relative proportions of the two units provide information about shifts in the probabilities of seeking to interact, especially in ways leading to contact, and of engaging in some sort of self-maintenance activity such as foraging or resting. Maintenance behavior, while incompatible with contact interaction, can be done while "associating" with another individual—and the singer does remain predisposed toward this sort of interaction.

More elaborate grammars of other species govern the sequencing of larger numbers of vocal units. Up to eight different song units are uttered in regular couplets and higher order combinations in the singing of yellow-throated vireos (Smith et al., 1978). These combinations provide even more detailed information about behavior. Various couplets and triplets occur only in correlation with particular classes of behavior, such as nest-centered activities and attempts to confront territorial opponents. Proportional representation of different song units shifts as singing correlates with different classes of activities, such as active or inactive attentiveness to the nest or nest region, patrolling without attempting to force confrontation, or moving widely about a territory while unmated. Other species of vireos have larger numbers of song units than *V. flavifrons* and may have more precisely predictive sequences or different kinds of sequencing rules (research in progress).

Dolphins sometimes produce sounds continuously for long intervals. The task is to discover if, when, and to what extent they structure formalized sequences of signal units. To determine whether they have a repertoire of grammatical rules that generates organized sequences will be difficult. It will be necessary to obtain extended and continuous recordings from known individuals in "stationary" conditions. That is, any patterns must not be caused by shifts in environmental events to which the dolphin is responding but rather must be imposed by the signaler itself while engaged in (what to it is) a single category of behavior. "Singing" behavior, often a matter of signaling to potential but distant recipients, provides our principal current examples of nonhuman grammars. Perhaps dolphins "sing," although not in the same ways known from phoebes or vireos—or from mysticetes. Can rhythms be detected in any of their sustained sound production? Suppose one dolphin was separated from others but allowed an acoustic link (as in an experiment by Lang and Smith, 1965). Might there be times, for example, after a long resting period or after a long interval in which one individual was deprived of sounds from the other tank, when one would "sing" in an attempt to establish contact with the others?

REPERTOIRES OF FORMALIZED INTERACTIONS

Some behavior patterns that are specialized to be informative cannot be performed by a single individual. A human handshake is a simple example. More elaborate formalized interactions appear as extended signaling routines typically

performed as participants greet, court, or jointly develop other carefully negoti-
ated events. These extended units have programs or frameworks that can include
many steps. Often their sequences are made flexible at points by optional or
conditionally available subroutines. They may incorporate many individual signaling acts, briefer formalized interactions, and nonformalized behavior.

The distinctive characteristic of all formalized interactions is that they are
mutually cooperative performances (Smith 1977, chapter 14, which gives many
examples from diverse species). Whether brief or having many steps, each
operates as a signal unit whose structure is produced by interacting individuals.
Each participant conforms to a more or less predictable "part" required by the
format of the unit. Each part provides its performer with what might loosely be
termed a role to play, specifying certain acts (or classes of acts) constructed in
cooperation with other participants to be performed in orderly sequences. Although there can be considerable flexibility, a participant becomes constrained
on assuming a part. It must perform only assigned kinds of acts and sequences
and must accommodate to the actions of other participants, regardless of how
much it may try to influence them to accommodate.

The cooperation required of participants enables performance of these signal
units to reduce the volatility of encounters. When extended formalized interactional frameworks govern the development of agonistic contests, for instance,
they tend to forestall uncontrolled fighting and reduce the frequency of disruption
by attack and fleeing when compared to events in which displays are performed
in the absence of a formal framework. Examples are common, from the chal-
lenges of wildebeest (Estes, 1969) to those of fighting fish (Simpson, 1968).

Various properties, in addition to mutual cooperation, typify formalized interactions. For instance, there are mutually synchronized actions by the participants, turn-taking, and mutual maintenance of spacing and such orientations as
aligning in parallel, antiparallel, or T-configurations. Extended formalized interactions have special procedures with which they are begun and, sometimes,
altered or terminated, as well as specified sets of choices at particular junctures.

A great many species of animals have formalized interactions, and probably
dolphins do too. The typical characteristics of such signaling could be sought by
watching and recording dolphins when formalized interactions are most likely to
occur, for instance when two are courting, or meet again after being held in
separate tanks.

CONTRIBUTIONS OF THE REPERTOIRES

Although this has been only an outline of the several kinds of repertoires, and we
are only beginning to learn their properties, it is already apparent that each
repertoire makes distinctive contributions to communicating, among which are
the following:

1. The signal acts (or "displays" in the sense of Smith, 1977, chapter 13) provide a limited number of information-carrying vehicles. These units have a number of important referents, apparently always including aspects of the identity of a signaler and some of the behavior it is performing or may perform.

2. The classes of form variation do two things. They alter the information already being made available, for instance, by giving more precision to the probabilities with which different kinds of behavior can be predicted or to the intensity of performance to be expected. In addition, some of them add to the kinds of information that a signal unit makes available; quavering, for example, adds information about behavior. Variations are implicated in recent demonstrations of the provision of information about environmental stimuli. For instance, the chatter vocalization unit of California ground squirrels does not distinguish between predators and conspecific opponents, but variant forms of it do, even distinguishing among some classes of predators (Owings & Leger, 1980).

Each species probably has only a limited number of classes of variations in its repertoire, just as it has a limited display repertoire. Nonetheless, within each class, variation in form is usually continuous and may permit a great many distinctions.

3. Combinations of signals provide signalers with some control over the sources of information available contextually to each component unit. Since responses to all signaling are context dependent, this is a potentially powerful procedure (and it is one that we depend on in speech). One special use of patterned combinations in the singing behavior of some bird species is to make evident the relative proportions of different signal units in segments of long continued sequences. These proportions appear to be important to interpretation of this singing.

The number of rules available to any species for formalizing combinations surely is limited. Nonetheless, the number of patterns, especially of sequences, that can be generated is sometimes very large. To generate even larger numbers of sequences the component units may have to be differentiable into functional categories that permit the sorts of interactive effects we get from nouns and verbs in human speech. No such differentiation is apparent yet in the natural signaling of other species.

4. Formalized interactions are basic vehicles for information in much the same ways as are individually performed "display" acts: They provide special units whose forms can be varied and combined. In addition, the more extensive formalized frameworks can even incorporate prolonged patterns of simultaneous and sequential combinations of briefer acts and thus are procedures for elaborately organizing signaling.

Formalized interactions appear to be performed in events that occur at or include times of change or involve potentially disruptive disparity in the contributions of their participants. Unless rendered orderly and predictable, these events can become not only functionless but also costly and sometimes even hazardous. Formalized interactions "bracket" (Goffman 1974) such events, setting them apart. The more extensive examples provide formats, with properties and bounds expected and accepted by each participant. They permit control to be shared as order is imposed and facilitate negotiation of disparities and the pace and direction of development toward some mutually acceptable state.

By adhering to the preestablished constraints of formalized interactions, participants reveal both their readiness to interact cooperatively and the way they will proceed. They specify and limit the extent and kinds of social access each will grant the others and the nature of accommodation. They thus enable individuals to join one another, to elicit information about each other's predispositions and expectations, to manage events that would otherwise be excessively unpredictable, and to begin new relationships or reaffirm, test, or alter existing ones. And all this can be done during performance of the extended signal units.

CONCLUSIONS

Although each of the repertoires appears to be limited in scope, the kinds of limitations differ among them. Their combined operation can yield rich communication. And, in any signaling performance, items from at least two and at times all of the different repertoires *are* brought to bear.

We cannot comprehend or analyze complex signaling without distinguishing the contributions made by each repertoire. This is something I previously have not emphasized sufficiently. In earlier writing I described some of the diversification of signaling specializations as comprising "repertoires of display units and of grammatical rules" (Smith, 1977, p. 423) and suggested that it was necessary to study the contributions of rules for the production of display units, variants of them, combinations, and formalized interactions, which yield "different classes of formalized information sources" (p. 464). Nonetheless, I developed a distinction among repertoires consistently only for the first and last presented in this chapter. Variation and combination were discussed in part as procedures that can make it difficult for ethologists to discern units of the basic repertoire of display acts. Although the importance of both as classes of formalized sources of information was stated (e.g., pp. 404, 408, 411, 423), the value of setting them forth as distinctive repertoires was not seen clearly. Yet it is just the recognition of such distinctions that may offer great promise as a conceptual framework for coming to grips with the enormous elaboration of dolphin communication.

By breaking down dolphin signaling into component units characteristic of the different kinds of repertoires, we can reduce the complexity that is now all but baffling. We could then distinguish the various units of each repertoire, what each repertoire contributes to dolphin signaling in different kinds of events, and how the characteristics of repertoires most used by dolphins influence the kinds of information in which they traffic.

How can we distinguish units from the various repertoires in the signaling of dolphins? It is very difficult to make naturalistic observations of these social, highly mobile marine creatures. But we now have some knowledge of widespread characteristics of the repertoires as they appear in communication of species more accessible to naturalistic observation. As a first step in assessing dolphin communication, it may be appropriate to use this knowledge in devising test situations (such as the few suggested above) designed to detect particular kinds of units: for example, quavered variants, formalized greeting interactions, rhythmical ''singing'' sequences. The results will not permit full interpretation of any single unit but could provide considerable guidance in subsequent studies of signaling.

REFERENCES

Beer, C. G. (1977). What is a display? *American Zoologist, 17,* 155–165.

Beer, C. G. (1980). The communication behavior of gulls and other seabirds. In J. Burger, B. L. Olla, & H. E. Winn (Eds.), *Behavior of marine animals, 4: Marine birds* (pp. 169–205). New York: Plenum.

Bernstein, P. L., Smith, W. J., Krensky, A., & Rosene, K. (1978). Tail positions of *Cercopithecus aethiops. Zeitschrift für Tierpsychologie, 46,* 268–278.

Caldwell, D. K., & Caldwell, M. C. (1977). Cetaceans. In T. A. Sebeok (Ed.), *How animals communicate* (pp. 794–808). Bloomington: Indiana University Press.

Dittus, W. P. (1984). Toque macaque food calls: Semantic communication concerning food distribution in the environment. *Animal Behaviour, 32,* 470–477.

Estes, R. D. (1969). Territorial behavior of the wildebeest (*Connochaetes taurinus* Burchell, 1823). *Zeitschrift für Tierpsychologie, 26,* 284–370.

Goffman, E. (1974). *Frame analysis.* New York: Harper & Row.

Gouzoules, S., Gouzoules, H., & Marler, P. (1984). Rhesus monkey (*Macaca mulatta*) screams: Representational signalling in the recruitment of agonistic aid. *Animal Behaviour, 32,* 182–193.

Green, S. (1975). Communication by a graded system in Japanese monkeys. In L. Rosenblum (Ed.), *Primate behavior: Developments in field and laboratory research, 4* (pp. 1–102). New York: Academic Press.

Lang, T. G., & Smith, H. A. P. (1965). Communication between dolphins in separate tanks by way of an electronic acoustic link. *Science, 150,* 1839–1844.

Morton, E. S. (1977). On the occurrence and significance of motivational-structural rules in some bird and mammal sounds. *American Naturalist, 111,* 855–869.

Morton, E. S. (1982). Grading, discreteness, redundancy, and motivation-structural rules. In D. E. Kroodsma & E. H. Miller (Eds.), *Acoustic communication in birds, 1. Production, perception, and design features of sounds.* (pp. 183–212). New York: Academic Press.

Moynihan, M. (1970). The control, suppression, decay, disappearance and replacement of displays. *Journal of Theoretical Biology, 29,* 85–112.

Nelson, D. A. (1984). Communication of intention in agonistic contexts by the pigeon guillemot, *Cepphus columba. Behaviour, 88,* 145–189.

Nelson, D. A. (1985). The syntactic and semantic organization of pigeon guillemot (*Cepphus columba*) vocal behavior. *Zeitschrift für Tierpsychologie, 67,* 97–130.

Owings, D. H., & Leger, D. W. (1980). Chatter vocalizations of California ground squirrels: Predator- and social-role specificity. *Zeitschrift für Tierpsychologie, 54,* 163–184.

Seyfarth, R. M., Cheney, D. L., & Marler, P. (1980). Vervet monkey alarm calls: Semantic communication in a free-ranging primate. *Animal Behaviour, 28,* 1070–1094.

Simpson, M. J. A. (1968). The display of the Siamese fighting fish, *Betta splendens*. *Animal Behaviour Monographs, 1,* 1–73.

Smith, W. John (1963). Vocal communication of information in birds. *American Naturalist, 97,* 117–125.

Smith, W. John. (1969). Messages of vertebrate communication. *Science, 165,* 145–150.

Smith, W. John. (1970a). Courtship and territorial displaying in the vermilion flycatcher, *Pyrocephalus rubinus. Condor, 72,* 488–491.

Smith, W. John. (1970b). Song-like displays in the genus *Sayornis. Behaviour, 37,* 64–84.

Smith, W. John. (1977). *The behavior of communicating. An ethological approach.* Cambridge, MA: Harvard University Press.

Smith, W. John. (1981). Referents of animal communication. *Animal Behaviour, 29,* 1273–1275.

Smith, W. John, Smith, S. L., Oppenheimer, E. C., & deVilla, J. G. (1977). Vocalizations of the black-tailed prairie dog, *Cynomys ludovicianus. Animal Behaviour, 25,* 152–164.

Smith, W. John, Pawlukiewicz, J., & Smith, S. T. (1978). Kinds of activities correlated with singing patterns of the yellow-throated vireo. *Animal Behaviour 26,* 862–884.

IV SOCIAL BEHAVIOR AND FORAGING STRATEGIES OF DOLPHINS

Forrest G. Wood

Less than 50 years ago virtually nothing was known about the social and feeding behaviors of dolphins. Their underwater activities were effectively hidden from view, and since scientists had little comprehension of the behavioral attributes and propensities of these small toothed whales there was neither incentive nor guidance for undertaking field studies that could have been made.

This situation changed rapidly when the first oceanarium, Marine Studios (later renamed Marineland of Florida), opened in 1938. Here, for the first time, scientists, along with the public, could observe bottlenose dolphins at close range and for extended periods from below as well as above the surface. The dolphins proved to be engaging creatures, adaptible, seemingly bright, curious, and playful. Their individual behaviors and social interactions suggested a higher order of mental caliber than had previously been suspected.

The success of Marine Studios led to the appearance of other oceanariums in the 1950s, to the benefit of the increasing number of biologists and psychologists who, on gaining first-hand acquaintance with dolphins, found them to be engrossing subjects for study. Knowledge gained from oceanarium observations has provided the foundation, interest, and incentive for studying free-ranging dolphins.

We now know more about *Tursiops,* the adaptible bottlenose, than we do about any other species, and the most detailed information about its behavior has come from captive specimens. However, as Johnson and Norris note in the following chapter, the validity of behavioral observations on captive dolphins has been questioned on the grounds that the captive situation may distort natural patterns. The oceanarium environment is seen as relatively sterile, and a captive colony may represent an unnatural grouping. Also, obviously, there are the constraints imposed by confinement—the inability to roam freely and interact with others of their kind.

These are, of course, well-founded concerns. However, the competent student of dolphin behavior will take into consideration the quality of the captive environment. Does it provide some simulation of natural conditions, such as rock formations and the presence of other forms of sea life? Is the dolphin colony relatively stable and do births occur regularly? Does the behavior of the animals appear unstressed and natural, as opposed to stereotyped and with indications of boredom?

Given optimal conditions, achievable at least with inshore dolphins such as the bottlenose, and with recognition of the constraints imposed by confinement, the behaviors of captive animals can furnish valuable information and insights, which can also be useful in interpreting observations of free-living animals made under much more difficult circumstances.

Nevertheless, there are two important features of captivity that are inherently and unavoidably unnatural. One of these, noted above, is confinement itself; we can learn nothing from captive animals about normal movement patterns, changes that may occur in group composition, and interactions between groups. The other is the lack of need—indeed the inability—to search for and capture prey. The elimination of this component of natural activity patterns must constitute a vacuum which, if not compensated for, may result in boredom and abnormal behavior. Feeding shows may provide diversion along with food but almost certainly are an inadequate substitute for natural foraging. The dolphins themselves, however, may have shown us their solution to the problem. It is not unreasonable to suppose that the many forms of play that have been observed, and the frequency with which such behavior occurs, can be attributed in large measure to the need to fill this vacuum.

For those who are interested in the cognitive capacities of dolpins, the games captive bottlenose dolphins have invented provide insights that could never be gained from attempts to observe them in their natural, usually turbid, environment. Because a scheduled chapter on dolphin play is unfortunately missing in this volume, it may not be out of place to cite here a few illustrative examples taken from my observations at the Florida Marineland.

Small innertubes were the most popular playthings. One dolphin was often seen tossing a tube in the air, obviously trying to make a ringer on her snout. Another would repeatedly toss an innertube onto the end of the narrow feeding platform extending over the water, persisting until the tube remained on the platform. The dolphins invented a game of catch with spectators (interspecies social activity, if you will); sometimes the person to whom the ring was tossed (usually the same individual among a number of people) was slow to learn that the innertube was to be returned to the dolphin's upraised snout instead of just thrown back randomly. Jets of water emerged at an angle from the floor of the tank; a dolphin would sometimes carry down a cast-off feather from one of the resident pelicans, release it into the jet, and go chasing after it. On one notable occasion I saw two young animals play this game cooperatively: one would release the feather for the other to chase, and the latter would then reciprocate.

The challenging games that captive dolphins invent, despite—even, in fact, enhanced by—their artifactual elements, certainly have cognitive significance. Observations of social relationships and interactions can also be revealing in this respect even when they present a somewhat altered and incomplete picture. However, only from field studies—difficult, demanding, and with their own inherent limitations—can we gain knowledge of the actions and activities of dolphins in the broad expanses of their natural environment.

In this section, Christine Johnson and Kenneth Norris provide a comprehensive review of what has been learned about social behaviors in free-ranging dolphins. Of particular interest is their account of the spinner dolphins that frequent a bay in Hawaii during daylight hours but depart in the evening to forage in offshore deep waters. Spinners are usually considered oceanic animals. The accessibility of this herd during the day has permitted the most extensive and detailed behavioral observations on a pelagic species yet made.

In the second paper, Bernd Würsig reviews what is known about the diverse foraging strategies of dolphins. The most striking feature of their food-finding activities is its cooperative nature, and the most detailed description of cooperative foraging has come from field studies of the dusky dolphin conducted by Bernd and Melany Würsig. Despite the distinction made in the title of this section it would appear that in at least some species foraging behavior can be subsumed under social behavior.

In the last paper, Jack Bradbury considers the economics of social systems, reciprocity exchanges, and evidence of altruism in odontocete cetaceans in comparison to the more easily studied terrestrial mammals and birds. He questions the commonly held assumption that delphinids have complex social structures based on cooperation but leaves open the possibility that dolphins are capable of much more sophisticated interactions than rigid reductionists may be willing to give them credit for.

Thus we progress.

17 Delphinid Social Organization and Social Behavior

Christine M. Johnson
Kenneth S. Norris
Center for Marine Studies, University of California, Santa Cruz

INTRODUCTION

Although there are over twenty genera of dolphins and porpoises in the rivers, lakes and oceans of the world, only about half a dozen of these have been the object of detailed study. Most of the schools whose behavior has been documented frequent coastal waters where they can be watched from shore, or reliably found by boat or plane. Riverine species often live in virtually opaque waters and rarely perform the aerial behavior patterns that help researchers locate their marine counterparts. The difficulty, in turn, of locating and accompanying open-ocean species has limited our knowledge of these animals to serendipitous sightings, extrapolations from related species found, for instance, off the coasts of islands, and from captive observations. In fact, the most detailed accounts of dolphin social organization and behavior involve animals held in captivity. Many researchers believe, however, that the captive situation may distort the natural patterns, and caution must be used in interpreting such evidence.

The logistics of studying these fleet, elusive creatures in their natural habitats are complicated and demanding. Observations have been made from aircraft, boats, and clifftops, the last often involving the use of surveyors' transits to track the animals' movements (e.g., Norris & Dohl, 1980a; Saayman & Tayler, 1979; Würsig & Würsig, 1979a). Identifying individuals often requires long hours of scrutinizing photographs for subtle scars and marks (e.g., Shane, 1977; Würsig & Würsig, 1977). Reliably determining the age and sex of wild dolphins may require the actual capture of the animals involved (e.g., Irvine, Scott, Wells, & Kaufamn, 1981; Perrin, 1975; Sergeant & Brodie, 1969). Killer whales (*Orcinus orca*) with their distinctive, ideosyncratic coloring and marked sexual dimorphism are a welcome exception; but, even here, positive identification may come only with an after-the-fact examination of photographs (e.g., Balcomb & Goebel, 1976). Boats with underwater-viewing capacity have occasionally been used to observe school structure and social interaction (e.g., Norris et al., 1982) and some underwater films and photos have been taken (e.g., Würsig & Würsig, 1979b). In addition, radio-tracking, with transmitters attached to the dolphins' fins, has provided some valuable data on group movement and dive times, especially offshore and at night (e.g., Evans, 1974; Irvine et al., 1981; Leatherwood & Evans, 1979). As a result of such efforts, along with captive observations, we have begun to piece together an understanding of the varieties of dolphin social organization and of the behavior patterns that maintain them.

SOCIAL ORGANIZATION

The most comprehensive studies of free-ranging dolphins have focused on accessible coastal populations. These include schools of Hawaiian spinner dolphins (*Stenella longirostris*) (Norris & Dohl, 1980a; Norris et al., 1982), dusky dolphins (*Lagenorhynchus obscurus*) off Argentina (Würsig & Würsig, 1980), humpback dolphins (*Sousa* sp.) (Saayman & Tayler, 1979), Indian Ocean bottlenose dolphins (*Tursiops aduncus*) off South Africa (Saayman & Tayler, 1973), Atlantic bottlenose dolphins (*Tursiops truncatus*) in Florida (Irvine et al., 1981), Texas (Shane, 1977) and Argentine waters (Würsig, 1978; Würsig & Würsig, 1979a), and killer whales (*Orcinus orca*) off the coast of Washington and western Canada (Balcomb, Boran, Osborne, & Haenel, 1980; Bigg, 1982; Bigg, McAskie, & Ellis, 1976). For an excellent review, see "The Social Ecology of Inshore Odontocetes" by Wells, Irvine, and Scott (1980).

One observation common to many of these accounts is a variability in association patterns. A school of fifty dolphins observed on a given day will often be a subset of a local population that may include hundreds of animals. In most species studied, school composition tends to vary somewhat from day to day and, except for mother-calf pairs, subgroups of even a few animals that are stable over extended periods of time are only rarely reported (although see Wells et al., 1980; Würsig & Wüsig, 1977). However, associations between individuals are often repeated—with some occurring more often than others—resulting in a complex pattern of rotation of the animals within a population. Of the well-studied species, only the killer whales of the Northwest maintain fixed groups, called pods, composed of multiple male, female, and young animals. These pods mingle frequently with other pods but consistently segregate back into what may be "extended family" units (Balcomb et al., 1980; Bigg et al., 1976).

In the broad overview of species, certain socioecological trends emerge. The mean water depth associated with a species, for instance, tends to be correlated with group size (see Norris & Dohl, 1980b). Only in some riverine and inshore species are dolphins regularly seen alone; most river-dwellers form groups of two to thirty animals. Inshore species are usually found in groups of less than fifty, although much larger aggregations are also seen. Pelagic dolphins tend to form the largest groups, involving hundreds or even thousands of animals. Body size is also a factor, however, with the larger species in a given habitat tending to form somewhat smaller groups. These correlations are probably a function both of feeding strategies (see Würsig, this volume) and of the risk of predation by sharks or killer whales. In shallow waters, large predators may be less likely to be found (although see Wood, Caldwell, & Caldwell, 1970) and the water volume requiring surveilliance is decreased. The typical response to a threat is the tight bunching of the dolphin school, and the more animals involved the greater the protection provided.

Security-dependent variability in dolphin school structure was observed in a study of spinner dolphins (*Stenella longirostris*) in Kealakekua Bay, Hawaii (Norris et al., 1982). Under normal conditions, in the protective environs of the bay, young animals were observed in a variety of social settings. Presumed mothers with calves could be seen in the midst of adult groups or in groups with other adult-young pairs. Alternatively, nurseries composed entirely of juveniles and calves, roughly surrounded by a loose-knit sphere of adults, were sometimes seen. In addition, isolated adult-young pairs were frequently seen well apart from the rest of the school, as when the majority of animals was resting but a particular youngster was intent on "practicing" its noisy leaps. However, at the first sign of a threat—for instance, at the appearance of speedboats or overzealous researchers—the classic defensive arrangement of mother-young pairs centrally located in a tight-knit, evasive school was quickly assumed.

This bunching response is seen regularly among startled dolphins in captivity, among those entrapped in fishing nets at sea (Norris, Stuntz, & Rogers, 1978; Pryor & Kang, 1980), and in other situations of surprise or danger in the wild. It is one illustration of the essential *communality* of these animals (cf. Jerison, this volume). It could be said that when the dolphins are most vulnerable—such as during rest when individual alertness is decreased, or during actual harassment—communality transcends individuality and the group responds as a unit. In this regard a dolphin school is very like a school of fish or, among terrestrials, a herd of ungulates. The absence of protective cover in the open ocean combined with the dolphin's lack of natural armor and limited weaponry make a reliance on integrated group response imperative in these animals.

Because of the difficulty in identifying the age, sex, and degree of relatedness of wild dolphins, the subtleties of social structure for most species are still unclear. In an exceptional study of bottlenose dolphins (*Tursiops truncatus*) off Florida's western shore, the capture and tagging of most of the resident population has provided a rare glimpse of social organization in this population (Irvine et al., 1981; Wells et al., 1980). Segregated subgroups of subadult males, small "bands" of adult males, females without young, and mother-young "nursery groups'' have been reported. Although intermingling both within and between these groups has been observed, somewhat overlapping ''home ranges'' were found to be monopolized by each of the groups. Most dolphin species studied do not seem to show this pronounced segregation and differential habitat use (although see Shane, Wells, Würsig, & Odell, 1982). However, it may well be that within what appear to be heterogeneous, free-mixing schools, spatial segregation or other dominance-related ordering does occur (e.g., Leatherwood, 1977; Norris & Dohl, 1980b).

When animals are placed in captivity, such subgroup segregation and/or differential positioning seem to translate into hierarchies that may govern feeding, mating, and threat behavior. (For discussion, see ''The Structure and Function of Cetacean Schools'' by Norris & Dohl, 1980b.) In most studies of captive bottlenose dolphins (e.g., Brown & Norris, 1956; Caldwell & Caldwell, 1967, 1972; McBridge & Hebb, 1948; Saayman & Tayler, 1973) male-dominated hierarchies have been reported. (For review, see Shane et al., 1982.) In such a system, the ''alpha'' male generally shows a seasonal priority of access to females and an active hostility towards, especially, subadult males. The aggression so often reported in adult male *Tursiops* towards infants in captivity (e.g., Caldwell & Caldwell, 1972; Essapian, 1953, 1963; McBridge & Hebb, 1948; Tavolga & Essapian, 1957) may reflect a tendency on the part of such adults to herd the young when threatened in the wild (e.g., Norris, Stuntz, & Rogers, 1978). This tendency may be transformed into obsessive hostility in captivity where the young can neither escape nor be buffered from the male by a tightly packed crowd of adults.

Several researchers (e.g., Bel'kovich et al., 1969; Caldwell & Caldwell, 1972; Tavolga, 1966; Tavolga & Essapian, 1957; Tayler & Saayman, 1972) report that the alpha *female* in a tank will often ''set the tone'' of the group's response to, for instance, a new object in the water; either by herding the others away or by being the first to investigate the novelty. Also, unlike the more often solitary alpha male, the high-ranking female *Tursiops* is rarely at a loss for companionship—although an aggressive male may dictate, at times, who is allowed to accompany her. It may be that both the males and females of this species play active roles in determining social structure in captivity because each of the sexes establishes its own social order in its respective group in the wild. In the free-living *Tursiops* studied in Florida, groups of females with young, some of whom maintain associations over years, may have little or no contact for months with the roving bands of adult males (R. S. Wells, personal communication, September, 1983). Also, the observation that these nursery groups occupy the ''optimal ranges'' and show the ''greatest degree of site-fidelity over time'' (Irvine et al., 1981), suggests that, in some sense, the dolphin society revolves around such groups. This corresponds with the common observation in captivity of the oldest, parturient female being ''more or less a focal point on which the social activity of the tank is centered'' (Tavolga, 1966).

One salient feature of most accounts of group behavior in captive dolphins is the *flexibility* reported in their social organization. That is, a simple "pecking order" does not suffice to predict all interactions. In a mixed school of captive spinner (*Stenella longirostris*) and spotter dolphins (*S. attenuata*), for example, researchers observed a dominance hierarchy based on threat behavior (Bateson, 1965). Under that system, 14 of 16 copulations seen were performed by the alpha male. However, the occurrence of other social interactions—including the reciprocation of sexual stimulation and even the initiation of chases—did not adhere to the threat-based dominance order. Participation in such activities by dolphins of widely varying social status indicates that although a dominance hierarchy exists it can, at times, be modified to favor more symmetrical relations.

SOCIAL BEHAVIOR

Dolphin gestures of aggression—seen more often in captivity than in the wild—can include the display of the teeth and the snapping of jaws, the sharp jerk of the head and/or tail, the extreme undulatory movement of the "S Posture" (Norris, 1967), as well as actual biting, swatting and ramming (e.g., Andersen & Dziedzic, 1964; Brown, 1960; Caldwell & Caldwell, 1972; McBride & Hebb, 1948; Tavolga, 1966). These exaggerated movements, which often increase the animal's *apparent* size, are blatant and intimidating signals. Most of the dolphin's gestural repertoire, however, is more subtle and ambiguous. These gestures include tilting and inverting the body, turning or "pointing" the head, and rotating and extending the flippers. Other social signals involve synchronizing tailbeats and surfacings with other animals, altering body position relative to others, and making tactile (and possibly tacto-acoustic) contact. In addition, dolphins will often release bubbles from their blowholes during social interactions and perform a variety of noisy body, head, and tail slaps on the surface of the water, which also produce underwater bubble fields.

Although many of the abovementioned behavior patterns are featured in courtship, most researchers agree that the dolphin's repertoire should be considered a set of social, as opposed to primarily sexual, signals. (For discussion, see Bateson, 1966; Bel'kovich et al., 1969; Norris & Dohl, 1980b; Saayman & Tayler, 1973). These signals can be used by animals of all sizes and sexes in a variety of social situations. The dolphin's streamlined form limits the number of possible gestures—as compared to terrestrial animals with their more flexible features and limbs—and, consequently, these few signals must serve a variety of purposes. A "belly tilt" (Norris et al., 1982), for example, where a dolphin rotates roughly 90° along its longitudinal axis, can be used as a greeting, as a precursor to mating, or as a final kinesic display when animals part. The proper interpretation, therefore, of many dolphin gestures is highly context dependent.

In addition to interanimal signaling, the geometrical arrangement of animals in their three-dimensional world is also an important factor in school integration (see Norris & Dohl, 1980b). Dolphins in a group are often staggered both horizontally and vertically. This may, in part, be related to hydrodynamic considerations (see Breder, 1976). Such a configuration also affords the animals a largely unobstructed view, in clear water, of the surrounding area while allowing them to maintain close proximity to one another. We have called this a "sensory window."

Observations of a group of captive spinner dolphins offered support for the notion that vision is an important factor in the arrangement of animals in the water (Norris et al., 1982). One of the captive dolphins, a male named Lioele, had broken his back upon hitting the concrete after performing a spin. As a result, his spine was permanently bent and, when he swam, the front half of his body was always tipped slightly to the right. It was interesting to note that his partners did not assume the normal below-beside position relative to his bulk in the water. The animal on his left was usually a little higher than normal and the one on the right a little lower. In this way, the partners achieved the "normal" position relative to his fields of vision. They may have been cued to this by the line of countershading where the middle grey area along the animal's flank meets the white of its belly. (For discussions of visual cuing, see Madsen & Herman, 1980; Mitchell, 1970; Norris & Dohl, 1980b.)

Depending on activity, level of arousal and prevailing environmental conditions, dolphin schools can assume a wide variety of configurations. The spinners in Hawaii, for instance, rest in bays in slow-moving, cohesive, roughly planar formations of up to about seventy animals. During active socializing, these same animals form several small, fluctuating subgroups scattered throughout the water-column and spread, at times, over scores of meters in the bay. A startled school will bunch together tightly, while members of an undisturbed school may spread over several kilometers of ocean offshore in search of food. High-speed traveling in many species has been observed with the animals rank-abreast in one or several rows (e.g., Shane, 1977; Tayler & Saayman, 1972; Würsig & Würsig, 1980) while dusky dolphins off the coast of Argentina have been reported passing in single file through shallow waters in an apparent attempt to avoid detection by nearby predators (Würsig & Würsig, 1980). In all of these situations, some sort of sensory contact is maintained in order that the animals may be quickly rallied for cohesive movement for feeding or defense.

The sense of hearing is of major importance to dolphins, especially when they are out of sight of one another, and the extended school is in large part an acoustic phenomenon. Vocalizations related to communication and/or echolocation tend to accompany most school activities. Many aerial behavior patterns involve distinctive splashes which are loud and more-or-less omnidirectional and probably convey information on the location and activity level of the animals involved (see, especially, Würsig & Würsig, 1980).

Listening to animals in captivity, it has long seemed obvious to us that dolphins poke and caress one another with sound and that some of the louder emissions can be extremely threatening. The highest energy in most dolphin vocalizations emanates forward in a beam from the animal's forehead (Au, Floyd, & Haun, 1978; Norris & Evans, 1967) and this may be a factor in the social rules governing the arrangement of animals in the water. A perpendicular approach, for instance, is an overtly interactive and potentially threatening one. In most cases, it is probably more "polite" to maintain a basically parallel orientation. In a frame-by-frame analysis of the films of wild spinners, we found that group turns were often initiated by a rear animal incling its head slightly in the direction of the turn just moments before the rest of the animals responded. Whether this was solely a visual cue or was accompanied by a sweeping beam of sound, we cannot say; the potential for the latter, however, is certainly there.

We also learned from the films that no one particular animal or position in a group was always the source of the cue to initiate a turn. That is, different animals in the same group, and not always those in the rear, could alternate directing the movements of that group. We also noted that not all such attempts to turn the group were successful but that even the younger animals could on occasion determine the direction of travel. This is reminiscent of the situation in a chimpanzee troop where low-ranking and even juvenile animals can initiate troop movement (Van Lawick-Goodall, 1971). It is also the case in fish schools in which turns may be generated from any position in the school (Breder, 1976). Perhaps the appropriateness of these two models depends on the level of integration in the dolphin school. That is, when the dolphins are socializing and interanimal relationships determine the group's activity, the chimp model is the more apropos. Alternatively, when coherent, overall school movement is involved, a fish school is, instead, the apt analogy.

"Turn initiator" is only one of the roles that are alternated among socializing wild spinners. In an active pair or trio, the role of belly-up animal can be assumed by any of the animals towards any other and can change repeatedly in the course of a single sighting. Once we even observed a trio of animals pressing their bellies together simultaneously. Subgroups of four to eight animals were also commonly observed in which the role of initiator in posturings and contacts was continually traded among the animals involved. Especially while watching the more active of these subgroups, observors shared the impression that the fluid and transient pairings were rather indiscriminate and that the basic unit of this activity was the group, not the individual. This reached an extreme in the formations we called "caressing groups," which involved as many as twelve animals in contact, rapidly interweaving and rolling together in the water. This rotation of roles has also been seen by us among captive spinners. The symmetrical relations implicit in such group-centered activity and role reversibility again indicate a communality and flexibility in these dolpins' social system.

THE SYMMETRY OF RELATIONS

One important situation in which symmetrical relations can be promoted is cooperative hunting. Cooperative hunting alone does not necessarily deemphasize social rank. On the contrary, terrestrial hunters that cooperate to take their prey often maintain rigid hierarchies which are reflected, for instance, in eating priorities at the kill. (For review, see Eisenberg, 1982.) However, such animals exist, for the most part, at the top of their respective food chains, whereas many dolphin species are subject to the threat of predation. Thus, communal feeding in these animals may require, in addition to the actual hunting and herding of prey, that at least some individuals continually monitor the activity of predators which could threaten the otherwise-occupied hunting and feeding adults.

Supervision of the young during cooperative hunting may likewise require a contingent of animals—for instance, mothers and/or "aunts"—that are not directly involved in the herding of the prey. Among dusky dolphins (*Lagenorhynchus obscurus*) nursery groups of several adult-young pairs have been observed, at times, to segregate from larger feeding aggregations, possibly to avoid competition with conspecifics or exposure to predators attracted to the scene (Würsig & Würsig, 1980; Würsig, this volume). However, it may also be that the animals involved in such supervisory activities could *vary,* allowing them to take turns feeding with the larger group. Observations of "babysitting" among the spinner dolphins (Norris et al., 1982)—by possibly related subadults, by another mother with a calf, and even by adult males—support this possibility.

If specific roles such as hunter, guard, or scout (e.g., Evans & Dreher, 1962) do, indeed, exist in cooperating dolphin schools, the question of whether these roles are rotated among the animals, assigned by sex, age, or social rank, or handled by some combination of such strategies, is still an open one. However, it is not unreasonable to suggest that the coordination of such activities would promote a sharing of both resources and responsibilities.

Connor and Norris (1982), in their paper on the question of reciprocal altruism in dolphins, suggest that "the dolphin school and all its changing geometry becomes a system devoted to ordering reciprocity for its members." Reciprocal altruism, as defined by Trivers (1971) and others (e.g., Hamilton, 1972; Williams, 1966), is the sociobiological model for a system in which an individual performs an altruistic act for another, nonrelated individual. Such an "altruistic act" is one that engenders a cost to the altruist. The compensating benefit for this act is delayed, and contingent upon the cooperation of others. Thus, such a system requires that the animals involved have frequent and recurrent interactions to provide them with opportunities to demonstrate altruism, to be reciprocated, and to identify "cheaters": those members who do not reciprocate. The system also requires that its members be fairly long-lived, experience a relatively extensive period of development in which they may learn appropriate responses in a variety of social contexts, and have memories adequate to the task of keeping track of other individuals and the status of their relationships. Dolphins apparently meet all of these requirements.

Participation in such a system also implies a cognizance of the effects of one's own actions on others and a high level of *empathy* that fosters reciprocation. This model may account for the occurrence of epimeletic—or care-giving—behavior in these animals. (For review, see Caldwell & Caldwell, 1966.) Dolphins have long been known to offer one another assistance, in the forms, for instance, of helping to raise a faltering animal up to the surface to breathe, of "standing by" when a schoolmate is captured, or of actively intervening to rescue or defend a threatened member of the group. Such behavior patterns have even been reported between members of different dolphin species (e.g., Brown & Norris, 1956; Caldwell, Brown, & Caldwell, 1963; Norris & Prescott, 1961).

The dependence, then, on cooperative feeding, the requirement of cohesive schools and consequent utility of symmetrical relations, and the occurence of assistance behavior, all support the reciprocal altruism model as an apt one for a principal force in structuring dolphin society. The challenge to us as researchers is to quantify the cost/benefit ratio involved—in terms of energy expenditures, changes in foraging efficiency or risk of predation, etc.—to determine if altruism, in the formal, theoretical sense, does indeed occur.

CONCLUSION

In summary, the key terms in a description of delphinid social organization and behavior are communality and flexibility. These qualities are evident in the animals' use of context-dependent signals, the alternation of social roles, the ability to respond differentially to a variety of individuals and, depending on the circumstances, to shift between hierarchical and symmetrical social interactions. In "The Social Function of Intellect," Humphrey (1976) suggests that the evolution of intelligence is adaptive in animals with complex social systems, where a proficiency at the subtleties of "social gamesmanship" is required. His proposal that "the chief role of creative intellect is to hold society together," suggests why the essentially communal and behaviorally variable dolphins may have been selected to develop certain complex cognitive abilities.

REFERENCES

Andersen, S., & Dziedzic, A. (1964). Behavior patterns of a captive harbor porpoise (*Phocaena phocaena*). *Bull. Inst. Oceanogr. Monaco, 63*, 1–20.
Au, W., Floyd, R. W., & Haun, J. E. (1978). Propagation of Atlantic bottlenose dolphin echolocation signals. *Journal Acous. Society America., 64*(2), 411–422.

Balcomb, K. C., Boran, J. R., Osborne, R. W., & Haenel, N. J. (1980). *Observations of killer whales* (Orcinus orca) *in Greater Puget Sound, State of Washington* (Report MM1300731-7). Washington, DC: U.S. Marine Mammal Comm.

Balcomb, K. C., & Goebel, C. A. (1976). *A killer whale study in Puget Sound: Final report* (Contract No. NASO-6-35330). Washington, DC: National Marine Fisheries.

Bateson, G. (1965). *Porpoise community research: Final report* (Contract No. N60530-C-1098). Kaneohe, Oahu, Hawaii: U.S. Navy Undersea Research and Development Center.

Bateson, G. (1966). Problems in cetacean and other mammalian communication: In K. S. Norris (Ed.), *Whales, dolphins and porpoises* (pp. 569–579). Berkeley: University of California Press.

Bel'kovich, V. M., Krushinskaya, N. L., & Gurevich, V. S. (1969). The behavior of dolphins in captivity. *Piroda, 11,* 18–28.

Bigg, M. A. (1982). *An assessment of killer whale (Orcinus orca) stocks off Vancouver Island, British Columbia* (Paper SC/Jn81/KW4). Washington, DC: International Whaling Commission.

Bigg, M. A., McAskie, I. B., & Ellis, G. (1976). *Abundance and movements of killer whales off eastern and southern Vancouver Island with comments on management* (Preliminary report). Ste. Anne de Bellevue, Quebec, Canada: Artic Biological Station.

Breder, C. M. (1976). Fish schools as operational structures. *Fishery Bulletin, 74,* (3), 471–502.

Brown, D. H. (1960). Behavior of a captive Pacific pilot whale. *Journal Mammalogy, 41*(3), 342–350.

Brown, D. H., & Norris, K. S. (1956). Observations of captive and wild cetaceans. *Journal of Mammalogy, 37,* 311–326.

Caldwell, M. C., Brown, D. H., & Caldwell, D. K. (1963). Intergeneric behavior by a captive Pacific pilot whale. *Los Angeles City Museum Contributions to Science, 70,* 1–12.

Caldwell, M. C., & Caldwell, D. K. (1966). Epimeletic (care-giving) behavior in cetacea. In K. S. Norris (Ed.), *Whales, dolphins and porpoises* (pp. 755–789). Berkeley: University of California Press.

Caldwell, M. C., & Caldwell, D. K. (1967). Dolphin community life. *Los Angeles City Museum Quarterly, 5*(4), 12–15.

Caldwell, M. C., & Caldwell, D. K. (1972). Behavior of marine mammals. In S. H. Ridgway (Ed.), *Mammals of the sea: Biology and medicine* (pp. 419–465). Springfield, IL: Thomas.

Connor, R. C., & Norris, K. S. (1982). Are dolphins reciprocal altruists? *The American Naturalist, 119*(3), 358–374.

Eisenberg, J. F. (1982). *Mammalian radiations: An analysis of trends in evolution, adaptation and behavior.* Chicago: University of Chicago Press.

Essapian, F. S. (1953). The birth and growth of a porpoise. *Natural History, 62,* 392–399.

Essapian, F. S. (1962). Courtship in captive saddleback dolphins, *Delphinus delphis,* L, 1758. *Zeitschrift Saugetierkd, 27,* 211–217.

Essapian, F. S. (1963). Observations on abnormalities of parturition in captive bottlenose dolphins, *Tursiops truncatus,* and concurrent behavior of other porpoises. *Journal of Mammalogy, 44,* 405–414.

Evans, W. E. (1974). Radio-telemetric studies of two species of small odontocete cetaceans. In W. E. Schevill (Ed.), *The whale problem: A status report* (pp. 385–394). Cambridge, MA: Harvard University Press.

Evans, W. E., & Dreher, J. J. (1962). Observations on scouting behavior and associated sound production by the Pacific bottlenose porpoise (*Tursiops gilli* Dall). *Bulletin Southern California Academy Science, 61,* 217–226.

Hamilton, W. D. (1972). Altruism and related phenomena mainly in social insects. *Annual Rev Ecology and System, 3,* 193–232.

Humphrey, N. K. (1976). The social function of intellect. In P. P. G. Bateson & R. Hinde (Eds.), *Growing points in ethology* (pp. 303–317). London: Cambridge University Press.

Irvine, A. B., Scott, M. D., Wells, R. S., & Kaufman, J. H. (1981). Movements and activities of the Atlantic bottlenose dolphin, *Tursiops truncatus*, near Sarasota, Florida. *Fishery Bulletin United States, 79,* 671–688.

Leatherwood, S. (1977). Some preliminary impressions on the numbers and social behavior of free-swimming bottlenose dolphin calves (*Tursiops truncatus*) in the northern Gulf of Mexico. In S. H. Ridgway & K. W. Benirschke (Eds.), *Breeding dolphins: Present status, suggestions for the future* (pp. 143–167). (Report MMC-76/07). Washington DC: Marine Mammal Comm.

Leatherwood, S., & Evans, W. E. (1979). Some recent uses and potentials of radiotelemetry in field studies of cetaceans. In H. E. Winn & B. L. Olla (Eds.), *Behavior of marine animals* (pp. 1–32). New York: Plenum.

Madsen, C. J., & Herman, L. M. (1980). Social and ecological correlates of cetacean vision and visual appearance. In L. M. Herman (Ed.), *Cetacean behavior* (pp. 101–147). New York: Wiley.

McBride, A. F., & Hebb, D. O. (1948). Behavior of the captive bottlenose dolphin (*Tursiops truncatus*). *Journal of Comparative Physiology and Psychology, 41,* 111–123.

Mitchell, E. (1970). Pigmentation pattern evolution in delphinid cetaceans. An essay in adaptive coloration. *Canadian Journal of Zoology, 48,* 717–740.

Norris, K. S. (1967). Aggressive behavior in cetacea. In C. D. Clemente & D. B. Lindsley (Eds.), *Aggression and defense* (pp. 225–241). Berkeley: University of California Press.

Norris, K. S., & Dohl, T. P. (1980a). Behavior of the Hawaiian spinner dolphin, *Stenella longirostris. Fishery Bulletin, 77,* 821–849.

Norris, K. S., & Dohl, T. P. (1980b). The structure and function of cetacean schools. In L. M. Herman (Ed.), *Cetacean behavior* (pp. 211–261). New York: Wiley.

Norris, K. S., & Evans, W. E. (1967). Directionality of echolocation clicks in the rough-toothed porpoise, *Steno bredanensis* Lesson. *Marine bio-acoustics: Volume 2.* New York: Pergamon Press.

Norris, K. S., & Prescott, J. H. (1961). Observations on Pacific cetaceans of Californian and Mexican waters. *University California Publications in Zoology, 63,* 291–402.

Norris, K. S., Stuntz, W. E., & Rogers, W. (1978). *The behavior of porpoises and tuna in the eastern tropical Pacific yellowfin tuna fishery: Preliminary studies* (Report No. MMc-76/12). Washington, DC: U.S. Marine Mammal Commission.

Norris, K. S., Würsig, B., Wells, R. S., Würsig, M., Brownlee, S. M., Johnson, C. M., & Solo, J. (1982). *The behavior of the Hawaiian spinner dolphin, Stenella longirostris: Final report* (Contract No. 79-ABC-00090). La Jolla, CA: National Marine Fisheries Service.

Perrin, W. F. (1975). Distribution and differentiation of populations of dolphins of the genus *Stenella* in the eastern tropical Pacific. *Journal of the Fisheries Research Board, Canada, 32,* 1059–1067.

Pryor, K., & Kang, I., (1980). *Social behavior and structure in pelagic porpoises (Stenella attenuata and S. longirostris) during purse seining for tuna: Final report* (Vse. Adm. Rpt. LJ-80-11C). La Jolla, CA: National Marine Fisheries Service.

Saayman, G. S., & Tayler, C. K. (1973). Social organization of inshore dolphins (*Tursiops aduncus* and *Sousa*) in the Indian Ocean. *Journal of Mammalogy, 54,* 993–996.

Saayman, G. S., & Tayler, C. K. (1979). The socioecology of humpback dolphins (*Sousa* sp.). In H. E. Winn & B. L. Olla (Eds.), *Behavior of marine mammals, Volume 3: Cetaceans* (pp. 165–226). New York: Plenum Press.

Sergeant, D. E., & Brodie, P. F. (1969). Tagging white whales in the Canadian Artic. *Journal of the Fisheries Research Board, Canada, 30,* 1009–1011.

Shane, S. H. (1977). *The population biology of the Atlantic bottlenose dolphin (Tursiops truncatus) in the Aransas Pass area of Texas.* Unpublished Master's Thesis. College Station: Texas A&M University.

Shane, S. H., Wells, R. S., Würsig, B., & Odell, D. K. (1982). *Behavior and ecology of the bottlenose dolphin: A review.* (Contract report). Long Beach: University of S. Mississippi at Gulf Port.

Tavolga, M. C. (1966). Behavior of the bottlenose dolphin (*Tursiops truncatus*): Social interactions in a captive colony. In K. S. Norris (Ed.), *Whales, dolphins and porpoises* (pp. 718–730). Berkeley: University of California Press.

Tavolga, M. C., & Essapian, F. S. (1957). The behavior of the bottlenose dolphin (*Tursiops truncatus*): Mating, pregnancy, parturition and mother-infant behavior. *Zoologica, 1,* 289–299.

Tayler, C. K., & Saayman, G. S. (1972). The social organization and behavior of dolphins (*Tursiops aduncus*) and baboons (*Papio ursinus*): Some comparisons and assessments. *Annals Cape Providence Museum of Natural History, 9,* 11–49.

Trivers, R. L. (1971). The evolution of reciprocal altruism. *Q. Rev. Biology, 56,* 35–57.

Van Lawick-Goodall, J. (1971). *In the shadow of man.* Boston: Houghton Mifflin.

Wells, R. S., Irvine, A. B., & Scott, M. D. (1980). The social ecology of inshore odontocetes. In L. M. Herman (Ed.), *Cetacean Behavior* (pp. 263–317). New York: Wiley.

Williams, G. C. (1966). *Adaptation and natural selection.* New Jersey: Princeton University Press.

Wood, F. G., Caldwell, D. K., & Caldwell, M. C. (1970). Behavioral interactions between porpoises and sharks: In G. Pilleri (Ed.), *Investigations on cetacea, Vol. 2,* (pp. 264–277). Berne, Switzerland: Brain Anatomy Inst., Univ. of Berne.

Würsig, B. (1978). Occurrence and group organization of Atlantic bottlenose porpoises (*Tursiops truncatus*) in an Argentine bay. *Biology Bulletin 154,* 348–359.

Würsig, B., & Würsig, M. (1977). The photographic determination of group size, composition and stability of coastal porpoises (*Tursiops truncatus*). *Science, 198,* 755–756.

Würsig, B., & Würsig, M. (1979a). Behavior and ecology of bottlenose porpoises, *Tursiops truncatus,* in the south Atlantic. *Fishery Bulletin, 77,* 399–442.

Würsig, B., & Würsig, M. (1979b). Day and night of the dolphin. *Natural History, 88*(3), 60–67.

Würsig, B., & Würsig, M. (1980). Behavior and ecology of dusky porpoises, *Lagenorhynchus obscurus,* in the south Atlantic. Fishery Bulletin, 77, 871–890.

18 Delphinid Foraging Strategies

Bernd Würsig
Moss Landing Marine Laboratories

INTRODUCTION

The *Delphinidae* Family of odontocete cetaceans includes about 30 species of small (< 4 m long) toothed whales generally termed dolphins, and four species of larger (4 to 6 m long) toothed whales. The smaller members of the family include the bottlenose dolphin, *Tursiops truncatus,* the common dolphin, *Delphinus delphis,* and several species of the genera *Lagenorhynchus* and *Stenella.* The larger members include the killer whale, *Orcinus orca,* and the pilot whales, *Globicephala* sp. (Leatherwood, Reeves, & Foster, 1983). The family is therefore represented by a large and relatively diverse group of mammals, having different modes of living and probably several different social systems as well. A brief review such as this can only provide examples of the better known feeding strategies of a few species, and I wish to emphasize that I make no attempt at an exhaustive survey of the family. It will become apparent, I hope, that some species have quite variable feeding behaviors, and some feed in complex cooperative ways which we are only beginning to understand.

Most delphinids are social mammals that almost always carry out their activities within the security and efficiency of a school of variable size (reviews by Norris & Dohl 1980a; Wells, Irvine, & Scott, 1980, Gaskin, 1982). Although schooling has many potential advantages, the primary ones for most species are presumably reduced predation and enhanced efficiency of finding and securing prey. Schools of dolphins—like other mammalian social units, but perhaps unlike most schooling fishes, invertebrates, and flocking birds—are composed of complexly interacting individuals, some of whom are likely to know each other, have preferred social and sexual partners, and often travel in long-term

347

associations with related animals (at least at the mother-calf level). This complexity makes foraging strategies particularly difficult to assess, but some broad statements are nevertheless possible.

Delphinid foraging strategies run the gamut from individual hunting and securing of prey to highly coordinated group activity. The manner in which food is gathered certainly depends in great part on the type and accessibility of prey. Where the type of prey availability is relatively constant, as for Hawaiian spinner dolphins, *Stenella longirostris*, feeding at night on organisms associated with a rising deep scattering layer, foraging strategy may also be relatively unvarying from day to day and season to season (Norris & Dohl, 1980b; Norris, Würsig, Wells, Würsig, Brownlee, Johnson & Solow, 1985). Where prey types change, strategies of finding and securing prey must change accordingly. For example, killer whales feeding on salmon often hunt in loosely coordinated groups (Bigg, MacAskie, & Ellis, 1976; Balcomb, Boran, Osborne, & Haenel, 1980), while killer whales feeding seasonally on pinnipeds appear to use complicated strategies to isolate and attack a particular vulnerable animal (Condy, Van Aarde, & Bester, 1978; Lopez & Lopez, 1985). Killer whales feeding on large whales also attack as a tight pod, harrying and harrassing a blue whale (Tarpy, 1979), for example, from different sides and in different ways. This behavior may be similar to wild dogs tiring and finally bringing to a standstill a wildebeest (for example, Kleiman & Eisenberg, 1973).

FINDING AND SECURING FOOD

I divide foraging into the two major categories of (1) finding prey, and (2) securing it. Food finding appears to rely mainly on eyesight, passive listening, and active echolocation (Gaskin, 1982). Nevertheless, recent evidence of a sophisticated sense of taste in bottlenose dolphins (Nachtigall, this volume) may mean that this sensory modality has more importance than previously thought. It is also becoming apparent that echolocation should not be thought of as the major sensory device. Dolphins are both acoustic and visual animals *par excellence,* and they appear to rely on echolocation mainly in murky water, at night, and at lightless depths. Sight appears primary in relatively clear and sunlit waters, however, and dolphins moving along under such conditions are often remarkably silent. This makes sense, of course, for there is usually no advantage to advertising oneself to potential prey or predators.

Delphinids in open water usually search for food in broad ranks which may be hundreds of meters wide, presumably to increase the chances of finding schools of fish or squid. Such ranks indicate that the animals are cooperating as a school in finding prey, and it is also likely that they have sophisticated methods of cooperative feeding once prey have been found. I have noticed that pilot whales often travel in ranks composed of individuals spaced close enough together for each animal to barely see its neighbor in the rank, and the entire school stays in contact by this method. It appears, for example, that pilot whales in the clear waters of Hawaii travel farther apart from each other than pilot whales which frequent the more murky shores of California, but no systematic investigation of this point has been conducted. Pilot whales, killer whales, Risso's dolphins, and bottlenose dolphins are frequently seen in rank formation in the open ocean (Norris & Prescott, 1961, and Norris & Dohl, 1980a provide these and other examples).

Dolphins near shore often find food in a less cooperative manner, with individual dolphins seeking out individual prey. For example, bottlenose dolphins studied in Argentina often traveled close to shore, in small groups of 6- to 10-animals (Würsig 1978, 1979; Würsig & Würsig, 1979a). Detailed observations from cliffs along shore allowed us to see that individuals pointed their snouts at and among nearshore rocks and boulders. Occasionally a dolphin brought a large rock-dwelling fish (usually of the genus *Pinquipes*) to the surface. The dolphin then repeatedly beat the fish against the surface while holding it in its teeth. This action apparently served to soften the prey (see also Norris & Prescott, 1961) before the dolphin bit off the fish's head and swallowed the body. Similar reports of apparent individual foraging are common in the literature, and have been perhaps best described for bottlenose dolphins feeding on mullet in Florida (Caldwell & Caldwell, 1972).

Bottlenose dolphins (like the aforementioned killer whales) are highly adaptive animals, feeding in different ways under different circumstances. This is perhaps best illustrated by the example from Argentina: The same dolphins that fed individually in a loose single-file formation near shore moved line abreast when farther from shore and appeared to be looking for schools of fish in a cooperative manner at this time (Würsig, 1979).

Perhaps most interesting in this story of shifting feeding modes is the fact that small groups coalesce when dolphins feed cooperatively. As a result, group size of bottlenose dolphins in Argentina increased up to 18 animals, all line abreast, in open water. It is probable that a larger group size increases the swath of sea being investigated, and it is also possible that more dolphins may more effectively feed on schools of prey once they have been found. We shall examine this possibility later for dusky dolphins.

A smaller group size during individual foraging may allow each animal a better chance at catching at least one of a limited number of large rock-dwelling prey in a particular area, but this is a tenuous and untested hypothesis. Wells et al. (1980) also found Florida bottlenose dolphin groups to be smaller near shore and larger offshore, and similar foraging differences as in the above example may be responsible for this shift in group size. The shift in group size is particularly interesting. Bottlenose dolphins have long-term affiliations, and it is likely that individuals of a group know each other well. How they make the decision to coalesce and to break apart depending on feeding mode is not known, but remains a fruitful area for research.

Bottlenose dolphins also chase fish onto gently sloping shores of mud or sand, and snap at the fish flopping about on land. During such chases the dolphins often cooperate in driving the fish onto land or enclosing the fish with their bodies in water less than 30 cm deep. This kind of feeding has been seen in many places, and has been described in detail for bottlenose dolphins in salt marshes of the southeastern United States (Hoese, 1971; Rigley, 1983).

It is likely that in most cases dolphins frequent particular areas where they have found food before. This is presumably especially true in areas where food can be reliably found. Common dolphins orient towards underwater seamounts and escarpments off southern California, where schools of fish are known to congregate (Evans, 1971, 1974). Since the water over the seamounts is deeper than the depths to which dolphins are thought to travel, Evans has postulated that dolphins orient to these areas by passive listening, using the difference in ambient sound of different ocean depths as cues. It is of course also possible that other factors—such as different fauna in different areas—may be cuing the dolphins onto such productive areas of ocean. Hawaiian spinner dolphins leave the relative safety of shallow bays in the afternoon in order to meet offshore pelagic prey rising out of depths with deep scattering layer organisms (Norris & Dohl, 1980b; Norris et al. 1985), and their behavior is part of a strict daily regime: resting in shallow water during the day and feeding in deep water during the evening and night. Norris and Prescott (1961) describe bottlenose dolphins which anticipated the arrival of garbage scows at an oceanic dumping site off San Diego Bay. Killer whales appear off sea lion and elephant seal breeding areas at those times of year when young pinnipeds first begin to enter the water (Condy et al., 1978; Lopez & Lopez, 1985). These and other accounts of dolphins orienting towards known areas of prey provide ample evidence that random search is under many circumstances augmented by memory of previous success.

COOPERATIVE FORAGING

Dolphins that search for prey singly probably secure prey by themselves as well. However, since dolphins are hardly ever alone, but are feeding "singly" in at least a loose school of at times vocalizing (and presumably communicating) animals, even bottlenose dolphins jumping after leaping mullet (Hamilton & Nishimoto, 1977) may be helping each other in some manner. Individual feeding may be enhanced by the presence of the group due to rapid and efficient information transfer concerning where, for example, the major concentration of prey is and what the extent of the prey school may be. Hawaiian spinner dolphins diving for fish and squid in loose aggregations spread over several kilometers (Norris &

Dohl, 1980b) may also be helping each other. This possibility is strengthened by the observation that spinner dolphins often dive synchronously while feeding, even though they may be separated from each other by 50 m or more. Perhaps they dive at the same time so that the entire group can stay in acoustic contact at night, and so that rapid information transfer regarding potential danger from deep-water sharks can always take place. At any rate, animals in social aggregation often cooperate to some degree even when particular actions, such as securing specific prey, take place on an individual basis.

Dolphins that hunt for prey cooperatively may also cooperate in the final securing of their food. Bottlenose dolphin schools observed in the Black Sea at times herd fish towards the surface (Morozov, 1970), and bottlenose dolphins off South Africa have been seen herding fish against a shoreline (Tayler & Saayman, 1972). The latter observations have been particularly well described: There appeared to be a division of labor as some dolphins crowded the fish towards shore while others patrolled offshore in order to keep the fish school from escaping. A colleague (Lisa Ballance) and I recently observed a particularly clear example of cooperative foraging in bottlenose dolphins off Bahia Kino, Mexico. Five dolphins which had been moving as a tight group close to shore detected a fish school about 3 m in diameter at a distance 50 m or more in front of them. Because water clarity allowed visibility to only about 4 m, this detection was presumably done by echolocation. At 50 m distance from the fish school, the dolphins split into two groups of two (nearshore) and three (offshore) individuals which changed direction in order to attack the school from two opposite sides. The two groups arrived at opposite sides of the school of fish at precisely the same time, and presumably this synchronized attack allowed for more efficient capture of prey. Other descriptions of cooperative feeding by bottlenose dolphins are found in Leatherwood (1975).

The most detailed description of cooperative foraging by dolphins has been made for the southern hemisphere dusky dolphin, *Lagenorhynchus obscurus* (Würsig & Würsig, 1979b, 1980). I present a synopsis of this work here, with further thoughts on foraging strategy.

In summer, dusky dolphins travel in small groups of 6 to 15 animals during night and early morning. Small groups are separated by 1 to 5 km, and there may be as many as 20 to 30 such groups in a 100 square km area of sea. There are occasional dashes by one group to the other, during which groups reach speeds of 22 km/hr for periods of 1 to 10 minutes. In such a case, the two groups usually join. There are also occasional random-appearing movements which bring groups close together, but in those cases they do not join. Usually, these small groups, moving slowly (average speed 6 km/hr) and changing direction frequently, simply stay apart. It appears that they have a moving "bubble" around them and that other groups will not intrude into that area. There is, in other words, a mutual change of movement by neighboring groups. If groups approach closer than 1 km, one or both will turn and move apart for some distance. Sounds that groups make (mainly composed of echolocation-type clicks) appear to travel underwater for about 1 km before attenuating, and it is possible that when groups hear each other they move apart. This dispersed formation allows dolphins as a widespread large group of 20 to 30 smaller groups to cover rather efficiently a large area of sea.

Slow movement in small groups continues from early morning to mid-morning. Suddenly, a slowly moving group stops and dives. Two to 10 minutes after the dolphins stop, a fish school—invariably southern anchovy, *Engraulis anchoita*—appears at the surface, with dolphins swimming around and underneath the fish school, and leaping at its sides. Birds—terns, gulls, cormorants, petrels, giant petrels, albatross—fly to the area and feed on fish near the surface. Underwater observations show that dolphins herd a school of fish to the surface and use the surface as a wall through which the fish cannot escape. While dolphins swim around and under the school, one dolphin at a time will break rank and rapidly move through the center or periphery of the ball of fish, coming out the other side with up to five anchovies in its mouth. Dolphins actually chase stray fish back into the ball of fish, and I have not seen dolphins taking stray fish. These strays could probably only be caught singly, and such pursuit away from the major concentration of fish might not be worth the effort. Besides, such diversion from the major task of keeping fish from escaping, and the fish school breaking up as a result, would certainly be detrimental to the dolphins' overall feeding effort (and therefore each individual's chance of feeding well), and may be selected against.

When a small group of dolphins (6 to 8) has found and herded a fish school to the surface, it is likely that it will not feed for long (average time 5 min). It appears that as feeding begins, the small dolphin group is not able to hold the school at the surface. The school escapes, and dolphins begin moving slowly in apparent search once again. If, however, the small dolphin group is joined by other nearby dolphin groups, the fish ball often becomes larger, and feeding activity may progress for several hours. This indicates that a group size greater than the basic searching group size is optimal for herding, and leads us to suspect that mechanisms for rapid aggregation of small groups may be present.

How do dolphins some distance from the group which has found food know about it? At close range, up to about 1 km distance, sound may be involved, and dolphins may make different sounds while beginning to herd fish. (There is some evidence that there are more whistle sounds at this stage than there were during the searching mode.) There is also much in-air leaping by dolphins in the group which found the fish, and these leaps are highly visible to human investigators in boats. Dolphins from as far away as 8 km (measured accurately by a shore-based theodolite) rapidly move towards a feeding group, and much of this rapid movement consists of in-air leaps towards the feeding activity. Although such leaping is thought to increase the efficiency of forward motion (Au & Weihs, 1980; Hertel, 1963), it is also likely that dolphins are using eyesight in air in order to cue onto the feeding activity. Human observers can, after some experience with dusky dolphins, determine approximately how many dolphins are involved in herding and how long the activity has gone on not just by the leaps of dolphins but by the number of birds and their concentration above the fish school. I suggest that far-off dolphins may be able to do the same.

In summary, birds and leaps (and, at close range, sound) may serve as cues to adjacent groups. At any rate, a lone small feeding group does not feed for long, but those groups which are joined by others may feed for up to three hours. A group which finds fish in mid-morning and is joined by others, may by noon have created a large feeding activity with 100 to 300 dolphins and thousands of birds. In such very large aggregations, there are usually four to five fish schools tightly balled at the surface, within a diameter of 200 to 300 m.

After feeding in such large aggregations, dolphins do not begin hunting for more food. Instead, much socializing and sexual activity takes place in the after-feeding large groups. As it is not a direct part of feeding, I did not detail it here. However, after-feeding social activity may be important to foraging if it helps to strengthen and reaffirm social bonds which could be necessary for smooth functioning of cooperative feeding.

If it is more efficient for more dolphins to herd fish (to an optimum dolphin group size), then we might expect that calling dolphin groups to the potential food would be of benefit: "Come and help us herd." This could be genetic or cultural or, of course, have components of both. Male chimpanzees (*Pan troglodytes*) will often call loudly upon finding a food source, and so attract other chimpanzees (Wrangham, 1977). In their case, males may be calling others in the hope of increasing their chances of encountering receptive estrus females. I am conjecturing about "calling" by dolphins, and have no proof for it at this time. We know that dolphins which have found food begin leaping, and we also know that other groups rapidly aggregate. Whether or not the leaps are at least in part designed to help show distant dolphins what is going on is not known. The birds above the activity are of interest, for they are usually even more visible than the leaping dolphins. Birds may thus be, at least close to shore and close to roosting sites, not just parasitic on the herding efforts of dolphins, but they may function as an interspecific cue to available food.

Apparent females with small calves (about one-third adult size) are only seen in the feeding activity early during herding and feeding. As more groups join, we no longer see calves in the active larger group, but instead encounter some noncalves, and calves separated from the feeding activity by 0.5 to 2 km. I have called these groups with calves "nursery groups." Many of the attendant non-calves in these groups appears small themselves—like subadults 1- to 3-years-old. I have wondered whether juveniles might be taking care of the calves, perhaps similar to alloparental care in scrub jays described by Woolfenden (1975), but I have no further information on this point. A possible reason for calves and attendant animals to leave the feeding area may be because it becomes "boisterous" as feeding progresses, with much contact and social-sexual activity. This may not be safe for the calves. As well, large sharks are attracted to the feeding area, and calves may be especially vulnerable. At any rate, calves leave the activity, and I suspect that some kind of babysitting may be taking place.

There is also a varying sequence of in-air leaps depending on feeding stage. *Herding dolphins* leap out head first, turn the body, and reenter the water head first. They make no splash, and underwater sounds of such leaps project only about 10 m. The leap appears designed for the dolphin to breathe rapidly, and go to depth at essentially the same place from which it just came. The leap is therefore a function of dolphins engaged in herding activity underwater. *During feeding,* leaps end mainly with animals slapping onto the water surface with their sides, belly, or back. These leaps create loud and sharp sounds underwater, and they occur mainly around the periphery of the fish school. They may serve to frighten fish and to cause them to school more tightly. *During late feeding and after feeding,* leaps become acrobatic—dolphins do head-over-tail flips, spins, spins and somersaults combined, etc. (Dusky dolphins may be the most aerially acrobatic of all the dolphin species.) At the same time, socializing increases, and it is possible that acrobatic leaps are an outgrowth of social "exuberance," with leaping serving a social facilitation function. Such activity may have a corollary in "chimpanzee carnival" behavior described by Henry Nissen (Emil Menzel, State University of New York at Stony Brook, personal comm.). All three leap types are distinguishable in air, and they tell an experienced human observer something about the stage of the feeding activity. It is possible that distant dolphin groups may be able to gain the same information.

A fright reaction causes bunching in many species of schooling fishes (Shaw, 1970). In the present case, this appears to be maladaptive for the fish, because predators more easily decimate a large portion of the fish school. Southern anchovy which are herded by dusky dolphins are usually very tightly bunched, with silvery sides almost touching. They also do not appear alert, as they are easily scooped out of the water with a small dipnet. Tight schooling may be causing anoxic conditions in the school, and thus affecting fish due to lack of oxygen (Moss & McFarland, 1970). Dolphins are creating slap sounds around the periphery of the fish school, and they are pushing the fish physically. Many fishermen believe that bottlenose dolphins are stunning fish by their boisterous activity at the surface (see Morozov, 1970, for example). Dolphins are also projecting sounds made internally, and it has been suggested by several researchers that such sounds could reach intensities sufficient to debilitate fish (Bel'kovich & Yablokov, 1963; Hult, 1982; Norris & Møhl, 1983). It is of course possible that any combination of factors—physical proximity of bunched fish, anoxia, stunning due to leap or vocal sounds—may be responsible for debilitating prey to the point where they can be taken more easily by dolphins. The sound debilitation hypothesis appears particularly provocative, for if it exists, this capability would give dolphins a special weapon which would have strongly affected their evolved predatory strategies (Norris & Møhl, 1983).

Dusky dolphin feeding behavior appears to represent an ideal situation for investigations of this point in the wild.

Much more work is necessary. We need to know relationships and sexes of members of the small hunting groups, whether they are in fact calling other groups to a feeding activity purposefully, whether in-air long-distance assessment of the status of a feeding activity is taking place, what the social rules are about which animals eat when, who is taking care of the young, etc. The system, in its broad generalities, may not be uncommon in the sea, and therefore I have detailed it here. Dusky dolphins off New Zealand form remarkably similar feeding aggregations with different fish and bird species from those seen in Argentina. Common dolphins also appear to feed in a similar manner in the Sea of Cortez; one sees balled fish, Brown and Blue-footed Boobies, Brown Pelicans, Yellow-legged Gulls, and Royal and Elegant Terns. Both common and dusky dolphins often have sealions feeding in their midst as well (Wells, Würsig, & Norris, 1981; Würsig & Würsig, 1980), but whether or not the sealions are contributing any herding efforts is not known. Fink (1959) described possible cooperation during feeding between harbor porpoises (*Phocoena phocoena*) and California sealions (*Zalophus californianus*).

There are other common interspecies associations which are probably largely food-based. For example, bottlenose dolphins and pilot whales often travel together, and it has been conjectured that the smaller dolphins take advantage of the presumably greater range of echolocation of the larger whales (Norris & Prescott, 1961). It is, of course, possible that both species may benefit due to a greater diversity in prey finding techniques. Risso's dolphins often travel at the periphery of dusky dolphin groups (Würsig & Würsig, 1980), and it appears that it is the larger Risso's dolphins who follow the smaller dusky dolphins. The larger animals may be feeding on large fish attracted to dusky dolphin feeding activities, but the true association is not known. Complicated interspecies associations exist in the tropical Pacific between spotted and spinner dolphins (*Stenella* sp.), common dolphins, yellowfin tuna (*Thunnus albacores*), and many species of pelagic seabirds (Green, Perrin, & Petrich, 1971; Perrin, Warner, Fiscus, & Holts, 1973). It is generally surmised that the tuna are taking advantage of the food-finding capabilities of the dolphins. This interaction may be especially important for spotted dolphins and tuna, since they both feed mainly during the day and on similar epipelagic and pelagic fish and squid. Spinner dolphins and spotted dolphins are often together in these aggregations and, since spinner dolphins feed mainly on mesopelagic creatures at night, it is likely that this latter association is not food-based. Perhaps they are together to enhance each others sensory capabilities (for detecting sharks, for example): Spotted dolphis are alert in the day while spinner dolphins are resting, and vice versa for nighttime (Norris, Stuntz, & Rogers, 1978).

Another well-known form of interspecies association is that between dolphins and humans (Mitchell, 1975). It appears between many different species and human fisheries; it is in many instances disruptive to the human fisheries, and in other cases of benefit or of neutral effect to human activity. In the disruptive category fall incidences of dolphins taking fish and invertebrates out of nets and long-lines, and into the beneficial category fall incidences of humans and dolphins apparently cooperating in order to herd or drive prey in some manner, usually against a shoreline. A particularly well-described account has been given of killer whales helping whalers of New South Wales ambush and drive humpback whales (Dakin, 1934). Nevertheless, in these accounts it is usually not possible to separate whether or not the actions of the two species were designed to be cooperative, or whether they were in their own ways simply working towards the common goal of herding or trapping the same prey. The fishing people involved in these interactions are usually very certain that they are cooperating with the dolphins, and they also believe that the dolphins are not simply taking blatant advantage of the human activity, but are exercising "temporary restraint" (Wilson, 1975) in order to herd prey and postpone feeding in a manner equitable to both groups. Neutral interactions involve dolphins feeding off human garbage (Norris & Prescott, 1961) or following shrimp boats while they are hauling in or sorting their catch (Gruber, 1981; Fulton, 1976, provides a particularly clear account of dolphins around a shrimp boat).

CONCLUDING REMARKS

This brief and incomplete overview of delphinid foraging strategies tells us that there is quite a bit of diversity between species, and for at least some species such as the bottlenose dolphin, quite a bit of feeding diversity within the same animal. The situation is not unlike that of social mammals such as wolves, wild dogs, and lions on land. These animals often cooperate in securing prey, and they do so not always in stereotyped fashion (Wilson, 1975, provides several good reviews; also Kruuk, 1972; Schaller, 1972). Our observations of foraging strategy related to the immediate finding and securing of prey tell us nothing about the possibility of such overall strategies as, for example, optimization of energy supplies by pulse fishing (Norris & Dohl, 1980a).

Cooperative foraging is not, of course, a trait only of social mammals. Excellent recent observations have shown that some predatory fish are more successful at catching schooling prey when they themselves are schooling (Major, 1976, 1978). Schmitt and Strand (1982) recently discussed cooperative foraging by the marine piscivorous yellowtail (*Serriola lalandei*). Yellowtails surround and herd jack mackerel (*Trachurus symmetricus*) toward shore, and they herd Cortez grunts (*Lythrulon flaviguttatum*) into open water. These two fish species are open-water fast swimming and nearshore reef-hiding species, respectively, and it appears that yellowtails change their strategies in order to herd fish to areas where their normal defenses of speed or hiding can no longer be used. The yellowtails show true cooperation, as in much cooperation in foraging mammals, by a division of labor among individuals, and by not feeding until prey have been made more vulnerable by their herding efforts (Wilson's "temporary restraint," 1975). The descriptions of herding by yellowtails appear remarkably similar to what I have observed of cooperative herding in dusky and common dolphins . Nevertheless, I do not mean to imply that the same mechanisms are operating in cooperating fish and dolphins. Both species are presumably cooperating because each individual has a greater chance of securing more food for itself. But beyond that, I would guess that dolphin cooperation can be more varied and tuned to the particular situation of the moment than fish cooperation. I would further guess that such mechanisms as kin-selected altruism (Hamilton, 1964) and reciprocal altruism (Trivers, 1971) may be involved in dolphin cooperation to a higher degree than in fish cooperation (see Connor & Norris, 1982). These assertions rely mainly, of course, on a perceived notion of a great phylogenetic difference in behavioral flexibility and capability between mammals and fishes. Mammals often live in long-term associations with their relatives, and they have a sophisticated long-term memory. Social mammals can also transmit knowledge about prey and predators (and a host of other things, such as social patterns and an understanding of the abiotic environment) by social tradition (Hendricks, 1983). There is little reason to suppose that dolphins are not at least as sophisticated as other social mammals in their individual interactions, but because relationships and details of behaviors are only incompletely known for even the best-studied delphinids, a thorough evaluation of their interactions and foraging regimes awaits further work.

ACKNOWLEDGMENTS

I thank Susan Shane, Randall Wells and Forrest G. Wood for their conscientious reviews of this paper.

REFERENCES

Au, D., & Weihs, D. (1980). At high speeds dolphins save energy by leaping. *Nature, 284*, 548–550.

Balcomb, K. C., Boran, J. R., Osborne, R. W., & Haenel, N. J. (1980). Observations of killer whales (*Orcinus orca*) in greater Puget Sound, State of Washington. *Final report for MMC contract MM1300731-7.* NTIS PB 80-224 728.

Bel'kovich, V. M., & Yablokov, A. V. (1963). Marine animals "share experience" with designers. *Nauka Zhizn, 30*, 61–64.

Bigg, M. A., MacAskie, I. B., & Ellis, G. (1976). Abundance and movements of killer whales off eastern and southern Vancouver Island, with comments on management. *Report of the Arctic Biological Station,* Ste. Anne de Bellevue, Quebec.

Caldwell, D. K., & Caldwell, M. C. (1972). *The world of the bottlenosed dolphin.* Philadelphia: J. B. Lippincott Co.

358 WÜRSIG

Condy, P. R., van Aarde, R. J., & Bester, M. N. (1978). The seasonal occurrences and behavior of killer whales *Orcinus orca* at Marion Island. *Journal of Zoology, London, 184*, 449–464.

Connor, R. C., & Norris, K. S. (1982). Are dolphins reciprocal altruists? *American Naturalist, 119*, 358–374.

Dakin, W. J. (1934). *Whalemen adventures*. Sydney, Australia: Angus and Robertson Ltd.

Evans, W. E. (1971). Orientation behavior of delphinids: Radio telemetric studies. *Annals of the New York Academy of Sciences, 188*, 142–160.

Evans, W. E. (1974). Radio telemetric studies of two species of small odontocete cetaceans: In W. E. Schevill (Ed.), *The whale problem: A status report* (pp. 385–394). Cambridge, MA: Harvard University Press.

Fink, B. D. (1959). Observations of porpoise predation on a school of Pacific sardines. *California Fish and Game, 45*, 216–217.

Fulton, G. (1976). Sounds in the night. *Waters, 1*, 30–31.

Gaskin, D. E. (1982). *The ecology of whales and dolphins*. London: Heinemann Press.

Green, R. E., Perrin, W. R., & Petrich, B. P. (1971). The American tuna purse seine fishery: In *Modern fishing gear of the world, 3*, 182–194. London: Fishing News Books Ltd.

Gruber, J. A. (1981). *Ecology of the Atlantic bottlenosed dolphin (Tursiops truncatus) in the Pass Cavallo area of Matagorda Bay, Texas*. Texas A&M University: M.Sc. thesis.

Hamilton, W. D. (1964). The genetical evolution of social behavior, I and II. *Journal of Theoretical Biology, 7*, 1–52.

Hamilton, P. V., & Nishimoto, R. T. (1977). Dolphin predation on mullet. *Florida Scientist, 40*, 251–252.

Hendricks, H. (1983). On the evolution of social structure in mammals. In J. F. Eisenberg & D. G. Kleiman (Eds.), *Advances in the study of mammalian behavior*. Shippensburg, PA: Special Publ. #7, American Society of Mammalogists, Shippensburg State College.

Hertel, H. (1963). Struktur-Form-Bewegung. Bd. 1, Biologie und Technik. Mainz: Krausskopf-Verlag.

Hoese, H. D. (1971). Dolphin feeding out of water in a salt marsh. *Journal of Mammalogy, 52*, 222–223.

Hult, R. (1982). Another function of echolocation for bottlenose dolphins (*Tursiops truncatus*). *Cetology, 47*.

Kleiman, D. G., & Eisenberg, J. F. (1973). Comparisons of canid and felid social systems from an evolutionary perspective. *Animal Behavior, 21*, 637–659.

Kruuk, H. (1972). *The spotted hyena*. Chicago: University of Chicago Press.

Leatherwood, S. (1975). Some observations of feeding behavior of bottle-nosed dolphins (*Tursiops truncatus*) in the northern Gulf of Mexico and (*Tursiops* cf. *T. gilli*) off southern California, Baja, California, and Nayarit, Mexico. *Marine Fisheries Review, 37*, 10–16.

Leatherwood, S., Reeves, R. R., & Foster, L. (1983). *The Sierra Club handbook of whales and dolphins*. San Francisco: Sierra Club Books.

Lopez, J. C., & Lopez, D. (1985). Killer whales (*Orcinus orca*) of Patagonia, and their behavior of intentional stranding while hunting nearshore. *Journal of Mammalogy, 66*, 181–183.

Major, P. F. (1976). *The behavioral ecology of predator-prey interactions in schooling fish*. Ph.D. thesis, University of California, Santa Cruz.

Major, P. F. (1978). Predator-prey interactions in two schooling fishes, *Caranz ignobilis* and *Stolephorus purpureus*. *Animal Behavior, 26*, 760–777.

Mitchell, E. D. (1975). Porpoise, dolphin, and small whale fisheries of the world: Status and problems. *IUCN Monograph No. 3*. Morges. Switzerland.

Morozov, D. A. (1970). Dolphins hunting. *Rybnoe Khoziaistvo, 46*, 16–17.

Moss, S. A., & McFarland, W. N. (1970). The influence of dissolved oxygen and carbon dioxide on fish schooling behavior. *Marine Biology, 5*, 100–107.

Norris, K. S., & Dohl, T. P. (1980a). The structure and functions of cetacean schools: In L. M. Herman (Ed.), *Cetacean behavior: Mechanisms and functions* (pp. 211–261). New York: Wiley.

Norris, K. S., & Dohl, T. P. (1980b). Behavior of the Hawaiian spinner dolphin, *Stenella longirostris. Fishery Bulletin U.S., 77*, 821–849.

Norris, K. S., & Møhl, B. (1983). Can odontocetes debilitate prey with sound? *American Naturalist, 122*, 85–104.

Norris, K. S., & Prescott, J. H. (1961). Observations on Pacific cetaceans of Californian and Mexican waters. *University of California Publications in Zoology, 63*, 291–402.

Norris, K. S., Stuntz, W. E., & Rogers, W. (1978). The behavior of porpoises and tuna in the eastern tropical Pacific yellowfin tuna fishery-preliminary studies. Springfield, VA: *NTIS Report PB-283 970*, U.S. Department of Commerce.

Norris, K. S., Würsig, B., Wells, R. S., Würsig, M., Brownlee, S., Johnson, C., & Solon, J. (1985). The Behavior of the Hawaiian Spinner Dolphin, *Stenella longirostris. National Marine Fisheries Service Report* LJ-85-06C, 213 p.

Perrin, W. F., Warner, R. R., Fiscus, C. H., & Holts, D. B. (1973). Stomach contents of porpoise, *Stenella* spp. and yellowfin tuna, *Thunnus albacores,* in mixed species aggregations. *Fishery Bulletin U.S., 71*, 1077–1092.

Rigley, L. (1983). Dolphins feeding in a South Carolina salt marsh. *Whalewatcher, Journal of the American Cetacean Society, 17*, 3–5.

Schaller, G. B. (1972). *The Serengeti lion.* Chicago: University of Chicago Press.

Schmitt, R. J., & Strand, S. W. (1982). Cooperative foraging by yellowtail, *Seriola lalandei* (Carangidae) on two species of fish prey. *Copeia, 3*, 714–717.

Shaw, E. (1970). Schooling in fishes: Critique and review: In A. R. Aronson, E. Tobach, D. S. Lehrman, & J. S. Rosenblatt (Eds.), *Development and evolution of behavior* (pp. 452–480). San Francisco: W. H. Freeman.

Tarpy, C. (1979). Killer whale attack. *National Geographic Magazine, 155*, 542–545.

Tayler, C. K., & Saayman, G. S. (1972). The social organization and behavior of dolphins (*Tursiops aduncus*) and baboons (*Papio ursinus*): Some comparisons and assessments. *Annals of the Cape Provincial Museum (Natural History), 9*, 11–49.

Trivers, R. L. (1971). The evolution of reciprocal altruism. *Quarterly Review of Biology, 46*, 35–37.

Wells, R. S., Irvine, A. B., & Scott, M. D. (1980). The social ecology of inshore odontoctes: In L. M. Herman (Ed.), *Cetacean behavior: Mechanisms and functions* (pp. 263–318). New York: Wiley.

Wells, R. S., Würsig, B. G., & Norris, K. S. (1981). A survey of the marine mammals of the upper Gulf of California, Mexico, with an assessment of the status of *Phocoena sinus*. Springfield, VA: NTIS. U.S. Department of Commerce.

Wilson, E. O. (1975). *Sociobiology, the new synthesis.* Cambridge, MA: Belknap Press.

Woolfenden, G. E. (1975). Florida scrub jay helpers at the nest. *Auk, 92*, 1–15.

Wrangham, R. W. (1977). Feeding behaviour of chimpanzees in Gombe National Park, Tanzania. In T. H. Clutton-Brock (Ed.), *Primate ecology* (pp. 504–538). London: Academic Press.

Würsig, B. (1978). Occurrence and group organization of Atlantic bottlenose porpoises (*Tursiops truncatus*) in an Argentine bay. *Biological Bulletin, 154*, 348–359.

Würsig, B. (1979). Dolphins. *Scientific American, 240*, 136–148.

Würsig, B., & Würsig, M. (1979a). Behavior and ecology of the bottlenose dolphin, *Tursiops truncatus,* in the south Atlantic. *Fishery Bulletin U.S., 77*, 399–412.

Würsig, B., & Würsig, M. (1979b). The day and the night of the dolphin. *Natural History, 88*, 61–67.

Würsig, B., & Würsig, M. (1980). Behavior and ecology of the dusky dolphin, *Lagenorhynchus obscurus.,* in the south Atlantic. *Fishery Bulletin U.S., 77*, 871–890.

19 Social Complexity and Cooperative Behavior in Delphinids

Jack W. Bradbury
University of California, San Diego

A persistent obsession in much of the cetacean literature is a justification for including these mammals in the ranks of the more sagacious organisms. Although claims have been made for sophisticated reciprocal altruism (Connor & Norris, 1982), elaborate social and moral capacities (Lilly, 1967), and considerable semantic abilities (this volume), one not privy to this obsession finds much of the literature a difficult mix of fact and fancy. There is frequent "bootstrapping" in this field. Sometimes it takes the form of an assertion that cetaceans arc "higher mammals" and then uses this assumption to interpret poorly described behaviors in favor of the assertion; while a good fit between the assertion and its consequences is necessary to prove the point, it is not a sufficient condition since other interpretations may give as good or better fits. Another form rests on a reciprocal empathy among cetacean investigators: Accepting that porpoises have "been shown" by psychologists and neuroanatomists to be intelligent, socioecologists interpret the highly unstable composition of delphinid groups as evidence of a very complex social order; psychologists and neuroanatomists then assume that because social organization in porpoises has "been shown" to be complex, the large brains of these animals must reflect high intelligence. We are all such "specialists" nowadays that it takes extraordinary breadth (or gall) to challenge the evidence from another discipline; for this particular taxon, the widely accepted faith in their status as "higher animals" makes the exercise of such cross-disciplinary critiques even less well received. The result is an edifice that, while intriguing, seems to an outsider quite fragile.

It seems to me that "complexity" can and ought to be defined in a way that is both operational and comparative. As referents, the more easily studied terrestrial mammals and birds can be invoked as counterpoint to the frequently

361

anecdotal and incomplete evidence for cetaceans. Given an observation on porpoises, what is the most likely counterpart in other taxa? Does a proposed interpretation fit within the likely economics known to apply in other groups? If one accepts this position, then several widely invoked arguments for cetacean status fall by the way. For example, one outcome of work on terrestrial forms is that there are no simple correlations between "complexity" of one aspect of an organism's biology and other aspects: Two species ranked according to encephalization quotient may well exhibit an opposite ranking on the basis of social organization. Similarly, a species exhibiting high flexibility and learning in foraging contexts may be quite inflexible and entrained in mating situations. Even humans show this mix of flexibility and conservatism. It may well be that, given appropriate comparative metrics, delphinids rank high for a variety of biological features; however, this must be shown, and cannot serve as a viable presumption for its own justification.

FORMS OF SOCIAL COOPERATION

In the area of cetacean social organization, the most striking claims in support of "complexity" revolve around the issue of cooperation. Again, some sophistication is required here since different cooperative acts have quite different economic constraints: Demonstration that a given species undertakes one form of cooperation in no way implies that other forms are also justified and likely. In Table 19.1 are listed most (but not all) of the types of cooperative behavior which have been described for birds and mammals. The list provides examples from terrestrial organisms and gives any cetacean examples known to the author. For references on terrestrial examples, see Krebs & Davies (1981), Wilson (1975), and Wilkinson (1984); for cetaceans, references are Best (1979), Caldwell and Caldwell (1966), Connor and Norris (1982), Würsig (1978), Würsig and Würsig (1979, 1980), Morejohn (1979), Leatherwood and Walker (1979), Benjaminsen and Christensen (1979), Norris and Dohl (1979), Saayman and Tayler (1979), Irvine, Scott, Wells, and Kaufmann (1981), Sergeant (1962), Gaskin (1982), Perrin, Brownell, and DeMaster (1984), and Donovan (in press).

This list is not meant to be exhaustive, either in terms of behaviors or in terms of examples. It is intended instead to show the diversity of cooperative behaviors which have been demonstrated in avian and mammalian groups and to point out that no species (except possibly humans) shows ALL possibilities. Each species appears to have its own peculiar mix from the available set. Cetaceans are no exception. It seems likely, given the extensive field and captive observations on these species, that smaller delphinids do not share suckling, even though the behavior is suspected in larger cetaceans (Donovan, in press; Perrin, Brownell, and DeMaster, 1984). Regurgitation of food between adults has also not been seen either in captive or wild individuals. On the other hand, a number of species exhibit standing by and some show postural support of injured school mates. Can

TABLE 19.1.
Cooperative Behaviors in Vertebrates

Behavior	Terrestrial Examples	Cetacean Examples
1. Shared guarding and tending of young.	Communal birds, ungulates, bats, elephants, primates, and carnivores	*Tursiops, Physeter, Orcinus,* etc.
2. Shared suckling	Elephants, lions, bats, hyaenas, walruses (?)	*Physeter* (?), *Globicephala*
3. Resource advertisement	Chimps; others may lead without display (bats, carnivores, primates)	Aerial displays (?) in odontocetes
4. Cohesive food searching	Many birds, carnivores, ungulates, bats	Many cetacean examples, including special school configurations and signals for synchronization
5. Coordinated prey capture	Carnivores, chimps, mixed bird flocks (?)	Many odontocete examples
6. Provisioning and regurgitation among adults	Carnivorous and vampire bats, canids	None known
7. Alarm signals	Most social birds and mammals	Tail slaps and probably some vocalizations
8. Defense of other adults	Ungulates, primates, elephants, bats	Standing by, but according to age or sex of recipient in many species
9. Postural support of sick or injured adults	Elephants	Some delphinids
10. Parasite removal	Bats, rodents, primates, some carnivores	None known
11. Shared thermoregulation	Many mammal and bird species	None known
12. Shared mate procurement	Turkeys (?), lions, baboons	None known
13. Shared defense of territory	Jays, tits, carnivores, primates, etc.	None known

an examination of which behaviors are performed by cetaceans be used to predict the kinds of neural capacities these animals must have in order to perform them? This is the premise utilized by several recent authors (e.g., Connor & Norris, 1982). I think that at best such predictions are quite limited, and those that are possible are not those currently in vogue in the cetacean literature.

ECONOMICS OF COOPERATION IN GENERAL

The presence or absence of given cooperative behaviors, particularly where a behavior is known in one species of a taxon but not in some others, is most likely to depend on the relative economics of that behavior. Put another way, the behavior is likely to be present if the weighted difference between the summed benefits and the summed costs when the act is performed exceeds the equivalent difference when it is not. The weighting of benefits and costs depends on the type of "accounting" which is relevant. A variety of accountings for cooperative behavior are possible: (a) mutualism (cooperators pay costs and gain benefits simultaneously); (b) nepotism (a "donor" benefits a "recipient" which is sufficiently closely related to the donor that any "genetic" costs to the donor are more than made up); (c) reciprocity (donor and recipient exchange roles sufficiently frequently that summed benefits received by each exceed summed costs suffered by each); (d) group selection (donor's cost is made up by population level concatenation of donors helping donors).

As noted above, an act is favored when the net profit (benefit minus cost) for performing the act is greater than that for not performing it. Usually the terms in this inequality are rearranged so that the ratio of the summed benefits to the summed costs of performing the act are compared to an index which combines all of the other terms. For example, the index in the case of nepotism is based on the relative degrees of relatedness between a donor and its own offspring, and the donor and the recipient's offspring (Hamilton, 1964). Constants in the nepotism index vary depending on whether the heritable aspects of the transaction are polygenic or not (Engles, 1983). Similar contrasts exist for the other accountings, although in the case of reciprocity, a wide variety of submodels must be considered (Axelrod and Hamilton, 1981; Boorman & Levitt, 1980; Brown, Sanderson, & Michod, 1982; Schaffer, 1978; Trivers, 1971). It should be noted that in real contexts several accountings may be appropriate concurrently and one must then quantify the contribution each makes to the performance of specific behaviors. This requires a large body of careful data, but it is a feasible task (Wilkinson, 1984).

ECONOMICS OF COOPERATION IN CETACEANS

Cetaceans, like other taxa, are diverse socially. In evaluating the kinds of processing required for the cooperative behaviors they do perform, it is important not to lump species indiscriminately as the differences are often more telling than the similarities. One cooperative behavior which ought to have high survival benefits in cetaceans is postural support of conspecifics which are sick or injured. Those species exhibiting such support (primarily delphinids) even perform it to other species such as man, sharks, or dead recipients (Caldwell & Caldwell, 1966; Connor & Norris, 1982). Mutualism can be immediately excluded as an appropriate accounting of this behavior. A group selection model for this behavior based on differential group reproduction would require a "strong selection" formulation; altruism would occur only if altruists sought each other out nonrandomly (Wilson, 1977, 1980). This is possible, but the compositional flux of delphinid groups argues against it. Nepotism could not explain the interspecific aid, but might apply on an intraspecific basis.

To go further, one needs some estimates of the relative costs and benefits of postural support. Connor and Norris (1982) have argued that the fluidity of smaller delphinid groups makes a nepotistic accounting for such aid unlikely. This is not necessarily true; while it may be that most members of a group are only weakly related, if the benefit-to-cost ratio is large enough, even a small level of relatedness may suffice to explain the behavior. It is likely that the recipient of support behavior receives a very large benefit; it is not clear to me, despite all the hints to the contrary, that the costs to the donor are often very large. Support of an injured conspecific when under attack would clearly be more costly to a donor than support of a sick individual which is shared with several other healthy members. The evidence suggests that support under attack is un-common, and often limited to specific sex/age class transactions. Cows will defend and support calves, and adult males will stand by and defend adult females they are accompanying (who may carry the male's offspring), but cows rarely stand by, defend, or support adult males (Caldwell & Caldwell, 1966; Connor & Norris, 1982). Most of the interspecific and irrelevant aid-giving appears to occur in contexts which are quite benign (and thus inexpensive) for the donor.

The possibility of a very high benefit-cost ratio for this behavior also affects the likelihood of a reciprocity accounting. Reciprocity is plagued with the need for proper cheater controls: A cheater in this context is an animal that accepts support when it needs it but does not support others when they need it. Note that this requires neither that every donation be repaid by a given recipient, nor that cheater controls be perfect. However, the sloppier the controls and the less complete the pay-backs, the higher the benefit-cost ratio must be to justify continued reciprocity (Brown et al., 1982). Thus support of dead sharks is not a challenge to standard reciprocity as long as it is neither frequent nor too costly. I know of no reciprocity model which would justify frequent and expensive indis-criminate aid without at least some cheater control (Connor & Norris, 1982).

The comments above apply to one necessary condition for reciprocity to occur: that is, the benefit-cost ratio must exceed a minimal value set by the rigor of any cheater controls and the payback probabilities or else it should not evolve. The benefit-cost ratio also affects the likelihood of reciprocity in another manner. No reciprocity behavior is a sure bet even if it meets the critical condition above. This is because the underlying economics always (to my knowledge) allow for two outcomes: a society of pure reciprocators and a society with no altruism. Which we see depends on what happens in populations with low frequencies of altruists. For any reciprocity model, there is a critical frequency of altruists at which altruism and cheating have equal payoffs. Should the population drift towards a lower frequency of altruists, the economics will then drive altruists out; should the population drift towards more altruists, then the economics will increasingly favor altruists until nonaltruists are gone. Where the costs of cheat-ing are very small relative to the benefits of reciprocating, the critical frequency of altruists is also small. In short, high benefit-cost ratios reduce the critical frequency and thus make it more likely that a population will by chance drift above this threshold and "take off" to a state of entirely altruists. Population subdivision may also facilitate this early evolution of reciprocal behaviors (Boorman & Levitt, 1980).

Where does this get us? The point is that whether nepotism or reciprocity or some combination of these accountings turns out to be the best explanation for supporting behaviors in cetaceans, if a donor's cost is usually low, no very sophisticated mechanism is required to justify the behaviors. In the case of nepotism, a very mild philopatry might generate sufficient levels of relatedness to meet the benefit-cost ratios involved. No fancy individual or kin recognition schemes need be proposed. In fact, the porpoises need have cognitive abilities no better than those of hedgehogs (Morgane, this volume). In the case of reciprocity, the lower the cost, the less sophisticated the cheater controls need be. Some individual recognition would be required, but it need not be perfect. This is certainly asking no more of the porpoises than that which we accept as reasonable in other vertebrates such as birds or bats. One could make similar arguments for the other presumably low-cost behaviors cited in the cetacean literature, such as advertisement of very rich food finds, without changing the basic conclusions.

The corollary is that if one wishes to look for sophisticated cheater controls, careful individual or kin recognition, and perhaps some memory of who did what in recent transactions, one should look to those species in which high-cost exchanges between adults have been recorded. (Exchanges between parents and young are often high cost, but so many organisms show this behavior that analysis of its economics is unlikely to distinguish cetaceans from other taxa.) Given the intense metabolic turnovers of nearly all cetaceans (Gaskin, 1982), one would expect such behaviors as shared suckling and regurgitation between adults to have the requisite low benefit-cost ratios. Physical defense of other adults under attack by large predators would also fit into this category. As noted, shared suckling is uncommon among cetaceans, and regurgitation has not been recorded at all. Physical defense of adults is known, but it varies with the nature of the predator, with the species of cetacean, and with the sex and age relationships of the individuals involved. Curiously, those higher cost transactions have been seen primarily in the larger odontocetes (*Orcinus, Physeter, and Globicephala*). The correlation must not be taken too seriously since many species have not been studied (especially most of the ziphiids). However, the correlation is reasonably easily interpreted economically: Larger cetaceans would suffer reduced risks in defense of conspecifics than smaller ones, and the allometric scaling of energy budgets would likely make sharing of acquired nutrients less costly, relatively speaking, for the larger species than for the smaller ones. Size might have the opposite effect on benefits, but the relationship between costs and benefits is rarely linear and thus their ratio is also likely to vary with body size.

As expected, it is also these larger odontocetes that seem to have the most stable groups. Stability of group composition is clearly a necessity for more expensive reciprocity exchanges, and is a consequence of the means of generating high degrees of relatedness where expensive nepotistic transactions are involved. This stability is reflected both in the (unfortunately scanty) census data available, and in the differences between the mating systems of the larger odontocetes and those of the smaller ones. Terrestrial mammals form the common mating pattern of several females and one breeding male in two ways (Emlen & Oring, 1977): (1) resource defense (in which males defend resources required by females and gain biased access to visiting females when the latter use these resources), and (2) female defense (in which males attach themselves to and defend an existing female group). Among mammals, unstable female groups are most commonly associated with resource defense; stable female groups facilitate female defense and the formation of "classical" harems (Bradbury & Vehrencamp, 1977). Resource defense is curiously absent in the cetacea. Grazing mysticetes surely experience a patchiness in the dispersion of food not unlike that of many ungulates which exhibit resource defense (Jarman, 1974). The mobile prey of odontocetes are also no less patchy than the insect prey defended by many bats and birds. Where food is not defensible, refuges such as those favored by spinner porpoises during the day are frequently the subject of defense by males in other taxa. For whatever reason, resource defense is not common, or at least has not been seen, in the cetacea. Long-term female defense is only known in larger odontocetes (NMFS symposia on behavior and reproduction, 1982 and 1981 respectively). The fact that those cetaceans which have female groups sufficiently stable to justify haremic defense by males are also those which are known to engage in higher cost cooperative behaviors argues (at least to me) that the kind of economic arguments developed earlier are probably valid.

There remains a set of intermediate cost behaviors which may or may not be useful in the resolution of this issue. Shared guarding of offspring is common in mammals and also occurs in some birds. Both nepotistic and reciprocity accountings have been invoked for the various terrestrial species in which it occurs (Vehrencamp, 1980). Whatever the accounting, it is not a behavior which requires unusual cognitive or intellectual abilities.

One exception in the latter case would be extensive communication of environmental information by symbolic means. Most animals do not exchange sophisticated environmental information with signals: Instead, good food finds are advertised with some simple broadcast signal, or one animal leads others to the find directly. Where environmental information is encoded in signals, the "vocabularies" are usually simple, e.g., a few types of alarm calls in monkeys and ground squirrels (Owings & Virginia, 1978; Seyfarth, Cheney, & Marler, 1980). The obvious exceptions are social hymenopterans and humans. I have nothing novel to say about human communication systems, but I do think the fact that bees and ants exhibit such sophisticated environmental communication while other organisms usually do not deserves some comment. One possibility is that the processing for such communication is sufficiently expensive neurally that benefit-cost ratios exceed critical values only when the communicating animals are very closely related. This explanation invokes a nepotistic accounting resting on the unusually high relatedness characteristic of hymenopteran societies (Hamilton, 1964). It may also be that the system is only worth the investment when error levels are low; perhaps high genetic relatedness guarantees sufficiently close matches between sender and receiver equipment to keep such errors infrequent. The point is that sophisticated communication of environmental information, if demonstrated in the fluid groups of smaller delphinids, would constitute a startling exception to much of what has been said here. It would not only be an unusual find, but it would also pose a difficult challenge to our current understanding of cooperative economics. As the evidence now stands, such communication in delphinids remains highly speculative.

How should the mix of cooperative behavior seen in cetaceans be viewed? In contrast to current views in the literature, it seems more reasonable to me that polygynous (harem) mating and compositional stability, not random mating and compositional fluidity, are the best markers for complex social transactions. As a corollary, it suggests that the fluidity of composition in smaller delphinids might best be interpreted as evidence of moderate anarchy, not as support for the existence of some complicated web of relationships. There are two possible reasons for the apparent correlations between body size and social structure in cetaceans. The foraging ecology of smaller forms might require such rapid and frequent exchange between sites that the critical indices of relatedness or association are never met, whereas foraging in larger species might favor local stability and therefore permit the evolution of costly cooperation. Alternatively, it may be that the allometric scaling of benefit-cost ratios sets a threshold in body size below which costly cooperation is never justified, that cooperation evolves wherever the threshold is exceeded, and that differences in group stability are consequences of prior evolution for or against costly cooperative networks. Were we to know which condition was the limiting constraint, it would greatly simplify the task of explaining the social diversity apparent in this group.

MEASURES OF COOPERATION COMPLEXITY

The thrust of the preceeding sections is that there is no current evidence to support the notion of highly complex social orders based on cooperation in smaller delphinids. There may well be elaborate patterns of reciprocity or nepotism in larger species with stable female groups, and available reports agree that these species do engage in the type of transactions which ought to require individual recognition, long memories, and the like. In short, the widely held presumption that cetaceans engage in complex social behaviors is at least justified for a few species. In a number of publications on cetaceans, and in much of the discussion at the conference generating this volume, the presumption that cetaceans engage in complex social behaviors is often followed by the conlusion that they must have large and complex brains to accomplish this. This jump contains two assumptions: (a) that cooperation is a sophisticated decision-making process; and (b) that the more complex the decision-making task, the more complicated the brains of the participants must be. I leave to the neuroanatomists the question of whether sophisticated tasks require sophisticated neural circuitry. But I do think some comment on how one might rank the complexity of social tasks is appropriate here.

There are two steps in the process of cooperation: deciding whether to cooperate and executing the cooperative acts themselves. Either might be complex or simple; there is no a priori reason to assume that complexity in one stage is coupled necessarily to complexity in the other. Looking first at the decision process, one can distinguish the following general situations:

A. Situations in which only a single type of transaction is involved; decisions might be made through either:

  1. Threshold Cooperation—This describes situations in which the donor's cost and the recipient's benefit are fixed at the outset and known to the participants. Cooperation would be justified only when the appropriate "threshold" index (that is, a combination of all terms in the inequality except cost and benefit) was less than the resulting benefit-cost ratio. Thus if the animal set the benefit-cost ratio at 10, it would cooperate with any kin related to it by 0.1 or more. Once the threshold was reached, close and distant kin would not be discriminated. If population substructure guaranteed a relatedness greater than this minimal index value, NO discrimination would be needed. Reciprocity analogues are obvious. As an example, a dolphin might support any injured conspecific in its usual area (assuming they are likely to be related sufficiently) as long as predators are not present and foraging time is not a limiting constraint on survival.

  2. Scaled Cooperation—This refers to situations in which a donor scales the cost it will accept, and in most cases, the benefit-cost ratio as a result, according to the index relating donor and recipient. Since the benefit-cost ratios for most types of cooperation decrease with increasing cost, a nepotistic donor would thus only undertake higher costs for more closely related kin. Again, reciprocity versions are immediate. This requires the ability to make several measurements and adjust output accordingly.

B. Situations in which several types of transactions are involved:

  1. Independent Currencies—In this case, a separate accounting is required for each type of exchange. Accountings could involve either threshold or scaled criteria, and one might find different types of criteria for different currencies. A delphinid might support injured comrades using some simple nepotistic threshold, but collaborate in foraging on the basis of scaled reciprocity.

2. Barter—This is a form of reciprocity in which a donor contributes to a recipient in one currency and is later repaid in another currency. One would expect barter to be scaled to some common "worth" to be justified, but the effective "worth" of any exchange might be different (relative to needs) for donor and recipient. Thus one female sperm whale might guard another's young in exchange for alloparental suckling of the first's offspring.

Holding execution economics constant, it seems reasonable that the tasks associated with cooperation ought to be considered more "complex" as one goes from single transaction biologies to multiple transaction ones. Similarly, barter presumably requires a more centralized accounting than do several concurrent and independent accounts. Where delphinids fall among these categories remains to be seen.

The cetacean literature has been more preoccupied with the sophistication of the decision stage in cooperation than in the execution stage. However, it is entirely possible that an organism which adopts quite simple decision processes may invest in quite sophisticated (and possibly neurally expensive) execution machinery. A case in point is the dance language of honeybees. By any standard, this is a highly sophisticated set of cooperative behaviors. The decision phase of bee dancing, however, is apparently a simple threshold process: Workers will dance for any worker in the hive (to which it is quite predictably related to a high degree) and not to workers of other hives (to which it has no predictably high relatedness). The complexity of the task thus lies in the performance of the dance and the subsequent read-out of information by attendant workers.

The point of the above is that any cooperative behavior is a mix of complex and simple programming tasks. This makes it difficult to rank the tasks overall on any single-dimensioned scale. Is the support behavior of dephinids really more complex than the dance of a honey bee? Is it worth belaboring this type of contrast? The problem is that cooperative behavior consists of several orthogonal components, any one of which may be complex or simple. This means that two species might have quite similarly complex brains, but for quite different reasons. It also means that we shall have to derive the second set of rules, that linking task complexity with neural complexity, not for a single scale but for a variety of measures of task complexity.

Compared to other chapters in this volume, the foregoing sounds like the grousings of a hard-nosed skeptic. The fact is that, like Griffin, I suspect that cetaceans are capable of much more sophisticated interactions than Morgan's canon would give them credit for. However, I shall be surprised if these marvelous mammals do not fit into the general patterns that are emerging from other taxa. If they do, it is no denigration since quite sophisticated social behaviors are now known from a variety of even "lower" animals; and if they do not, then the clarification of their exceptional status can only be extremely illuminating for both behavioral and physiological biologists.

REFERENCES

Axelrod, R., & Hamilton, W. D. (1981). The evolution of cooperation. *Science, 211,* 1390–1396.

Best, P. (1979). Social organization in sperm whales, *Physeter macrocephalus.* In H. E. Winn & B. L. Olla (Eds.), *Behavior of marine animals* (Vol. 3). *Cetaceans* (pp. 227–289). New York: Plenum Press.

Benjaminsen, T., & Christensen, I. (1979). The natural history of the bottlenose whale, *Hyperoodon ampullatus.* In H. E. Winn & B. L. Olla (Eds.), *Behavior of marine mammals* (Vol. 3). *Cetaceans* (pp. 143–164). New York: Plenum Press.

Boorman, S., & Levitt, P. (1980). *The genetics of altruism.* New York: Academic Press.

Bradbury, J., & Vehrencamp, S. (1977). Social organization and foraging in emballonurid bats. III. Mating systems. *Behavioral Ecology and Sociobiology, 2,* 1–17.

Brown, J. S., Sanderson, M. J., & Michod, R. E. (1982). Evolution of social behavior by reciprocation. *Journal of Theoretical Biology, 99,* 319–339.

Caldwell, M. C., & Caldwell, D. K. (1966). Epimeletic (care giving) behavior in cetacea. In K. S. Norris (Ed.), *Whales, dolphins, and porpoises.* (pp. 755–789). Berkeley: University of California Press.

Connor, R. C., & Norris, K. S. (1982). Are dolphins reciprocal altruists? *American Naturalist, 119,* 358–374.

Donovan, G. P. (Ed.). (in press). *Behavior of whales in relation to management.* Reports of the International Whaling Commission (special issue 8). Cambridge, England.

Emlen, S. T., & Oring, L. W. (1977). Ecology, sexual selection and the evolution of mating systems. *Science, 197,* 215–223.

Engels, W. R. (1983). Evolution of altruistic behavior by kin selection: An alternative approach. *Proceedings of the National Academy of Sciences, USA, 80,* 515–518.

Gaskin, D. E. (1982). *The ecology of whales and dolphins.* London: Heinemann Educational Books.

Hamilton, W. D. (1964). The genetical evolution of social behaviour. *Journal of Theoretical Biology, 7,* 1–52.

Irvine, A. B., Scott, M. D., Wells, R. S., & Kaufmann, J. H. (1981). Movements and activities of the Atlantic bottlenose dolphin near Sarasota, Florida, *Fishery Bulletin, 79,* 671–688.

Jarman, P. J. (1974). The social organization of antelope in relation to their ecology. *Behaviour, 48,* 215–267.

Krebs, J. R., & Davies, N. B. (Eds.). (1981). *An introduction to behavioural ecology.* Oxford: Blackwell Scientific Publications.

Leatherwood, S., & Walker, W. A. (1979). The northern right whale dolphins, *Lissodelphis borealis,* in the Eastern North Pacific. In H. E. Winn & B. L. Olla (Eds.), *Behavior of marine mammals* (Vol. 3. *Cetaceans* (pp. 85–141). New York: Plenum Press.

Lilly, J. C. (1967). *The mind of the dolphin: A nonhuman intelligence.* New York: Doubleday.

Morejohn, G. V. (1979). The natural history of Dall's porpoise in the North Pacific Ocean. In H. E. Winn & B. L. Olla (Eds.), *Behavior of marine mammals* (Vol. 3). *Cetaceans* (pp. 45–83. New York: Plenum Press.

Norris, K., & Dohl, T. P. (1979). Behavior of the Hawaiian spinner dolphin, *Stenella longirostris. Fishery Bulletin, 77,* 821–849.

Owings, D. H., & Virginia, R. A. (1978). Alarm calls of California ground squirrels (*Spermophilus beecheyi*). *Zeitschrift für Tierpsychologie, 46,* 58–70.

Perrin, W. F., Brownell, Jr., R. L., DeMaster, D. P. (Eds.). (1984). *Reproduction in whales, dolphins, and porpoises.* Reports of the International Whaling Commission (special issue 6). Cambridge, England.

Saayman, G. S., & Taylor, C. K. (1979). The socioecology of humpback dolphins (*Sousa sp.*). In H. E. Winn & B. L. Olla (Eds.), *Behavior of marine mammals* (Vol. 3). *Cetaceans* (pp. 165–226). New York: Plenum Press.

Schaffer, W. M. (1978). A note on the theory of reciprocal altruism. *American Naturalist, 112*, 250–253.

Sergeant, D. E. (1962). The biology of the pilot or pothead whale, *Globicephala melaena*, in Newfoundland waters. *Bulletin of the Fisheries Research Board, Canada, 132*, 1–84.

Seyfarth, R. M., Cheney, D. L., & Marler, P. (1980). Monkey responses to three different alarm calls: Evidence of predator classification and semantic communication. *Science, 210*, 801–803.

Trivers, R. A. (1971). The evolution of reciprocal altruism. *Quarterly Review of Biology, 46*, 35–57.

Vehrencamp, S. L. (1980). The roles of individual, kin, and group selection in the evolution of sociality. In P. Marler & J. G. Vandenbergh (Eds.), *Handbook of behavioral neurobiology* (Vol. 3). *Social behavior and communication* (pp. 351–394). New York: Plenum Press.

Wilkinson, J. (1984). Reciprocal food sharing in the vampire bat. *Nature, 308*, 181–184.

Wilson, D. S. (1977). Structured demes and the evolution of group advantageous traits. *American Naturalist, 111*, 157–185.

Wilson, D. S. (1980). *The natural selection of populations and communities.* Menlo Park: Benjamin/Cummings Publishing Company.

Wilson, E. O. (1975). *Sociobiology: The new synthesis.* Cambridge, MA: The Belknap Press.

Würsig, B. (1978). Occurrence and group organization of Atlantic bottlenose porpoises (*Tursiops truncatus*) in an Argentine bay. *Biological Bulletin, 154*, 348–359.

Würsig, B., & Würsig, M. (1979). Behavior and ecology of the bottlenose dolphin, *Tursiops truncatus*, in the South Atlantic. *Fishery Bulletin, 77*, 399–412.

Würsig, B., & Würsig, M. (1979). Behavior and ecology of the dusky dolphin, *Lagenorhynchus obscurus*, in the South Atlantic. *Fishery Bulletin, 77*, 871–890.

Author Index

Numbers in *italics* indicate pages with complete bibliographic information.

Davis, M. B., 88, *112*
Dawkins, R., 209, *217*
Dawson, W. W., 39, 54, *56,* 83, 85, 86, *109,*
110, 111, 112, 226, 242, *249*
Defran, R. H., 254
DeGaaf, A. S., 53, *56*
Deglin, V., 43, 46, *55*
Delius, J. D., 210, *217, 218*
Demarest, J., 171, *180*
DeMaster, D. P., 362, *371*
Descartes, R., 265, *269*
Desmond, A. J., 210, *217*
de Villiers, J. G., 294, *298*
de Villiers, P. A., 294, *298*
deVilla, J. G., 324, *330*
Dewdney, A. K., 148, *164*
Dewsbury, D. A., 175, *180*
Diamond, I. T., 147, *164*
Dilger, J. P., 126, 127, *134*
di Sciara, G., 102, *113*
Dittus, W. P., 316, *329*
Dobkin, D. S., 291, *298*
Dohl, T. P., 340, *345,* 347, 348, 349, 350,
351, 354, 355, 356, *358, 359,* 362, *371*
Don, M., 54, *56*
Donaldson, B. J., 104, 105, *110*
Donchin, E., 61, 74, *76*
Donovan, G. P., 362, *371*
Donskov, A. A., 130, *135*
Dooling, R. J., 291, *298*
Doty, R., 43, 46, *56*
Dral, A. D. G., 85, 86, *110,* 226, *249*
Dreher, J. J., 274, *286, 287,* 342, *344*
Dubrovskiy, N. A., 127, *133*
Dziedzic, A., 274, 275, *286,* 339, *343*

E

Ebbesson, S. O. E., 151, *164*
Eberhardt, C., 291, *298*
Egan, J. P., 125, *133*
Eibl-Eibesfeldt, I., 306, 308, *312*
Eimas, P. D., 159, *164*
Eisenberg, J. F., 144, 150, *164,* 262, 263,
267, *269, 270,* 342, *344,* 348, *358*
Elias, H., 33, *56*
Ellis, G., 336, *344,* 348, *357*
Elmasian, R., 66, 72, *77*
Elsner, R., 37, 39, 41, *57, 59*
Emlen, S. T., 367, *371*
Epstein, R., 174, *180,* 210, *217*
Erickson, H. I., 209, *218*
Erulkar, S. D., 125, *133,* 145, *164*

Essapian, F. S., 338, *344, 346*
Estes, R. D., 326, *329*
Evans, W. E., 32, 48, 54, *56, 59,* 88, *110,*
126, 127, 129, 132, *133, 134,* 144, *166,*
273, 274, *287,* 336, 341, 342, *344, 345,*
350, *358*

F

Fantino, EJ., 209, *217*
Fantz, R. L., 176, *180*
Farley, G. R., 62, 72, 74, *76, 77*
Fenton, M. B., 159, *164*
Fiala, K. L., 291, *301*
Filimonoff, I. N., 6, 7, 9, *28*
Fink, B. D., 355, *358*
Fiorelli, P., 269, *270*
Fiscus, C. H., 355, *359*
Fish, J. F., 55, *56,* 131, *134*
Fish, J. R., 88, *109*
Fisher, H. D., 40, *59*
Flanigan, N. J., 221, *249*
Flanigan, W. F., 35, 41, 42, *56, 58,* 62, 63,
76
Fleischer, G., 96, 97, *110*
Fletcher, H., 124, *134*
Flottorp, G., 124, *136*
Floyd, R. W., 126, 127, 128, 129, 130, 131,
132, *133, 134,* 341, *343*
Fobes, J. L., 81, *110,* 175, *180*
Folds, D. L., 128, *134*
Fodor, J., 203, *204,* 208, *218*
Foote, S. L., 62, *76*
Forestell, P. H., 237, *250*
Foster, L., 347, *358*
Fouts, R. S., 227, 248, *249,* 294, *298*
Fowler, H., 209, *218*
Fraenkel, G. S., 143, *165*
Francis, D., 259, *260*
Fraser, F. C., 95, 96, *110,* 119, *134*
French, N. R., 123, 124, *134*
Friberg, V., 105, *109*
Friedman, M. P., 143, *164*
Fulton, G., 356, *358*
Fulwiler, R. L., 294, *298*

G

Gailey-Phipps, J., 88, *113*
Galaburda, A. M., 12, 17, *28*
Galambos, R., 52, 53, 54, *58,* 61, 62, 72, 74,
75, 76, 77
Galdikas, B. M. F., 210, *217*

Y, Z

Subject Index

Color
  discrimination, 87
  perception, 188–189
"Communal" cognition, 160–162
Communication, 271, 340
  competence, anomalous, 295–297
  human-animal
    comparisons, 304–305
    and reinforcement training, 257–259
  natural, 285–286
  sophistication of, 212
  systems
    anomalous, 290, 293
    exceptional, 290, 293
  tactile, 272
  two-way, response mode, use of mimicry
    as, 282–285
Communicative acts
  intentional informative, 309–310, 311
  unintentional emotive, 310
Communicative behaviors, 310–312
Comparative cognition, suggestions for re-
    search, 207–217
Concept learning, 212
Confinement, 332
Consciousness, 332
Conspecific signaling system, 290–291
Constancies, maintenance of, 148–149
Context, variation of, 238
Convexity cortex, 23
Cooperation, decisions related to, 369–370
  scaled, 369
Cooperation, *see* Social cooperation
Cornea, 81
Cortex, intermediate, 8, 9
  laminated, 12
  limbic, 10
  paralimbic, 10, 19, 23
  parinsular, 10, 19, 23
  periallo, 12, 16
  primary, 10
  proiso, 12
Counterclockwise swimming, 42–43
Courtship, 339
  repertoire in, 211
Creodonta, 22
Critical band theory, 124–125
Currencies, independent, 369

D

Delphinapterus leucas
  brain symmetry, 45

audiogram, 102
chemoreception, 105
Delphinus delphis
  brain
    asymmetry, 45, 46
    growth, 35
    lateralization, 46
  delphis, 48, 52, 226, 347
    chemoreception, 105, 106
Dendrites, 16
Detector system, transient, 86
Dimensions, discrimination of, 188
Displacement, linguistic concept of, 236–237
Display(s), 321–322
  integrating of, 322–324
  referents, 322
Distance senses, 150
Dolphin(s)
  audition, *see* Audition
  female social behavior, 338
  vision, 84–87
Domestication, 253–254
Dominance hierarchy, 339
Doppler resolution, 130
"Dysgranular," 13

E

Ear
  anatomy and transduction mechanisms, 117–
    119
  sound transmission through, 119–122
Ear drum, 117
Echolocation, 101, 103, 115, 152, 154, 159,
    163, 340
  and brain size, 146
  for knowledge of external world, 144–146
  models, theoretical, 130–132
  recognition of, 95
  signals, 129–130
  sound production, 126–130
  in water, 99, 117
Electrocardiogram, 106
Electroencephalogram (EEG), 39–40, 46
Electrophysiological mapping studies, of brain,
    27
Electrophysiological recording experiments, 2
Elements, number of, 212
Elephas maximus, 269
Emotion(s), 162–163
  range of, 213
Emotional responses, variety of, 213
Empathy, 343

Encephalization, 153–154
high values, and social and cognitive attributes, 268, 269
and social organization, 262–263
structural, 142
Enhancements
auditory and visual objects, 158–159
"communal" cognition, 160–162
self as an object, 159–160
Environment, 79
interacting with, 210–211
ERP, *see* Event related potentials
Essentialism, 178, 202–203
Ethological cognition, suggestions for research, 207–217
Event related potentials (ERPs), 31, 61–62,
see also Auditory event related potentials
Evoked potentials
from central auditory nervous system, 98–100
cerebral, 99–100
hearing and, 50–55
pinniped, 89
Somatosensory, 47–48
Exceptional communication system, 290, 293
Exploration, 211
External auditory meatus, 95
External world, 163
knowledge of, echolocation for, 144–146
sense of, 151
Eye, 80
disconjugate movement, 38–39
preference, 43–45

F

Features, distinct, multiplicity of, 208–209
Feeding, 79
strategies, 337
Fish, herding of, 353
Fitness, inclusive, 264
Fixed action patterns (FAPs), 303, 306–307
FM sweeps, 68, 74
Folk taxonomy, 167–169, 178
Food, finding and securing of, 348–350, 351
Foraging behaviors, 159, 333, 347–348, 356, 357
cooperative, 350–356
finding and securing food, 348–350
Frequency distribution

dolphins, 102–103
pinnipeds, 91
Fright reaction, 354

G

Galvanic skin response (GSR), 48, 106
Game(s), 332–333
learning of, 212
Ganglion cell, 86
Gene(s), for parental care, 264
Generalization, semantic, 238–239
Gestures, 339
Globicephala sp., 347
Grammar(s), 305
Grampus, 32
Gravity, information on, 151–152
Growth rings, 23

H

Halichoerus grypus, audiograms, 94
Hearing, *see* Audition
Herding dolphins, 354
Hedgehogs, 19
Heterocephalus glaber, 262
Higher mental processes, and cognition, 265–269
Human codes, 289
inculcation, 291–294
validity and implications, 289–291
Human language
as model of sensory enhancement, 154–156
and self consciousness, 156–158
Human qualities, 214
Humor, 214
Hunting, cooperative, symmetrical relations in, 342–343

I

Imaging, 199
Independence, modality, 248
Independent currencies, 369
Infants, aggression to, 338
see also Calves
Inferior colliculus, evoked potentials in, 99
Information
perception and interception, 79
processing, 147, 244
Information bearing parameters (IBP), 49, 50

Multidimensional scaling (MDS), 188–192
Music, 214

N

N200, 66
Natural selection, 266
 and social dynamics, 263–264
Nearest neighbor classification rules, 191, 192
Need, 332
Neocortex, 7, 9, 162–163
 development and formation, 5, 6, 7
 evolution, concepts, 10–18
 "growth rings," 11, 12
 "original architectonics," 22
Nerve endings, prominent, 48
Neurons, extraverted, 16
Nominalism, 178
Non-self, 212
Novelty, desire for, 210–211

O

Object
 internal representation of, 188–191
 labeling and reporting of, 247–248, 278–279
 manipulation, 211
 self as, 159–160
 selection, 294
Observation-learning, 211
Olfactory apparatus, 104
Olfactory data, absence, 150–151
Olfactory system, enhancement, 154
Orcinus, 32
 brain growth, 35
 counterclockwise swimming, 42
 orca, 54, 271, 336, 347
 auditory thresholds, 101
 vision, 87
Optic nerve fibers, total crossing of, 37–38
Organization, social, 335, 336–339
Otter, vision, 81–82

P

P300, 65, 73
 -like activity, 62, 63
P550, 66, 71
 components, 71, 73–74
 latency, 74
Pagophilus groenlandicus, audiograms, 92

Paleocortex, 7, 9, 10
Paralimbic cortex, 10, 19, 23
Parental care, genes for, 264
Parinsular cortex, 10, 19, 23
Parrot, communication, 290–291
Pattern recognition, 148–149
Perception, 267
 and large brains, 147–149
Perceptual world, 141–142
 echolocation for knowledge of external world, 144–146
 umwelten, 143–144
Perianal glands, 271
Phoca vitulina, 82, 83, 89, 269
 angular discrimination, 91
Phocoena phocoena, 355
 brain asymmetry, 45
 audiogram, 100
 phocoena, 355
 chemoreception, 106
 sound localization, 103
Phocoenoides, 271
Phonations, 318
"Phylogenetic ranking," 170
Pigeons, auditory matching, 245
Pinna, 117
Pinnipeds
 audition, 89–94
 chemoreception, 104
 vision, 82–84
Pitch discrimination, 91
Platanista, 32
Play, 211
Pontoporia, 32
Predation, risk of, 337
Predator avoidance, 79
Prevarication, 214
Probe tones, 68
Problem solving, 195–201, 202, 213
 goal-oriented, 200–201
Production systems, 195–196
Prototype classification, 191–192
Pseudorca crassidens, 255
Psittacus erithacus, human vocalization, 292
Pulse sound stimuli, 91
Pupil, constriction, 85–86
Pyramidalization, 13

Q

"Quantism," 178
Quavering, 219–321